I0876595

# A GREAT REVOLUTION IN CHURCH AND STATE

The Revolutionary Age

Francis D. Cogliano, Christa Breault Dierksheide, Eliga H. Gould, and Patrick Griffin, Editors

# A GREAT REVOLUTION IN CHURCH AND STATE

## Religion, Government, and Property in the Chesapeake, 1700–1830

Alyssa Penick

University of Virginia • *Charlottesville and London*

The University of Virginia Press is situated on the traditional lands of the Monacan Nation, and the Commonwealth of Virginia was and is home to many other Indigenous people. We pay our respect to all of them, past and present. We also honor the enslaved African and African American people who built the University of Virginia, and we recognize their descendants. We commit to fostering voices from these communities through our publications and to deepening our collective understanding of their histories and contributions.

University of Virginia Press

Printed in the United States of America on acid-free paper

*First published 2026*

9 8 7 6 5 4 3 2 1

LIBRARY OF CONGRESS CATALOGING-IN-PUBLICATION DATA

Names: Penick, Alyssa, author
Title: A great revolution in church and state : religion, government, and property in the Chesapeake, 1700–1830 / Alyssa Penick.
Other titles: Revolutionary age (Charlottesville, Va.)
Description: Charlottesville : University of Virginia Press, 2026. | Series: The revolutionary age | Includes bibliographical references and index.
Identifiers: LCCN 2026024167 (print) | LCCN 2026024168 (ebook) | ISBN 9780813955308 hardback | ISBN 9780813955315 paperback | ISBN 9780813955322 ebook
Subjects: LCSH: Church of England—Chesapeake Bay Region (Md. and Va.) | Church and state—Chesapeake Bay Region (Md. and Va.) | Slavery and the church—Church of England | Church and state—Maryland—History | Church and state—Virginia—History | Disestablishment of churches—Maryland | Disestablishment of churches—Virginia | Chesapeake Bay Region (Md. and Va.)—Race relations
Classification: LCC BX5157 .P46 2026 (print) | LCC BX5157 (ebook)
LC record available at https://lccn.loc.gov/2026024167
LC ebook record available at https://lccn.loc.gov/2026024168

Publication of this volume has been supported by the Jefferson Scholars Foundation and the Walker Cowen Memorial Fund.

*Cover art: Burning of Old South Church, Bath, Maine,* John Hilling, c. 1854. (Courtesy National Gallery of Art, Washington)
*Cover design:* Cecilia Sorochin

*To Owen, thank you for everything*

# CONTENTS

# ACKNOWLEDGMENTS

This book would never have been finished (let alone started) without the support of many mentors, colleagues, friends, and loved ones.

At the University of Michigan, I benefited from a vibrant intellectual community and tremendous mentorship. My deepest thanks go to Sue Juster, who read countless drafts and pushed me to sharpen my arguments and explain why history matters. Her wisdom, humor, and kindness over the past decade have been invaluable. This project began in Mary Kelley's History of the Book seminar. Her rigorous questions and cheerful reminders to "find the people" made me a better historian. David Hancock's expansive perspective and searching questions encouraged breadth and depth in my work. His seminars and dinner parties are among my fondest memories of graduate school. Bill Novak introduced me to legal history, and his enthusiasm and advice have inspired me to keep pursuing it. In every conversation, Val Kivelson taught me how to think and talk about religion more effectively. She has been a generous mentor, and I am grateful for the many ways she and Tim Hofer made Ann Arbor feel like home. Paul Johnson, Kit French, Greg Dowd, Rebecca Scott, Scotti Parrish, and Clem Hawes all offered exceptional models for teaching and scholarship during my graduate training. My undergraduate mentors, Annelise Orleck and Joseph Cullon, treated me like a historian from day one and taught me to follow my questions into the archives.

I couldn't have asked for a better fellow early Americanist than Hunter Harris, who always exudes kindness, curiosity, and a sense of fun. Disagreeing about almost everything we read and studying for prelims together over beers made graduate school so much fun. Meeting Kate Waggoner Karchner on the first day of graduate school was one of the luckiest moments of my life. From starting grad school to finishing this book amid early parenthood, Kate has been the greatest friend. I treasure her generosity, intelligence, and humor.

Arriving at the Jefferson Scholars Foundation at UVA introduced me to Christa Dierksheide. Her humor and warmth made my time at the JSF so enjoyable, and her thoughtful advice and incisive questions refined this project immeasurably. My time in Charlottesville began with a fellowship at the International Center for Jefferson Studies at Monticello, where John Ragosta helpfully shared his wide-ranging knowledge. Feedback from the Early American Seminar, particularly from Max Edelson, Alan Taylor, Johann Neem, Frank Cogliano, and Peter Onuf, propelled my thinking forward. Thanks to Emily Sackett, Bethany McGlynn, and Alice King for making my time in Charlottesville so much fun; learning from their work was also a pleasure. Ann Brown and Terry Birkel offered me a home away from home in Charlottesville. Their open-heartedness and generosity embody the UVA spirit.

It has been a joy to work with Nadine Zimmerli at UVA Press. Her expertise, patience, and perspective strengthened my work at every turn. I am also grateful for the manuscript workshop hosted by UVA Press and the feedback given by scholars I deeply admire, Mary Sarah Bilder, Kate Carté, Sarah Barringer Gordon, David Konig, Jessica Lowe, Rob Parkinson, and Doug Winiarski. Thank you, also, to the anonymous reviewers whose insights improved this manuscript from start to finish.

The generosity of numerous institutions made this book possible, including Rackham Graduate School, the Doris G. Quinn Foundation, the Berkeley Center for Religion, Peace, and World Affairs at Georgetown University, the Fred W. Smith National Library for the Study of George Washington, the International Center for Jefferson Studies at Monticello, and the Jefferson Scholars Foundation at UVA. I received helpful feedback on many portions of this project over the years at conferences and seminars hosted by the Institute for Thomas Paine Studies, Sons of the American Revolution, the University of Oklahoma Law School, Omohundro Institute for Early American History and Culture Annual Conference, Association for the Study of Law, Culture, and the Humanities, Missouri Regional Seminar on Early American History at the Kinder Institute, American Society for Legal History, the Annual Law and Religion Roundtable at the University of Virginia Law School, American Philosophical Society, the Virginia Consortium of Early Americanists, the Washington Early Americanists Seminar, and the Michigan Early Atlantic Seminar.

I am also deeply indebted to the expertise of the archivists at the Library of Virginia, the Maryland State Archives, the Bishop Payne Library at Virginia Theological Seminary, the Maryland Historical Society, the Virginia Museum of History & Culture, the Maryland Center for History and Culture, the Swem Special Collections at William and Mary, the Maryland Province Archives at Georgetown University, the Lambeth Palace Library, and the Small Special Collections at the University of Virginia. Special thanks to Mary Klein at the Maryland Diocesan Archives for her expertise and kindness.

Many friends outside of academia cheered me on at every stage of writing this book. Big thanks to Claire Dugan, Kristina Petersen, Caroline Raul, Maggie Birkel, Juliana Katinas, Adrienne Lerner, Bridget McNamara, Alex Abington, Adele Hedden, Ann Baum, Meghan Carter, Sarah Hutcheson, Lucy Zuraw, Sarah Stanton, Elizabeth Trandel, and Carrie Ryder.

To my family, Beth, Larry, Joyce, Jimmy, Liz, Julia, Nancy, Tony, Mary, Eric, Priscilla, and George, thank you for your constant enthusiasm and support. Jennifer, thanks for always encouraging me to keep going with this project and asking great questions along the way. Dad, thanks for being a paragon of intellectual curiosity and *joie de vivre.* I wouldn't be who I am or where I am without your love and support. My mom radiated compassion, tenacity, and wit. She remains my greatest role model, and I only wish she were here to read this book, which owes so much to the values she instilled in me.

Hugo never left my side on long days spent writing and reminded me that walks are the best way to think through a problem. Fen arrived mere hours after I finished the complete manuscript. Watching him discover the world during his first year has been the greatest joy and privilege of my life. Finally, thank you, Owen, for standing by my side every step of the way. No list of superlatives can convey my love and appreciation. Thank you for being my tireless cheerleader, kindest editor, and best friend. On to the next adventure!

# INTRODUCTION

Upon his death, John Yeates, a wealthy Virginia planter, bequeathed a thousand acres of land and three enslaved people to Suffolk Parish in Nansemond County. In his 1731 will, he tasked the parish vestry with managing his bequest "forever," in effect creating a perpetual endowment of land and unfree Black labor to benefit the parish. He directed his legacy to support a variety of causes, including the minister's salary, the purchase of communion silver and legal books, poor relief, and a parish school. A dynamic picture of religious life in Virginia emerges from Yeates's final instructions. Anglican parishes like Suffolk closely governed their local communities, provided spiritual care to parishioners, executed the laws, and administered public services. Yeates's words also pointed to a civic and spiritual culture sustained through enslaved labor and plantation agriculture; the parish vestry invested heavily in material property and embraced racial slavery. Importantly, the terms of this donation in no way distinguished religious purposes from other public works. Such a division between the spiritual and the civic would have made no sense to Yeates, who lived under the legal system of religious establishment in which the Church of England governed as an arm of the imperial state and Anglican orthodoxy suffused colonial law. There were no hard-and-fast lines between religion and government in the colonial Chesapeake.[1]

More than seventy years later, in 1802, residents of Nansemond County demanded that the state of Virginia seize Yeates's bequest, including the enslaved community that had grown to include more than twenty men, women, and children. According to the petitioners, Yeates could have had "no idea of the great Revolution in Church as well as state" that would transform Virginia into a republic and remove the Church of England from its privileged position as the established church. They insisted that the parish was now just one of many religious communities in the state and had lost any claim to Yeates's public-spirited donations, which were "designed for the general and mutual advantage" of "the people at large."

According to these petitioners, so long as this property remained in the hands of the parish, a pernicious form of religious establishment attenuated their religious freedom. Despite protests from the Suffolk Parish vestry and parishioners, Virginia's republican legislature authorized the transfer of parish lands and the enslaved community from Suffolk Parish to the Nansemond County Overseers of the Poor, an elected board of secular officials who would administer the colonial bequest moving forward.[2]

The seizure of Suffolk Parish's landholdings and enslaved community was part of a massive confiscation project intended to dismantle the Anglican establishment. In the wake of the American Revolution, Virginia's counties claimed enslaved people, demolished churches, sold glebe lands, and auctioned off church bells and communion silver in their quest to overthrow the Anglican establishment and create an establishment of religious freedom in its place. Many of the loudest cries for confiscation came from white communities hoping to secure their hold over church property, including Black people enslaved as chattel, in the name of religious liberty. The Virginia legislature appropriated at least one hundred enslaved people (though likely many more) and more than forty thousand acres of land across the state. Revolutionary appeals for religious freedom were in no way a clear-cut vindication of fundamental rights for all. Framed then and often discussed now as a fight for individual liberty, the process of disestablishment secured only some individuals' liberties and did so at a high cost.

In contrast to Virginia, no parish property was seized in Maryland after independence. However, the postwar debates in Maryland were no less concerned with the inextricability of religious liberty and property. Like Virginia, until the Revolution, colonial Maryland had been governed by an active Anglican establishment, which bestowed numerous legal privileges on the Church of England and sharply restricted the rights of nonconformists.

Most importantly, common law conferred corporate powers on the established church, enabling it to hold and convey property securely. Colonial Anglican parishes exercised these powers to amass wealth across the Chesapeake. But nonconforming communities of faith there had no such corporate rights under statute or common law. Property thus became a source of acute anxiety for dissenting Protestant and Catholic communities, which struggled to secure land, sanctuaries, buildings, and enslaved people. In the words of John Carroll, a longtime Jesuit leader in Maryland who would become the first American Catholic bishop, the legal vulnerability of nonconformists' property was an "ever present danger."[3]

In 1802, the very same year Virginians were forging ahead with plans for the confiscation of parish property across the state, Marylanders were instead enacting a program of general incorporation for Christian churches. For religious communities long worried about losing their property, general incorporation offered a reliable way to gain legal standing and secure their assets for future generations. Moreover, Presbyterians, Methodists, Catholics, and other religious communities argued that extending incorporation to all Christian denominations would deliver equal recognition and protection of their rights under the law. Reformers in Maryland set their sights on general incorporation rather than confiscation, but concerns about property were still the driving force behind this movement.[4]

Fundamental to confiscation in Virginia and incorporation in Maryland was the belief that the revolt against the English monarchy had been a war against the Anglican establishment. Anglicanism had underpinned the social, legal, and political order of the colonial Chesapeake, and the war took aim at the joint foundation upon which imperial religious and political authority rested.[5] Yet the Revolution toppled the Anglican status quo in the Chesapeake colonies without clarifying what would take its place. There was no blueprint for dissolving the church-state union nor any coherent plan to guide reformers as they rebuilt their governments, religious institutions, and public life in the absence of both monarchy and establishment.

As they began dismantling their established churches, newly independent Americans grappled with a fundamental concern: how to replace an establishment of religion with an establishment of religious freedom. They sought not just to remove Anglican legal privileges but to enact positive laws and create new institutions to guarantee individual rights to free exercise and to protect religious pluralism. This upheaval was not a straightforward "separation of church and state" in which Americans tore along the dotted line between two already distinct entities. Instead, as reformers pulled down the establishment, they reconceived the fundamental premises on which both religion and government rested and forced a reallocation of their powers and responsibilities. This fraught process remade church, state, and the relationship between them.

I HAVE made several deliberate choices about the chronology, geography, scale, and themes of this book to contribute something new to the rich literature on church and state in the era of the founding. A large body of scholarship has emphasized the social dynamics of Anglicanism and characterized the established church as a powerful instrument of elite control in the colonial era.[6] These studies of Anglicanism emphasize the social and political power of the church but not necessarily its spiritual vibrancy.[7] Closely related are studies of evangelical dissenters in Virginia and their challenge to Anglican hegemony, which dovetailed with the overthrow of the English monarchy.[8] Subsequent revisionists, in turn, emphasize the dynamic religious culture of Anglicanism by looking at parochial culture, the clergy, devotional practices, sermons, and print culture.[9] Another important body of work has read Anglicanism through the lens of material culture and architecture, again highlighting both the depth of religious commitment and the dominance of Virginian elites who oversaw the established church in local communities.[10]

By contrast, comparatively less has been written about Anglicanism in Maryland. Instead, Catholicism remains the dominant feature of the literature, an emphasis that both distinguishes Maryland from other English colonies and privileges the seventeenth century over the eighteenth century.[11] My work shines a new light on religion in the Chesapeake through a comparative study of Virginia and Maryland. By bringing both colonies into a single frame, this book explores the shared culture of Chesapeake Anglicanism and religious dissent across the region while highlighting important distinctions between the two colonies. The significance of these differences only becomes clear in a comparative narrative that closely examines Maryland and Virginia together.

My primary focus is not religion per se but religious establishment, a difference in emphasis that presents new interpretive opportunities. Establishment was the legal system that knit together the Anglican Church and English state and underwrote the operation of imperial and local government in the Chesapeake. The evolving connection between church and state over two centuries of ideological and institutional change remains the centerpiece of this story and adds a new perspective to the existing literature. In part, I offer this new angle by drawing on an overlooked set of sources: parish vestry books. Too bureaucratic for scholars of religion and too religious for scholars of the state, these parish records have been mined for demographic data but rarely studied as evidence of

This engraved map of Maryland and Virginia orients the two colonies around the Chesapeake Bay, revealing how this single waterway defined the entire region. Francis Lamb, *A map of Virginia and Maryland*, from John Speed, *A prospect of the most famous parts of the world*, 1676. (Courtesy of the Boston Public Library)

spiritual vitality or of legal power. As the legal records of church activity, these manuscripts reveal the church to have been a vital and active part of imperial government. I situate these parish records among numerous other original documents: dissenting church records, legal treatises and handbooks, court records, poor-relief accounts, letters, newspapers, legislative petitions, architectural records, and property inventories. By drawing on this array of sources, my discussion reveals just how present Anglican institutions were in daily life and foregrounds their essential role in the operation of the imperial state in the Chesapeake. Anglican bureaucracy was central to the smooth operation of the British Empire, and the established church carried out the essential functions of law enforcement on the ground in both colonies.[12]

These records also led me to focus foremost on the local institution of the parish. Many scholars of Anglicanism have pointed out the ingrained localism of Chesapeake Anglicanism, but they tend to concentrate on other aspects of religious life without centering the parish as a legal institution.[13] Far removed from the oversight of English bishops or any other ecclesiastical administration, the parish took on a newfound prominence in the Chesapeake. A young Thomas Jefferson once referred to Virginia's religious establishment as "the churches of our government."[14] This phrase neatly captures the operation of religious establishment in the Chesapeake: Every parish acted as an agent of the transatlantic state but exercised its power on a local scale. All colonists—male and female, free and enslaved, conforming and dissenting—were considered parishioners. They were bound to the transatlantic church through their allegiance to the monarch as head of church and state while living under the watchful eye of parish ministers, vestries, and churchwardens in their communities. Parishes distributed poor relief and public patronage, collected taxes, oversaw indentures, inspected tobacco, punished moral crimes, publicized, sanctioned, and executed the laws, administered processioning, and announced elections. Their many bureaucratic duties knit together political authority and religious orthodoxy and reflected the church's mandate to oversee an orderly society. Focusing on the parish underscores just how powerful a force Anglicanism was in the colonial Chesapeake.

The question of revolutionary disestablishment has also received significant attention from scholars. Two main topics dominate this field: first, the state-by-state process of disestablishment in the 1780s and, second, the drafting of the Constitution and the First Amendment at the federal level.[15] In both camps, scholars tend to cast disestablishment as a political achievement driven by an ideological movement for individual rights and a vindication of the Revolution's highest ideals. Moreover, discussion of Virginia dominates this literature while Maryland has received less attention.[16] Presenting Virginia as the archetype of disestablishment, however, has significant drawbacks. Because this approach connects events in the Old Dominion to national politics through the involvement of Jefferson and Madison, it can lose sight of how local dynamism drove the process. It also reduces the story in other states to a laundry list of dates.[17] Any attempt to provide a single date for a state's disestablishment misrepresents a meandering process as a single event. Just as no single act established the Church of England in either colony, no single act that disestablished the church in either state. Moreover, accounts of disestablishment often employ different markers to pinpoint when disestablishment occurred. There have been no consistent criteria from state to state.[18] By certain definitions of disestablishment used in the literature about Virginia, Maryland has never fully disestablished its colonial Anglican Church.[19] This approach implies a uniformity that did not exist. Stating that Maryland disestablished the Anglican Church in 1785 and Virginia disestablished the Anglican Church in 1786 gives the impression that the two states simply enacted the same policies a year apart. Investigating events on the ground reveals the contradictory terms of their legal settlements. There was no coherent or agreed-upon definition of disestablishment adopted by the Chesapeake states.

The story of disestablishment becomes far richer in a comparative geographic frame. While both Maryland and Virginia began to dismantle the established Anglican Church during the Revolution, they did so in distinct, often contradictory ways. The significant differences between the two colonies prompted reformers in either state to pursue very different postwar agendas. This divergence only registers in a comparative account.

This book also takes a longer chronological approach by following events from the founding of the Chesapeake colonies in the seventeenth century through the Revolution and several decades into the nineteenth century. Much of the scholarship on the established church in colonial Virginia cuts off at the Revolution or shortly thereafter. Conversely, most of the scholarship on disestablishment begins on the eve of independence. Studies that connect state disestablishments to the drafting of the First Amendment suggest that the struggle for religious freedom reached some sort of terminus with ratification. These studies do not follow the ongoing and rapid changes in church-state settlements that continued unabated for decades into the nineteenth century. Drawing together insights from scholars of both the colonial establishment and its dismantling after independence into a single narrative offers far more explanatory power about how religious freedom grew out of colonial establishments and revolutionary turmoil.

Another key difference in my approach to church and state is an emphasis on property.[20] Under the establishmentarian laws of both colonies, Anglican parishes raised taxes annually and amassed a significant amount of wealth using public funds, including numerous church buildings, poorhouses, glebes (plantations of at least two hundred acres), communion silver, and enslaved people. Parishes also received property through charitable bequests made for the support of public worship or to benefit the parochial welfare system. Dismantling the established church wrought an extraordinary material transformation across the religious landscape. Financial gain and material concerns animated many of disestablishment's most bitter contests because property expressed the very real interests of rightsholders. By underscoring the tangible stakes of disestablishment, this study does not seek to cheapen or tarnish the ideological arguments made in the debates over religious freedom. Rather, acknowledging their material dimensions underscores the concrete consequences of personal liberties in the early republic.

Parish property holding was distinguished not only by its scale but also by the established church's unique corporate privileges. Incorporation is a legal tool that provides a group or organization with the ability to exist as a single person in the eyes of the law. Corporations can own property in perpetuity, sue and be sued, and sign binding contracts. Access to the corporate form preserved the parishes' institutional continuity independent of the succession of individual vestrymen, churchwardens, or ministers. When a vestryman resigned or a minister died, the parish itself lived on, and its property remained secure. Incorporation was, thus, a cornerstone of the colonial Anglican establishment because it allowed parishes to safeguard the significant wealth that funded their wide-ranging statutory and ecclesiastical duties. Denied any corporate privileges, nonconforming faith communities in Maryland and Virginia struggled to protect their property using other methods. Quakers, Catholics, and Presbyterians complained about their inability to incorporate and feared that individual trustees could misappropriate assets or that heirs might challenge bequests. Property and the right to secure it through incorporation were constitutive elements of establishment because they created and enforced powerful legal distinctions between Anglicans and everyone else.

On both sides of the Atlantic, many local bodies of the Anglican Church exercised corporate privileges under common law, rather than through formal charters. The leading eighteenth-century English theorist of the common law, William Blackstone, explained that Anglican bishops, churchwardens, and parsons, "by common law have ever been held . . . to have been corporations" by the "King's implied consent."[21] The unusual nature of customary incorporation means these bodies have largely been left out of the history of American corporations.[22] Several scholars have examined English parishes and debated whether and when they began exercising corporate powers. Historians of colonial Anglicanism have devoted less attention to the issue.[23]

The historical record, however, clearly shows that ordinary people and jurists alike in the colonial Chesapeake regarded Anglican churchwardens, rectors, and vestries as corporations.[24] The gentlemen who served as parish vestrymen and churchwardens understood and exercised these corporate powers to great effect. Churchwardens and rectors were traditionally treated as corporations in English common law. The vestries' assumption of corporate powers in the colonies marked a significant local innovation and became a point of contention with imperial authorities.[25] The vociferous protests of non-Anglicans after independence over their exclusion from corporate privileges revealed their sense that incorporation conferred enviable and unfair advantages to the established church. Moreover, early national jurists affirmed the corporate standing of colonial Anglican parish vestries and churchwardens.[26]

Incorporation became a flashpoint during disestablishment precisely because the established church had exercised exclusive corporate powers in the colonial era. Reformers in both Maryland and Virginia launched campaigns to redress this disparity after independence, either through confiscation or general incorporation. The prominence of incorporation as a pressing legal and political issue during disestablishment only makes sense in light of this history. Recognizing the corporate privileges of the colonial establishment better explains why property—and the precise legal powers to secure it—was a central battleground in disestablishment.

Too often, historians silo disestablishment from other areas of legal history, but questions about religious property and incorporation better integrate the history of church and state into larger narratives of early American law. Removing the church from its customary position of power raised vexing legal questions about slavery, suffrage, common law, corporations, the absolute right to property, and the ties between citizens and the state. Disestablishment dovetailed with other transformations in American law, such as the end of entail and primogeniture, debtors' relief, changes in corporate and criminal law, and the entrenchment of racial slavery in the South.[27] Americans energetically pursued numerous opportunities to remake the law in their new republic. Reforms to church and state need to be recognized within the broader movement of legal reform in the early republic. Religion was just one of the many venues in which newly independent Americans grappled with how to reconcile conflicting claims to property and liberty in their new republic. This book reorients the discussion of disestablishment beyond its familiar context of constitutional law and integrates it more fully into the legal, political, and social history of the early republic. Deliberations over church and state queried how republicanism's abstract premises ought to shape actual laws in the new republic.[28]

Finally, historians of race and slavery have also made significant contributions to our understanding of Southern Anglicanism. Their work demonstrates that the established church not only sanctified slavery but also actively participated in and profited from slaveholding.[29] My work adds to this conversation by showing how parishes were an essential part of the legal entrenchment of slavery. The clergy reiterated that submission to earthly superiors was a form of obedience to God, which grafted racial slavery neatly onto the theological foundation of establishment. Ministers recited the slave code from the pulpit during divine service while parish vestries and churchwardens advertised fugitives from slavery, punished interracial sex, and oversaw the indenture of mixed-race children. By carefully controlling not only who had access to the rite of baptism but also whose baptisms were officially recorded in the parish register, parishes hardened racial boundaries and equated parochial belonging with whiteness. Parishes were also acquisitive slaveholders, and more than half of Virginia's parishes owned enslaved people. While there are fewer surviving sources in Maryland, it is clear that a handful of parishes enslaved dozens of people. Many more parishes in both colonies hired enslaved laborers from year to year or paid to accommodate people enslaved by parish ministers at the glebes. The wealth produced by enslaved laborers went directly back into the parish by augmenting the minister's salary, supporting the poor, purchasing prayerbooks and communion elements, and maintaining sanctuaries. In all these ways, the established church in the Chesapeake relied on racial slavery to carry out its spiritual and civic work and sanctified racial hierarchy in the process.

Accounts that paint disestablishment as a triumphant struggle for individual rights can overlook the Black men and women held in bondage as white communities fought over their bodies and labor. Throughout this book, I integrate the history of slavery more fully into the revolutionary reform of church and state. In Maryland, Anglican and Catholic institutions enslaved hundreds of people after disestablishment. In Virginia, counties seized enslaved men and women from parishes and used their labor to support new civic institutions for the benefit of the white community. A desire to win control of church property, particularly enslaved people, animated many of the most bitter fights and sweeping reforms during disestablishment. Relatedly, as legislatures transferred powers from parishes to counties, county officials redeployed the traditional legal tools of moral control—indentures, bastardy laws, and welfare—to surveil and control free people of color. Originally utilized to oversee a godly community under the watchful eye of religious institutions, these legal technologies enabled republican governments to police the racial order, even in the absence of a religious mandate.

ULTIMATELY, THIS book makes three key arguments. First, an "establishment of religion" was a contingent concept in early America.[30] Though both Chesapeake colonies had established the Church of England in their laws, the establishment operated differently in Maryland and Virginia. Americans brought distinct experiences of the established church into their fight for independence and ensuing efforts to build a new republic. While Virginia and Maryland championed the end of the established church during the Revolution and enshrined religious freedom in their new constitutions, their actual state laws diverged drastically in practice. The shared rhetoric of religious freedom obscured how differently disestablishment was implemented in these neighboring states. In Maryland, the state could extend legal privileges to Christian denominations, so long as it did so equally. In Virginia, any formal tie between church and state came to be viewed as an unconstitutional vestige of the Anglican establishment. Maryland's revolutionary definition of establishment rested on state partiality toward particular denominations over others, whereas Virginia's framework rejected any close connections between church and state. There was no stable or shared definition of an impermissible "establishment of religion" between the states, nor was there any unified agenda or agreed-upon platform driving the movement we now call disestablishment.[31]

The definition of establishment continued to evolve rapidly in both Virginia and Maryland. Both Chesapeake states' 1776 constitutions represented a snapshot in time amid the turmoil of the Revolution. In the 1780s, widespread dissatisfaction with these wartime settlements sparked a new wave of debates and reform. By the early nineteenth century, state laws continued to change in response to emerging concerns about incorporation and confiscation. Within a generation, Maryland's position came to align more closely with Virginia's separationist model, as the state instituted more insulation between church and state. Moreover, Baltimore's booming growth brought large numbers of Jews to the state for the first time, whose demands for religious liberty broadened Maryland's church-state settlement to afford greater rights to non-Christians. And even in Virginia, where policies sought to uncouple church from state, the two often remained entangled. In short, establishment was a moving target, a contingent concept that evolved swiftly during and after the Revolution.

My approach to disestablishment carries significant implications for how we understand the First Amendment's Establishment Clause. Contemporary materials reveal the absence of a singular or stable meaning of this term at the time of the founding. The constitutional concept of *an* establishment of religion evolved from the acrimonious and negotiated process of dismantling *the* established Anglican Church, which varied widely from one community to the next. The legal category of establishment remained nebulous as it evolved rapidly and unevenly in response to events in real time. Any appropriate definition of the concept must acknowledge that "an establishment of religion" was a hotly contested and demonstrably capacious category at the time of the founding.

Second, this book follows the story into the nineteenth century to consider how Americans replaced the Anglican establishment of religion with an establishment of religious freedom. Reformers were not satisfied with merely removing the legal privileges of the Church of England from their laws; they went further by demanding that positive laws preserve and protect religious liberty. Thomas Jefferson, James Madison, and John Carroll all borrowed the vocabulary of establishment but inverted its meaning by calling on the state affirmatively to establish religious freedom.[32] Coupled with this new body of law to guarantee religious freedom was a series of ambitious projects to remake public institutions fit for the American republic.

Gone was the established church and all it had represented, but questions lingered about what would take its place. Disestablishment sparked debates about how government ought to support the common good in the absence of state-enforced orthodoxy. While this transformation was less disruptive in Maryland because its parishes did not lose their property, significant changes still swept over the state. Determined to build new republican institutions, Episcopalians and Catholics in the state moved away from their traditional reliance on plantation agriculture and sold hundreds of enslaved people South in the first decades of the nineteenth century. In Virginia, counties used the proceeds of confiscation to fund a wide variety of republican civic projects, such as poorhouses, academies, and even colleges like the University of Virginia. But most often these funds offset the cost of poor relief. Most Virginians were intent on lowering taxes above all else and sold off the buildings, land, and enslaved people as quickly as possible. In both states, counties assumed the duties of parishes—collecting taxes, maintaining vital records, and distributing poor relief—but did not undertake the close regulation of the moral behavior of white citizens. Free Black citizens, however, were subjected to intense scrutiny. As part of disestablishment, secular officials appropriated the tools of ecclesiastical governance—warning out, indenture, surveillance, and welfare—to enforce racial order. Removing the established church from the foundation of government and demolishing its institutional framework, therefore, did not upend the traditional social hierarchies that Anglican parishes had upheld in either state. If anything, the new republican settlement left less room for women in communal life and made racial hierarchy the single most important organizing logic of antebellum government in the Chesapeake.

Third, the Anglican establishment was a property regime, and disestablishment necessarily became a fight over material property as much as ideological principles. The legally established church in the colonial Chesapeake was undeniably a material project. The rich material culture of Chesapeake Anglicanism promoted obedience and order as interlocking spiritual and political values. Parishes expressly invoked state power to manage and invest resources on behalf of the community. The sacred spaces and liturgical objects essential to Anglican spirituality were also a valuable form of communal property. The established church invested heavily in land and enslaved people to support its sweeping civic and spiritual program. It was not just the immense wealth of the established church but its unique privileges of incorporation that entwined property rights with religious establishment. Parish vestries, churchwardens, and ministers each had a unique corporate status under common law that allowed them to hold and pass property securely. Catholics and Protestant dissenters in both colonies were denied the ability to secure their property through incorporation, and this prohibition remained one of the most potent legal disadvantages facing nonconformists in the Chesapeake.

Given the centrality of property and property rights to the workings of the establishment, it should come as no surprise that debates over material property—how to secure it and to whom it ought to belong—drove the process of disestablishment forward. Property was never a secondary concern but propelled the most significant divergences between the two states' disestablishmentarian laws and the ongoing development of "establishment" as a legal concept. Maryland offered general incorporation to all Christian denominations, which suited the state's Episcopalians and Catholics, who were anxious to safeguard their colonial-era holdings. In stark contrast, Virginia's evangelicals had comparatively little property and saw little benefit to winning formal incorporation. Instead, they pressed the state not only to strip the Episcopal Church of its incorporation but to prohibit any religious society from becoming incorporated in the state. In 1802, Virginia's legislature went even further and authorized counties to confiscate parish property, which included tens of thousands of acres of land, scores of enslaved people, sanctuaries, and objects worth thousands of pounds sterling. Property moved the needle of religious reform in both Chesapeake states.

By framing religious liberty as a contest over property rights, reformers married the most conservative impulses of the Revolution to its most radical promises. As a result, disestablishment was radical insofar as it removed orthodoxy from republican government and abandoned denominational conformity as a goal of statecraft, but it did not pose a threat to the social order. A commitment to absolute private property rights and legal entrenchment of racial slavery worked hand in hand in the dismantling of the established church. The established church had bolstered and participated in slavery. The newly republican state would continue to promote and profit from slavery using many of the same legal technologies. This story of property and power underscores how the American Revolution gave way to republicanism without unleashing a radical social revolution. The expansion of religious freedom was not accomplished in spite of the revolutionaries' conservative instincts but in accordance with them.

# 1

# ESTABLISHED BY LAW

THE LAST recorded witch trial in colonial America took place in 1706, when forty-six-year-old widow, midwife, and mother of three Grace Sherwood was convicted of witchcraft in southeastern Virginia. Local legends recall her dancing naked at night, her supernatural ability to fly, and her prowess as an herbalist and healer.[1] Meanwhile historians of early America have invoked Grace's ordeal to extend the narrative of witchcraft beyond the infamous events at Salem and show that belief in witchcraft was deeply rooted in Anglo-American culture and widespread across the colonies.[2] But Grace's story also demonstrates the full force of the established Church of England in the colonial Chesapeake. Her experiences reveal the extent to which Anglican orthodoxy permeated colonial law and Anglican parishes carried out the essential work of the state. Under the establishment, church and state governed together without any clear boundaries between religion and government.

Later known as the Witch of Pungo, Grace White was born in 1660 in Lynnhaven Parish near present-day Norfolk. The daughter of a respected carpenter, she married James Sherwood and raised three sons. Sherwood became the subject of persistent local suspicion in the 1690s as tales spread about her nighttime conjuring and shapeshifting alongside allegations that she had cursed her neighbors' livestock and crops. She was widowed in 1701 and became a rare female landholder in the parish, two facts that made her an even more likely target for ostracism.[3] By the time she was formally charged in court with witchcraft in 1706, the clerk of the court neatly summarized years of accusations by observing that she had been "a long time Suspected of witchcraft."[4] Before proceeding to a trial, the court impaneled a jury of women to inspect Widow Sherwood's body for physiological signs of evil. These female jurors declared that she had two unusual "titts," a damning piece of evidence according to the tradition that female evildoers suckled the devil and his familiars.[5] After some tussling over jurisdiction, the county court proceeded to a witch trial.

In June 1706, the court heard testimony against the accused witch, "proving Many Cercumstances to which She could not make any excuse."[6] According to local lore, she was then taken to the church, placed on a stool, and ordered to repent for her crimes. Rather than admit any wrongdoing, Sherwood vowed, "I be not a witch, I be a healer."[7] After she refused to confess, the justices of the peace resorted to a water trial. Still known as Witchduck Point today, the site chosen for her ducking was close to both the courthouse and the parish church. The authorities bound Sherwood's hands and feet and plunged her underwater, but she managed to escape and began "swiming . . . contrary To custom & the Judg[men]t of all spectators."[8] To the assembled onlookers, her watery escape was unassailable proof of her wickedness. Just as damning was a second bodily inspection by five "ancient" women who concluded she was "not like them nor noe Other woman that they knew of having two things like titts on her private parts of a Black Coller being Blacker [tha]n [th]e Rest of her Body."[9] While the records do not indicate Sherwood was of African descent, a darker complexion might suggest another reason for her isolation in a society increasingly obsessed with maintaining racial boundaries. Convicted of witchcraft, Sherwood was swiftly imprisoned.

The criminal prosecution of witchcraft epitomized the legal framework of religious establishment. Parliamentary witchcraft statutes bracketed together moral, religious, and social deviance and underscored that individual sin threatened the entire community. A Virginian legal handbook published a few decades after Grace Sherwood's trial summarized the Anglo-American definition of witches as "persons of either sex, who have real Correspondence and familiar Conversation with Evil Spirits."[10] Colonial officials enforced Anglican orthodoxy and corrected heterodoxy in their pursuit of the public good. They framed punishing women like Sherwood as necessary to preserve the moral order of the community.

The local institutions of church and state worked hand in hand during her case. Nine county justices of the peace presided over the trial, four of whom were also parish vestrymen.[11] These JPs appointed Maximillian Boush, a wealthy planter, militia officer, and one of Lynnhaven Parish's two churchwardens, to act as the Queen's Attorney, or the chief prosecutor, in the case. The overlap between parish vestrymen and county magistrates has often been used to illustrate the hegemony of Virginian elites.[12] But we can add more nuance to this conclusion when we recognize that Grace Sherwood, her accusers, the JPs, the vestrymen, the female jurors, and the many community members who had swapped suspicions over the years were *all* parishioners. Enforcing moral law relied on vigilant communal oversight as much as hierarchical deference. The parish acted as a vehicle of neighborly surveillance and retribution in this watchful society.

The story of the so-called Virginia Witch usually ends with Sherwood's conviction, but she and her descendants continued to live in Lynnhaven Parish long after her trial ended. After her release from jail, Sherwood continued to participate in the life of the parish. As one of the few female landowners in Lynnhaven, she partook in processioning, the ritual of surveying of all private property lines in the parish.[13] All property holders in the parish were required to process (that is, to literally walk along) their property boundaries accompanied by adjoining landholders and parish-appointed inspectors. Processioning, like other parish duties, expressed the established church's mission to safeguard social harmony and maintain order by drawing all parishioners into legal agreement.[14] The parish carried out this local work without distinguishing its civic and religious duties. While Lynnhaven Parish participated in Widow Sherwood's condemnation and marked her as a social pariah, it also recognized her communal membership and protected her property claims.

After Sherwood died in 1733 at the age of eighty, her family fell on hard times and turned to Lynnhaven Parish for support. Parishes in Virginia administered a social safety network by providing poor relief to orphaned, elderly, sick, and indigent persons. In 1748 and 1749, John Sherwood was given an annual allowance by the parish to help maintain his wife's aged mother.[15] After Grace Sherwood's son James Sherwood died in 1752, his two orphaned children were taken in by three different parishioners, each of whom received regular payments for supporting the children until they came of age.[16] Among the vestrymen who made the final decisions about these disbursements were the sons and grandsons of the men who presided over Grace Sherwood's witch trial. The bonds of communal reciprocity could be as strong as those of censure.

The Sherwood family's wide range of experiences in Lynnhaven Parish reveal the full force of religious establishment in the colonial Chesapeake. By foregrounding establishment as a legal system that fused church and state, this chapter offers a novel account of the eighteenth-century Chesapeake. Establishment functioned both on an ideological level and an institutional level as Anglican orthodoxy provided a basis for and justification of state power while Anglican parishes took on active roles in executing the law and governing daily life. None of the church's duties were auxiliary to its religious work; rather, a key premise of establishment was the exercise of state power to oversee a moral and orderly society. Ministers carried out civic duties and preached obedience to the state as a spiritual and moral obligation. Vestries and churchwardens publicized and executed the laws, raised and invested public funds, regulated the local economy, and policed moral crimes. Establishment touched nearly every facet of daily life in colonial Virginia and Maryland.

By looking at church and state together, this chapter makes three key arguments. First, church and state both were far more powerful than has often been represented in the scholarship. Historians who study the established church in the Chesapeake from a transatlantic or top-down perspective tend to overlook the most powerful Anglican institution: the parish. The church operated most powerfully at the local level of the parish. Anglican parishes carried out essential work as part of the imperial state in the Chesapeake and were often the most immediate form of government in the daily lives of colonists. These local bodies coordinated public worship and carried out a wide range of legal and civic duties. We can only grasp the extensive reach of religion and government when establishment is central to the story of the Chesapeake.

Moreover, a careful study of how establishment functioned on the ground in the Chesapeake furnishes a much sharper definition of an "establishment of religion" in the eighteenth century. Most often, the scholarship on church and state focuses on the use of state power to curb religious liberty or advantage particular religious communities above others. In short, this emphasis approaches religion through the lens of individual rights. But my analysis expands the definition of religious establishment by calling attention to the fact that power flowed in two directions: from state to church and from church to state. Establishment not only entailed governmental oversight of religious matters but also meant that Anglicanism undergirded the state ideologically and institutionally. Anglican orthodoxy infused and sanctioned the law, and the established church exercised tremendous discretionary authority in daily life.

Finally, this chapter reveals the outsized role of the Anglican Church in building and maintaining the legal system of racial slavery in the Chesapeake. Nearly every facet of the parish's work—its use of doctrine to demand obedience, its regulation of marriage and sexual behavior, its distribution of patronage to white parishioners, its publication and enforcement of the laws, and its regulation of the tobacco economy—strengthened slavery as a legal institution and framed racial hierarchy as an expression of a godly society. The church gave divine sanction to the cruelest laws of man by endorsing and enforcing slave law.

This chapter begins by exploring the evolution of establishment in the Chesapeake through the early eighteenth century. The distinct origins of Maryland and Virginia as English colonies determined the legal parameters of religious establishment in each, and this seventeenth-century history provides essential context for the longer story of church and state. While key differences between Virginia and Maryland endured, several important features of Anglican practice had coalesced across the region by the early eighteenth century, and Chesapeake Anglican practices and institutions had come to differ from their English counterparts in several significant ways. Then, I survey the vast power deployed by local parishes in both colonies by looking closely at the local parish system and reviewing the church's authority over public worship, taxation, census records, marriage, moral crimes, and the tobacco economy. In each of these domains of parish power, the church operated as an essential part of the imperial state to enforce laws and govern communal life.

## Empire and Establishment in the Chesapeake

The underlying logic of Anglican establishment maintained that church and state were symbiotic, and political loyalty amounted to spiritual obedience. In the words of the Rev. James Maury, an eighteenth-century Virginian clergyman, the Church of England was "incorporated and blended with the state," and this union safeguarded "Peace, Unity [and] Order."[17] Maury's eighteenth-century understanding of establishment was the product of two centuries of religious and political turmoil. When Henry VIII left the Catholic Church in 1534 and declared himself the Supreme Head of the Church of England, he plunged England into a long and often violent process of reformation.[18] For generations afterward, English men and women wrestled with the divine nature of sovereignty, the boundaries of legitimate religious dissent, and the structure of the church-state relationship. When Elizabeth I took the throne in 1558, she tried to usher in a moderate religious settlement that prioritized allegiance to the monarch as head of church and state and compelled outward conformity. As

Richard Hooker, a chief defender of the queen, put it, "There is not any man of the *Church of England* but the same man is also a member of the *Commonwealth,* nor any member of the *Commonwealth* which is not also of the *Church of England.*"[19] Under this idealized model of establishment, all English subjects were Anglican parishioners who comprised a single English church and nation.

Of course, religious dissent persisted and with it came disagreement about how to deal with those who refused to conform. William Cecil, another advisor to Elizabeth I, advised against toleration, declaring that "the state could never be in safety, where there was toleration of two religions."[20] After acceding to the throne in 1603, James I faced violent challenges from radical Protestants and Catholics alike. In response, the King and his government endorsed the view that he was "lesser than God onely, from whom he immediately reeceieved his power over all men, and all sorts of men, Priest and people, in all causes, Civill and Spirituall."[21] This expansive assertion of royal sovereignty rooted in divine favor underwrote the partnership of church and state and legitimized the established church's exercise of legal power. Amid this long reformation, the English also embarked on the conquest of North America. The ongoing crises in England over church and state cast long shadows over the English imperial project.

There was no single model of Anglican establishment across the British Empire; rather, the precise terms of the church-state relationship in each colony reflected the needs and preferences of local populations and evolved in response to political and religious upheavals on both sides of the Atlantic. This transatlantic process of reformation created distinct Anglican establishments in Virginia and Maryland stemming from key dissimilarities in the early histories of the two Chesapeake colonies.

In Virginia, the Church of England was established from the colony's inception. James I granted the Virginia Company a charter in 1606 vaunting the English invasion in providential terms, and the first set of instructions issued for the colony's governance later that year required adherence to "the doctrine, rights, and religion now professed and established within our realme of England" and forbid "any person to withdrawe . . . from the same, or from their due allegiance, unto us . . . as their immediate soveraigne under God."[22] Virginia's leaders put this establishmentarian vision into practice in their initial legal code, the *Lawes Divine, Morall, and Martiall* (written and revised between 1610–12). Introduced after the notorious Starving Time when a majority of Jamestown's residents died from disease, violence, and starvation, these new laws aimed to compel capitulation from a society on the brink of collapse. Hearkening back to James I's comprehensive assertion of divine sovereignty, the *Lawes* proclaimed that "all power and authoritie is derived, and flowes" from God and thus colonists owed complete obedience to every "publike Officer" acting in the colony on the king's behalf.[23] Criticism of any official or insubordination of any kind was deemed at once treasonous and sacrilegious. Even the syntax of this early legal code with sweeping references to "*the* true religion," "*the* ministers," and "*the* church" [emphasis added] recognized only one legitimate faith and papered over the pressing spiritual differences among settlers.[24] The *Lawes* set an important precedent by giving lay political leaders direct control over the established church and oversight of its clergy and adopting several domains of ecclesiastical law into the colony's statutes under civil jurisdiction. An expedient solution to the absence of either bishops or ecclesiastical courts in the colony, this model of lay political control over the church would persist after Virginia became a royal colony under the control of a Crown-appointed governor after 1624 and last for the rest of the colonial era.

Early leaders painted Virginia as an orthodox Anglican colony, but the established church floundered for much of the early seventeenth century. There were very few Anglican ministers in the colony, parishes received public funds sporadically, and many of the colony's establishmentarian laws were not enforced. But the lack of official support for the established church did not suggest that Virginians were irreligious. Quite the opposite, in fact. Spiritual vitality flowed from the ground up, and the Anglican Church grew in an improvised fashion through popular support. Lay colonists took their religious needs into their own hands, and local communities formed parishes and supported lay readers and ministers of their choosing. When the House of Burgesses eventually did strengthen laws organizing parishes, regulating clerical duties and salaries, punishing moral crimes, and standardizing the collection of parish levies, their efforts codified decades of Virginian custom.[25]

This locally grown system of establishment could also effectively cloak religious difference, and Virginia was never as homogenous as its boosters claimed.[26] Puritans who came to Virginia in the early 1620s settled in separate parishes and recruited like-minded clergymen.[27] Far away from the supervision of bishops or ecclesiastical courts, this locally organized establishment offered significant religious latitude. But the cascading violence of the English Civil Wars inflamed tensions over religion in the colony. In 1642, royalist Gov. William Berkeley reportedly tried to force Puritan colonists to take oaths in support of the king and threatened those who declined with imprisonment or expulsion. The leader of the Powhatan Confederacy, Opechancanough, recognized the colony's internal divisions as an opportunity to reclaim their territory and launched the Third Anglo-Powhatan War. One eyewitness claimed that "if the Indians had forborne for a month longer, they had found us in such a combustion among our selves that they might with ease have cut of[f] every man if once we had spent that little powder and shot that we had among our selves." From this turmoil over religion, Virginians imbibed the belief that dissent invited danger.

In the wake of King Charles I's execution and the establishment of the Commonwealth, Berkeley's government in Virginia defiantly continued to compel obedience to the traditional forms of the Church of England, and local communities cooperated in these efforts. Several county courts prosecuted Puritan ministers who refused to abide by the colony's establishmentarian laws, and some parishioners withheld tithes from Puritan clergymen. Ultimately, this hostility drove a Puritan exodus from Virginia to Maryland. By the Restoration of the monarchy in 1660, Virginia was more religiously uniform than at any point in its earlier history.

There were dissenting communities in Virginia, particularly Quakers, after the mid-seventeenth century, but their numbers remained low through the early eighteenth century.[28] The author of a legal handbook for Virginia's local officials admitted that he had "purposefully omitted" an exhaustive list of all prohibitions against nonconformists "because this Government has hitherto enjoied the singular happiness, that all the subjects here agree in uniformity of Worship, according to the Doctrine of the Church of England, which is here by Law established."[29] The legal regime of establishment worked not only by punishing nonconformists in the colony but also by dissuading them from coming in the first place.

Unlike Virginia, Maryland was a proprietary colony under the control of a single family, the Calverts. A Catholic convert and close ally of the Stewarts, the second Baron of Baltimore, Cecil Calvert, received a charter from King Charles I to establish a province in Maryland in 1632. The Maryland Charter skirted around Calvert's Catholicism by referring broadly to "God's holy and true Christian Religion" and framing English conquest as an ecumenical Christian enterprise.[30] But the charter still likened the proprietor to an Anglican bishop and insinuated that any formally established church in Maryland would have to be Anglican. The Calverts adroitly sidestepped this issue by affirming nonsectarian Christian doctrines in law while eschewing any form of ecclesiastical administration in the province.

Though Maryland never established Catholicism, Calvert privately recruited the Society of Jesus to minister in the province. In the 1630s, Jesuit priests traveled to Maryland like any other private persons and received private land grants of more than nine thousand acres under the colony's headright system by paying to transport dozens of indentured servants. With this significant investment in land and unfree labor, the Jesuits signaled their intent to finance their missions through private plantations in the absence of state support. The priests held this land as individuals, but the growth of landed Jesuit estates nonetheless alarmed Protestant colonists as an affront to English law, which had sharply restricted Catholic property ownership and other public expressions of "popery" since the Henrician Reformation. The Jesuit clergy even angered some Catholic colonists, who complained that they devoted too much energy to proselytizing Indigenous peoples and not enough attention to the pastoral care of English settlers.

The relationship between the Catholic proprietor and his chosen ministry soured over the following decade, particularly after the Jesuit Order purchased additional lands directly from the Patuxent tribe and received gifts of land from the Piscataway tribe. Calvert viewed this acquisition of land directly from Indigenous peoples as an infringement of his sovereignty over all land granted in the Maryland Charter. As tensions mounted, he forbade these Catholic institutions from acquiring property without his express permission, a development that will be discussed in detail in chapter 2. Calvert asserted the primacy of his proprietary rights under the charter and curbed Catholic ecclesiastical autonomy in the province.[31]

The colony's broad policies of toleration offered a refuge for Catholics fleeing England's harsh penal laws but also attracted nonconformists of all stripes to the colony. Dissenting Protestants and conforming Anglicans arrived in large numbers, and Maryland was majority-Protestant from the outset. During the Civil Wars, Calvert briefly lost control over the province in a revolt led by Protestant settlers in 1646. To mollify the ascendant Puritan administration in London and unhappy Protestants in Maryland, the proprietor appointed a Protestant governor and instructed the assembly to enact a policy of religious toleration. The resulting statute, "An Act Concerning Religion," reiterated the traditional form of sovereignty—namely, that all subjects must show obedience to civil authorities—but took a novel approach to the question of dissent by asserting that state coercion in "matters of Religion hath frequently fallen out to be of dangerous Consequence in those governments." In effect, Calvert blamed the violence of the Civil Wars on a regime too intent on compelling conformity.

This statute instead fashioned an ecumenical Christian establishment in which no one could be "compelled to the beleife or exercise of any other Religion against his or her consent." As long as colonists were Christians and did not "molest or conspire against the civill Governement," they would be granted toleration in the colony. Furthermore, the new act made it a criminal offense for one colonist to call another any "name or terme in a reproachfull manner relating to matter of Religion" by including an exhaustive list of forbidden monikers. Anyone caught calling another a "heritick Scismatick, Idolator, puritan, Independent, Prespiterian, [or] popish," could be fined, whipped, or imprisoned. Calvert's solution to the problem of religious conflict was functionally a gag rule that prohibited public discussions or displays of religious difference. Driven by self-interest in preserving his authority as well as quelling disagreement, Calvert paired coercion of speech with toleration of belief as a strategy to preserve public peace in a diverse society.[32]

However, the Calvert family came under increasing pressure in both Maryland and London over the lack of Anglican establishment in the colony following the restoration of the monarchy in 1660. The exertions of Rev. George Yeo, an Anglican minister in Maryland, exemplified the lobbying campaign for greater support of Anglicanism in the colony. To Yeo, the problem was not a dearth of faithful Anglicans but the absence of any institutional support for their spiritual practices. He warned the Archbishop of Canterbury that without access to public worship or pastoral care, "many daily fall away either to Popery, Quakerism, or Phanaticism."[33] Yeo argued that the lack of an established church had made Maryland into a "Sodom of uncleanness" where "the Lord's day is profaned, religion despised and all notorious vices committed." In his view, Maryland's social fabric lay in tatters without an established church.

In this 1793 allegorical engraving, Cecil Calvert presents the 1649 Maryland "Act Concerning Religion" to a pantheon of lawmakers, including Lycurgus and Marcus Aurelius, as William Penn watches. The image celebrates Calvert and emphasizes that Maryland, not Pennsylvania, was the first colony to protect the rights of conscience. James Barry, *Religious & civil liberty established in Maryland in 1649*. (Courtesy of the Library of Congress)

This criticism overlooked local efforts to strengthen Anglicanism in the colony, where voluntary contributions supported clergyman and funded the construction of fifteen Anglican churches.[34] Lay Protestant colonists also resented the lack of an Anglican establishment in the colony and chafed at the privileges bestowed on Catholics and Quakers. Protestant polemicists began accusing the proprietor of serving a "secret Councell of priests" and plotting with the French to "turne the Province to the Pope's devotion."[35] These farfetched allegations found a ready audience during the Exclusion Crisis as the English public wrestled with whether a Catholic monarch could legitimately rule over Protestant subjects.

The Glorious Revolution would ultimately answer this question in the negative as the Protestants William and Mary deposed the Catholic King James II in 1688. This political revolution set off a parallel revolt in Maryland when a group of rebels proclaiming themselves the Protestant Association overthrew Calvert's proprietary government. They legitimized their coup by making it an extension of the imperial Protestant struggle against Catholicism, exalting the new monarchs as "the glorious instruments of the Protestant Religion" and pleading with them for a "Protestant Government in this your Majesties Province, whereby our Religion, Lives, Liberties and Properties may be secured."[36] The Crown ultimately seized the colony from the Calvert family, and only after Charles Calvert, the fifth Baron of Baltimore, converted to Anglicanism in 1715 were the Calverts restored as the proprietors of Maryland. The imperial acquiescence to the Protestant Association and the requirement that the Calverts conform to the Church of England underscored the extent to which these two revolutions—England's and Maryland's—enforced a confessional requirement on sovereignty and loyalty.

In the wake of these two revolutions, the Maryland Assembly tried unsuccessfully to establish the Church of England three times before finally succeeding in 1702.[37] The first of the so-called Church Acts marked the colony's initial commitment to an Anglican establishment. This 1692 law imposed an annual tax for supporting Anglican ministers, created a system of parishes, and codified moral crimes.[38] Before the new governor had even signed it into law, the established church began to operate on the ground. Parishes were formed, vestrymen appointed, and levies collected.[39] However, the Crown formally repealed the act in 1695, citing a purportedly ambiguous clause in the law's opening proviso. This weak excuse did little to conceal that intense lobbying by Quakers and Catholics in London had killed the statute.[40] After two more colonial acts and two further royal vetoes on similar grounds, the Maryland Assembly passed a fourth version of the act in 1702 that complied with the Crown's demands. Despite this transatlantic clash, the overturned laws had already created a durable establishment on the ground, and many parishes had been operating since 1692 without serious interruption. As in Virginia, Maryland's establishment took root first as a locally governed institution through its parishes.

In fact, Maryland's longtime policy of toleration was muted by the colony's adoption of the 1689 English Act of Toleration. New measures accompanying the Church Acts in the following decades barred Catholics from voting, holding office, serving on juries, enlisting in the militia, worshipping publicly, or proselytizing.[41] New taxes were imposed on any "Irish Papist servants" imported to the colony. By making Protestantism a prerequisite for membership in the body politic and stripping Catholic Marylanders of longstanding rights and privileges, the province conformed to the 1689 parliamentary Act of Toleration. Discrimination against Catholics was part and parcel of English toleration, and conforming Marylanders embraced anti-Catholicism as a pillar of their new Anglican establishment.

Virginia was slower to adopt the English Act of Toleration in the wake of the Glorious Revolution, apparently because the act was deemed too lenient toward Protestant dissenters. Not until 1699 did the Burgesses acknowledge the parliamentary statute, and, even then, many Anglican Virginians insisted that the law did not apply to the colony. County courts sought to blunt its effects by often refusing to license more than one dissenting meetinghouse per county. By the mid-eighteenth century, Virginia's continued repudiation of toleration for Protestants looked regressively out of step with the rest of the British Empire.[42]

Out of this long transatlantic reformation emerged eighteenth-century religious settlements in Virginia and Maryland that were distinct from the English model and from one another. Virginia's established church was present from the colony's infancy, and its parishes governed alongside its counties. The Old Dominion's establishment was horizontally organized as church and state acted in parallel. Maryland's establishment, on the other hand, was grafted onto a provincial government that had been in operation for sixty years, and the Anglican Church sat squarely beneath civil government. This vertical structure meant that parishes had less independence and operated under the colony's counties. Moreover, the fault lines between orthodoxy and heterodoxy differed. In Maryland, the laws extended greater toleration to all Protestants while fixating on the suppression of Catholicism. In Virginia, Protestant dissenters remained the focus of the state's animus.

Still, there were important shared features of Anglican establishment across the region. Of course, there was the faith itself—the doctrines and orthodoxy of the Church of England, its emphasis on order, liturgy, and ritual, and its rich materiality in which spaces and objects enabled communion with the divine. But there were also important commonalties in how the church-state union functioned. First, both colonies drew bright lines around civic membership by making spiritual conformity the test of political loyalty and framed sovereignty through a spiritual lens. Second, lay leaders effectively ran the church in the absence of bishops and ecclesiastical courts in both colonies. The assemblies passed laws regulating the clergy and worship, carving out the boundaries of legitimate dissent, and delegating wide-ranging authority of parishes.

Governors had the formal power to appoint ministers in the absence of a bishop. Still, though, the church operated most powerfully on the local level through its parishes, and this localism is the third defining feature of the Chesapeake establishment. These three key characteristics–the fusion of the civic and the spiritual, the power of the laity, and the enduring localism—distinguished the Anglican establishment across the eighteenth-century Chesapeake.

## Parishes

The most important institution in the Chesapeake's locally governed and lay-dominated Anglican establishment system was the parish.[43] It is easy to miss the strength of the establishment when the Anglican Church is viewed from a transatlantic or colonywide perspective. The paucity of ministers, the idiosyncrasies of local practice, and the absence of ecclesiastical oversight can make the established church appear absent or ineffectual. But studying the church from the ground up furnishes us with a view of a robust and omnipresent institution.

At once a government institution, a legal body, a geographic division, a social community, and a religious fellowship, the parish was the local division of the established church on both sides of the Atlantic. The social realities of the Chesapeake meant that colonial parishes departed significantly from the English model.[44] Anglican clergymen lamented that colonial "parishes are so large, the Inhabitants so dispersed, and so distant from the Church" that colonists often missed divine services, neglected to bury their dead in the churchyards, or failed to baptize their children.[45] To accommodate these far-flung communities, Chesapeake parishes built several churches and chapels within their bounds. Parish ministers would rotate where they conducted services from week to week, and in the absence of the minister, the clerk or a lay reader would lead worship. These practical adaptations tailored the English parish and its spiritual program to the unique environment and culture of the tobacco colonies.

The term "parishioner" had several connotations in the colonial Chesapeake. English theologians and political leaders had traditionally imagined that English subjects and Anglican parishioners were one and the same, and in this sense, "parishioner" was a legal status that denoted residency within the geographic bounds of an Anglican parish. This all-inclusive framing was practically realized in the legal authority of parishes over all residents. But the universalizing nature of this legal term was also ill-suited to the Chesapeake, where religious dissent abounded and racial slavery made comprehensive spiritual fellowship a nonstarter for many white Anglicans. In practice, the term "parishioners" referred to active members of the spiritual community who attended worship, male freeholders who voted in parish elections, or white community members whose births, baptisms, and deaths were recorded in the parish register. The mutability of the term "parishioner" reflected the fuzzy boundaries between spiritual and civic identities and the limits of parochial belonging in the Chesapeake.

Parishioners lived under the authority of an array of civil and ecclesiastical parish officers. The responsibility of supervising the colonial parish fell first and foremost to the vestry. Vestries had long existed in England, but in the Chesapeake, the institution morphed into something altogether novel.[46] The absence of bishops, church courts, or other traditional loci of ecclesiastical power made colonial vestrymen far more powerful than their English counterparts. Virginia's vestries were composed of twelve laymen, who were generally appointed in a self-perpetuating fashion known as co-optation; when a vestryman died or resigned, the remaining members of the vestry voted to fill his spot. Vestrymen were the same elite gentlemen who served as justices of the peace, as officers in the militia, and as elected members of assembly. Virginia vestries taxed residents annually and wielded the power of the purse on par with county courts. They oversaw land processioning and distributed lucrative patronage. Virginian vestries also claimed the right to accept or reject ministerial candidates before the governor inducted them, thus functionally controlling the choice of clergymen.[47] In a hostile standoff with the vestry of St. Anne's Parish in Essex County over the dismissal of a clergyman, one Virginia governor famously derided the vestry as the "twelve Bishops of St. Ann's" for their presumptuous behavior, a jibe that perfectly captured just how much power Virginia's vestries had come to command.[48]

The vestry system in Virginia seemed to serve as cautionary tale to the Maryland Assembly when it formally established the Church of England in 1692, and the province curbed the autonomy of parish vestries in four ways. First, Maryland's vestries consisted of only six members, including the incumbent minister, whose presence introduced an important check on the laity. Second, Maryland's vestrymen were elected each year by the parish freeholders, which made the institution answerable to the larger community.[49] Third, Maryland's vestries had to seek permission to impose an annual levy exceeding ten pounds of tobacco per person and thus remained financially dependent on county government for most expenses.[50] Finally, Maryland's governor appointed clergymen without respecting the vestry's right to refuse a candidate.[51] Still, Maryland's vestries exercised important discretionary power, including overseeing worship, appointing tobacco inspectors, awarding valuable building contracts, and allocating public funds. Maryland's vestries were less autonomous than their counterparts in Virginia but nonetheless exercised wide-ranging authority in their parishes.[52]

Much of the day-to-day administration of parish life fell to another set of parish officers, the churchwardens.[53] These parochial officers maintained all houses of worship and oversaw any necessary upkeep on the glebe. They managed parish finances, signed contracts, represented the parish in lawsuits, removed strangers, distributed parochial funds, and paid for parish expenses throughout the year, including bibles, prayer books, and bread and wine for communion. Their responsibility over all the parish's real property was founded in common law and will be discussed at greater length in chapter 2. Finally, churchwardens surveilled the behavior of parishioners and presented offenders to the county court for an array of moral crimes, including fornication, bastardy, drunkenness, and swearing. Invested with this significant discretionary authority, churchwardens came to know many of the most intimate details of their parishioners' lives and superintended their behavior closely. Robert Carter, one of Virginia's wealthiest planters, wrote a revealing manuscript entitled "Rules for the Conduct of Churchwardens," which outlined all the statutory responsibilities of churchwardens. For example, he noted that churchwardens could prosecute any parishioner "willfully absenting him or her self from divine service, at his or her parish church or chapel" and included a citation to 18 George II Chapter 2, 1744.[54] Carter's careful attention to the legal "power and duty" of every churchwarden emphasized their role in local law enforcement.

In Virginia, the churchwardens carried the additional responsibility of distributing poor relief and arranging the indenture of bastard and orphaned children. When George Washington served as churchwarden of Truro Parish in 1764, he directed the construction of a new church, oversaw the care of "Sarah Mill's crippled son," distributed clothing and relief payments to a dozen families, and reimbursed Dr. James Laurie, who provided medical care to the poor.[55] Transactions like these signaled the reciprocity of parochial membership; parishioners were monitored and governed by parish churchwardens but could also demand their attention and support.

Finally, the parish rector was a public officer invested with important civic responsibilities and rewarded with valuable benefits. Parish rectors were required to conduct divine services regularly at all the parish churches, perform baptisms and marriages, and keep accurate vital records. The choice of rector was fiercely contested because the rite of induction vested an Anglican rector with lifetime tenure, freehold over the glebe property, and a salary guaranteed by statute and funded by taxes. Inept, corrupt, or dissolute rectors could not be easily dismissed.[56] In an extreme example, the rector of Coventry Parish in Maryland, the Rev. Nathaniel Whitaker, spent much of his twenty-five-year tenure in jail for crimes ranging from violent assault to libel and debt and was suspected of murdering an enslaved person. He was unwilling or unable to carry out his basic pastoral duties but nonetheless continued to collect a staggering annual salary of fifty thousand pounds of tobacco, making him one of the highest paid officials in the province. "Under this deplorable situation," the Coventry vestry complained, parishioners had to raise additional funds to hire outside ministers to preach and baptize their children while their minister languished in prison still collecting his annual salary.[57] Once inducted, ministers were powerful public officials in both colonies.

Together, vestries and rectors superintended and served parishioners by carrying out many essential public responsibilities. Their wide-ranging authority expressed the mission of the established church to govern a moral, orderly community. The remainder of this chapter will consider how parishes exercised state power through public worship, taxation, vital records, moral crimes, the regulation of land and tobacco, and the enforcement of racial slavery. These arenas of parochial authority were mutually reinforcing. Orthodoxy preached from the pulpit bolstered the state's moral authority to discipline sinners and enforce slave law. The collection of parish taxes was framed as a direct means of supporting the clergy, providing for worship, and rewarding upright parishioners. The close oversight of land, tobacco, and slavery sought to promote communal order and strengthen the economy. The church's sanctification of racial slavery and the role of the parish in enforcing the slave code propped up the racial caste system of the Chesapeake. There were no clear distinctions between the parish's spiritual work and its civic duties.

## Public Worship

Defenders of establishment argued that the church-state union bolstered the rule of law. As Virginian clergyman Rev. Robert Paxton explained in a sermon, "Religion hath a good influence upon the people to make them obedient to government & conformable to laws. . . . Whosoever resisteth Authority resisteth the ordinance of God."[58] For this reason, Virginia Governor Alexander Spotswood argued in a letter to the Board of Trade that "those poor people who are deprived of the benefits of the publick worship, will either degenerate into Paganisme or Atheism, or at best give opportunity to [sectarians] to establish their opinions amongst them, and thereby shake that happy establishment of the Church of England. . . . Once schism has crept into the Church, it will soon create faction in the Civil Government."[59] Under this logic, the state acted out of self-interest in facilitating public worship to guard against disorder, promote unity, and maintain public peace.

Public worship was carefully choreographed and regulated by the state. Parliamentary and colonial laws required parish ministers or readers to perform divine services according to *The Book of Common Prayer* and obliged parishioners to attend authorized divine services regularly.[60] The orthodox Anglican liturgy reminded worshippers that the monarch was God's "chosen servant" invested with divine "authority" whom all subjects should "faithfully serve, honour, and humbly obey."[61] From the pulpit, parish ministers instructed worshippers they were "Members of the church," and "likewise Members of the State," and the king's coat of arms was often prominently displayed alongside the Ten Commandments above the altar.[62] In all of these ways, the ritual of public worship and the space of the parish church conveyed that obedience to political power was a spiritual dictate.

Anglicans also argued that the established church promoted spiritual devotion and encouraged public morality. Under the laws of both Maryland and Virginia, parish ministers conducted divine services and provided pastoral care, vestries built churches and chapels, and churchwardens purchased prayerbooks and the communion elements. Anglican clergymen argued that public worship ensured that religious beliefs and practices remained "agreeable to Sound doctrine . . . proper and lawful."[63]

If worship was left to private judgment, one Virginian clergyman predicted that "every house would soon have its own religion" and "the doctrine of true religion & virtue" would be compromised.[64] The Rev. James Blair likened ordered prayers to "the Direction of so skillful a pilot" that could "steer" souls to God and prevented the "nonsense, Rashness, and other inconveniences of extemporary Effusions."[65] Blair and others emphasized the dangers of unregulated preaching, particularly the "noisy clamours & extatick raptures," and the loss of public virtue brought by evangelical itinerants starting in the mid-eighteenth century.[66] By drawing together the community and regulating its observances, public worship was meant to keep the faithful from straying from the flock.

As much as public worship encouraged obedience and deference, there was also a sense of reciprocity between parish and parishioner. Communities expected the services and spiritual care guaranteed by law and expressed this demand in pointed ways. A 1732 arson attack on a newly constructed but inconvenient church in Virginia's Spotsylvania County demonstrates this sentiment. Former Gov. Alexander Spotswood chose a location "so remote" for the new parish edifice that none but he and his servants could easily attend divine services.[67] In response, a local mob "wilfully and maliciously burnt" down the building, apparently hoping "to have another instead thereof in their neighbourhood." Driven to violent protest, parishioners demanded the spiritual care required by law and paid for by their taxes. Unmet spiritual needs could spark anger from communities who viewed orthodox worship as a public benefit to which they were entitled.

Law infused the rituals of parish worship. In both colonies, ministers or parish clerks were required to recite entire colonial statutes aloud several times a year in the sanctuary after the sermon. The Maryland General Assembly required the entire text of the "Act to punish Blasphemers, Swearers, Drunkards, and Sabbath-Breakers," which outlined a host of moral crimes and gruesome penalties, to be read aloud every three months after the sermon.[68] In Virginia, the parish minister or clerk was required by law to recite the entire 1705 slave code twice a year during public worship. The act included a long list of violent punishments against any enslaved person who ran away or any free person who aided them.[69]

The arrival of print in the colonies made it easier for parish officials to fulfill this duty. Less than a year after William Parks began publishing Virginia's first newspaper in 1736, he printed a letter purported to be from a parish clerk, Witudle, riddled with spelling errors: "I am Klark of a Church, and am to rede the Laws about Fornecasion and Nigers to Times in the Yere in the Church; whech laws are in wreten Hand, which I can't rede. . . . I have sin your Gasset, and can rede it in as wel as in the Bible, for it is wreten in prenting Hand; and desir you wel send the Laws."[70] The bumbling Witudle was, of course, an invention of Parks's imagination meant to advertise his printed editions of Virginia's laws. But this spoof also demonstrated the parish clerk's legal responsibility to pronounce the colony's laws "as well" and recite from the Bible and conveyed Parks's low estimation of their competence in matters of law or religion.[71] The repeated proclamation of these laws at church became an important rite, albeit one outside the liturgical calendar, that wove civil law into divine worship and imbued earthly punishments with the patina of divine retribution.

The case of Jane Ham reveals why requiring parishes to promulgate new laws could be an important procedural safeguard. A single white female servant, Ham was sentenced to death in 1713 for concealing the death of her newborn child. When Ham's case came before the court, it found no evidence that she had committed any "violence" against her "child to occasion its death," but since she could produce no witnesses to prove her innocence, she was convicted of willful murder under the colony's new infanticide statute.[72] Moved by her plight, some of the judges later lobbied Governor Spotswood to pardon "the unfortunate woman." The governor reviewed the facts and found she had an even "more reasonable excuse to plead for her ignorance of that law, which makes the concealment penal, than I at first imagined, for . . . an express clause therein appointed to be read yearly in all churches, I find it never was published in any church in that county wherein she lived."[73] Because the law had not been read in Ham's parish church, the governor concluded she was "ignorant of the law, being but lately enacted here" and pardoned her in 1714. Parish publication was an essential form of legal notice in a colony without print.

The church did not simply broadcast legislation but had a statutory duty to execute numerous laws. In both colonies, statutes required the announcement of debts, public auctions, property sales, elections, militia musters, and lawsuits be posted on the parish church door, and a flurry of legal notices greeted parishioners whenever they crossed the threshold for worship.[74] The assembly periodically ordered parishioners to bring their weapons to church, a custom that suggested parish worship was seen as a uniquely vulnerable practice for white Virginians worried about the threat of violence in "tymes of danger," including indigenous warfare, slave rebellions, or foreign invasion.[75] This wide range of public activity was authorized only after it had been published on the parish door.

The 1705 slave code also carved out a specific role for the parish church in enforcing racial slavery. A chilling clause required the parish clerk or reader to publish a proclamation at the church door "immediately after divine worship" to warn parishioners about any enslaved people who had recently run away in the vicinity and might be hiding out or "committing other injuries to the inhabitants."[76] Once such an announcement was made, "it shall be lawful for any person or persons whatsoever, to kill and destroy such slaves by such ways and means as he, she, or they shall think fit, without accusation or impeachment of any crime for the same." The parish had the authority to deputize residents as slave catchers to undertake rough justice with impunity. The parish did not just endorse slavery from the pulpit but had a clear statutory role in executing this key portion of the slave code.

## Order and Exclusion

Public worship purportedly united "all the People of the Land, whatever Rank or condition" as "members of the same Church," but it also exposed and hardened the extreme stratification of Chesapeake society. The parish church was one of the few public gathering spaces in the Chesapeake, and divine services offered colonists a rare opportunity to congregate and socialize. The gentry performed their authority by coming in late, sitting apart, and outfitting their private pews with expensive decorations. White families sat together while enslaved people and free people of color stood in the back or on raised balconies. In Maryland, the St. James Parish vestry in Anne Arundel County adopted a plan to segregate worship in 1747 by ordering the churchwardens to "prevent the Negroes from going in among the white people to disturb them as they frequently have done." But it was not merely social clout that kept order in the church. For example, when the Lynnhaven Parish vestry assigned church seating in 1736, "according to their Several Stations, the most proper Seats or pews," they also specified that anyone who took "the Liberty to place themselves or others in any other Seats or pews in the Said Church: Shall be Esteemed a Disorderly person & may Expect to be dealt with according to Law."[77] The vestry claimed the full force of the law to maintain a strict social order at church. Common membership in the parish did nothing to diminish social differences; if anything, the assembly of every person in the parish recapitulated the social order to affirm its righteousness. Public worship took on a profound importance not only as a legal and political act but as a key means of preserving traditional hierarchies.

Membership in the parochial community certainly benefited white women. Wealthy white female parishioners could secure loans from the vestry, left legacies to adorn parish churches, built private pews, and welcomed clergymen into their homes to minister to the women privately and even administer the sacraments.[78] Parishes often employed middling and poor white women as cleaners, caretakers, midwives, and nurses, which will be discussed later in the chapter in more depth. While gender structured parochial life, white women of all classes were acknowledged formally as members of the parish and reaped spiritual and material benefits from their inclusion.

The prospect of including Black parishioners in their spiritual fellowship was far more troubling for white Anglicans. In the early eighteenth century, many Chesapeake enslavers tried to prohibit Black people from attending worship or being baptized. In Virginia, the vestry of Lynnhaven Parish, for one, forbade all enslaved people from attending Sunday services after the discovery of a purported rebellion in 1730. Gov. William Gooch described the incident in a letter to the Duke of Newcastle, reporting that the enslaved community of Princess Anne "had the boldness to assemble on a Sunday while the people were at church." Thereafter, he ordered "every man to bring his arms to church on Sundays and Holydays, lest they should be seized by the slaves in their absence, if the same mutinous spirit should be revived amongst them."[79] Gooch's words embraced a militant form of proslavery Christianity and made clear that in his mind "the people" gathered for worship referred only to the white community. Segregation during or total exclusion from parish worship signaled another powerful means of denying Black Virginians membership in the body politic.

However, in the following decades, the conversion of enslaved people to Catholicism and evangelicalism aroused the antipathy of white Anglicans. Jesuits in Maryland were accused of provoking slave rebellion in the 1750s by "preaching publicly to large mixed Congregations" and converting "the Negroes of Protestant Inhabitants" while lay Catholics were accused of acting to "pervert Servants and Negroes of Protestants, and keep them under their Command and Authority, which, upon any Insurrection (from their well known Principles), may become of dangerous Consequence to his Majesty's Protestant Subjects in Maryland."[80] Similarly, evangelicals in both colonies were accused of drawing "slaves from the obedience of their masters" and destroying "those little societies from which the greater is drawn" during the revivals of the 1760s and 1770s.[81] Defenders of establishment dreaded the prospect of enslaved people joining nonconforming faiths and acknowledging some form of higher authority beyond or outside their enslavers' control. Religious dissent raised the awful specter of slave insurrection in the minds of Anglican elites, and this argument seemingly convinced many white Anglicans it was wiser to keep enslaved people in the established church than to stomach any form of heterodoxy within their ranks.

Ministers like Thomas Bacon buttressed this expedient rationale with theological arguments that Christianity would make Black men and women into more "*excellent* slaves."[82] Anglican clerics like Bacon helped cement the tradition of proslavery Christianity by naturalizing racial slavery and instructing Black listeners that God had intentionally "made them" slaves and expected them to accept their station in this life. Bacon's sermons treated racial slavery as yet another form of social difference in the great chain of being in which "Masters and Mistresses are God's Overseers" and enslaved people owed them obedience as part of their submission to "your great Master in Heaven."[83] His sermons touted the promise of heaven as the just reward for earthly subservience.[84] The established church's ambivalent inclusion of Black believers was exemplified in St. Anne's Parish's plan to build a new church in Annapolis, Maryland, in 1774. The proposed sanctuary included separate pews for the vestry, churchwardens, and other gentlemen, along with three additional galleries: "A common gallery, or place for parishioners in general, another place for servants, and a third for slaves."[85] Class and racial hierarchies organized this holy space as the rich sat away from the poor, and the enslaved were set apart from white churchgoers. The parish comprised the entire community and recapitulated its hierarchies.

Of course, the universal church was a fallacy in the Chesapeake. A significant number of nonconformists, particularly Quakers and Catholics, emigrated to Maryland throughout the seventeenth and eighteenth centuries. In Virginia, the number of dissenters remained low before 1740 but grew rapidly in the decades before the Revolution. The toleration laws of the two colonies protected or denied the nonconformists' civil and religious rights to varying degrees. By the mid-eighteenth century, Protestant dissenters in both colonies were exempted from the monthly requirement they attend Anglican services, so long as they attended public worship at another meeting house licensed by the county instead.[86] Catholics, however, were barred from worshipping publicly in Virginia from its founding and in Maryland after 1704.[87] In addition to curbing religious practice, inductees to all public offices and positions of trust in Virginia and Maryland swore the Oaths of Allegiance and Abjuration and signed the Test, in which they denounced the Papacy and disavowed transubstantiation.[88] Adopted as part of the English Declaration of Rights, these oaths rehearsed the constitutional crises of the seventeenth century and knit together religious difference with the threat of political treachery into a public performance of loyalty. These public pledges excluded Catholics, Quakers, and other nonconformists from full participation in the body politic and reminded the public yet again that legal rights and political authority rested on religious obedience. Powerful state mechanisms enforced the confessional regime by limiting numerous rights and privileges to conforming Protestants.

Though both colonies' laws acknowledged nonconformity as a practical reality, the parish still operated under the legal fiction of universality in which the English church comprised English society, and a small group of local elites invoked their legal, spiritual, and social power to rule the rest. No matter their faith, nonconformists of all kinds were still legally parishioners and subject to the church's jurisdiction and required to pay parish taxes. The parish levying system, which imposed compulsory assessments on all nonconformists and enabled the church to carry out its wide-ranging public activity, will be examined next.

## Laying the Levy

The parish's varied legal, spiritual, moral, and administrative duties were funded by taxes. The annual parish levy was an essential source of parochial power and a key to understanding how parishes governed as part of the state. After raising significant public resources through the levy, parishes disbursed these funds and acted as powerful patrons in local communities.

In both colonies, the vestry gathered in the late autumn to review annual expenses of the parish and calculate an annual tax to cover their costs. This ritual, called laying the levy, coincided with the tobacco-growing season; planters had finished their harvesting but not yet shipped their crop. At this meeting, the vestry would agree to reimburse expenditures from the previous year as well as raise funds to cover anticipated spending for the coming year. The parish levy was a poll tax, meaning each householder paid a per-person tax on themselves and any dependents deemed tithable. Gendered and racialized expectations around labor in the Chesapeake colonies deemed all men and Black women over sixteen tithable; white women were exempt because they were understood to be unable to support themselves.[89] Parish vestrymen kept a close eye on their parishioners to ensure that they paid taxes on all tithable persons. For example, the Christ Church vestry in Middlesex County, Virginia, admonished Widow Perrott for not paying taxes on Dick, a man she held in bondage, and added his name to their list of tithables.[90] Some vestries also heard petitions from enslavers who sought exemptions from paying parish levies on enslaved people who were unable to labor; an example was George Baker, who asked the Blisland Parish vestry in Virginia's New Kent County "that his Negro; Girl (who thro. the infirmity of nature is render'd incapable of doing any Service) be exempted Paying her Parish Levy."[91] Parish levies were due early in the new year along with the county levy and other taxes at the same time and were usually collected by the county sheriff. The authority of the vestry to determine tithable status, impose taxes, and spend public funds handed parishes significant discretionary power.

The annual parish levy in Virginia ranged from ten to one hundred pounds of tobacco per poll and was typically the highest annual tax.[92] In Maryland, by contrast, parish levies were significantly lower, usually under ten pounds of tobacco. The average parish levy in Prince George's County, Maryland, between 1734 and 1760 was just eight pounds of tobacco per poll.[93] However, this apparent difference simply reflected different methods of funding the church in each colony. The two biggest line items in many Virginian parishes' budgets—the minister's salary and poor relief—were not included in Maryland's parish levies. While Virginia's parishes compensated ministers with an annual salary of sixteen thousand pounds of tobacco directly through the annual levy, Maryland's counties collected a separate "clergy tax" of forty pounds of tobacco per poll (eventually decreased to thirty) to pay to every parish rector.[94] Thus, after parishioners in Prince George's County paid both the clergy tax and their parish levy each year, they contributed between thirty-eight and forty-eight pounds of tobacco per poll to the established church. In fact, this per-person funding scheme that tied parish population to clerical compensation meant that Maryland's Anglican clergymen could earn significantly more than their peers in Virginia, whose salaries were fixed no matter the size of their parish.

Moreover, Virginian parishes funded the poor relief system directly through the parish levy. A catch-all term to describe a broad range of public assistance, poor relief drove up the annual levy in Virginia over the course of the eighteenth century and accounted for 30–40 percent of Virginia's parochial spending by the 1770s. However, things worked differently in Maryland, where the county courts had already begun administering welfare before the province established the Church of England, and poor relief was never transferred from counties to parishes. Marylanders paid just as much, if not more, on average to support the established church and welfare programs, but not all these funds flowed through the parish.

The power to impose taxes and disburse public funds made parishes into powerful public patrons in both colonies. The discretionary power of Virginia's vestries to award poor relief and provide care was perhaps the parish's most visible form of patronage. Individual parishioners could apply for various forms of relief from the vestry, including financial support, and the churchwardens were tasked with providing needy parishioners with food, clothing, medicine, and other necessities out of a general fund throughout the year. Parishioners had to personally apply to the vestry or churchwardens requesting relief, and the vestry had complete discretion over who received assistance. Widows, the elderly, and orphans along with the sick and the suffering often received parish welfare when they were deemed "worthy" of support and unable to support themselves. Poor relief was understood as the civic expression of Christian charity and the care of the poor a spiritual duty for all Christians. However, as the petition of one Virginian, Samuel Ferguson, made clear, Christian charity in Virginia sometimes had to be compelled by the state. Ferguson's request for relief explained that he was "by reason of his age . . . and weakness . . . entirely unable to" support himself.[95] He lamented, though, that "when he applys to Christian neighbours they seem not willing to supply him but in the Legal way altho' they look upon him as a real object of charity." Ferguson's neighbors, though perhaps viewing him sympathetically, deferred to the legal relief system to determine whether he deserved their support.

Race and religion circumscribed access to parish welfare in Virginia. In the fifty-two years of poor relief records from Lynnhaven Parish, including more than 1,200 individual payments, the sole recorded instance of an individual identifiable as Black receiving relief came in 1773 when the parish paid William Capps for keeping "Mary Lester (Orphan of James Lester) and her negro one year."[96] The distribution of poor relief reflected and reinforced the hierarchical and racialized boundaries of this slave society. Parishes also excluded nonconformists from poor relief. For example, no Friends whose names appeared in the Henrico Monthly Meeting of Friends between 1731 and 1776, nor any individuals appearing in the Presbyterian Hanover Synod between 1755 and 1776, received welfare payments from nearby Henrico Parish or St. Paul's Parish Hanover.[97] Instead, nonconforming religious groups in Virginia made separate provisions for the poor of their communities.[98] Dissenters were thus forced to contribute to a relief system that did not support them, just one of the many reasons they referred to parish taxes as "sufferings."[99] Despite the supposed universality of the parish, vestries imposed bright lines around parish relief to exclude Black people and religious dissenters.

The relief system depended on neighbors to provision and care for one another. When parishioners provided the needy with care, goods, accommodation, or services, they requested reimbursement from the parish. In a region with dispersed settlement and few towns, financial compensation for relief services helped incentivize neighborly conduct. Claimants often presented dramatic accounts replete with gory details. For example, when Nathan Gilliand petitioned Augusta Parish in April 1762 to pay him for taking care of an ill neighbor, he vividly wrote about "attending Wm Scott in a deep Consumption being obliged to sit up day & Night, washing his most Loathsome cloaths, 7 or 8 times a night."[100] For the parish, the overriding aim was to keep the cost of relief as low as possible. The churchwardens of Bristol Parish sought to "let out the poor of this parish to the lowest bidder" each year.[101] White female parishioners were rewarded for their labor and pocketed public funds year in and year out. For example, a Virginia midwife, Barbara Keeling, received annual payments from Lynnhaven Parish every year between 1743 and 1753 for nursing or looking after her fellow parishioners.[102] Female carers took in their neighbors, nursed infants, looked after the elderly, and worked as medical practitioners who offered specialized forms of care.[103] In these capacities, white women were essential public actors, and their labor sustained Virginia's economy of care.

Even though Maryland's parishes did not pay the minister directly or distribute poor relief, they still played an important role as public patrons that raised, invested, and distributed public funds.[104] St. James Parish in Anne Arundel County regularly lent money at 8 percent annual interest to male and female parishioners. The parish apparently kept running lists of "debitors to the vestry" who had received these personal loans, and debt collection with interest provided an additional source of revenue for the parish.[105] In one instance, the vestry lent a whopping 31,282 pounds of tobacco to Dr. William Chapman.[106] It took the unlucky Dr. Chapman five and half years to repay his loan, and the parish received a good return on its investment by collecting 13,764 pounds of tobacco in interest on top of the principal.[107] Parishes were uniquely well-positioned in the cash-scarce Chesapeake to act as lending institutions. The levy gave the parish ready access to cash year in and year out, a rare type of security in the boom-and-bust economy of the tobacco colonies. And with a legally ensured means of raising funds each year through the levy, the parish was a particularly secure creditor.

Parishes in both colonies kept numerous parishioners on their payroll. Parish clerks were essential state bureaucrats and were paid handsomely for their work. They kept the parish register, maintained accurate financial records, took minutes at vestry meetings, and served as a lay reader when the minister was absent. Sextons (church caretakers) cleaned the church, maintained the churchyard, and did other odd jobs as custodians of parish property. These allowances could either be doled out as a form of charitable patronage to needy parishioners or claimed by vestrymen who appointed themselves, forced their enslaved workers to perform the labor, and pocketed the payments.[108]

The construction of a new church or chapel was another lucrative source of parochial patronage. Vestries saw the high cost of sanctuaries as a worthy investment in the public good by providing a space for orthodox worship. As vestries purchased material and employed workmen, these building projects infused cash into the local economy and would have been an important source of revenue for local artisans. For example, Lynnhaven Parish used public funds to finance major construction projects including churches, chapels, a glebe-house, and a poorhouse seven times in just fifty-five years.[109] Each project cost tens of thousands, if not hundreds of thousands, of pounds of tobacco. To raise these funds, the parish typically appropriated a higher-than-normal levy over the course of two to four years. The ease with which Virginian parishes could raise funds unchecked by any other public institution stands in stark contrast to the bureaucratic oversight that restrained parochial action in Maryland, where vestries had to request permission from the assembly to raise a levy exceeding ten pounds.[110] Though supported by taxation, Maryland's parishes also relied on voluntary contributions for a significant proportion of their spending. Parishes across the province resorted to selling pews to raise money, as well as soliciting private donations from parishioners to supplement funds raised through the levy. The vestry of Shrewsbury Parish in Kent County raised more than 11,400 pounds of tobacco for a new chapel in the late 1740s through private subscriptions after receiving permission to raise only 8,000 pounds of tobacco through a levy from the assembly. The necessity of resorting to private donations to fund construction suggests either that Maryland's vestries were reluctant to request or the assembly was unwilling to approve extraordinarily high taxes for parochial building projects.

Certainly, Virginian vestries had far more autonomy over their spending than did those in Maryland. Still, parishes in both colonies imposed levies and allocated public resources in order to perform their statutory duties. The power to tax is one of the most fundamental expressions of state power. Thus, the parish levying system conveyed the crux of establishment: that the Anglican Church was an arm of the imperial state. By exercising the power of the purse, the church demonstrated its legal authority and wielded its mandate to govern communal life.

Parish taxation, like all taxes, relied on gathering and recording reliable information about the population, and local officials could only effectively collect taxes by closely overseeing their residents. Thus, parishes' levying power went hand in hand with its administration of important rites like marriage and baptism and careful record-keeping. The power to tax drew the established church into surveilling local communities and governing daily life.

## Seasons of Life

Parishes shepherded parishioners through the different seasons of life by administering baptismal, matrimonial, and funeral rites. These holy rituals marked membership in the spiritual body of Christians and maintained the supposed good order of society, but they were also instrumental to imperial statecraft. Without accurate vital records, the state could not collect taxes, determine residency, record parentage, or prove legal status. To this end, ministers and clerks performed these rites and kept careful records, which entwined the legal and spiritual authority of every parish. Establishment delegated a dual mission to the church to oversee a moral and orderly society and to assist the smooth functioning of local government and imperial administration.

Laws regulating these rites explicitly connected the goals of statecraft to spiritual orthodoxy. As early as 1632, statutes ordered parish ministers to perform all burials, baptisms, and marriages. Churchwardens had to keep careful records of these rites. The Burgesses invoked divine retribution as an enforcement mechanism and reminded parishioners that "Almighty God may justlie punish his people for neglectinge this good and wholesome lawe."[111] The ministry, for its part, emphasized that the ritual rhythms of the church preserved "the good rule of peace" and bolstered "the Order and Authority of the Government in Church or State, under which we live" while also nurturing believers and drawing them closer to Christ.[112] Parishes coerced popular participation in the rituals of Anglican life while simultaneously carrying out the necessary work of imperial governance.

By carrying out these duties, parishes also took on an outsized role in enforcing racial hierarchy and bolstering the legal institution of slavery. A slave society built on a racial caste system relied on accurate vital records to determine legal status. In both Virginia and Maryland, a tithable person was any man sixteen or above and any Black woman, either free or enslaved, sixteen or above.[113] Because the tithable status of an individual depended on age and race, accurate birth records were essential to the project of taxation. The 1702 Church Act in Maryland explicitly linked the establishment of the Church of England to the keeping of vital statistics by requiring every parish to employ a clerk to "make due Entry of all Vestry Proceedings, and of all Births, Marriages and Burials (Negroes and Mulattoes excepted) *that is to say,* the Christian and Sir-Name, with the Day, Month and Year of every such Births, Marriages or Burials."[114]

By excluding Black men and women from the rites of the church and the records of the parish, parishes played a critical role in enforcing a racial litmus test for communal belonging. For John Anderson, a Black man living in Virginia's Augusta Parish, his very freedom rested on the accuracy of parish records. In June 1763, Anderson petitioned the court, accusing parish minister "Rev. John Craig [of] detaining him as a slave."[115] The Augusta County Court relied on evidence from the vestry records of Saint Andrew's Parish in Brunswick County, more than 150 miles away in the southeastern part of the colony, to prove that "Anderson is the son of a free white woman and was bound by the Church Wardens of the Parish of Saint Andrews, in Brunswick County, to serve till 21, and he is now of that age." His mother's crime of bearing a mixed-race child and the facts of his indenture were preserved in the parish records, but not his birth. Based on this evidence, the Augusta Court ordered that he be released immediately. Thus, white individuals were guaranteed the means to prove their parentage while free Black or mixed-race colonists often lacked official documentation of their births.

Like births, marriages were regulated and documented by parishes. Matrimony was not only a sacred rite performed before God but also a legal institution authorized by a representative of the state. Holy matrimony served the needs of both the individual and society as a whole by ensuring "the propagation of the world" and promoting moral and "Christianly" life.[116] The Maryland Assembly laid out its views on the political significance of marriage, declaring, "Forasmuch as Divine Institutions ought to be strictly observed in every well-regulated Government . . . entering into the holy Estate of Matrimony may tend to the more orderly Propagation of Mankind, it ought, not only in a religious, but political View, to be promoted"[117] This language expressed the political and spiritual weight of marriage as well as the assembly's authority to regulate it closely.

In Virginia, performing the rite of matrimony was a legal privilege granted only to Anglican ministers for much of the colonial era. Couples had to pay a fee of twenty shillings in Virginian currency for the minister to perform their marriage in Virginia, and Anglican clergymen were eager to protect this valuable source of revenue.[118] In one exceptional instance, the parish rector of Augusta Parish, the Rev. John Jones, sued the minister of the neighboring Botetourt parish, Rev. Adam Smith, for fees collected by Smith after marrying eight couples from nearby Augusta

Parish. The law was clear that no matter who performed the ceremony, the marriage fees went to the rector of the parish where the bride resided prior to marriage. Jones won his case and recovered 2 pounds, 2 shillings and 6 pence.[119]

Though the colony overhauled its marriage laws in 1748 to allow licensed dissenting ministers to marry parishioners, the Anglican rector in the parish still pocketed the twenty-shilling fee for these weddings.[120] The parish not only regulated the rite of matrimony but also carefully superintended marriage records. Every rector had the legal duty to publish marriage banns, either by reading them from the pulpit or posting a notice on the courthouse or church door. Failure to publish such a notice could mean a marriage was not legally formalized. In 1767, the court of Augusta County, Virginia, charged a yeoman named Joseph Bell with tampering with the parish marriage records. Perhaps the act of a spurned suitor or simply a prank gone too far, the young man purportedly forged the marriage banns between a single woman, Anne Wallace, and Edward Sampson, whom the records called "a deformed little tailor." Bell purportedly slipped a false marriage announcement to the unwitting parish clerk, who read the banns out loud during a Sunday service, without the "knowledge or consent" of either party. The court unleashed a torrent of adverbs against Bell by accusing him of "falsely, unlawfully, and wickedly devising, contriving and intending . . . maliciously and injuriously to aggrieve, oppress, ridicule, and to bring [Anne Wallace] and her parents into discredit and disgrace." The mischief-maker had not only caused "discredit and grief" to Wallace and Sampson, but his prank amounted to an attack on "the peace of our said Lord the King, his Crown, and dignity," and Joseph Bell faced criminal charges. Marriage records were essential to maintaining moral order and enforcing the laws.[121]

Maryland's marriage statutes exempted Protestant dissenters, but not Catholics, from being married by Anglican parish rectors. The province's accommodation of Protestants made its exclusion of Catholics all the more targeted. Jesuit priests in the province were not entrusted with the authority to perform a binding legal act, a prohibition that underscored the belief that Catholicism was incompatible with public faith or trust. Amid the crescendo of anti-Catholicism during the Seven Years' War, the Maryland General Assembly further imposed a penalty on all bachelors over the age of twenty-five by arguing that those who "are not burthened with the Charge and Expence that usually attends a

Matrimonial Condition, they may be better enabled to contribute a larger Tax towards the Support of the Community."[122] This statute took conspicuous aim at the vow of celibacy taken by Catholic priests and financially targeted young Catholic laymen. The bachelor tax was accompanied by other anti-Catholic provisions, including an additional tax on all Catholic landholders over eighteen who refused to take the oaths of allegiance.[123] To accomplish this political end, the assembly turned to vestries, which readily complied with this law and regularly presented unmarried parishioners to county sheriffs for the additional tax.[124] For example, in St. James Parish, the vestry removed Richard Brown, Richard Lewing, and Robert Norris in 1761 from the initial list of bachelors after consulting the parish register to confirm their ages.[125] Not surprisingly, many young men objected to the tax and claimed that the vestry had gotten their ages or amount of property wrong, and they mounted "legal" appeals, which were heard by the vestry.[126] Vestries had intimate knowledge of their parishioners' lives and longstanding power as a taxing body, which enabled them to carry out the political agenda of the Protestant state.

Parishes drew on their wide-ranging authority over baptism, marriage, taxation, and vital statistics to bolster the workings of the state. Their dual authority over religious and civic life cut to the heart of establishment in which church and state governed together. The Janus face to administering moral order was punishing disorder, and as we shall see, colonial parishes played a critical role in enforcing moral order and punishing offenders.

## Punishing Sin

Established religion had been defended on the grounds that only a state church vested with legal power could enforce moral order in society. Parishes' regulation of births and marriages was accompanied by the power to punish illicit sexual behavior. English ecclesiastical courts had long enforced a wide range of moral crimes—drunkenness, blasphemy, profaning on the Sabbath, marital and sexual law, and nonattendance at worship. But without the traditional system of church courts in the colonies, county courts in both Maryland and Virginia began prosecuting this misconduct, thereby muddying the jurisdictional boundaries between ecclesiastical and criminal law.

Seventeenth-century supporters of establishing the Church of England in Maryland had insisted that only an established church could safeguard public morality and social order, and the acts passed between 1692 and 1704 establishing the church prohibited swearing, drunkenness, profaning the Sabbath, missing worship, and bastardy. While counties had the jurisdiction to prosecute moral crimes and received all monetary fines, Maryland's established church investigated and punished illicit behavior.[127] The crimes of adultery, lewdness, and fornication were known euphemistically as "incontinent" living, and the parish served as the first line of defense against these crimes. Parish vestries were also instructed to investigate and condemn relationships that ran counter to colonial marriage statutes or "violated the Rules and Canons of the Church," such as incest.[128] By aggregating a growing body of colonial laws, particularly against interracial relationships, with the canons of the Anglican Church, Maryland's parishes lent moral weight to the laws of slavery and other colonial legal innovations.

Maryland's parish system of moral oversight not only invoked the authority of the church's teachings but also harnessed the power of communal surveillance to police moral behavior. If someone suspected their fellow parishioner of having committed one of these crimes, he or she reported their allegations to a churchwarden, the minister, or the vestry for further investigation.[129] The vestry then summoned the suspects, questioned them, and could opt to present them for prosecution. The vestry of Shrewsbury Parish in Kent County, Maryland, summoned eleven couples for unlawful cohabitation, as well as a man and two women for individual offenses, between 1746 and 1756.[130] In all fourteen cases, the vestry found the charges credible and admonished the offenders. This remarkable rate of guilty outcomes suggests that these investigations were not a forum for discovery and adjudication but a display of moral censure. The Shrewsbury churchwarden chose to present offenders to the county court for prosecution only in the four instances when parishioners refused to attend the vestry proceedings. What mattered in these proceedings was deference to the parish as the arbiter of morality and willingness to accept public condemnation.

When convicting couples of fornication and single women of bastardy, the Kent County Court proclaimed these acts brought forth "the high Displeasure of Almighty God," set an "Evil Example of all others," and breached "good rule and Government."[131] This reproach was a familiar script used time and again in Maryland court judgments and suggested that sin was a contagion that could infect the entire body politic if left unchecked. Wayward parishioners defied the authority of church and state and threatened order and well-being of the entire community.

In Virginia, parish churchwardens not only had the legal power to make presentments but also had the added responsibility of collecting criminal fines. Virginia's county courts convicted individuals of moral crimes like gaming and bastardy, but, unlike Maryland, parishes were the recipients of their fines. When the court convicted, the church collected. A few brief entries in the vestry book of Bristol Parish from January 1757 recorded that: "John Jones, Haulkey Pride, Sheppyallen Puckett being fin[e]d for gameing by the Judgement of Pr[ince] George Court, Order'd that the Churchwardens receive the said Judgment."[132] The churchwardens of Upper Parish in Nansemond County raised anywhere from five to fifteen pounds current money each year through criminal fines in the 1750s and 1760s and used this money, in turn, to fund poor relief.[133] For example, in 1751 the two churchwardens, Daniel Pugh and William Moore, collected fines from each of three women convicted of bastardy by the Nansemond County Court, which they promptly redistributed to several other needy parishioners.[134] Every instance of swearing, drunkenness, bastardy, gaming, dishonest dealing, and Sabbath-breaking funded an additional allowance to the poor at no cost to the taxpayers. This system engendered a transactional morality in which the sinful paid the virtuous and the established church policed the line between the wicked and the worthy. Indeed, these payments were often made on Easter, which tied the liturgical calendar to the material welfare of the poor. While the pious marked the resurrection of Jesus Christ each year, the poor must too have celebrated receiving a material form of deliverance.

Scholars have shown that Virginian churchwardens' presentments to the court became less common after 1750, when grand juries began presenting the majority of offenders.[135] However, records from several county courts underscore that churchwardens still made presentments. The Fairfax County Court order book from 1754 to 1756 shows that both grand juries and the county's two parishes presented women for bastardy. Cameron Parish presented three women: Margaret Anderson, Patience Graham, and Jane Slater. Truro Parish also presented three female parishioners: Elizabeth Barry, Phebe Cole, and Sarah Pardis. Grand juries presented an additional four women in the same time span. The court dismissed the charges against all of the women who came before the court; however, the outcome was different for those who refused to attend the proceedings. Joyce Tomlin was one of at least five women convicted for bastardy in that eighteen-month period after failing to appear before the Fairfax County Court. As was the case in Maryland, the pattern of dismissing charges against those who appeared while convicting absentee individuals suggests that the primary reason for bringing the charge was to publicly shame women suspected of bastardy, either in a public hearing or through a conviction, rather than determining their guilt.[136]

In addition to presenting parishioners and collecting court-imposed fines, Virginia's churchwardens also arranged indentures for the children of women convicted of bastardy as well as for poor and orphaned children. Customarily, a single woman who was pregnant or had recently given birth could name the father voluntarily or could be required to name him after being presented by the court. The churchwardens then sought out the alleged father and attempted to force him to sign a bond with the parish promising to provide financial support for the child with steep penalties for nonpayment.[137] Parish churchwardens also frequently bound children whose parents died or proved unable to support them until they reached adulthood (ages eighteen for girls and twenty-one for boys), as was the case of Elizabeth Glidewell, who apparently petitioned the Bristol Parish vestry in 1729 to arrange an indenture for her son, Robert, because she was a "poor Widow and Not able to Take Care of her Children."[138] In the case of bastardy, churchwardens sought to prevent unwed mothers and their children from becoming financially dependent on the parish. Churchwardens brought lawsuits against fathers if they failed to make adequate child support payments.[139] There are also instances in which churchwardens would indenture children to their reputed fathers.[140] When arranging indentures and signing bastardy bonds, Virginia's churchwardens sought to protect the financial interests of the community first and foremost and exercised a significant amount of discretion over the lives of their most vulnerable parishioners.

Bastardy law was a crucial plank in Virginia's slave code, and parish churchwardens became central administrators of slave law in this capacity. The 1705 slave code branded mixed-race children born of white women as an "abominable mixture and spurious issue," drawing on a half century of discourse about the dangers of interracial sex.[141] White women who gave birth to mixed-race children were not only guilty of bastardy but also faced a heftier fine or an extended term of servitude. Children born to white mothers and Black fathers were technically free people of color, but they faced decades of forced labor as Virginia law required them be bound out until the age of thirty-one.[142] Parish churchwardens played a crucial role in this process by arranging the indentures of mixed-race children.[143] Churchwardens had complete discretion to make these arrangements and sometimes exploited the circumstances for personal or parochial benefit. For example, the churchwardens of Bristol Parish bound two "Mulotto children, Named Philip and Betty son and Daughter to Ann Evans," to the rector, the Rev. Robert Ferguson.[144] Doing so provided the rector with decades of free labor. Under the aegis of religious establishment, the state had long legislated morality and tasked parishes with policing sexual behavior. By adapting the traditional domain of bastardy law to punish interracial sex, colonial legislators made the novel labor regime of racial slavery seem both familiar and righteous. They contextualized the codification of white supremacy within the traditional moralizing framework of Anglicanism and relied on the usual administrators of moral law, parishes, to enforce these new provisions.

In both colonies, parish churches also served as sites of public retribution for moral crimes. While the traditional rituals of shaming and penance—appearing before the church in white robes and making a public confession on the Sabbath—were uncommon by the early eighteenth century, parishes continued to maintain visible sites of public punishment. St. James Parish in Anne Arundel, Maryland, built a pair of stocks in its churchyard in 1720.[145] Twenty-seven years later, in 1747, the vestry approved the construction of a new "p[ai]r of stock & a whipping post" while renovating the church. St. Peter's Parish in New Kent County, Virginia, likewise ordered a "good and substantial" pair of stocks in 1734 "to be forthwith erected near the Church yard Wall for the Restraint of licentious and disorderly Persons several such having lately appeared."[146] Although the vestry records do not record specific instances of punishment, presumably when the county courts meted out public lashings or time in the stocks for moral crimes, these punishments were inflicted on the bodies of parishioners on the grounds of the church. The parish church was a symbolically potent site for moral condemnation where parishioners faced punishment for their transgressions in the presence of God and the community.

## Economic Regulation

The parish not only bolstered the tobacco economy through its enforcement of the slave code but also in its oversight of the two most important forms of private property in the Chesapeake: land and tobacco. When exercising key powers of economic regulation, the church acted as a steward of the public good.

In Virginia, the most important regulatory role of the parish was its oversight of land processioning. A custom dating back to medieval England, processioning was a ritual in which the community reviewed and recorded all private property boundaries every four years. Under the terms of a 1705 statute, vestries were ordered to appoint certain parishioners as processioners to confer with all landholders and process, or literally walk, along all private property boundaries to establish agreement among neighbors about the limits of their property every four years. Processioners documented the proceedings, and the parish collated these records for safekeeping.[147] This ritual was essential in the mete-and-bound landholding system of the Chesapeake, where property boundaries were often demarcated through mutable natural landmarks like trees, creeks, or stones. Processioning records also noted who held patents and deeds over undeveloped tracts of land, which was particularly important in a western parish, where speculators and residents clashed over competing land claims. While the custom certainly benefitted Virginian elites, it also ensured that the claims of more marginalized landowners were publicly acknowledged. For example, Grace Sherwood participated in processioning after her release from prison in Lynnhaven Parish, and the records of Henrico Parish also show that Black landholders like William and Jane took part and had their property lines recorded.[148] Processioning was time-consuming and difficult to coordinate, but its continuation over generations attested to its value.

While processioning sought to prevent disputes over land, there were instances when it failed to achieve a peaceful resolution, and neighbors turned to the courts for resolution. In one contested property case, *Bradford v. Bradford,* heard by Virginia's General Court in 1769, two litigants (likely relatives given their shared surname) went to court over the precise boundary between their claims. The plaintiff stated that the property lines had been improperly recorded during the previous five processionings, when he had been absent from the parish. George Wythe, who represented the defendant, argued that the twenty years of processioners' returns had legally established the defendant's claim to the disputed property. Wythe argued that invalidating the recorded boundary would undermine the integrity of the custom. The lawyer defended processioning as the best means of "preserving boundaries in quiet" and suggested that "institutions tending to promote public utility, must prevail, though injurious in particular instances." On the other side, another esteemed attorney, Edmund Pendleton, represented the plaintiff. He did not dispute the importance of processioning but insisted that the value of the practice stemmed from the participation of all parties. The absence of any interested landholder intrinsically invalidated the act. The court sided with Pendleton, and its decision reiterated that the deeper purpose of processioning was securing consensus among community members. Only through the participation of all individual landholders could processioning achieve "the harmony of the whole." In this regard, the supervisory role of the parish over private property represented the larger purpose of establishment to act as a steward of the public good by maintaining communal unanimity.

Maryland's parishes exercised an important role in the tobacco economy by appointing tobacco inspectors. In both Chesapeake colonies, tobacco was not only the staple crop but the central currency, and its regulation was of paramount importance to colonial officials and local planters.[149] In order to improve the quality of exported tobacco and increase prices, Maryland's Tobacco Inspection Act of 1747 required all tobacco to be inspected at one of seventy-five public warehouses by two parish-appointed inspectors.[150] Inspectors were required to unpack all hogsheads of tobacco, burn any "trash" tobacco, and repack the high-quality remainder for export. Boosters of the inspection system attached moral value to tobacco production, decrying growers of poor-quality tobacco as "slovens."[151] This terminology blamed low-quality harvests on the rectitude of the men who grew it, rather than on the quality of the soil, weather patterns, or availability of labor.[152] By rooting out the sale of trash tobacco, the inspection system was designed to improve the quality of Maryland's cash crop and reform the characters of the Marylanders who grew it. The legislature relied on parishes to appoint tobacco inspectors annually. Most years, the vestrymen and churchwardens appointed four inspectors, though there was some variation from year to year and parish to parish. This delegation of responsibility reflected the assembly's trust in parish vestries to select the right gentlemen for the office.

With this new responsibility, the vestry and churchwardens received an opportunity for lucrative patronage. Tobacco inspectors not only received impressive annual salaries but also wielded significant personal

In this cartouche from a 1755 map of Virginia, wealthy white gentlemen inspect tobacco leaves and conduct business while enslaved laborers serve them wine and pack hogsheads of tobacco for shipment. Joshua Fry and Peter Jefferson, cartographers; Thomas Jefferys, engraver and printer; cartouche designed by Francis Hayman, *A map of the most inhabited part of Virginia containing the whole province of Maryland*, 1755. (Courtesy of the Library of Virginia)

discretion over the fortunes of their neighbors. The records of several parishes show that vestrymen often appointed themselves and their family members for the position. For example, Shrewsbury Parish made sixty-seven appointments for tobacco inspectors between 1750 and 1770, and of these, only thirteen individuals were ever chosen for the post. Eleven of the thirteen men selected were also vestrymen or churchwardens during this twenty-year stretch. All the men chosen were pew-holders in the church and made private donations to church construction and maintenance.[153] Apparently, when looking for the most "able and sufficient planters," Maryland's vestrymen felt no need to look beyond themselves.[154] These gentlemen had no qualms about using their civic power to promote their own interests. The vestry's total discretion in the process also made the appointment of non-Anglicans unlikely and further advantaged Anglicans over dissenters. Perhaps the most visible and powerful administrator of the local economy, the tobacco inspector embodied yet another privilege of the gentry and underscored the link between spiritual conformity and civic power.

Parishes took on active roles in regulating and supporting the tobacco economy through their supervision of land and tobacco. Whether these responsibilities grew out of longstanding custom or reflected new legislative initiatives, the established church's exercise of power reflected its mandate to secure accord and promote order. Every domain of the church's power—its control over public worship, its collection of taxes and recordkeeping, its regulation of marriage and punishment of sin, and its economic regulation—underlay slavery as a legal institution.

ORTHODOXY WAS woven into Anglo-American law institutionally and ideologically. The smooth operation of the imperial state relied on the established church in both Chesapeake colonies by the eighteenth century. Parishes were busy centers of civic administration that carefully watched over their communities, maintained social order, and oversaw moral welfare. The regulatory power and administrative authority of parishes made them a key part of the state and knit together religion and government. Through these many responsibilities, parishes enforced orthodoxy and justified the exercise of state power through the spiritual dictates of Anglicanism.

By the eighteenth century, Chesapeake Anglicanism had grown distinct from its English counterpart in several conspicuous ways. The extreme localism and power of the laity made parishes the most important institutions of the Chesapeake establishment. But perhaps the most striking innovations to religious establishment as a legal regime in the Chesapeake stemmed from the church's role in bolstering slavery. Every domain of the parochial power—overseeing public worship, publicizing statutes, collecting taxes, keeping vital records, overseeing moral order, punishing sin, and regulating land and tobacco—was used to sanction and strengthen racial slavery as a legal institution in the Chesapeake.

The established church derived much of its power from its extensive property. Using the annual levy and charitable donations, Anglican parishes managed funds, built churches and glebes, acquired silver and prayer books. But more than that, they enslaved hundreds of Black men and women who labored on parish glebes for the benefit of the church and white community. The next chapter will examine this propertyholding in detail as a key buttress of the Chesapeake establishment.

# 2

# PROPERTY AND POWER

THE REV. JAMES Blair came to Virginia in 1685 to serve as rector of Henrico Parish. An ambitious Scotsman, Blair soon convinced seventeen-year-old Sarah Harrison to break off her engagement to another man and marry him instead. Despite some raised eyebrows, Blair's marriage secured his entry into Virginia's elite circles. His star continued to rise after he was appointed commissary, the personal representative of the Bishop of London in the colony, and gained a seat on the colony's executive council. Wily, quarrelsome, and unrelenting, Commissary Blair dominated Virginian politics for the next half century as he outmaneuvered and outlasted four royal governors.[1]

Troubled by the anemic state of the established church when he first arrived in Virginia, Commissary Blair put forward a plan to improve "the bad constitution in this country as to its Church and Clergy" in 1699.[2] Blair blamed the colony's laws for providing meager salaries and poor living conditions to the ministry, which meant that only "ignorant, scandalous, and negligent" clergymen were willing to emigrate. To recruit "worthy men" to Virginia, Blair proposed that every parish provide the clergy with guaranteed incomes and comfortable houses on glebe plantations, which would be "stocked [with] four or five Negroes under an overseer and with a stock of cattle of seven or eight milch cows or calves."[3] Virginia's clergymen would profit from the glebe during their lifetimes, and "the parish negroes and cattle shall never be subject to attachments . . . but shall be annexed to the freehold" to benefit the parish in perpetuity.[4] Under this system, glebe plantations worked by Black enslaved people would provide a durable source of financial support for future generations of white parishioners. In short, Blair planned for Anglican clergymen to join the genteel ranks of white Virginians by turning parish glebes into plantations reliant on enslaved labor.[5] Blair's proposal, which predated the 1705 slave code in Virginia by six years, underscores the significant role played by the established church not only by sanctifying racial slavery but also by commodifying enslaved people. There was no pretense of

Christian paternalism or missionary zeal here, just a blunt appraisal of enslaved people as bodies fit for labor without souls worthy of pastoral care.

Important assumptions about establishment underlay this proposal. As Blair inventoried the shortcomings of the colonial established church, his proposed solution lay in a new property regime. Although the legislature did not adopt all the specifics of Blair's plan, its general contours became the status quo for funding the establishment. Parishes leveraged their legal power to raise taxes to invest heavily in property. Using the funds raised from compulsory taxes and gifts from charitable donors, vestries and churchwardens invested in glebe plantations, built churches and chapels, enslaved people, and purchased prayerbooks, vestments, church silver, and libraries. Vestrymen and churchwardens framed the acquisition of this expensive real estate and chattel as the best means to care for the spiritual needs of parishioners, provide for the minister, and oversee the local community. Property underlay the church's many public functions and the exercise of its spiritual work.

The unique privileges of the established church were not only expressed in parishes' immense wealth but also in the relative security of its holdings. Statutory law required parishes to raise taxes, manage public funds, construct churches, and buy land for glebes. Common law, in turn, protected parish property by recognizing the corporate standing of parish vestries, churchwardens, and ministers of the established church. This bundle of customary corporate rights meant that parishes not only held extensive amounts of valuable property but also could secure it indefinitely into the future, defend it in court, and contract securely. The perpetuity of the corporate form was particularly appealing in the context of racial slavery, which sought to class people as legally heritable property from one generation to the next. Customary incorporation and the secure property rights it conferred were essential to the extraordinary power exercised by the established church.

Establishment operated not only through the privileges extended to the Church of England but also through the many legal disadvantages dealt to all other religious groups.[6] White Anglicans were not alone in building a material faith nor in enslaving Black people to support their spiritual communities. Dissenting Protestants and Catholics in both Chesapeake colonies invested in enslaved people and plantations to finance their ministry and devotional practices. But under the legal strictures of establishment, these nonconformists faced higher hurdles to secure their property claims. While Anglican parishes relied on common-law incorporation to hold property, nonconformists complained bitterly about their inability to incorporate. They were not satisfied with holding property in trust or as individuals; they wanted secure corporate privileges equivalent to those of parish vestries, churchwardens, and clergymen. Without the benefit of incorporation, Catholics, Quakers, Presbyterians, and other nonconformists struggled to secure their assets. Religious establishment was a property regime built on and enforced through the legal privileges exclusively granted the Church of England and denied to all others.

This chapter explores how property—both the material wealth itself and the legal rights to secure it—served as a crucial plank in the legal establishment of religion. I begin by overviewing the material culture of Chesapeake Anglicanism and the extent of parish wealth before looking specifically at parish slavery. I then turn to the corporate privileges conferred to the established church in common law and statute and mechanisms by which parish officers exercised their unique corporate rights to protect and secure their property claims. Finally, the chapter concludes by looking at how nonconformists—Catholics, Quakers, and Presbyterians in Maryland and Baptists and Presbyterians in Virginia—struggled to hold property without the benefit of incorporation and how the insecurity of religious property snowballed into a significant grievance against establishment on the eve of the Revolution.

## Material Faith

For millennia, Christians have debated the relationship between spirit and matter. These deliberations took center stage amid the Protestant Reformation as rosaries, icons, relics, crucifixes, and stained glass all fell victim to the iconoclasm of sixteenth- and seventeenth-century radical Protestants, who deemed them "popish idolatry."[7] But as much as they tried to ground their faith in the Word rather than the world, reformers came up against the inescapable materiality of their devotional practices. Prayerbooks, Bibles, and printed sermons all existed as material objects. While radical Protestants reconfigured their meetinghouses to emphasize the sermon, they still furnished these spaces with pews, reading desks, or even communion tables that enabled the fellowship of believers. Baptism required water, and communion still needed bread and wine. Meanwhile English Catholics held fast to traditional practices, and devotional objects perhaps took on an even greater presence amid penal policies that drove Catholic practice underground in much of Anglo America. A rosary or a crucifix allowed access to the divine in the absence of mass. Even as images were defaced, railings torn down, and windows smashed, the sacramental power of objects endured and offered a continued communion with the divine. Triangulating between the traditional materiality of medieval Catholicism and the reformed practices of Protestants, Anglicans attempted to follow a middle way. This settlement was reached less by a carefully guided compromise than a series of violent paroxysms over 150 years of reform and revolution.

The eighteenth-century Anglicans living in the Chesapeake practiced a "comfortable" faith born of the previous centuries' storms.[8] Chesapeake Anglicans took a "both/and" approach to worship that emphasized the sermon and the sacraments as vehicles for sanctification. *The Book of Common Prayer* carefully scripted the liturgy, which took place in refined and ordered sanctuaries.[9] Parish churches often featured large windows and painted interiors, which offered light-infused, bright spaces for public worship. Anglicans used ornate details to elevate their churches and chapels—gilded altars, velvet cushions, wainscoted pews, ceilings adorned with angels, and marble fonts. Divine services culminated in a sermon delivered from pulpits that themselves were often works of art, ornately carved and raised high in the air above listeners. Communion was offered a handful of times a year, and ornate paintings of the Ten Commandments, the Lord's Prayer, and the Creed adorned the wall behind the altar.[10] These decorations quite literally elevated the Word above the congregation and called attention to it with artful lettering, gilded details, and carved frames. Text became a form of beautiful embellishment, and the space itself offered religious instruction. Chesapeake Anglicans followed a twofold approach that embraced the material and the textual as essential elements in their faith practice.

The architectural language of Anglican churches made worship an arresting departure from the ordinary lives of most colonists, nearly all of whom lived in small, semipermanent wooden homes far from public spaces and one another.[11] Grand and impressive, parish churches and chapels were visible from a great distance and stood out from the built environment. Scholars have examined these spaces and objects as part of a

Completed in 1773, Christ Church in Alexandria, Virginia, hung hand-lettered tablets of the Ten Commandments, the Lord's Prayer, the Apostles' Creed, and the Golden Rule behind the altar and pulpit. These catechetical texts were required to be exhibited in parish churches and chapels under the canons of the Church of England. (Photograph by Alyssa Penick, 2025)

rich literature on the material culture of Chesapeake Anglicanism. Upper balconies seated enslaved people or others deemed socially inferior, while local grandees sat apart, often in private pews constructed personally for their families.[12] The ordering of this space reinforced social hierarchies by imbuing racial, financial, and class distinctions with divine sanction. More recently, Louis Nelson has argued that the material dimensions of Anglican parish churches enabled believers to "sense the sacred," or as Lauren Winner puts it, "Material cues reminded parishioners that they were in church not just to meet neighbors but also to meet God."[13] A layered and richly material faith practice, Anglicanism used objects and spaces in public worship and private devotions to communicate social authority and to aid access to God.

Parish vestrymen created spaces for public worship that communicated the authority of the state and its established church. The power of parishes to undertake such large construction projects reflected their ability to raise revenue through taxation. These building programs required a significant outlay of capital and could triple or quadruple the annual levy paid by parishioners for several years. The vestry saw the high cost of these churches as a worthy investment in public welfare and the stability of the state. The construction of new worship spaces infused cash into the local economy as vestrymen contracted with builders, purchased materials, and employed workmen. The parish's patronage would have been an important source of revenue to a local artisan, and the frequency of costly parochial building programs would have outpaced the expenditures of many gentry families over the course of the century.

While this rich material culture has received significant attention from scholars, less attention has been paid to the connections between this material faith and the legal establishment of the Church of England. Parochial wealth in the mid-eighteenth century reflected the robust property regime to fund the official religion, much as James Blair had envisioned it decades earlier. The extensive wealth of Lynnhaven Parish in present-day Virginia Beach serves as a typical example. At the start of the American Revolution, Lynnhaven boasted a large brick church on a two-acre churchyard. The parish also had two brick chapels of ease with their own churchyards, Pungo Chapel and the Eastern Shore Chapel, in more remote corners of the parish. The vestry was intimately involved in designing these spaces. When commissioning the Eastern Shore Chapel, the vestry gave detailed instructions about shape, scale, and materials, right down to requesting that the church's interior to be painted "a sky colour."[14] They requested that the building have a raised gallery, large glass windows, "wainscoted" pews, a "railed and ballastered" communion table, and a "decent" pulpit. In addition, Lynnhaven owned three sets of liturgical silver for communion, liturgical vestments, and a valuable parish library. Furthermore, Lynnhaven Parish also held two pieces of real estate—a glebe and a poorhouse. The first was a two-hundred-acre plantation where the parish rector lived complete with a furnished brick house, a kitchen and other outbuildings, and a garden. The second was a fifty-acre poor farm, where recipients of poor relief were sent starting in the 1760s.

The wealth of a parish like Lynnhaven was derived from and in turn reinforced by its privileged legal status and position of public authority. Its visible grandeur was framed as an investment in the public good. By collecting fines, building spaces for public worship, procuring communion elements and prayer books, providing for the minister, and collecting funds for the poor, the material property of parishes reflected their mandate to provide for the welfare of the community. At the same time, these spaces and objects must also be understood as valuable property and the by-product of legal establishment.

## Parish Slavery

Conspicuously absent from this survey of Lynnhaven Parish's property claims are the half dozen people whom the parish enslaved. Indeed, nearly half of parishes in Virginia directly enslaved Black people who labored on the glebe and in the poor house, and any discussion of parish property must foreground parishes' role as enslavers. Vestry books elide parish slaveholding to an astonishing degree. In many Virginian vestry books, only one or two references across hundreds of pages are made to the enslaved people who belonged to the parish; some make no mention at all.[15] Maryland's vestry books also offer little evidence of slavery, though other contemporary sources mention parish slaveholding.[16] One possible explanation for this marked absence in vestry books is that slaveholding was recorded in churchwardens' accounts, nearly all which are lost. These silences remind us to remain circumspect when estimating the total number of enslaved people held by parishes and how many parishes were slaveholders.

Though evidence in Maryland's extant parish records is slim, clear examples of parish slaveholding can be found in other sources. A 1768 debt action against John McPherson, rector of William and Mary Parish (also known as Piccowaxen Parish) in Charles County, revealed the extensive property held by the parish. According to the records, "one hundred and fifty acres of glebe land . . . and about thirteen or fourteen working negroes, and six or eight negro children belonging to the incumbent of said parish for the time being."[17] McPherson was "languishing [as] a Prisoner in said County Goal for larger sums than he was unfortunately able to pay" and sent a pitiful petition to the assembly requesting assistance.[18] The assembly brokered a complicated deal whereby the minister gained his freedom, and in exchange his creditors received "his whole Estate real and personal and his future Income as Rector of William and Mary Parish . . . also the Rents and Profits of the Glebe Land and the Profits arising from the Labour of the Slaves thereto belonging." The indebted minister was left with just "his wearing Apparel and Library" and a small annual allowance for his "Support and Maintenance." A decade later, McPherson was apparently still the incumbent minister of William and Mary Parish when he placed an ad seeking the recapture of an enslaved man named Will Wage. A talented banjo player who was "well-acquainted with the area," Wage had been hired out along with the rest of the "Piccawaxon glebe slaves" to work near Port Tobacco, presumably under the settlement made by the assembly.[19] Though McPherson no longer pocketed the income earned by Wage and the other enslaved people held by the parish, he hoped to apprehend the escaped man.

Somerset Parish in Somerset County, Maryland, also enslaved a large number of persons. Though the exact number of people held in bondage by the parish is unknown, the parish vestry aimed to sell "so many of the said slaves belonging to their parish as will enable them to build a dwelling house, and such other houses as may be fit and convenient for a clergyman."[20] Given that this proposal came in 1783, it seems likely that the parish had engaged in slaveholding before the Revolution and was seeking a new way to raise funds after the war. However, the precise details of how and when the parish first claimed these people are not recorded in the parish vestry book. These two examples demonstrate that at least two of Maryland's thirty parishes enslaved people as chattel property, but the absence of evidence from parochial records in either case again underscores that silences in the records do not indicate a lack of slaveholding.

Extant records from Virginia reveal that over the course of the eighteenth century, roughly half of the colony's parishes enslaved Black people.[21] Parishes most often began slaveholding either after receiving bequests from parishioners or when opening poorhouses.[22] Wealthy benefactors left money to parishes, which vestries used to purchase enslaved people; sometimes parishioners directly gifted enslaved individuals to parishes. Numerous parishes received enslaved people as part of charitable endowments for "the poor of the parish" or to support a specific charitable institution like a free school.[23] In an effort to lower the cost of poor relief, after 1750 parishes increasingly moved away from out-of-door assistance and began constructing poorhouses. Vestries purchased enslaved people in the hopes of lessening the tax burden of providing for the poor. What went unsaid, of course, was that the poor who benefited from charitable bequests and poor relief were overwhelmingly white. Parishes treated bonded Black labor as an endowment for the financial welfare of white parishioners rather than as a benefit for their ministers. Whether parishes claimed enslaved people from bequests or purchased them outright to work at poorhouses, enslaved people labored to support the white poor.

The example of Lynnhaven Parish exemplifies both routes to slaveholding. Using the proceeds from a bequest from former vestryman Anthony Walke in 1757, the vestrymen of Lynnhaven Parish purchased several "young slaves for the support of the said parish" in 1761.[24] It was no coincidence that in the same year the parish opened its poorhouse on a fifty-acre farm. Lynnhaven and other parishes relied on enslaved laborers at their poorhouses to work the land and care for white parishioners. Recipients of parish poor relief in Virginia were overwhelmingly white, and the labor and bodies of Black men and women served their good. Parochial welfare was built on and reinforced racial hierarchy.

Six years later, the Lynnhaven vestry ordered the churchwardens "to sell the Negro wench Rachal belonging to the Parish & that the Money Ariseing thereby be applyed towards buying another Negro." Rachal may have been one of the women purchased in 1761, but her fate, along with that of any other individuals belonging to Lynnhaven, is missing in the records. In the 1770s, the longtime minister Robert Dickson left four more enslaved people, Harry, Lewis, Gefford, and Lydia, to the parish. The parish debated selling these men and women but instead determined that "their labour and service at this time will be more Adventitious than the interest of the money ariseing from the sale thereof."[25] The Lynnhaven vestry valued enslaved people as form of capital or labor. No mention was made in any of these discussions of the spiritual lives of any of the enslaved community, nor do they appear among the baptisms in the church register.

Parishes expected enslaved laborers to bring in short-term revenue, but they also anticipated benefitting from hereditary enslavement for generations to come. Legislation, wills, and vestry books referred to enslaved persons as "stock" and planned for their future "increase." Many parishes stipulated that they hoped to purchase "young female slaves," "wenches," and "breeding negroes," which underscored their expectation that these women would bear children who would also be held in bondage by the parish.[26] This language closely resembles the terms commonly used to describe livestock in similar bequests—"breeding mares" and "the increase of cattle"—a disturbing similarity that underscores how the language used in these discussions sought to normalize slavery by denying the humanity of enslaved people. The language used to describe enslaved women emphasized their ability to bear children and treated women's bodies and reproductive labor as long-term assets whose value would appreciate over time. Commissary Blair had tried to lump the cattle and human chattel together in his dehumanizing discussion of "stock" in his 1699 proposal. Enslaved men and women were not only labor and property in the short term but regarded as investments who promised future value as their descendants would remain in bondage.

Parishes that did not directly enslave people still frequently benefitted from enslaved labor. In Virginia, bastardy laws required churchwardens to bind out any mixed-raced child born to a white mother until she or he reached the age of thirty-one.[27] The churchwardens of Bristol Parish, for example, apprenticed two "Mulotto children, Named Philip and Betty son and Daughter to Ann Evans," to serve the rector, the Rev. Robert Ferguson.[28] Doing so provided the minister with unpaid labor for the glebe lands for decades. Thomas Jefferson briefly hired the labor of two mixed-race men, Isaac Jackson and George Manly, who had been bound out by his parish churchwardens.[29] Later, Jefferson even represented Manly in a suit for his freedom after he was illegally held until the age of thirty-four.[30]

Maryland's establishmentarian laws had initially created a similar system in which mixed-race children were bound out by the parish. At a meeting on February 15, 1698, the vestrymen of St. James Parish in Anne Arundel County made a long list of objects and improvements they sought for their newly built church. Charged with formalizing public worship under the colony's new system of Anglican establishment, the vestry and churchwardens appointed one of their number to send to England for a fine green altar cloth, a chalice and plate for communion, a pewter baptismal font, and a large folio to register births, marriages, and deaths. In addition to purchasing these sacred materials, the St. James vestrymen also hoped to install locks on their pews and to upgrade the church's windows with lead and glass. While the construction of their new sanctuary had been funded by taxpayers over the previous four years, this new investment in materials and renovations would be funded by the "sale [of] the women having Mallattoe Children."[31] A few months later, the vestry noted that the "produce of the three women Servants sold by [the] vestry being adjudged for their having Mallattoe children amounting in all to [the] sum of thirty & two pounds," and stated that they could now proceed with their planned renovations and purchases.[32] Indeed, in the span of just four years, from 1697 to 1701, at least five female servants convicted of bastardy and five mixed-race children were handed over to the parish vestry "to be disposed off [*sic*]" at their discretion.[33] Three-year old Margaret and another young mixed-race girl, along with Mary Budd and her child, were sent to work for the parish minister, Mr. Henry Hall, while Katherine Worley, her child, and several other women "condemned by the law at Ann Arundell County Court" and their offspring had their terms of service sold. The St. James vestry funded its early spiritual work by selling the service of women convicted of bastardy and their mixed-race children.

Maryland's counties took over the indenturing process in the early eighteenth century under a new slave code. The Maryland commissary complained in the following decades that "Mulato's [were] . . . once the right of the Church" and ought to "be restored for Servants to manage the Glebe."[34] Such a system would be "serviceable to Religion and conduce to the ease of the Clergy and their more comfortable subsistence." Despite this clergyman's suggestion, this source of free forced labor was not returned to parishes in Maryland.

Parishes in both colonies also hired enslaved people on a short-term or annual basis to provide additional labor.[35] When Petsworth Parish in Gloucester County, Virginia, hired an enslaved woman from John Wiatt to work at the parish poor house for a term of one year in 1767, the vestry specified that she would wear "cottin" clothing, whereas the poor, white children whom she tended wore "blue or green."[36] The required uniform of this enslaved woman marked her out as distinct from the poor. At Whitehall Plantation, which served as the glebe for St. Margaret's Parish in Anne Arundel County, Maryland, from 1749 to 1761, parish historians estimate that as many as one hundred enslaved people were hired to cultivate the extensive glebe lands each year.[37]

The glebe system sought to make parish rectors into Chesapeake planters, and a majority of Anglican ministers personally enslaved people.[38] Parishes often built slave quarters on their glebes, and the men and women enslaved by ministers labored on parish lands. Carol Van Voorst estimates that 60–80 percent of Maryland's Anglican ministers held enslaved people between 1710 and 1776 and that by the 1760s, parish ministers typically held a dozen men and women in bondage as personal property.[39]

Individual ministers also hired enslaved men and women on an annual basis to work on glebes. For example, the accounts of Rev. Charles Clay of St. Anne's Parish in Albemarle County, Virginia, show that he hired an enslaved woman named Sukey from her enslaver, Rebecca Tucker, on an annual basis to work on the glebe.[40] The account book of William West, rector of Westminster Parish in Anne Arundel County, shows at least six people held in bondage by the minister: Nan, Priscilla, Jenny, Austin, Bob, and Tom.[41] By 1776, Reverend West had moved to St. George's Parish in Harford County and enslaved nine people, who lived in the quarters on the glebe land.[42] These enslaved men and women cultivated corn, wheat, potatoes, and pork and produced cider on the glebe. Reverend West then sold or bartered these goods to his neighbors to raise additional income. Parish vestries and clergymen were acquisitive landholders and slaveholders like so many of their white parishioners.

The colonial parish had access to several forms of capital—taxes collected in pounds of tobacco, glebes held in acres of land, and the bodies and labor of the enslaved—because of its privileged position as a public body. The annual levy gave the parish liquid capital that was scarce in the colonies and allowed it to weather the boom-and-bust economic cycles that affected great planters.[43] The levy enabled parishes to convert tax revenue into long-term investments in land and goods and to extend credit. But it was not only the amount of property parishes held but the relative security of their investments that expressed the special status the established church, which I will explore next.[44]

## Incorporation in Custom and Statute

The extraordinary wealth of the established church was rendered secure through incorporation, and corporate privileges were a key plank of Anglican establishment. Statutes, common law, and custom together underpinned the ability of parishes to hold property securely. Parish officers were endowed with unique corporate standing that enabled their parishes to accumulate wealth and safeguard it from one generation to the next. Colonial parishes exercised immense power in the dispersed landscape of the tobacco colonies through the incorporation of their vestries, churchwardens, and ministers.[45]

The Church of England was not a single corporation but a constellation of corporate bodies. Individual vestrymen and churchwardens came and went, but these parish officers existed as corporate bodies in perpetuity. They had standing in law and could enforce contracts and recover debts in court. They could buy, hold, and sell property securely. Parish officers signed contracts and deeds that secured obligations and property over generations. These powerful corporate entities existed in every Chesapeake community, whether coastal or mountainous, densely settled or thinly populated. In fact, only through the exercise of corporate privileges could parishes effectively carry out their many legal duties. Vestrymen and churchwardens needed to hold funds jointly, secure their assets, and pass on property to provide communities with the religious services and civic oversight required by statute. In the colonial Chesapeake, where there were few corporations and individuals went to great lengths to preserve familial wealth from generation to generation, customary incorporation conferred security on parochial wealth from one generation to the next. Incorporation was a necessary privilege in the scaffolding of religious establishment because it allowed the church to consolidate and hold property over time.

The general resistance of elite colonists to forming towns and other corporate bodies, both private and public, did not prevent them from exercising immense corporate power through their own parishes as vestrymen and churchwardens.[46] These men made savvy use of the incorporated powers of their parishes to further their own standing as patrons and administrators. They built grand churches that closely resembled their homes and the courts they oversaw as justices of the peace.[47] They helped elevate the parish church to one of the few public spaces serving the dispersed population of the tobacco colonies and appointed their sons and favorites to fill open seats on the vestry. These grandees were not allergic to all corporations, simply those that might displace them one day.

For colonists living under the Anglican establishment, there was simply no question that parish officers had corporate standing. Vestries could hold property, churchwardens could recover debts in court, and the vestry, churchwardens, and minister existed in perpetuity, notwithstanding changes in their personnel. The natural persons who served as rectors, churchwardens, and vestrymen lived and died, but these legal personalities endured in perpetuity. Several types of evidence highlight the widely accepted corporate status of colonial parishes, including legal treatises, colonial legislation, political debates, and the records of lawsuits, contracts, and deeds. A careful examination of these sources shows how commonplace unchartered corporations were in the context of colonial religious establishment.[48]

The legal foundations of parochial incorporation rested in English common law. As the preeminent eighteenth-century English jurist William Blackstone observed, incorporation ensured that "the present incumbent and his predecessor who lived seven centuries ago, are in law one and the same person; and what was given to the one was given to the other also."[49] The construct of corporate personhood meant that the "endowment of parish churches, the freehold of the church, the churchyard, the parsonage house, the glebe, and the tithes of the parish" remained securely in the hands of the parish and provided "temporal recompence" for "spiritual care."[50] The ability to hold and pass property securely, to sue and be sued, and to be known in law in perpetuity allowed a parish, cathedral, or diocese to raise funds, acquire property, and manage their investments through the ages.

These many bodies of the established church did not rely on charters for their incorporation but existed under common law. As Blackstone wrote, "The king's implied consent is to be found in corporations which exist by force of the *common law* . . . being nothing else but custom, arising from the universal agreement of the whole community."[51] These customary corporations "by common law have ever been held (as far as our books can shew us) to have been corporations, *virtute officii*." For these church institutions, "incorporation is so inseparably annexed to their offices, that we cannot frame a complete legal idea of any of these persons, but we must also have an idea of a corporation."[52] Practically, the established church could not have fulfilled its public duties without the capacity to hold property, to exist in perpetuity, and to bring suit. Religious establishment naturalized these powers and expressed the de facto consent of the Crown upon which custom rested.

These unchartered forms of incorporation relied on the prerogative of the king as head of church and state, but they also invoked the pretext of universal membership in a state church. Conformity in matters of religion was certainly a legal fiction, as was the assertion that the Church of England's powers stretched back to time immemorial. But this imagined church—national, unanimous, and ancient—strengthened the pretense of consensus on which customary incorporation rested. Under this framework of illusory agreement, there was no space for dissent. Thus, privileges of customary incorporation could only extend to the established church for which the King's consent was assumed.

Blackstone detailed many of the corporate bodies that made up the established church in his chapter on corporations. Bishops, deans, parsons, and other "spiritual persons," were incorporated "for the furtherance of religion, and perpetuating the rights of the church," and classed as ecclesiastical corporations. But lay civil corporations, which carried out "temporal purposes," were also essential to the practical operation of the established church, in particular the churchwardens, who held "the goods of the parish."[53] Another key distinction Blackstone laid out was between corporations sole and aggregate. The former type included bishops, deans, and rectors. These clerics were "one person only and his successors . . . incorporated by law, in order to give them some legal capacities and advantages, particularly that of perpetuity, which in their natural persons they could not have had." Incorporation lent these natural persons the artificial quality of perpetuity, which was essential to preserving the institutional wealth of parishes and dioceses over generations. Corporations aggregate, comprised of "many persons united together into one society, and . . . kept up by a perpetual succession of members," also operated on behalf of the established church, such as the dean and chapter of a cathedral. The established church was known in law through these many distinct corporate forms, ecclesiastical and civil, sole and aggregate.

Blackstone's *Commentaries,* though an essential compendium of common law, appeared in 1765, after generations of Anglican establishment in the Chesapeake. Colonial legal sources help clarify how English law had been enacted and adapted in the Chesapeake. One of the earliest publications of Virginia's first printer, William Parks, was a handbook for Virginian justices of the peace entitled *The Office and Authority of a Justice of Peace.*[54] The book's author, George Webb, had been born in London before emigrating to Virginia in the early eighteenth century, where he served as a vestryman of St. Peter's Parish, a militia officer, and a justice of the peace in New Kent County. Webb's work provided an essential summary of English and Virginian law for the use of local officials, most of whom had no formal legal education.[55] This colonial handbook provided clear descriptions of the corporate status of various Anglican bodies. Webb noted that churchwardens "by the Common Law, are made a Corporation to take Care of the Goods of the Church. . . . They are a corporation, only as to Moveables, vis to take Goods, but not Lands, for the Use of the Church."[56] The vestry was tasked with the purchase of glebe lands "for the use of minister of such parish, for the Time being and his successors for ever." Glebe lands were vested in the parish in perpetuity, and the duty to purchase and maintain its "lands and tenements" fell to the vestry.[57] Once inducted, the parish rector was treated as a sole corporation, a *persona ecclesiae*, who had freehold over the glebe during his tenure.[58] The churchwardens, vestry, and minister existed as three distinct bodies operating on behalf of the parish. Each exercised different rights under common law, which were reflected in their distinct responsibilities in the parish.

Even a brief comparison of the discussion of the different parochial institutions in the colonial *Office and Authority* and the English *Commentaries* highlights how colonial Anglicanism had deviated from English practices, and this evolution is certainly reflected in the differences between Blackstone's and Webb's discussions of church corporations. Importantly, Webb's Virginian treatise focused significant attention on the legal powers of vestries, something which Blackstone does not detail. This difference in emphasis signaled how much more powerful vestries had become in the colonies than they were in England (see chapter 1). Another key difference was the relationship of churchwardens to the vestry. In England, parishes held separate elections to choose churchwardens annually. The common-law division between the corporate powers of the churchwardens and the vestry underscored that English vestries and churchwardens represented separate institutions. However, in Virginia, the vestry simply appointed two of its members to act as churchwardens each year, and the time-consuming job often rotated among the vestrymen. While churchwardens were elected separately in Maryland, they still gathered with the vestry to make decisions for the parish. In the Chesapeake colonies, the formal distinction between churchwardens and vestrymen was often a legal fiction; together, these men interchangeably acted as representatives and custodians of their parishes to purchase goods and real estate.

Colonial legislation practically recognized the customary incorporation of parish bodies described in these abstract treatises. The assemblies of Virginia and Maryland frequently passed statutes that enabled and even required parish officers to exercise corporate rights. These acts recognized without question the customary rights of standing of parish vestries, churchwardens, and ministers under common law. In turn, these parish bodies exercised corporate rights to carry out the many legal duties delegated to them by the assemblies.

Virginia's colonial legislature never passed anything resembling a formal act of incorporation for the established Anglican Church or its parishes. Indeed, there had never been a systematic program of legislation that established the Anglican Church in Virginia; rather, the legislature passed a piecemeal series of laws over a 150-year period that recognized the establishment status of the church from the colony's founding and accommodated English customs to colonial realities. The lack of specificity in Virginia's statutes about the corporate status of the church suggested the strength of common-law tradition made express acts of incorporation unnecessary.

Still, Virginia's laws frequently recognized the corporate status of parochial bodies. The power of parishes to tax all inhabitants through an annual levy was granted by statute in 1631/2 and reaffirmed by additional laws in 1655/6 and again in 1696.[59] The 1655/6 act empowered churchwardens to "dispose of" funds raised in the levy and required them "to give securitie" to the vestry for the parish levy. A year later, a new law required parishes to construct churches and arranged for churchwardens to purchase "gleabes and stock" for ministers.[60] By instructing churchwardens to manage and transfer cash and moveables and to buy real estate, the assembly recognized their customary rights as a corporate entity. Moreover, by requiring the vestry and churchwardens to sign a contract each year to ensure the proper collection of the levy, the law recognized two distinct corporate bodies that acted on behalf of each parish. Legislation passed at the end of the seventeenth century gave parishes "the liberty to make lawes for themselves."[61] The right of passing bylaws was a unique privilege typically extended to corporations.

Another important statutory recognition of the corporate powers of Virginia's parishes came in the form of acts empowering specific vestries to sell glebe lands. The seventeenth-century statutes requiring parishes to buy glebes had not specified which body held title to the glebe lands. The vagueness of these laws proved problematic for Virginian vestries trying to sell their glebe lands decades later.[62] In response, the assembly began issuing separate acts empowering any vestry that petitioned to sell their glebes. The assembly acquiesced to more than a hundred petitions from parishes over the colonial period to sell glebe lands.[63] By passing specific acts authorizing vestries to sell their glebe lands, the assembly sought to clarify that the vestry of every parish held title to glebe lands for the use of the minister during his lifetime. In this respect, these specific acts simply reiterated the longstanding principles of common law.

The involvement of the assembly in the transfer of parochial property further underscored that parish vestries were public corporations. Towns like Williamsburg, which had been formally incorporated by acts of assembly, received similar governmental oversight when they sought to expand their boundaries or sell lands.[64] In another analogous example, a chartered corporation that produced and sold wine also had to receive the assembly's approval before selling its land.[65] Virginia's public corporations, whether manufacturers, towns, or parishes, could buy or dispose of real estate only with the assembly's approval.[66]

Virginia's legislature superintended the personnel of parishes across the colony and exercised the right to "dissolve" incompetent vestries. The assembly received dozens of petitions over the eighteenth century from parishioners who accused their vestrymen of holding office unlawfully, or of being idle, illiterate, dissolute, oppressive, or, perhaps most damning of all, religious dissenters. In response to these reports, the assembly had the power to dissolve vestries and call for new elections. However, the terms of these acts highlight that the process of "dissolving a vestry" did not destroy the corporation itself or interfere with its legal rights. For example, in 1772, the Virginia legislature "dissolved" the vestries of St. John's Parish in King William County and St. Martin Parish in Hanover and Louisa Counties.[67] The act called for new elections in the coming months; however, it noted, "notwithstanding any thing in this act contained, any suit or suits brought by or against the vestry or churchwardens of either of the said parishes, and now depending, may be prosecuted in the same manner as if this act had not been made."[68] Dissolving the membership of the vestry did not actually destroy the vestry or churchwardens as corporate bodies, nor did it affect their legal powers or property.

There are instances when the corporate status of parish officers under common law was bolstered by legislative intervention. For example, Rev. William Meldrum won a sizeable judgment against the vestry of Frederick Parish after a long-fought lawsuit over back pay.[69] The minister argued that the vestry had unjustly lowered his salary, and he sought a remedy from the court. Some of the vestrymen had covered the costs of prosecution out of pocket, and after losing their case, they sought legislative assurance that they personally were not accountable for repaying the minister. Their nonliability should have been clear-cut without any legislation under common law, as vestries and churchwardens commonly raised funds in the levy to repay themselves for any costs they incurred while carrying out their parochial duties. The minister had won a judgment against the vestry as a corporation, not the vestrymen as a group of individuals. However, perhaps to quiet any possible complaints from parishioners about the increased parish levy, the vestry petitioned and received an act empowering them to raise funds specifically to repay themselves for the court costs and the judgment through the levy. Growing hostility toward the established church in the western region of Virginia, where Frederick Parish lay, might further explain why the vestry sought legislative affirmation of their corporate standing.

By the early eighteenth century, Virginian lawyers began to assert that vestries were corporations under the colony's statutes and its custom. In 1718, the Vestry of Bruton Parish sued Gov. Alexander Spotswood over the issue of advowson, or the right to present and select the parish rector. The vestry hired "the ablest lawyer" in the colony to argue their case.[70] Citing Virginia's distinctive custom and acts of assembly, this attorney maintained that "a Corporacon may be seised of Advowson And that the Vestry here in behalf of the parishioners are such a Corporacon."[71] He explained how Virginian law augmented the traditional English common law:

> In Common Cases Church Wardens are by Law a Corporation for [the] benefit of the Parish. But the Acts of Assembly in 1662 & 1696 having appointed a Vestry to be chosen for [the] making Assessments, for the building of Churches and purchasing a Glebe, Do thereby make them a Corporation for those purposes, and they are Enabled to Act of a body corporate in all things which relate to & depend thereon. And as the Right of presentation is a Consequential Right arising from the Founding Building and Endowing, that will likewise vest in them as a Corporation.[72]

Commissary Blair and other members of the Virginia Council "strenuously" supported this view, arguing that "the Practice of the Country . . . be of more force than the power granted by the Crown."[73] Defenders of royal prerogative and legal formalists were aghast at Virginians' claims that their customs of their own "Country" overrode either the Crown or the traditional doctrines of English common law. Before the general court had come to a decision, Spotswood was replaced by Hugh Drysdale as governor, who decided not to continue the case. Drysdale and subsequent royal governors did not try to insist on the advowson.[74] Vestries had thus successfully claimed the advowson and in so doing asserted the corporate rights of Virginia vestries. A novel departure from English common law, which recognized the incorporation of churchwardens and rectors, the customary incorporation of vestries became widely accepted in Virginia in the eighteenth century.[75]

Unlike in Virginia, where incorporation remained customary and implicit in statute, the Maryland Assembly explicitly addressed the corporate standing of vestries and churchwardens. The series of laws establishing the Church of England in Maryland, known as the Church Acts, mentioned the corporate rights of the church directly. As discussed in chapter 1, the assembly tried unsuccessfully to establish the Church of England three times—in 1692, 1696, and 1700—before finally succeeding in 1702. The first of these laws, the 1692 "Act for the Service of Almighty God and the Establishment of the Protestant Religion," stipulated that every vestry should act "in the nature and amply as a body Politick or corporate" to manage their assets.[76] The act went into effect immediately in Maryland. Parish vestries began exercising their corporate privileges right away by collecting levies and managing parish property. However, the law was repealed by the Crown following intense pressure, both from Quakers and Catholics.[77] The second iteration of the Church Act (1696) elaborated on the corporate status of vestries in much greater detail. The act specified that vestries in each parish "be hereby Constituted and appointed in the nature of a body Corporate" in order to manage the levy, to build and repair church property, to receive "any Lands Tenements Hereditaments money Tobbacco Goods Cattle or Chattells . . . whatsoever of what nature" and to sue and be sued.[78] Parish vestries could act "fully and Amply to all intents and purposes as any Body Corporate might or could do." The same statute also declared that churchwardens "of each respective parish are by this Act Impowered to sue" on behalf of the parish for the nonpayment of fees owed to the parish. This act explicitly recognized the corporate status of both the vestry and the churchwardens and acknowledged their distinct powers to act on behalf of the parish. However, the council yet again interceded on behalf of non-Anglicans in the colony and killed the law.

On the heels of the repeal of the 1696 law, the assembly passed a third Church Act in 1700. This version of the statute declared that vestries were "bodys corporate . . . hereby made capable of sueing and being sued" and that the annual levy was due to "the Vestry of each respective Parrish by this Act Constituted and incorporated a body Pollitick."[79] The third rendition of the law did not detail the exhaustive rights of vestries but simply "confirmed" their rights under standing practice, which underscored that their corporate status had already been well-established in the province. However, the 1700 Church Act was likewise overturned in London; this time the Board of Trade recommended a veto because under the law, "the Vestrys of the several Parishes are thereby incorporated, and made a Body Politick, Which is not so in England."[80] Finally, the assembly passed a revised statute in 1702 that simply referred to "the body of the Parish" and then instructed parishes to continue collecting the levy and managing parochial funds "as they have beene."[81] Yet with these oblique references, the Maryland Assembly endorsed the parochial system already in operation. The 1702 Church Act recognized in statute what had already taken root in practice and affirmed the customary corporate privileges of parish officers without any further explicit discussion of incorporation.[82]

Lingering uncertainty over whether the final 1702 statute had supplemented or displaced the customary rights of Maryland's parish vestries became a point of contention on the eve of the Revolution. Two of the colony's most able jurists, future Supreme Court justice Samuel Chase and his fellow signer of the Declaration of Independence William Paca, insisted that Maryland's churchwardens and vestries retained their corporate capacity in common law beyond the express terms of the statute. These lawyers were also vestrymen of the most visible and powerful parish in the province, St. Anne's, located in its bustling capital, Annapolis. Their letters expressed both their formal training as lawyers and their experience running parish affairs on the ground. In a series of public letters published in the *Maryland Gazette,* Chase and Paca argued that the corporate standing of Maryland's vestries and churchwardens rested on "custom" from "time immemorial" and formed part of Maryland's constitution. They explained that "the parishioners, by common law, founded upon publick utility, become a *body politic.*" When "particular persons by custom are . . . chosen and elected for Vestrymen, the government of the parish devolves upon them, and they, as the representatives of the people of the parish, may in their corporate capacity of Vestrymen" carry out a wide range of activity. Churchwardens, too, they explained were also "considered in law as a corporate body to many purposes" founded upon the "common right in all the parishioners." Much like the vestrymen of Bruton Parish sparring with Governor Spotswood in Virginia half a century earlier, Paca and Chase were eager to assert that by "common law and common right," Maryland's distinctive customs, including the corporate powers of vestries, were authoritative and constitutional.[83]

Chase and Paca's description of the customary incorporation of Maryland's parish vestry and churchwardens was not an academic exercise but a vigorous defense of local powers amid a fierce battle between Maryland's Anglican clergy and the laity in the early 1770s. Initially a dispute about how much parishioners were obliged to pay the clergy after the expiration of the Tobacco Inspection Act, the clash boiled over into a broader struggle over the proprietary government's rights in the colony, the prospect of an American bishop, the abuses of Parliament, and popular anger at the established church in Maryland.[84] The question of corporate standing became not just a legal point but a political one, as Paca and Chase tied incorporation to other rights, such as the right of trial by jury, and implored, "May THE COMMON LAW prevail triumphant!" against imperial overreach.[85] Stoking the fires of anti-imperial indignation, Paca and Chase insisted on the customary privileges of their parishes as a way of bolstering the laity's power vis-à-vis the clergy and local power against the perceived proprietary government and Parliament.

Their primary public opponent was the Rev. Jonathan Boucher, an Anglican clergyman born in England who had come to the Chesapeake a decade earlier. After a brief stint as rector of St. Anne's, Boucher had departed for a higher salary in Queen Anne Parish in Prince George's County. Bad blood festered between the minister and the vestrymen of his former parish.[86] Boucher would go on to become one of history's most famous loyalists after his vehement Toryism made him the target of increasingly violent threats before he fled for England in 1775.[87]

Shades of this staunch royalism can be found in Boucher's formalist rejection of Paca and Chase's claims, including their understanding of parish rights founded in custom. He offered a formalist view that only statute could extend incorporation to vestries and rejected the "supposed custom" invoked by Chase and Paca.[88] He flatly rejected their claim to customary rights, including incorporation. St. Anne's and other vestries, he declared, had not existed in Maryland before the 1692 statute, and their rights were limited to what had been expressly conferred by the final text of the 1702 statute establishing the Church of England. The divergence between colonial practice and English formalism created longstanding disputes about how authoritative colonial custom really was within Anglo-American law.[89] Despite Boucher's objections, colonists' insistence on customary incorporation reflected the realities of their homegrown establishment and signaled the stakes for protecting it against English incursion.

## Exercising Corporate Privileges

Just as Paca and Chase were proclaiming vestries' corporate standing in the *Maryland Gazette,* the two men were also busy exercising corporate powers as vestrymen by disbursing funds, managing bequests, and hiring a minister for the parish.[90] To these vestrymen and their parishioners, incorporation was never an abstraction limited to legal treatises or political disputes. Customary incorporation gave parishes the ability to sue and be sued and the right to contract. These powers were mutually reinforcing and proved essential to safeguarding property over the generations.

Whether employing builders, day laborers, physicians, or painters, parishes used contracts to secure the terms of a labor agreement and securely transfer property. Their ability to contract protected a valuable investment over multiple years. Contracts were particularly important for expensive and lengthy construction projects like building a new church. Signing an agreement allowed the builder to receive a monetary advance, often necessary to purchase materials, while also allowing the parish to set down exact terms before work got underway. The vestry of St. Paul's Parish in Prince George's County, Maryland, signed a contract on October 27, 1742, with Daniel Page to build a new church for the parish.[91] The St. Paul's vestry outlined its requirements for the new church in a detailed contract that stretched over four pages. The vestrymen specified the types of materials to be used throughout the project: walls of well-burnt bricks, windows of glass and lead, carpentry of poplar or white oak timber, and roof shingles made from cypress. Perhaps it was their relatively reliable status that explains how vestries could get men like Daniel Page to agree to conditions like the final clause of this contract, which prevented the accruing of interest on the amount the parish owed the builder if they did not have all the necessary cash to pay him on time. As public bodies, parishes were uniquely positioned to drive a hard bargain.

By the time the new St. Paul's Parish church was finished several years later, different individuals were serving as vestrymen. The original contract remained in full effect because vestries existed in perpetuity, no matter their personnel. While the individual men serving as churchwardens and vestrymen changed from year to year, the courts recognized the corporate standing of the churchwardens as an independent legal body that existed in perpetuity.

Parochial wealth was secured under statutory and common law, but property transactions in the Chesapeake sometimes deviated from the forms laid out in legal treatises. The distinct powers of churchwardens and vestries were not always observed in property transactions. Colonial deed books list vestries, churchwardens, or the parish as whole as purchasing and selling glebe lands and church buildings. In Princess Anne County, Virginia, there are deeds for real estate giving title alternatively to "Lynnhaven Parish," "the vestry of Lynnhaven Parish," and "the churchwardens of Lynnhaven Parish."[92] This irregularity likely reflected the lacking legal education of many county clerks; while clearly intending to vest property in some parochial body, these transactions were inconsistent and reflected a situation far messier on the ground than in formal law. But the variety in these contracts also reflect the assumed corporate standing of parish bodies; the accepted corporate powers of the established church apparently meant the lack of exactitude was not considered a problem.

Contracts were only powerful tools if they could be enforced by the courts, and the ability to sue and be sued went hand in hand with parishes' ability to contract. The responsibility to represent the parish in lawsuits fell to the churchwardens, and county courts treated parish churchwardens as corporations without question.[93] Numerous parochial lawsuits appear in vestry books and county court records.[94] As the custodians of the parish's moveable property under common law, the churchwardens were responsible for managing the parish's finances and thus acted to recover damages or recoup debts. Churchwardens' responsibility of representing the parish in lawsuits was distinct from their power to present parishioners to the court for moral crimes such as drunkenness, Sabbath-breaking, fornication, and bastardy.[95] When charging parishioners with crimes, churchwardens appeared in court as representatives of the Crown and served as an arm of the state. In these instances, their prosecutorial powers to bring charges were equivalent to those of grand juries. When they sued for breach of contract, churchwardens acted in their corporate capacity to recover debts due to the parish.

When necessary, churchwardens pursued lawsuits for breach of contract. These included unpaid debts or the failure to perform the specific terms of a contract. In 1772, the churchwardens of Virginia's Henrico Parish were ordered by the vestry to sue a former vestryman, Samuel DuVal, who had failed to build a new church per an agreement he had made with the parish the year before.[96] The churchwardens withdrew their lawsuit and awarded the contract to another builder after DuVal relented and forfeited his advance. In addition to lawsuits over incomplete construction projects, parishes also sued for unpaid bills arising from the extensive system of parochial poor relief. Every year, parishes made dozens of appropriations to provide food, clothing, allowances, and medical care to poor parishioners in their communities. Virginian parishes were responsible for providing poor relief and medical care to their parishioners, but they were also required to cover these costs for "strangers," or nonresidents, if they fell ill or became injured while in the parish. For example, Upper Parish provided expensive medical care to a sick "saylor" named Joell Brown in 1745. The vestry paid for the sick man to see a doctor using parish funds and put him up while he recuperated; meanwhile, the churchwardens sued to recover the cost from his ship captain, John Meredith, who was legally responsible for his sailors' care.[97] The churchwardens won their suit and recovered the costs of Brown's care.

Parishes extended loans to parishioners and sometimes turned to the courts to enforce the repayment of these financial agreements. The vestry of St. Peter's Parish in New Kent County, Virginia, noted in 1751 that the vestry "ordered that all persons indebted to the Parish do account with the Church Wardens and Pay to their Hands the Several Sums due from them, and in failure of Payment the church wardens are required to bring suit for the recovery of the same."[98] Parishes could extend credit safely because they were possessed of a legal remedy to recover unpaid debts.

Churchwardens even turned to the courts to collect the public money due to them from county officials. The churchwardens were legally entitled to collect all fines for moral crimes but often relied on officers of the county court to collect this money from convicted individuals. In 1761, the churchwardens of Bristol Parish in Prince George County, Virginia, recovered 12 pounds, 12 shillings and 8 pence after winning "a Judgm't of P. Geo. Court ag't Mr. Jam. Murray as Sherriff for fines Rec'd by Peter

Peterson his under Sherriff Due the Parish including Cost of suit & att. fee."[99] The Bristol churchwardens were forced in this instance to sue the county's sheriff to recover the money owed the parish. Sometimes, the threat of a lawsuit was enough to pressure public officials to settle. In 1758, the churchwardens of Petsworth Parish in Gloucester County, Virginia, "appl[ied] to Major Tomkies and Mr. Francis Stubbs for the money in there [*sic*] hands belonging to the poor of this parish" and reminded the two men that "if they refuse[d] payment," the wardens would "bring sute for the same."[100] Tomkies and Stubbs, both former churchwardens, apparently had held onto the parish funds after leaving parochial office. The prospect of legal action apparently prompted both men to turn over the money in their hands, and the parish did not pursue the matter further. Tensions between parish and county officers underscored that the abstract model of establishment built on the union of church and state did not always operate seamlessly in practice. While the established church was an extension of the state, conflict could still arise between different public officers and institutions.

Under the program of religious establishment, parishioners experienced parochial corporateness as a daily reality in which they together comprised one entity under the authority of a small group of vestrymen. In return, everyone (at least purportedly) received moral and spiritual benefits, and a few received more material returns through poor relief, salaries, or loans. The program of religious establishment made parishes powerful legal institutions and expressions of collective wealth and power familiar to colonists. All members of the community—male and female, elite and poor, free and enslaved, and even religious dissenters—theoretically comprised one parish. Their individual taxes amounted to the collective wealth of the parish. When the vestry built fine churches, distributed charitable relief, regulated the production and export of tobacco, or performed a multitude of other civic tasks, they acted on behalf of the community. The parish derived its civic power from the imagined universality of its spiritual membership and its legal power to compel communal resources. The institution of the parish constituted individuals into one spiritual community, a body politic and religious, and its legal privileges as a corporation relied on the presumption of spiritual universality.

## Nonconformists and Property

Yet just as a corporation was an artificial person—a person in the eyes of the law only—the mandate of religious universality and spiritual unity was likewise a legal fallacy. Race circumscribed parochial belonging as the bodies of enslaved Virginians were taxed by the parish while these men and women were largely excluded from any sort of spiritual inclusion, as discussed in chapter 1. The spiritual body politic involuntarily included all residents, no matter their religious persuasion. Legally, all nonconformists in both colonies were parishioners. In Maryland, the religious wars of the seventeenth century and the powerful communities of Catholics and Quakers made clear the fallacy of religious cohesion. In Virginia, it was not until the mid-eighteenth century that a growing number of evangelical dissenters pointedly opposed the establishment and undermined the illusion of religious unanimity. The Great Awakening brought significant numbers of dissenters to Virginia for the first time. Nonconforming communities confronted discrimination under the establishment, not just in restrictions of their free exercise but also in the difficulty to secure property, hold it as jointly as a spiritual community, and pass it onto future generations.

All dissenting communities encountered difficulty holding property securely because they lacked the powerful tool of incorporation. While parish vestries could buy, hold, and sell property securely, nonconformists had no legal mechanism to protect their property. Shut out of statutory incorporation and unable to take advantage of customary incorporation, dissenting Protestant and Catholic communities had to rely on creative solutions to manage and protect property. The difficulty faced by unincorporated religious communities in holding and transferring property reveals how common law and statutory law worked hand in hand as part of the legal establishment to hinder nonconforming religious groups.

The property held by Maryland's Jesuits was a long-running source of tension in the province. As mentioned in chapter 1, the colony's headright system awarded Jesuit missionaries thousands of acres for transporting indentured servants to the colony in the 1630s. While they held this property as individuals like any other colonists, the clergy expected that living in Maryland under a Catholic proprietor would unshackle them from the many constraints of post-Reformation English law. They were eager to restore the privileges and immunities of the Catholic Church and hoped Maryland would operate as if it were any other Catholic country.

But these expectations set the Jesuits on a direct collision course against the proprietor in the late 1630s. At issue were several parcels of land the Jesuits had purchased directly from the Patuxents and had received as gifts from the Piscataways. The fight between the proprietor and the Jesuits intensified after the order asserted its right to hold this property as a corporation. But Calvert viewed this acquisition of real estate directly from Indigenous communities as a violation of his sovereignty in the colony under the Maryland Charter and bristled at the Jesuits' presumption that the church's rights trumped his own. Moreover, the brewing tensions of the English Civil Wars made Calvert particularly concerned about losing his colony and led him to hew as closely as possible to English legal norms.[101]

Calvert moved to curb the Jesuits' ability to hold property by introducing restrictions on mortmain in 1641.[102] Literally meaning "dead hand" in French, mortmain referred to the inalienable and perpetual condition of property held by ecclesiastical (and later other) corporations. Unlike natural persons, corporations could not die and so retained their property indefinitely. The English Crown typically collected taxes and fees whenever land was inherited or sold, so such perpetual holdings deprived the state of a significant source of revenue. The first English statutes to restrict mortmain were passed in 1279, forbidding ecclesiastical corporations from acquiring property without the king's express permission. These restrictions on mortmain limited the ability of religious bodies to amass untaxable wealth without approval from the Crown.[103]

After Henry VIII's break with Rome that initiated the English Reformation, prohibitions against mortmain also became a valuable tool for the Crown to strip Catholic institutions of their property. According to Henrician statutes, all Catholic institutions supported "superstitious uses," and therefore the Crown had the right to expropriate their property and revoke their corporate standing. Thus, by the mid-sixteenth century, laws limiting mortmain had become synonymous with the politics of expropriation leveled against English Catholics and served as yet another plank in the legal establishment of the Church of England. These statutes were not just a means of raising revenue for the state (though they certainly did that) but also became a way to assert the authority of the state to regulate religion.

The proprietor's decision to introduce these traditional English restrictions on mortmain in Maryland signaled to Jesuits that Maryland would not be a Catholic country that safeguarded the ancient rights of the church. Instead, the proprietor asserted his chartered rights derived from the authority of the king and affirmed an Erastian vision of law—placing the state above the church—by denying Jesuit clergymen the ability to hold property corporately. The extensive landholdings that Maryland's Jesuit missionaries accrued in the seventeenth century were thereafter held privately by individual Jesuit priests or lay trustees rather than by any religious community or corporation.[104]

Calvert introduced mortmain in Maryland in 1641, well before the establishment of the Church of England in Maryland, and these restrictions applied to all ecclesiastical bodies, including those of the established church. The laws establishing and regulating the church expressly empowered parishes to acquire and stock glebes and receive donations, thus giving the proprietor's consent to parish property-holding under a specific regulatory framework.[105] Contemporary legal thinkers identified these regulations as some of Maryland's mortmain statutes.

Despite the province's restrictions on mortmain, the Jesuit Order still managed to acquire a significant amount of property over the following century. An official audit of their property conducted on July 23, 1765, listed eight different estates belonging to the order, which totaled 12,677 acres.[106] Five of the plantations exceeded 1,000 acres. The largest, at Port Tobacco, was 4,400 acres. There were also two smaller farms, Deer Creek, which was 127 acres, and Tuckahoe, which was 200 acres. The Jesuits enslaved nearly two hundred persons, who lived and worked on these plantations. The total income produced by the enslaved population, along with income generated by renting land to tenants, was an estimated £696 annually. As landlords and enslavers, Maryland's Jesuits relied on the plantation economy of the Chesapeake to fund their spiritual communities and in many ways hewed closely to the social norms of the Chesapeake. Jesuit priests became planters who "dressed like gentlemen," according to one visitor, and oversaw mission plantations that had shifted by the early eighteenth century from relying on white indentured servants to enslaving Black men and women.

After the establishment of the Church of England in Maryland, the Jesuit missions also became a haven for Catholic spiritual life within Maryland. The province's newly empowered Protestant assembly had outlawed the public celebration of Catholic mass in 1704, and Catholics began gathering on the missions or in private chapels for worship. Maryland's Jesuit missions offered a refuge for Catholic spiritual activity amid the increasingly hostile landscape of establishment while also operating as profit-driven plantations fueled by the labor of enslaved people. Their dual purpose exemplified the inextricability of religious liberty and property rights as the missions financially and spiritually shielded Maryland's Catholics.

However, without the benefit of incorporation, this property was not held by the Catholic Church, the Jesuit Order, or any institution at all. Instead, all Jesuit property belonged to individuals who acted as trustees. Father Peter Atwood, SJ, wrote instructions for his fellow Jesuit priests in 1726/7 about how best to secure their property under these legal constraints. He noted that Jesuit property "descends by conveyance or will; for all other right of succession or inheritance in common we are deprived of by the Statute of Mortmain."[107] Atwood continued, "Hence it is very adviseable that each possessor have always a will by him, whereby he bequeathes all his estate, both real and personal, to N. N. and his heirs for ever; and, in case of his [viz. N. N.] dying first, to [another] N. N. and his heirs for ever; and so name two or three of ours, least possibly our land become escheat." To protect the order from this "dangerous" legal and political climate, Atwood advised his fellow priests to practice constant vigilance in their legal transactions. All priests were instructed to make multiple copies of their wills and deposit them at different locations across the colony for safekeeping. The Jesuits took every possible precaution to ensure their transactions were irrefutably lawful. Their wariness contrasts sharply with the nonchalant, even sloppy, nature of Anglican parish property records. Parishes of the established church could be complacent in their property transactions—interchangeably listing the rector, the vestrymen, the churchwardens, or the parish on the title to real estate and chattel—because their power rested comfortably on common-law custom and legislative partiality. Nonconformists were forced to rely on the less secure instruments of personal deeds and wills, which could be more easily compromised or challenged.

This arrangement ran the risk of someone swindling the Jesuit Order out of its rightful property. Relying on individuals fostered an aura of suspicion that "those persons, who enjoy the legal title to the lands" might one day "appropriat[e] the whole income of them to themselves, their friends and relations" and cheat the community out of its property.[108] An ordinance sent to all of the clergymen in 1759 again urged them to "carefully make their wills" to "better to preserve from danger our lands and settlements."[109] In fact, the circular letter also required every Jesuit vested with property to sign a bond to "two or three of ours" for the sum of £40,000 if he made a will "in favour of any other person."[110] Jesuits sought to ensure that priests did not abuse their legal power over the estates by imposing a severe financial penalty on anyone who tried to improperly sell or gift property away from the order. Thus, for all their wealth, the property of the Jesuit missionary project rested on a precarious legal foundation.

One dramatic example of the Jesuits' legal vulnerability can be found in a desperate letter sent in 1773 by Fr. Matthias Manners, SJ, the Superior at Bohemia Manor, one of the eight mission plantations, to the Rev. John Lewis, SJ, the Provincial Superior. Manners warned despairingly, "We are likely to be ruined intirely at Bohemia."[111] Father Manners detailed lawsuits challenging the original conveyances of land that had come to form St. Francis Xavier Mission at Bohemia Manor. The first litigant, Daniel Heath, argued that over half of Bohemia rightfully belonged to him, "because it was only a gift to us, and not purchased," while the other, Sidney George, claimed that his father improperly donated land to the estate when he had "no right to dispose of it."[112] In both cases, unhappy heirs challenged the Jesuits' legal title to Bohemia, a plantation where twenty-six men, women, and children were enslaved that stretched more than 1,600 acres on Maryland's Eastern Shore.[113]

Unwilling to wait for the county court to rule, Heath had already begun demolishing outbuildings on the estate and hauling the materials back to his plantation. When Father Manners confronted Heath, things turned violent. The trespasser attacked the priest and then beat a pregnant, enslaved woman named Rachel with his loaded gun while "swearing by God that he would shoot the d[a]m[ne]d bitch."[114] The plantation overseer and another enslaved man managed to subdue Heath, but not before Rachel endured life-threatening injuries. Heath showed no remorse and vowed that if he lost his lawsuit, he would still encourage the local community to trespass and cut "firewood upon [the Jesuits' land] . . . under pretence that they don't know where our line is."[115] Heath's violence coupled with his litigation mounted a direct attack on the mission at Bohemia—its land, buildings, timber—as well as on the Black persons like Rachel held as property whose labor raised income and whose bodies were treated as valuable investments. Father Manners lamented that if either lawsuit proved successful or if he could not prevent future vigilantism, "we shall have little or nothing at all left to ourselves to live upon."[116]

Aware that he had no legal standing to defend the claim to Bohemia, Father Manners expressed confusion about his role in the legal proceedings against Heath. Bohemia was privately held by Manners's superior, Father Lewis, and Manners therefore assured him, "I have done nothing else, nor do I intend to do anything before I hear from you; for I don't know whether [to appear in court] in my own, or in your name." A recent émigré from Germany, Father Manners worried further that "being a *foreigner*. . . . I am afear'd that this circumstance might be prejudicial to the cause *because I can hold no land*."[117] The collective or corporate existence of the Jesuit Order was never recognized in Maryland law, which made the assets of Catholic faith communities far more susceptible to challenge. Neither Manners nor the Jesuit Order had legal claim to Bohemia, which left the priest powerless to respond to litigation or vigilante violence. Most vulnerable of all was Rachel, whose life and pregnancy came under attack from popular violence aimed at dispossessing Jesuits of their property. Rachel was treated as part of the Bohemia property and expected to bear children who would likewise be enslaved and labor for the estate, yet Rachel personally was left out of Manners' discussion of legal redress. Because the plantation system of spiritual support in the Chesapeake relied on enslaved laborers, Black people themselves were caught in this struggle without clear avenues for recourse.

Though Calvert's introduction of mortmain statutes in Maryland had targeted the Jesuits, they equally stymied Protestant dissenters in Maryland from securing property. The shaky legal standing of Third Haven Monthly Meeting of Friends, a Quaker congregation in Talbot County, illustrates the broader legal dilemma faced by dissenting groups in Maryland in the eighteenth century. The Talbot Friends acquired several tracts of land and built four separate meetinghouses during the seventeenth and eighteenth centuries.[118] The congregation completed its Great Meeting House in 1684, which remains the oldest surviving Quaker meetinghouse in the United States. These simple frame structures stood in sharp contrast to the fine parish churches. Inside, the differences were even starker. In place of the altar and pulpit were simple wooden benches, which enabled Friends to meet face-to-face in fellowship. These spaces

The oldest surviving Quaker Meeting House in the United States, the Third Haven Meeting House, was completed in 1684 in Talbot County, Maryland. Its plain architectural style conveyed the Friends' emphasis on simplicity and humility. (Photograph by Alyssa Penick, 2017)

were not only places for Friends to practice their faith but were, in fact, a material expression of their closely held values: simplicity, equality, and community.

The congregation also held a significant amount of land. They received three more acres of land in 1701 and built the Bay Side Meeting House.[119] Then, in 1705, they were deeded two more three-acre plots, where they built the Tuckahoe Meeting House.[120] Finally, in 1745, they bought another half-acre of land nearby in Tuckahoe.[121] The 1705 deed buying the site for the Monthly Meeting House stated that the transaction was undertaken by the "direction and appointment of the members or persons belonging to Monthly Meeting of the people called Quakers called by the name of their monthly meeting in Talbot County" and referred to their "unity and religious fellowship."[122] However, the property itself was vested in private individuals. Legally, none of the properties belonged to the congregation as a whole or to a recognized entity before the law; instead, a dozen different men and their heirs named in four deeds spread across forty years held title. The result was a legal mess.

Similarly, in 1723, Charles Ballard, a member of Manokin Presbyterian Church in Somerset County, Maryland, gave three hundred acres of land "for the Support Maintenance and Continuance of a meeting house for the worship and Service of Almighty God according to the Presbyterian persuasion and for no other use whatever."[123] He conveyed the lands to the "present Pastor and Elders of above said congregation and their successors."[124] While Ballard's intention was for the land to be used only on behalf of the congregation, the unincorporated church did not exist as a legal entity capable of holding property. Though he referred to the elders as a collective, the deed technically vested the property in the nine elders and their reverend, Alexander Stewart, as individuals. The deed referred to "successors" rather than "heirs," which suggested an attempt to bolster the congregation's future legal claim over the property. However, without incorporation, this title remained vulnerable.

Frustrated by their inability to hold property, the elders and minister of the First Presbyterian Church of Baltimore sought incorporation in 1774. They attempted to bypass the legislature by petitioning Governor Eden directly for an act of incorporation. They explained that the church had used a lottery scheme to finance the construction of their new church but ran into trouble trying to collect unpaid debts from the unlucky losers in the draw. Their plea explained that because they had "no legal consideration in a Congregational capacity, we are unavoidably subject to many inconveniencies in recovering, and securing such subscriptions, as become, due in the ordinary management of our affairs."[125] They even appealed to Maryland's "Government & Laws, which breathe the Spirit of Toleration." After they finally purchased the land and built the church, the elders still lacked a "clear and indisputable title" without the benefit of incorporation, nor could they easily bring lawsuits to collect debts. Their petition went unmet before the outbreak of the Revolution.[126]

While Maryland had long been home to populous non-Anglican communities, the nonconformist denominations in Virginia did not become populous or powerful until the 1750s.[127] Itinerant evangelical ministers travelled through the colony as the Great Awakening moved south, and Virginians began to leave the Anglican Church in greater numbers to join dissenting faiths. The rapidly changing religious makeup of Virginia posed new challenges to the legal establishment of Anglicanism. Despite the host of other legal penalties enacted against dissenters, Virginia never explicitly passed any kind of mortmain statute in the colonial era.[128] The assembly may have assumed the English mortmain laws were in effect in the colony, and without a large dissenting population until the mid-eighteenth century, additional legislation may have seemed unnecessary.

Even without the explicit adoption of laws restricting mortmain in the colony, there were no incorporated dissenting churches in the Old Dominion. Instead, Virginia's dissenters relied on the same techniques that Maryland's Jesuits had been using for more than a hundred years by vesting their property in individual trustees. As early as the 1670s, communities of Quakers in Virginia were designating trustees to hold property to build meeting houses.[129] In Augusta County, the Presbyterian congregation of Tinkling Spring listed a number of individuals named as "trustees" on its deed for the land on which its meetinghouse and cemetery stood.[130] In Princess Anne County, the Baptist Meeting House of Princess Anne also placed lands in the hands of nearly a dozen trustees.[131] These transactions mimicked many of the ways that an incorporated church might have held property. The deeds mentioned the congregation and referred to individual trustees. But despite the attempts to emphasize that these lands belonged to the church as an institution, these transactions technically vested the title to property in specific individuals who lacked any form of a recognized, corporate standing.

Issues over legal titles would continue to surface in the years to come. For example, in 1761, the Fincastle Presbyterian Church in Botetourt County came into possession of eighty acres of land known as the Meetinghouse Land. However, the congregation was unable to sell the property later because the church was not a corporate body and lacked any clear claim to the acreage.[132] Instead, the individuals named on the deed, and later their heirs, actually held title. While the members of the congregation agreed that selling the land would be a great "advantage," they were unable to proceed with the sale under the terms of these colonial-era deeds. Augusta Presbyterian Church faced similar problems proving title to its property. A congregation worshipping in Virginia's Shenandoah Valley, they were "long since . . . possess'd of two small tracts of land upon which their house of worship is erected and their grave yard inclosed." However, "the legal Title of which Lands are still vested in particular Individuals" because the colonial congregation had never been "a body corporate or known in law." A "conveyance to" a board of trustees "would only be a conveyance to individuals and subject to the same Inconveniences as heretofore." This direct invocation of corporate rights compared the liability of nonconformists to the stature and power conferred by customary incorporation on the institutions of the established church. Without incorporation, they argued, there was no way to secure their church's property or future.[133]

The Virginia Assembly received its first ever petition for incorporation from a dissenting church in 1774 from the Peaks of Otter Presbyterian Church in Bedford County. Their petition stated that "many well disposed Persons of their community had made Contributions to which others are willing to add, for supporting their Clergy in a method more convenient than the ordinary one by subscriptions."[134] However, "the pious intentions of such benefactors cannot be effectually carried into execution, the elders of the Church not being incorporated, so as to be capable of taking care and holding lands and Slaves for the use of the minister." The petition suggests that the congregation had traditionally relied on a voluntary subscription system to support its minister but had decided it would be more "convenient" to replicate a glebe system in which the minister was supported by enslaved persons laboring on a church estate. They hoped that the "said Elders may be enabled to take and hold Lands and Slaves to such use, under proper Regulations." This appeal suggested no theological discomfort with the state's involvement in incorporation, nor did it suggest that the process improperly muddied the waters between secular and sacred authorities. Unfortunately for this Presbyterian congregation, the legislature was dissolved before it had responded either affirmatively or negatively to the church's request.

That the Virginia legislature received its first petition for incorporation from a dissenting group at the tail end of the colonial era underscored just how effective the colony's disestablishmentarian laws had been at dissuading dissenters from settling in the colony or from seeking legal rights. Virginia's growing community of dissenters was just beginning to encounter difficulties holding property without the security of legal incorporation. The timing is particularly striking when compared to other Anglican colonies. The New York and South Carolina legislatures had both received and rejected numerous petitions for incorporation from dissenting congregations throughout the eighteenth century.[135] In

Maryland, the legislature had settled the matter in the mid-seventeenth century by passing mortmain statutes, though renewed appeals still reached the governor in the 1770s.

What is perhaps most striking is this widespread evidence of a desire to incorporate. Trusts were flexible and powerful legal mechanisms that enabled communities to hold property jointly without incorporation.[136] Yet dissenters argued that the legal device of the trust had proven insufficient and set their sights instead on corporate rights equal to those exercised by the established church. Nonconformists' mounting appeals for incorporation in the Chesapeake underscored their pragmatic reasons to seek corporate privileges on par with Anglicans and signaled a desire to overturn a traditional plank in the legal regime of Anglican establishment.

THE EXPERIENCE of living under the Anglican establishment taught colonists that property rights and religious liberty were inseparable. The established church's legal power was reflected in the wealth and corporate privileges of its parishes. Vestries could buy and sell property with ease, execute contracts and deeds, and secure their investments in perpetuity. Churchwardens brought lawsuits to recover damages and enforce their contracts. Nonconformists in the Chesapeake were excluded from these provisions. In Maryland, the Jesuits held extensive and valuable property, but their assets were legally vulnerable. Though Maryland's Protestant dissenters faced far fewer restrictions than Catholics on their religious practices, their inability to incorporate and secure their property presented a significant restriction on their free exercise in practice. In Virginia, dissenting faiths had begun to expand rapidly and had just begun chafing at their inability to incorporate in the colony. Without the benefit of incorporation, all these nonconformists worried their wealth could be misused or abused by private trustees or the aims of pious donors might be ignored by future generations.

But as much as these debates about property and materiality were part of a larger transatlantic reformation, the embrace of chattel slavery in the Chesapeake transformed the debates over religious property into something new. Nonconformists were not just fighting to secure devotional objects, churches, or cemeteries but also for the right to hold enslaved people and land to finance their spiritual communities.

This legacy cast a long shadow over the relationship between church and state in the early republic. During revolutionary disestablishment, church property, particularly enslaved people, and the right to incorporate became central issues in the question of how the state ought to dismantle the establishment and ensure religious liberty. Ultimately, it was the issue of church property that would drive the Chesapeake states to take divergent paths to reform church and state.

# 3

# PULLING DOWN THE CHURCH

AFTER SEVERAL months of skirmishes, Patriot regiments forced Lord Dunmore and his British troops from the city of Norfolk, Virginia, on New Year's Day 1776. Virginians justified their armed resistance by pointing to Dunmore's "attempts to infringe their rights and liberties, by proclamation declaring freedom to our servants and slaves, and arming them against us."[1] As the fighting in Norfolk drew to a close, St. Paul's Church stood smoldering, a cannonball lodged in its facade.[2] The real damage came weeks later when the Virginia Convention, the colony's provisional government, ordered the entire city to be burned as a defensive measure against British reinvasion.[3] St. Paul's was torched along with the rest of Norfolk by the end of February 1776, and the church's brick walls were among the few left standing. The sanctuary's fine interior—its altarpiece, windows, and woodwork—lay in ashes.[4] Begun by the British in battle and finished by the Virginians themselves, the demolition of this parish church signaled the transition of the Revolution in Virginia from a political revolt to a bloody civil war. An act of self-immolation, the convention's decision to burn Norfolk revealed how far white Virginians were prepared to go to secure their liberties and property, including their property in persons, and what they were willing to cast aside in the process. Their revolution had begun in earnest.

The Anglican establishment fell victim to popular attacks during the war even before it was legally dismantled by the new state governments. Dissenters and many Anglicans embraced religious reform as an essential part of their Revolution against the Crown and understood themselves to be engaged in a "great Revolution in Church as well as state."[5] Loyalist and neutral clergymen fled their parishes, and clergymen were put in the agonizing position of renouncing their ordination oaths to the king in order to swear loyalty to the Patriot governments. Church buildings were frequently abandoned or desecrated; communion silver was buried. Vestries stopped meeting, and the gears of local government ground to a halt. Parishes were at the center of this fight because they had been the most powerful institutions of religious establishment in the colonial Chesapeake. Parish vestries had forcibly extracted wealth for generations and decided how to spend it, whether on fine churches, prayer books, or the purchase of enslaved people. Every person—enslaved and free, male and female, Anglican and nonconformist—had fallen under the lawful authority of the parish and their social station anchored within a divinely ordained great chain of being. The Revolution stripped away the basis for parochial authority and left communities to grapple with what now bound them together in the absence of an established church led by the English monarch.

The destruction of St. Paul's materialized popular allegorical demands for the established Church of England to be "pulled down" during the war. At the same time, reformers also declared their goal of "establishing religious freedom" in their laws. In an inversion of the traditional legal framework of establishment, many Virginians and Marylanders now called on the state to guarantee religious liberty rather than to police orthodoxy. Scholars often bracket this dual revolutionary movement as "disestablishment," but this label can lend events a false sense of order and cohesion. Throughout the war, the drive for religious reform remained a contingent and inchoate process. The destruction of the former establishment and the drive to rebuild a new establishment of religious freedom in its place certainly gained momentum amid the battle for American independence, but the process was far from complete by the time fighting ended.

This chapter considers wartime disestablishment from 1774 to 1782. This periodization returns disestablishment to its context during a bloody civil war with an unknown outcome. In all its violence and dislocations, its compromises and contradictions, the Revolution moved the needle toward dismantling the established church in significant ways, but it did not represent an ideologically coherent movement. Widespread ambivalence underlay this breach and fueled contention about what would take root in its place. By narrating the story of legislative change through statutes, petitions, and constitutions and reading this evidence alongside material and local sources, this chapter shows how the rupture between church and state transformed communal life. Military expediency and material concerns determined the direction and pace of reform, and the most controversial church-state issues would be tabled and addressed only after the war ended.

## Defining Disestablishment

Disestablishment was not a clearly defined concept in 1776, and reformers did not possess a roadmap for the process. Instead, nonconformists and their political allies moved to redress longstanding grievances law by law at the start of the war. The Baptist Church in Occoquan, Virginia, submitted a list of demands to the convention in the spring of 1776 and made it clear that their participation in the war would be contingent upon the redress of these grievances. These Baptist brethren asked "to be allowed to worship God in our own way, without interruption . . . permitted to maintain our own ministers and no other . . . [and to] be married buried in the like without paying the parson of any other denomination."[6] Historians have summarized this petition as an appeal for "the end of establishment" or a call "to disestablish the Anglican Church." These characterizations are somewhat misleading, though.[7] This label suggests that the Occoquan petitioners expressed their concerns as a single platform and implies an ideological coherence that was absent at the beginning of the war. Moreover, using the broad term "disestablishment" might suggest these Baptists demanded the many reforms we now associate with the movement in Virginia.

In fact, the legislature would act on all the Occoquan petitioners' requests during the war but did so without removing the Church of England from its favored position nor stripping it of its unique legal privileges. Their appeal made no demands for church property to be seized or for the legislature to ban the incorporation of religious bodies, both views that would take hold among Baptists in the 1780s. They did not ask to end the vestry system or to transfer poor relief from parishes to county courts. Many of the legal privileges discussed in chapters 1 and 2 that underpinned establishment went untouched during the war. It is essential to avoid the teleological trap of assuming that what we now call disestablishment was recognizable as such in 1776.[8]

Scholars use the word "disestablishment" to describe the dismantling of the Anglican Church after the Revolution, but this term was not used by contemporaries. In fact, the word "disestablishment" first entered popular usage in the 1860s in British debates about the Church of Scotland and only later came to the United States.[9] Despite often being credited as the architects of Virginia's disestablishment, neither James Madison nor Thomas Jefferson ever used any form of the word "disestablish" in their correspondence or notes.[10] Perhaps the closest Jefferson came was writing about his hope that "the establishment of the Church of England by law in this commonwealth be discontinued," while Madison described the movement as having sought to "pull down" the religious establishment.[11] The term did not appear in any of the legislative acts passed by Virginia or Maryland in the half century after the Revolution, nor was it used in private correspondence or public debates. No unified platform of demands or shared vocabulary for reform existed when the war began.

In fact, liberal reformers and evangelicals often relied on architectural metaphors to convey their goals, clamoring for the established church to be "broken," "overthrown," "pulled down," "abolished," and "justly exploded."[12] The physicality of their language—breaking, tearing, pulling down, pushing—recalled the iconoclasm of past religious struggles but also reflected that parish churches were quite literally coming under fire in 1776. It also underscores the sense of an active struggle they had to undertake to win disestablishment. The outcome was not foreordained but the result of an ambitious process of deconstruction.

Many campaigners turned to enslavement as a metaphor for religious establishment. They called on the legislature to "relieve us from our long night of ecclesiastical bondage" and declared "having long groaned under the Burden of an ecclesiastical Establishment, [we] beg . . . every other yoke may be broken, and that 'the oppressed may go free.'"[13] Looking back on the struggle only a few years later, John Carroll, the future first Catholic archbishop in the new United States, celebrated having fought "with might and main" against "the lash of an established church."[14] Virginian Baptist minister Robert Semple described his fellow dissenters as having "shaken off their fetters," never to be "bound again." Many white Patriots used the language of bondage throughout the Revolution to characterize their struggle against the Crown.[15] Slavery was a potent metaphor in the Chesapeake because of the utter familiarity of the institution.[16] The continuity of this symbolic language after the war to frame a new set of demands for religious freedom underscored that dismantling the established church extended their revolutionary fight for liberty to the realm of religion. Of course, these calls to end the metaphorical enslavement of white nonconformists in the Chesapeake did not insist on individual liberties for Black Americans.

Alternatively, advocates for reform in both Maryland and Virginia also expressed their desire to affirmatively "establish religious freedom." They spoke of their ambitions in the familiar language of "establishment" but inverted its meaning by seeking to use state power to protect religious freedom, rather than to punish dissent. John Carroll wrote in 1785 that "as soon as the laws of England were abrogated, freedom of religion was established" in his home state.[17] Jefferson drafted a "Bill for Establishing Religious Freedom" in the 1770s, and Madison would secure its passage in 1786. By borrowing the terminology of an "establishment," Carroll, Madison, Jefferson, and other advocates employed the traditional phrase but inverted its aim; they would pass laws to ensure religious freedom rather than to privilege the state-sponsored church. The stated goal of establishing religious freedom wielded state power to enforce religious freedom, which did not necessarily mean that government and religion would be separate. The tensions between separating church and state institutionally and establishing religious freedom in law would continue to complicate the process of rebuilding.

These two vocabularies, one destructive and the other constructive, point to two distinct processes for reforming church and state in law. This regime change required the established Church of England to be pulled down while an establishment of religious freedom was built up in positive law. The language of construction and deconstruction underscores the translation of principle into practice as Americans wrestled with disestablishment as both an ideological movement and a pragmatic process of reform in which personal rights, state power, and valuable property were at stake. Moreover, it provides a useful way to define and delineate the dual processes at work before, during, and after the Revolution to remake the church-state relationship.

## Securing Loyalties

The dismantling of the religious establishment became a legal reality only once Patriot leaders needed the support of religious nonconformists in their struggle against the Crown. The 1776 conventions of both Maryland and Virginia would offer concessions to dissenters before the war that unwound some of the crucial powers of the established church and destabilized the logic of confessional uniformity on which it rested.

Popular foment against the established church had intensified in the third quarter of the eighteenth century in both Maryland and Virginia. The Great Awakening had posed a fundamental challenge to the power of the establishment as evangelicalism spread across the Chesapeake in the 1750s and 1760s. But despite mounting pressure from Presbyterians and Baptists in Virginia for reform, many county courts continued to persecute dissent, sometimes violently. The House of Burgesses maintained numerous restrictions on evangelical worship when it considered revising the colony's Act of Toleration in 1772. Although the assembly was dissolved before the law could pass, the proposed bill had revealed how little ground the colony's leaders were willing to give to religious dissent just a few years before the war.

Maryland had long granted more liberal exemptions to dissenting Protestants than had Virginia, but its communities of nonconformists were still denied equal status in the province's laws and lived in a system in which their religious rights rested on the continued good grace of the legislature. Evangelical dissenters published diatribes attacking the "disagreeable burden" placed on them by the laws and argued that the much-loathed poll tax to support the Anglican clergy only degraded the spiritual life of the established church.[18] However, the colony's persecutory regime was far harsher toward Catholics, who made up about 10 percent of Maryland's population. They faced "inveterate" harassment from the government, as one Catholic observed in 1759, through restrictions on their rights to worship, own property, bear arms, and vote, as well as facing double taxation.[19] Future Patriot leader Charles Carroll of Carrollton, who hailed from one of the colony's most powerful Catholic families, lamented the situation and openly discussed the possibility of leaving Maryland altogether.

But there was also discontent inside the Anglican Church about the terms of its legal establishment in the colonies. The fluctuation in tobacco prices had sparked political crises in both colonies over clerical salaries, which spiraled into full-blown legal challenges to the Two-Penny Act in Virginia (1758) and the Tobacco Inspection Act in Maryland (1773). These controversies pitted the clergy against lay leaders and ultimately exposed deep frustrations among Anglicans about the operation of the church.[20] Heated debates about the proposal to create an American episcopate became entangled with local controversies about reprobate rectors as well as the brewing imperial crisis after the Seven Years' War.[21] But the church was still enormously powerful, particularly as a local institution. The defeat of the proposal for an American bishop exposed the aversion to imperial oversight but did nothing to weaken the local establishment.

A crowd brandishes weapons and chases an Anglican bishop onto a ship in this 1768 cartoon, which captures the animosity of many colonists toward the proposed establishment of a colonial episcopate. *An attempt to land a bishop in America. United States,* 1768. (Courtesy of the Library of Congress)

Expensive building programs were underway in both states, and clerical salaries remained high. While there was an appetite for reforming the establishment from within and outside the church on the eve of the Revolution, the church was still extraordinarily powerful in 1774. While there was pressure for greater toleration, there was no sign yet that it was in jeopardy of losing its public status as an arm of the state.[22]

Between 1774 and 1776, in both Maryland and Virginia the conventions and Committees of Safety formed rival governments, and extralegal bodies vied for authority. Driven by the need to recruit as many people as possible to the American cause, leaders in both Maryland and Virginia granted concessions to non-Anglicans and explicitly made the Revolution a gateway to religious reform. Both colonies drafted new oaths of loyalty that did away with the traditional religious tests of the British constitution and defined political loyalty in secular terms. Oaths had long been a means for the government to legitimize its authority. By appropriating these traditional rituals to the cause of American independence, the new oaths of loyalty were a means of moving from extralegal mob to sovereign state. These expedient policies were an essential step in securing Catholic and evangelical support for the war and made way for the formal regime change in the two states' 1776 Declarations of Rights.

The traditional mechanisms used to enforce orthodoxy across the far-flung British Empire were the Oaths of Allegiance and Abjuration, as well as signing the Test oaths. Any oath-taker had to pledge loyalty and obedience to the monarch, deny the authority of the pope or any other "prince or prelate," and disavow Catholic doctrines, including transubstantiation.[23] In return, the monarch would ensure the "safety and welfare of this Protestant kingdom" and grant liberties and rights to "good subjects being Protestants." Together, these oaths drew bright confessional lines around the body politic and made Protestant conformity a premise of political stability. But these oaths did more than serve as gatekeepers to Catholics, Quakers, and other nonjurors who refused to take oaths on principle. Dissenting Protestants were granted the "indulgence" of practicing their faith "only upon" taking these oaths. These rituals thus reified toleration by making religious rights something the state could legitimately grant or restrict as it saw fit.

In a bid to win a broad coalition of support, the conventions and Committees of Safety abandoned a religious framework of loyalty by crafting new nonconfessional oaths of loyalty. The Maryland Convention signaled this new policy when it seated three Catholic delegates in December 1774.[24] One of these delegates was Charles Carroll of Carrollton, a wealthy Catholic landholder, who emerged as a popular champion of representative government in a highly publicized debate with Daniel Dulany in 1773. Scions of two of Maryland's most genteel families, the two men squared off in the pages of the *Maryland Gazette* about whether Governor Eden should bypass the assembly and set the salaries and fees paid to provincial officers by proclamation.

Dulany defended the governor's action on constitutional grounds, citing the proprietor's prerogative and English precedents. Dulany's arguments seemed foolishly out of touch with the popular mood amidst both the economic downturn and the ongoing imperial crisis over parliamentary taxation. Meanwhile Carroll found a ready audience for his rebuttal when he argued that Maryland had a distinctive constitution in which fees had always been under the jurisdiction of the assembly. Dulany attempted to discredit Carroll as a "papist by profession" whose "religious principles" were "inconsistent with the security of British liberty."[25] Carroll countered that Dulany had resorted to these "popular prejudices" because his constitutional arguments were unconvincing. Carroll's election to the Maryland Convention the following year suggested that he had won in the court of public opinion. The Maryland voters repudiated any suggestion that Catholics like Carroll posed a threat to British liberty.[26]

When Carroll was elected to the 1774 Maryland Convention, he was still not legally able to vote in Maryland, let alone hold office. But that convention did away with the Oaths of Allegiance and Abjuration and the Test oath, which would have prevented Carroll and the other elected Catholics, Ignatius Fenwick and Thomas Semmes, from taking their seats. With this move, the Maryland Convention discarded traditional mechanisms for excluding Catholics from the body politic. Carroll's fellow members appointed him to the Committee of Correspondence, a mark of their significant respect. Without referencing either the oaths or Carroll specifically, the convention still acknowledged that they had embraced an ecumenical policy: "As our opposition to the settled plan of the British administration to enslave America, will be strengthened by an union of all ranks of men in this province, we do most earnestly recommend, that all former differences about religion or politics, and all private animosities and quarrels of every kind, from henceforth cease and be forever buried in oblivion; and we intreat, we conjure every man, by his duty to God, his country, and his posterity, cordially to unite in defence of our common rights and liberties."[27] By declaring in December 1774 that religious difference was now a thing of the past and vowing to defend common rights and liberties, the Maryland Convention made an enticing bid to the colony's Catholics for their support.

The unspoken boundary, of course, was race. When these delegates declared their desire to unite "all ranks of men" to fight off British slavery, they did not include the actual Black men and women whom they enslaved. The need to unify white Marylanders took precedence over everything else and did away with the traditional framework of religious exclusion that had divided Maryland's society for nearly a century. This drastic departure was driven by expediency and certainly did not herald the defeat of anti-Catholicism. An item in *Dunlap's Gazette* warned that Papists would soon be "sheathing swords in the bowels of Protestants."[28] But in practice, the war abolished Protestantism as the basis for the body politic and further distinguished the constitution of Maryland as articulated by the Patriot movement from the British constitution.

In Virginia, militia enlistees were likewise freed from the traditional confessional oaths. They only had to declare to be "faithful and true to the colony and dominion of Virginia; that I will serve the same . . . in defence of the just rights of America . . . obey the orders of such others who may be set over me, and lay down my arms peaceably when required so to do, either by the General Convention, or the General Assembly, of Virginia. So help me God."[29] While soldiers still had to swear their oaths before God, allegiance to Virginia and participation in its defense required no confessional commitments. The need to secure loyalty against the Crown had led to a rapid overthrow of one of the key premises of religious establishment—conformity as a precondition of loyalty.

Aware that some dissenters in North Carolina had rallied to defend the king after years of local persecution, the Virginia Convention passed several measures to win support from evangelicals.[30] In August 1775, the convention received a pointed petition from the Baptist General Committee, noting that however "distinguished from the body of their countrymen," Virginia's Baptists considered "themselves members of the same community" engaged in a "common cause" against "Great Britain in her unjust invasion, tyrannical oppressions, and repeated hostilities." The missive noted that many Baptists "had enlisted as soldiers, and many more were ready to do so, who had an earnest desire their minister should preach to them during the campaign." The petition promised enlistment but only if their brethren were truly granted equality "in respect to civil matters" by giving their ministers "the liberty of preaching to the troops at convenient times, without molestation or abuse."[31] The Baptists leveraged their potential enlistment to exact promises of greater liberty.

During the turmoil of 1774 and 1775, non-Anglicans secured important concessions from their de facto governments. The fact that these policies were driven by expediency does not diminish their ideological significance. Rather, it demonstrates how wartime exigencies helped ease the adoption of new principles and explicitly tied the success of the Patriot cause to the expansion of religious liberty.

## Constitutions

What started as pragmatic policies to appease dissenters and secure popular support for the Patriot movement grew into a much more substantial reform to the basic premises of government. In 1776, the conventions of Virginia and then Maryland declared independence and drafted new state constitutions. These founding documents provide a helpful benchmark for how the concessions made to non-Anglicans became constitutional guarantees in the new states, replete with ideological defenses grounded in popular sovereignty and natural rights. Wartime exigencies thus provided the essential opportunities for ideological change. Religious liberty would be baked into the founding constitutions of the new states.

Overthrowing the monarchy and establishing that sovereignty lay only in the people fundamentally challenged the religious status quo. Principally authored by George Mason, Virginia's 1776 Declaration of Rights began by pronouncing that "all men are by nature equally free and independent and have certain inherent rights," which included life, liberty, property, and the pursuit of happiness.[32] The text reaffirmed numerous natural, procedural, and political rights of Englishmen, drawing on centuries of constitutional evolution from the Magna Carta to the English Bill of Rights. The opening of Maryland's Declaration of Rights, drafted and passed in the wake of Virginia's, echoed these sentiments. Despite their revolutionary context, these principles rested comfortably on the accepted tenets of the British constitution.

However, both these new state constitutions rejected the imperial past by proclaiming popular sovereignty as the highest law of the land. Virginia's Article II stated "that all power is vested in, and consequently derived from, the people," while Maryland's First Article likewise declared

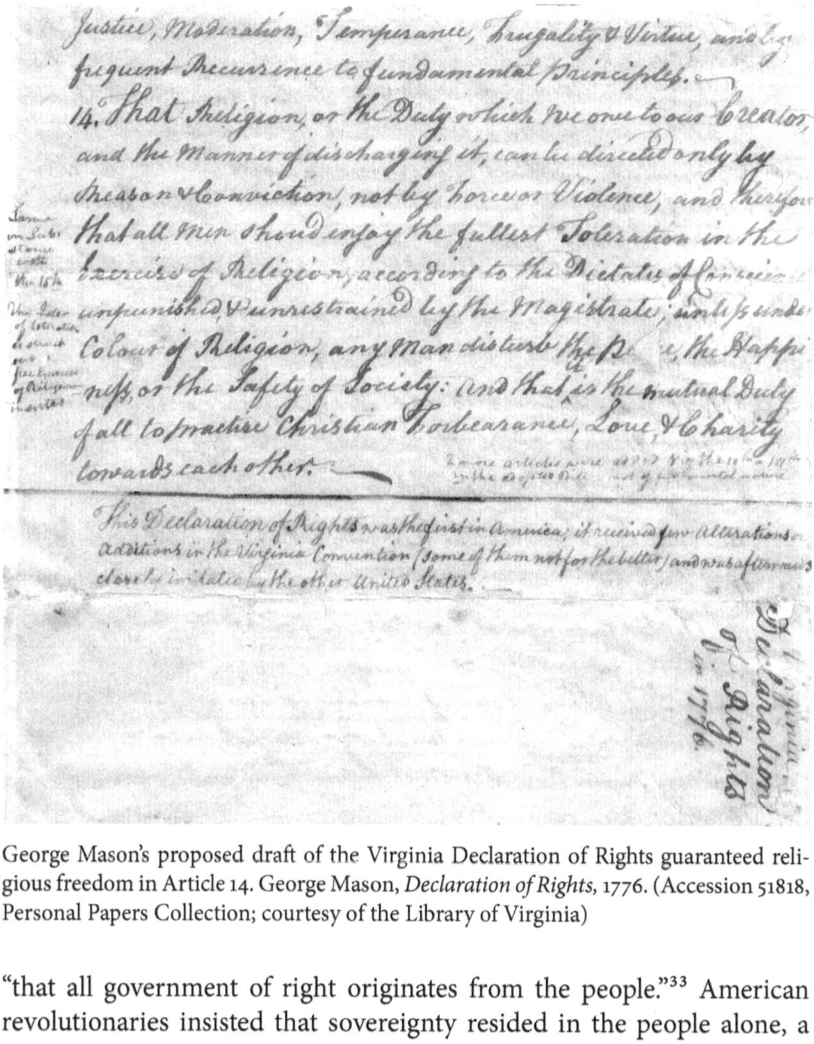

Justice, Moderation, Temperance, Frugality & Virtue, and by frequent Recurrence to fundamental Principles.
14. That Religion, or the Duty which we owe to our Creator, and the Manner of discharging it, can be directed only by Reason & Conviction, not by Force or Violence; and therefore that all Men should enjoy the fullest Toleration in the Exercise of Religion, according to the Dictates of Conscience, unpunished & unrestrained by the Magistrate, unless under Colour of Religion, any Man disturb the Peace, the Happiness, or the Safety of Society: and that it is the mutual Duty of all to practice Christian Forbearance, Love & Charity towards each other.

This Declaration of Rights was the first in America; it received few Alterations or Additions in the Virginia Convention (some of them not for the better) and was afterwards closely imitated by the other United States.

Virginia Declaration of Rights in 1776.

George Mason's proposed draft of the Virginia Declaration of Rights guaranteed religious freedom in Article 14. George Mason, *Declaration of Rights,* 1776. (Accession 51818, Personal Papers Collection; courtesy of the Library of Virginia)

"that all government of right originates from the people."[33] American revolutionaries insisted that sovereignty resided in the people alone, a direct repudiation of the principle of divine right on which the legal establishment of religion had long been justified. As one Maryland clergyman put it, obedience to God's chosen monarch was "the dictate of religion, and certainly the doctrine of the established church, and still also the law of the land."[34] The rituals of the English state, the tenets of Anglo-American law, and the liturgies of the established Anglican church had all tied the Crown's authority to God and mandated political and religious submission from the people.[35] By claiming that sovereignty emanated only from the will of the people, these constitutions rejected the first principles of Anglican establishment.

The two states' Declarations of Rights also broke from their colonial past in their explicit discussions of religion. Virginia's Article 16 declared "that religion, or the duty which we owe to our Creator, and the manner of discharging it, can be directed only by reason and conviction, not by force or violence; and therefore all men are equally entitled to the free exercise of religion, according to the dictates of conscience; and that it is the mutual duty of all to practise Christian forbearance, love, and charity toward each other."[36] While this framework of free exercise characterized certain civic virtues as "Christian," its sweeping language endorsed a robust version of free exercise that protected all religions. Virginia's embrace of a fundamental right to free exercise rejected the colonial model of establishment, which had so recently prosecuted religious dissent and mandated adherence to the established church as a qualification for full participation in government. Moreover, Mason explicitly stated that force and violence were futile to command religious convictions, and, by extension, the state should have no power to employ either force or violence to compel religious belief or practice. The concessions made to evangelicals had moved from the indulgences of a tolerant state to exigencies made amid a military crisis and finally become fundamental and irrevocable guarantees of rights. Thus, the Virginia Declaration of Rights undercut the ideological framework of establishment without outlining specifics of a revised church-state arrangement. This text explicitly protected religious freedom in law without addressing the project of pulling down the church.

By contrast, Maryland's articles about religion traded the philosophical transcendence of Mason's words for many more specifics about the immediate task of dismantling the established Anglican Church. The document offered a qualified protection of free exercise but also stripped the Anglican Church of numerous longstanding privileges and powers. Maryland's Declaration of Rights included forty-two articles, four of which explicitly concerned the relationship between religion and government. Article 33 declared

> That, as it is the duty of every man to worship God in such manner as he thinks most acceptable to him; all persons, professing the Christian

> religion, are equally entitled to protection in their religious liberty; wherefore no person ought by any law to be molested in his person or estate on account of his religious persuasion or profession, or for his religious practice; unless, under colour of religion, any man shall disturb the good order, peace or safety of the State, or shall infringe the laws of morality, or injure others, in their natural, civil, or religious rights; nor ought any person to be compelled to frequent or maintain, or contribute, unless on contract, to maintain any particular place of worship, or any particular ministry; yet the Legislature may, in their discretion, lay a general and equal tax for the support of the Christian religion.[37]

This constitutional framework lacked the sweeping ideological commitment of Virginia's Declaration to separating religious belonging from political rights. Article 33 carved out some space for the state to censure immorality and to police religious practices deemed to be "disturb[ing] the good order." The bulky and limited language of this provision stood in stark contrast to the far-reaching scope of Virginia's declaration. The Maryland text invoked God rather than the more abstract "Creator" of Mason's version.[38]

Moreover, Maryland's document laid out a version of religious freedom that extended explicitly to Christians. In Articles 35 and 36, the state proclaimed it had ended the system of religious tests that had barred Catholics from voting and officeholding before imposing a new test: "A declaration of a belief in the Christian religion" for "admission to any office of trust or profit."[39] Together, Articles 33, 35, and 36 set out a highly moderated version of free exercise that still required adherence to Christianity for full civic rights and religious freedom. These provisions satisfied the longstanding grievances of Catholic and Quaker communities by placing all denominations of Christianity on par with Anglicanism but failed to include the growing Jewish community in Baltimore in its full protections.[40]

Unlike Virginia's broad and ideologically framed declaration, Maryland's Articles 33 and 34 included specific provisions that began to dismantle the exclusive status of the Anglican Church. The Anglican Church would no longer have any special relationship with the government, but parishes would be able to retain their real and personal property. Baking this provision into the new constitution made it much harder for Marylanders to seek the confiscation of parish property in later decades.

Importantly, the Maryland legislature also maintained the power to impose a "general tax" that would support the Christian denomination of the individual's choosing. The state government also claimed the right to regulate the property transactions of all denominations, much in the way it had always overseen the property of Anglican churches. The legislature required that any "gift, sale, or devise of lands, to any minister, public teacher, or preacher of the gospel, as such, or to any religious sect" exceeding two acres required legislative permission.[41] From the outset, Maryland's legislature took an active role in superintending religious denominations while also guaranteeing the property rights of parishes.

Maryland's declaration went further than Virginia's in laying out a specific plan to reform the relationship between the established church and the state government. Having addressed parish levies, church property, and a general assessment in its constitution, Maryland would later avoid the hostile debates about these issues that so divided Virginians in the 1780s. Yet this document went less far in disentangling religion from government. Virginia's sweeping statements noticeably used the broadest possible terms to protect "religion" rather than specifically referring to Christians, and the state implemented policies in terms that actively protected the rights of non-Christians. Maryland, on the other hand, restricted the rights of non-Christians, which denied Jewish citizens a wide variety of political and legal rights including holding office, serving on a jury, or being admitted to the bar as an attorney in the state by requiring all public officials to swear an oath to their "belief in the Christian Religion."[42] With this oath, the Maryland constitution adopted a new religious test that would remain on the books in some fashion until the mid-twentieth century.

These constitutions sounded the death knell for the traditional Anglican establishment. By grounding sovereignty solely in the people, they certainly repudiated that civil authority had divine origins. In Virginia, there was an explicit commitment to guaranteeing free exercise and a move to disentangle government and religion. But the specifics of this plan were not addressed, and the work of deconstructing the establishment was left to the legislature. In Maryland, the constitution undertook active steps to strip the former establishment of its legal privileges. And the state's establishment of religious freedom was so far limited to Christians and focused on levelling the playing field for all Christian denominations in the state. These constitutions envisaged different church-state relationships and would ultimately set the states on different courses of disestablishment.

## Wartime Reform

In the five years following 1776, the legislatures of both states attempted to translate these constitutional guarantees into new laws. Wide-ranging debates about proposed reforms revealed a wide variety of views about what exactly the declarations mandated or prohibited. The process was fraught as political leaders, religious groups, and ordinary citizens sought to enact their preferred version of an establishment of religious freedom and to demolish privileges they thought contradicted the spirit and letter of their constitutions. The exigencies of war also slowed the pace and limited the scope of change. State leaders treaded carefully and sought only to implement reforms that would not risk alienating members of the war-weary public.

Many of the same issues were raised in the two states between 1776 and 1781. Parish taxes, vestries, oaths, and marriage laws were all addressed in new statutes. These laws reflected a piecemeal and responsive legislative process in which petitioners asked for specific reforms. In Virginia, much of this energy came from the organized campaigns of evangelical dissenters, who were indefatigable in pressing the legislature to remove vestiges of favoritism from the laws. There were fewer concerted campaigns for reform in Maryland, too, but individual petitioners appealed for redress, and the legislature amended the laws in return. Partially, this difference in agenda reflected the fact that many pragmatic reforms to church and state had already been passed as part of the Maryland's constitution, while Virginia had deferred this responsibility to the legislature. However, Maryland's Catholics also hesitated to protest as forcefully or as publicly as Virginia's evangelicals. Having so recently gained admission to the body politic and aware that popular prejudice against "papists" still abounded, Catholics relied on their political leaders to work quietly behind the scenes during the war. This difference in approach seemingly reflected the hierarchical nature of Catholic church governance but also underscores that Catholics did not yet trust the state to uphold the constitutional equality of all Christians.

Even so, there was a recognition in both states that religion was far from the only topic needing legislative attention during the war. The most controversial issue, general assessment, was on hold during the war. Maryland's constitution had abolished the right of parishes to raise levies and eliminated the public salaries paid to parish rectors. However, it explicitly permitted some form of general tax to fund the "Christian Religion." After the loss of state support in 1776, several Anglican vestries set to work to secure state funds for some form of general assessment in 1777.[43] But their efforts went nowhere during the war, and the issue was punted until after the war.

Virginia's constitution did not specifically address religious taxation, but many dissenters read Article 16 as a promise to end the parish levies and church attendance requirements. They besieged the legislature with petitions demanding both, and the state complied quickly in December 1776. New laws exempted dissenters from paying levies to support the established church while also temporarily suspending the levy for Anglicans.[44] Anglican sympathizers reacted with alarm to these changes. A printed petition circulated in Mecklenburg County described the "undue means taken to overthrow the established church" by denying "the usual mode of her support."[45] For these petitioners, the state constitution had not necessarily promised disestablishment. Rather, they blamed the political machinations of evangelicals in securing these laws. This petition also signaled that these measures were publicly justified because "withholding fixed salaries is the most likely means to make men unanimous in the defense of liberty." Given the highly controversial nature of the issue, these petitioners urged the legislature to defer from making any more changes until "a time when you have nothing of more importance to engage your attention." The assembly received numerous petitions about assessment over the next five years, some demanding the abolishment of all religious taxes and a few urging them to adopt a general assessment. The difficult economic conditions made any sort of tax unpopular, and the legislature was savvy enough to read and heed the public mood. The state did not take up the question again until after the war.

While shying away from the question of a general assessment, the Virginia legislature made permanent the law abolishing parish levies in 1779. However, the act did not eliminate the taxing power of parishes entirely. The state left parishes with the responsibility to provide "provision for the poor in their respective parishes as they have hitherto by law been accustomed to make, and levy the same in the manner heretofore directed by law."[46] Parishes were still able to raise taxes in support of the poor. This awkward arrangement represented the inchoate nature of disestablishmentarian reform up to this point. While the law freed individuals from having to support parishes in their religious functions, it also continued to treat episcopal parishes as civic bodies and vestrymen as state actors. The church retained the power to tax and administer welfare as a civic but not a religious body. By attempting to cleave poor relief from religion, this law initiated a profound shift in the civic fabric of Virginia, where poor relief had always been legally mandated as a form of "Christian charity."

## Dismantling Parishes

These statutory changes presaged reforms to the church-state relationship, but they still had to be institutionalized at the local level. Anglicanism in the Chesapeake had always been a local affair, and the colonial church's power resided in its parishes rather than any central organization. Thus, it is essential to consider how disestablishment took hold in communities. Despite the many ideological inconsistencies and ambiguities of wartime disestablishment, parishes were unrecognizable by the war's end.

Take the example of Norfolk's Elizabeth River Parish, which opened this chapter. The parish not only lost its largest house of worship, St. Paul's Church, when Norfolk burned, but its rectory, poorhouse, and other properties also went up in the blaze. Without a home or a church, or even a sizable community of parishioners left to serve, the parish rector left with his family in 1776. The curate enlisted as a chaplain in Virginia's Fourth Regiment and was only periodically in the area during the next four years. The parish owned several enslaved people, whose fate during and after the destruction is unknown. The rector or churchwardens may have forcibly moved them out of Norfolk, though their proximity to Dunmore's forces also offered some possibility for escape. There was no active vestry between 1776 and 1778, which also meant there was no functioning poor relief system or organized collection for the church. Many of these officials had left the area during the hostilities, and some never returned to rebuild after the fire. The population fluctuated between 40 to 60 percent of its prewar levels during the next five years. Although the parish received funds from the state to restore their "public buildings," they were unable to begin repairing the church until after the war.[47] By the 1790s, the old poorhouse was nothing more than a "useless" ruin. The old parish church still belonged to Elizabeth River but would soon be abandoned and taken over by a congregation of Baptists.[48]

Though particularly dramatic, the story of Elizabeth River Parish represents a larger pattern of parochial unraveling across the Chesapeake between 1776 and 1781. The dislocation of people due to exile, military service, or temporary removal destabilized the parish as a durable spiritual community. While private devotion certainly continued, the rituals of public worship were irregular. Churches and glebes were abandoned. Parishes across Virginia stopped providing poor relief during the exigencies of war and the dissolution of vestries. Much of the administrative and spiritual work of Virginia's parish system ground to a halt during the war.

Circumstances were similar in Maryland. In one telling example from 1776, the vestrymen of Durham Parish in Charles County expressed their utter confusion about how to proceed without clarity about who was in charge in the province. When trying to appoint tobacco inspectors for the coming year, they hedged their bets and addressed "the Governor for the time being, or the Convention, or the Council of Safety—The Vestry and Church Wardens have nominated and recommended as inspectors." Eager to carry out their legal duties, these parish officers deferred to anyone who might conceivably hold power in Maryland. The war continued to cause significant disruptions when parish vestries tried to continue with their usual business. Five years later, the Durham Parish vestry noted the delay in their parish elections because an "invasion of the enemy [had] prevented a meeting of the Parishioners to choose a Vestry on Easter Monday 1781." The institutional chaos of the early period of independence and the violent dislocation of its later years upended the traditional authorities and legal procedures that had anchored parish life.[49]

In both states, the departure and disaffection of the ministry dramatically impacted the spiritual lives of parishioners. In Virginia, roughly 15 percent of parishes were vacant after the war.[50] Far worse off were the parishes in Maryland. Fewer than half of the church's parishes had a rector in 1780, and there were only fifteen ministers left when the war ended. The other thirty-nine clergymen had died, fled, or left the ministry. To compound this exodus, new clergymen stopped arriving in the colonies once the war started. By and large, British clergymen refused to emigrate to the Chesapeake, and American-born candidates ceased traveling to England for orders amid the turmoil. Moreover, many Anglican ministers were unwilling to take the state oaths of loyalty in 1777 because they came into direct conflict with their ordination vows. Faced with the dilemma of these oaths, at least a third of Anglican clergymen in both colonies chose to resign their positions or leave altogether. When a local committee of safety tried to compel Rev. John Bowie, the rector of Worcester Parish on Maryland's Eastern Shore, to take the oath, he retorted that he would rather "suffer his right arm to be cut off, and wished if he took it his tongue might cling to the roof of his mouth and never come loose."[51] Bowie would later be jailed for his anti-American preaching, but other neutral clergymen also found it impossible to swear these oaths.

The end of the levying system and declining numbers of parishioners left parishes to rely on their glebe properties for the support of their ministers, and in many instances, on enslaved people who belonged to parishes and ministers. These Black men and women raised additional income for the parish through being hired out or working on glebe plantations. At the same time, the Revolution disrupted slavery everywhere in the Chesapeake. The British were actively trying to recruit enslaved men by offering them freedom in exchange for their military service. Of course, the act of arming Black men was meant to terrify white Americans, but this strategy was also intended to hamper the American economy and provide the British with local knowledge and manpower.[52] Enslaved people made for British lines or used the disruption and dislocations to their advantage as cover for escaping elsewhere. The estimates vary widely, but even the most conservative numbers suggest that six thousand enslaved people escaped the Upper South during the war.[53] Particularly once ministers lost their tax-supported annual salaries, income from the glebe lands became a financial lifeline for the clergy, and thus slavery became even more central to funding the parish system.

There is evidence that several enslaved people belonging to ministers fled during the war. John McPherson, the rector of William and Mary Parish (also called Piccowaxen Parish) in Charles County, Maryland, placed an ad in the *Maryland Journal* in October 1778 looking to recapture "one of the Piccawaxon glebe slaves, commonly called Will Wage or Will Crack," who had been hired to work at a nearby plantation.[54] In addition to a physical description of the "tall stout young fellow," the minister also noted that Wage played banjo and was "well acquainted with all parts of the country." The timing of Wage's escape in August 1778 occurred in the years when the highest number of enslaved people fled from bondage in Maryland, and there were reports of British raids regularly recruiting enslaved persons.[55] Given his extensive local knowledge of the area along the Potomac River, he would certainly have been an asset to British forces. While Wage seemed to have evaded recapture, numerous people were still enslaved by the parish as late as 1796.[56] Clearly, the parish continued to rely on enslaved labor for decades after the war. Likewise, Rev. Thomas Lundie, the rector of St. Andrew's Parish in Brunswick, Virginia, placed a notice looking to recapture Tom, whom the minister described as "strong . . . sensible, [and] cunning."[57] The nineteen-year-old Tom had been working for Lawrence Washington in Stafford County and departed sometime in February 1778. Tom's parents lived nearby, and the minister assumed the couple had helped conceal their son. More than a year later, Reverend Lundie was still looking for Tom.[58]

For an enslaved community living on the glebe of St. Patrick's Parish in Virginia's Prince Edward County, Lt. Col. Banastre Tarleton's destructive raid in the summer of 1781 provided a chance for escape. Tarleton was certainly no committed liberator of Black men and women. His family had made their fortune in the slave trade, and he went on to become an ardent proslavery advocate in his later parliamentary career representing Liverpool.[59] But nonetheless his raid in Virginia offered enslaved people a means of escape.

Tarleton had been dispatched by Cornwallis to raid Southside Virginia and cut off supplies destined for Gen. Nathanael Greene's forces in South Carolina. Tarleton was ordered to seize "ammunition, cloathing, or stores of any kind intended for the public. . . . Do everything in your power to destroy the supplies destined for the rebel army. All public stores of corn and provisions are to be burnt."[60] During their march through Prince Edward County, Tarleton's dragoons targeted the St. Patrick's Parish glebe. The rector, Rev. Archibald McRoberts, fled, apparently leaving behind at least five enslaved persons on the property. British soldiers broke into the glebe house, destroyed its fine mirrors and featherbeds, and confiscated provisions. They purportedly made camp at the glebe before "carr[ying] off five valuable negroes, and all his horses" and setting fire to the house.[61] Purportedly, the glebe was only saved by a sudden rainstorm, which put out the flames. This miraculous act of deliverance led the minister to rename the glebe "Providence."[62] The scant record does not clarify whether these enslaved persons were the property of the parish or minister, but clearly they performed essential labor on the parish plantation, as McRoberts' letter expressed his concern about "sav[ing] his crop and doing the necessary farm work."[63]

While McRoberts squarely blamed the dragoons for "carrying" off enslaved persons from the glebe, Tarleton's own account states that enslaved people took it upon themselves to escape. The officer observed that "all the negroes, men, women, and children, upon the approach of any detachment of the King's troops, thought themselves entirely absolved from all respect to their American masters, and entirely released from servitude: Influenced by this idea, they quitted the plantations, and followed the army."[64] By Cassandra Pybus's estimates, nearly a third of all enslaved people from the Upper South who escaped during the war did so during the British march to Yorktown in the summer of 1781.[65] The community who fled St. Patrick's were among two thousand who escaped that summer and headed for Yorktown, where they may have been put to work bolstering British defenses.[66]

The flight of enslaved people from glebes and the efforts of ministers to recapture them is a further reminder of the reliance of the established church on racial slavery to exploit the parishes' extensive property holdings. The loss of levy support and subsequent dependence of parishes on glebe lands and enslaved people thrust the issue of church property into the spotlight during the war. Purchased using public funds in the colonial era, parish property came to symbolize the ongoing favoritism toward the established church in the eyes of many evangelicals and became one of the next crucial issues for reform after the war.

By THE time the fighting ended in 1781, the church-state relationships in the Chesapeake had evolved in profound ways. Wartime concessions had become constitutional guarantees. Spiritual and civic life were unrecognizable by the Revolution's end. But despite all this change, many issues remained unsettled, particularly surrounding the general assessment and church property. Located at the intersection of religious liberty and private property rights, these issues would dominate public debates over the church-state relationship in the following two decades. Virginians and Marylanders alike agreed that the process of toppling the church and establishing religious freedom would continue, but the paths of the two states would ultimately diverge sharply in the next decade.

# 4

# THE ESTABLISHMENT OF RELIGIOUS FREEDOM?

John Carroll wrote in 1785 that "as soon as the laws of England were abrogated, freedom of religion was established" in his home state.[1] Across the Potomac River in neighboring Virginia, Thomas Jefferson drafted a "Bill for Establishing Religious Freedom" in the 1770s, and Madison would secure its passage in 1786.[2] By appropriating the term "establishment" and inverting its meaning, Carroll, Madison, and Jefferson expressed their aspiration to construct a new framework of positive law to enshrine religious freedom. As the establishment of religion fell, an establishment of religious freedom would be assembled in its place.

The terms of this new establishment, though, were not yet clear as the Revolution drew to a close. After 1782, public debates about church and state in the Chesapeake centered around three hot-button issues: general assessment, the incorporation of religious societies, and church property-holding. The first of these questions, general assessment, has received by far the most attention from scholars, and many narratives concerning disestablishment in the Chesapeake frame the rejection of a general assessment as the conclusion to revolutionary disestablishment and a final vindication of the religious liberty guaranteed in the 1776 state constitutions.[3] Many classic accounts present disestablishment as a singular event achieved by a unified ideological movement. The emphasis on Virginia across the literature exacerbates this tendency, as Virginia often stands in for a national story to which other states are treated as mere footnotes.[4] This narrative construction implies that the states eventually arrived at comparable religious settlements, simply doing so a few years apart.

I offer a revised approach to revolutionary disestablishment by examining assessment, incorporation, and property together. All three issues were inextricably linked in the minds of those who had lived under the colonial establishment. Anglican parishes in the Chesapeake had long collected taxes and reinvested the proceeds in valuable property, including glebe lands, costly church buildings, communion silver, and enslaved people. This wealth had been secured through the corporate privileges conferred on vestries and churchwardens in common law. Dissenters of every persuasion, including Catholics, Protestants, and Jews, had been forced to contribute their taxes to support the established church while they were unable to secure their own property through incorporation in either of the Chesapeake colonies.

However, the corporate rights of vestries, churchwardens, and ministers in common law had rested on "the king's implied consent," rather than any formal charter.[5] But the revolutionary overthrow of the king destabilized this legal foundation, and the new state constitutions abandoned the customary fiction of "universal agreement" about religion. In the absence of either monarchical framework of consent or the continued exclusive establishment of the Church of England, the future of the church's privileges and property was ripe for debate.

Disestablishment was not foreordained, and reformers lacked a clear blueprint for how to achieve it. Political leaders and religious groups embarked on the project of dismantling the established church without a consensus about their end goal. While Marylanders and Virginians both rejected general assessment, incorporation drove a wedge between the two states during the 1780s. Prohibiting religious incorporation became as important to Virginia's evangelicals as securing incorporation did to Maryland's Catholics. As Marylanders and Virginians diverged over concrete policies, they ultimately embraced different notions of how to guarantee religious freedom in state law and what constituted an impermissible religious establishment. In Maryland, an establishment of religion was defined as any use of state power to favor or disadvantage one sect over another, and thus reformers constructed an establishment of religious freedom premised on equality in the laws. However, in Virginia, an establishment of religion came to be defined by the formal connections between church and state, and the establishment of religious freedom was built by separating and insulating religion from government. These debates drove events in the two states and carried important implications for the meaning of "establishment" in the First Amendment of the Bill of Rights. As they overturned colonial laws and debated how to ensure religious freedom under republican government, Americans constructed powerful, if not fully coherent, legal categories. Dismantling *the* established Anglican Church gave shape to the constitutional concept of *an* establishment of religion.

## Jesuit Property in Republican Maryland

The scion of an elite Maryland family and an early supporter of the Revolution, John Carroll was ambivalent about the reformed relationship between church and state in the aftermath of the war. At times, the Jesuit priest sounded jubilant, proclaiming that in Maryland "our Religion has acquired equal Rights & privileges with that of other Christians."[6] Under the state constitution, "every person has a right to worship Alm. God in that religious mode or form which his conscience dictates, as most agreeable to the divine will: that no person shall be compelled to support any minister, or form of worship, which he does not approve."[7] Still, he remained wary, an attitude born of a lifetime enduring "deep hatred and suspicion" toward Catholicism.[8] While Catholics had come to "enjoy the same rights as other citizens," he wondered just "how long we shall continue to have these benefits" as "many of our people, especially in Maryland, fear that there is a desire among non-Catholics to exclude us altogether from holding office" or that they would be denied other legal privileges. Carroll worried that his newfound rights remained revocable under the terms of Maryland's constitution.

Amid this uncertainty, Carroll's first priority was securing Jesuit property through incorporation. Trying to clarify the confusing legal situation to a Vatican official, Carroll explained, "The possessions by which the priests are supported are held in the name of private individuals, and by will they are transferred to their heirs."[9] He observed that "this procedure was dictated by the dire necessity" in the colonial era, when "the Catholic religion was restricted by laws." Since the end of the war, the Jesuits had "sought in every way to obtain a law permitting Catholic priests to form a corporate body and hold property in common. . . . We hoped to bring it about that property acquired from individuals would pass into the perpetual legal right and use" of the church.[10] Voicing a long-running concern of Jesuits in the colony, Carroll sought to prevent the "ever present danger when an individual could transfer these properties to relatives or anyone else by legal instrument or will." To Carroll, incorporation provided the only means of firmly safeguarding the church's property and thus securing their foothold in Maryland.

Two other issues animated Carroll's fixation with securing incorporation. First, the papacy had disbanded the Jesuit Order in 1773.[11] The suppression of the Jesuits left colonial Catholic clergymen struggling without any formal leadership or organization. Carroll hoped that forming a corporation under new bylaws would restore much-needed order to priests living on isolated manors scattered across the state. Second, the 1776 Maryland Declaration of Rights had prohibited religious societies from holding more than a few acres of land without legislative permission, a provision that echoed the earlier mortmain statutes and preserved a key means of legislative oversight of religious life.[12] The Jesuits sought an act of incorporation to consolidate their individual holdings under a single corporate entity and protect it from the whims of majoritarian politics.[13] In 1783, Carroll organized a convention of Maryland's Catholic clergy at Whitemarsh to draft a constitution to govern the church and make a plan for the "preservation of their property."[14] Acting on the resolutions from Whitemarsh, Carroll and others tried hard to secure a charter from the legislature to recognize the terms of the Whitemarsh agreement. As a member of one of Maryland's most powerful families, he lobbied privately for the law but warned "it must not appear that our Clergy do any corporate act, before they are a legal corporation."[15] Carroll moved forward cautiously.

## The Clergy Bill

Just as Carroll was carefully taking steps to secure Jesuit property, the leaders of the formerly established church were also navigating the murky waters of their reformed relationship to the state. During the war, it was not clear just how independent the Church of England was from the new republican state. In 1779, the Maryland General Assembly had passed the Vestry Act, which had overseen the election of vestries, reiterated the role of parishes in keeping vital statistics and registering marriages, and yet again confirmed the title of parish vestries to all their assets.[16] But the 1776 state constitution had abolished the levying system that exclusively benefitted the established church. Nearly three quarters of Maryland's Anglican clergymen had fled during the war, and without an active ministry, most parishes had stopped collecting funds. The church faced desperate financial straits by the end of the war and an uncertain legal standing vis-à-vis the state.

New questions arose when the American branch of the Anglican communion reorganized as the Protestant Episcopal Church in 1782. Episcopalians expressed concern about whether they were required to abide by almost a century's worth of statutes still on the books regulating their liturgy, rites, and administration. Moreover, the clergy worried that their restructuring had jeopardized their standing as the legal successor to "the Church of England" and thus risked parishes' claims to their colonial-era property as guaranteed in the Maryland constitution and subsequent legislation.

Events in 1782 gave the Episcopal Church reason to hope. That spring, William Paca, the former vestryman and vocal defender of vestries' rights, became governor of Maryland and publicly threw his weight in support of a general assessment. Under the terms of Article 33 in the Maryland constitution, "No person ought by any law to be molested in his person or estate on account of his religious persuasion or profession" nor "compelled to frequent or maintain, or contribute, unless on contract, to maintain any particular place of worship, or any particular ministry; yet the Legislature may, in their discretion, lay a general and equal tax for the support of the Christian religion."[17] Paca's proposal for a general assessment would have allowed Maryland's citizens to decide which Christian denomination their annual levy would support and would have exempted non-Christians from the tax.[18] Paca argued that a general tax in support of all Christian ministers would benefit both religion and government. A parish vestryman and lay leader of the statewide denomination, Paca was personally invested in securing aid for the Episcopal Church as part of an ecumenical Christian establishment. Paca's advocacy on behalf of his own church underscored the challenge in dislodging public favoritism from a church whose members had been leading the state for generations, or from any particular religious group in a system of plural establishment.

Paca's proposal quickly became mired in a much broader proposal of the Episcopal clergy. Buoyed by Paca's support for general assessment, the Episcopal clergy sought permission from the state to draft a new church constitution in May 1782. The clergy hoped to restructure their governance, alter their "liturgy and Service, in order to adapt the same to the Revolution," and affirm their "Subordination to the State."[19] The legislature assented, and the clergy gathered in August 1782 for that purpose. The clergy apparently saw no contradiction in proclaiming "ecclesiastical and spiritual Independence" of all denominations while also asking for the state to codify their refined doctrine, liturgy, and organization in statute.[20] The document repeatedly affirmed that the Episcopal Church held the "Churches, Chapels, Glebes, or other Property, formerly belonging to the Church of England in this State." They endorsed Paca's plan for a general assessment and closed by recognizing they had changed "from a daughter to a sister-church." While the Episcopal Church claimed no longer to be a sole daughter but one of many sisters, it still professed to be a child of the state. This proposal, quickly branded the Clergy Bill by its opponents, would soon be met with intense opposition.

At the same meeting, the Episcopalian clergymen also drew up an act of incorporation, which empowered the Episcopal Church to act "as a Body Corporate, to hold Goods, Lands and Chattels, by Deed, Gift, Devise" and to manage a charitable fund to support widows and orphans.[21] This proposed charter affirmed that the Episcopal Church was the lawful successor to the Church of England, no matter what "name" had been used in prior legislation. The Episcopal clergy explicitly framed religious liberty as security over one's "person and estate," a phrase which neatly articulated what so many historians of republicanism have told us: namely, that property was a fundamental expression of liberty. The material stakes of disestablishment were made plain in these proposals, just as they had been in Carroll's urgent campaign for incorporation.

Weeks later, Governor Paca quickly recommended the Episcopal clergy's constitution and request for a charter. He expressed his commitment to "advancing the interests of Religion in general" and "placing every Branch of the Christian Church in this State, upon the most equal and respectable Footing."[22] Episcopalians and their political allies like Paca insisted that these proposals did not lend unfair support to the formerly established church. Their vision of religious freedom here rested on the equality of Christians rather than separation of religion from government.

Patrick Allison, the minister of the First Presbyterian Church of Baltimore, became the most vociferous public opponent of the Clergy Bill when he published a rebuttal, *Candid Animadversions,* on October 28, 1783. Writing under the pseudonym Vindex, Allison rejected any type of general assessment. Better for religious denominations to be left to themselves, which would offer "a more complete permanent security, than even legal sanctions or constitutional provisions" could provide.[23] He also wrote with evident scorn about the provision in Article 33 of Maryland's constitution that expressly reserved "the churches, chapels, glebes, and all other property" to the Church of England "forever."[24] By asking for permission from the state to regulate "peculiarly spiritual" matters, the Episcopalians had invested the legislature with the "authority . . . to grant or refuse" rights that all Christians assuredly had under the state constitution.[25] Worse yet, the legislature had assented to the petition and thus "presume[d] itself vested with this authority."[26] Such a course had made the legislature a potential "usurper" of constitutional rights and in effect allowed them to hijack the document.[27] Allison's pamphlet quickly set off a firestorm in the Maryland press and prompted numerous responses.[28] Sensing popular opposition, the legislature dispensed with the request to approve church doctrine, or issue a charter of incorporation, or affirm parishes' claims to their property.[29]

Some form of statewide religious tax remained on the table, though. Carroll regarded the proposal for a general assessment as a thinly veiled ploy by "contriving" Episcopalians to reinstate the established church. If the law had been "truly formed upon the principle of the Constitution, we R.C. should have no very great objection to it: but from certain clauses in it, and other circumstances, we, as well as the Presbyterians, Methodists, Quakers, and Anabaptists are induced to believe, that it is calculated to create a predominant and irresistible influence in favour of the Protestant Episcopal Church."[30] An ecumenical tax may have been constitutional on its face, but its detractors saw it as a Trojan horse designed to chip away at religious equality. A petition printed in the *Baltimore Gazette* went further and attacked the proposed bill as explicitly unconstitutional. The anonymous writer reasoned that general assessment may have been abstractly allowed under the state constitution but that such a plan could never be implemented in practice without engendering an unconstitutional form of religious favoritism. Such a tax gives "one church a preeminence above others" by granting its wish for state support at the expense of other religious societies "who do not desire it" and indeed viewed it as an infringement of their rights.[31] This line of argument suggests that a general tax for religion would have been permissible in Maryland only if all religious societies favored it. Requiring unanimity turned the provision in Maryland's Declaration of Rights allowing a general assessment into a dead letter. Any form of assessment had become inseparable from establishment in the minds of many Marylanders. The proposed general assessment was soundly rejected in 1785, though the state's power to impose a general tax in support of religion remained constitutional for the time being.[32]

## General Incorporation

Reverend Allison would soon turn his attention to a more ambitious project—securing general incorporation for all religious denominations.[33] In 1784, Presbyterian State Senator James McHenry introduced a bill for general incorporation in the Maryland Senate, where it remained stalled until 1788 when it was revised and reintroduced.[34] The 1788 bill's preamble underscored that its purpose was to make the same legal rights available to all Christian denominations "without partiality, preference, or distinction."[35] This proposal sought to give all Christian denominations the same legal privileges long held by the established church by codifying equality in law. But it also specifically addressed the property of the Catholic Church and provided a means for priests who had held land as individuals to transfer it to a joint trust, which would then be held by the Catholic clergy as a corporation. John Carroll had not yet been able to secure an act of incorporation for his church in 1788, and this proposed law gave him and his brethren everything for which they had hoped. But it also offered concessions to the Episcopal Church by reaffirming their title to parish property, something that they had yet to receive after the controversy of the Clergy Bill. The former established church could also have received incorporation under its terms. The framework of general incorporation explicitly favored Christians over other religious groups and certainly did not try to sever ties between religion and government. Rather, it sought to use state power to bolster church property-holding for all Christians, in their view strengthening religious liberty and delivering religious equality.

Wary of reviving the turmoil over incorporation and church property, the House of Delegates demurred, claiming it would be impossible to "give it that attentive consideration which the importance of the subject requires. Complicated and extensive in its nature, it ought to undergo a very deliberate discussion."[36] The legislature agreed that the entire proposed bill should be published "for the consideration of the people."[37] Newspapers published a full-page copy of the bill the following month.[38]

Episcopalians strongly opposed the proposal for general incorporation. They claimed that the legislation might undermine their claims to parish property, although there was no clear basis for this fear. The General Convention of the Protestant Episcopal Church in Maryland tasked two of its most influential members and high-ranking state leaders, William Paca and his longtime ally Samuel Chase, to keep a close eye on general incorporation or any incursion on the rights of vestries to their property.[39] Ultimately, the bill was tabled for several years before dying in committee.[40]

Observers like Patrick Allison warned that the creeping reestablishment of the Episcopal Church in Maryland could only be prevented through general incorporation. Allison hoped to revive the prospect of passing a general act of incorporation and republished his 1783 *Candid Animadversions* in a new edition along with several additional essays in 1793. Still brimming with revolutionary fervor, Allison excoriated the many ways in which Maryland's postrevolutionary laws violated Article 33 and upheld a de facto establishment of the Anglican Church. Recent "legislative crimes" committed by "wicked rulers" had brought "ignominious slavery on a free people."[41] But he chastised his fellow citizens whose meek acceptance of these policies led them to "concur in the treason, by tame unmanly submission."[42] He pointed to a recent bill to use state funds to complete the construction of an Episcopal Church in Annapolis and highlighted the fact that laws regulating marriage still employed the phrases "dissenter" and "parish," which preserved a two-tiered religious order in the law.[43] But what most incensed Allison was the noticeable lack of public outrage among Marylanders, and he aimed to rouse them from what he saw as extreme complacency about their hard-fought rights.

The minister turned again to the question of parish property but did so in service of his arguments about incorporation. While Episcopalians had long worried that their claims to parish property might be challenged, Allison understood that the state constitution had upheld parishes' property claims and that the 1779 Vestry Act had unequivocally asserted vestries' ongoing rights to "glebe-lands, churches and chapels, books, plate, and other ornaments" as well as "Negroes and debts."[44] To Allison, this policy exhibited "the bigoted zeal of the delegates" in favor of the Episcopal Church. By passing a law only to protect Episcopalian property while stymying the act for general incorporation, the assembly expressed that "other denominations . . . were not worthy of legislative attention."[45] The failure of general incorporation amounted to unconstitutional favoritism for one church. Allison's arguments made the protection of parish property a metric for the continued inequality of religious denominations. The only solution was to secure incorporation for all sects.

Maryland's Catholics were also disappointed by the failure of general incorporation. Instead of issuing public jeremiads like Allison, a determined Bishop Carroll quietly won a separate Act of Incorporation for the Catholic clergy in Maryland in 1792. Much of the language in the 1792 law came word for word from the 1788 bill for general incorporation. The law declared that "it is highly reasonable and just to grant ministers of the Roman catholic religion, who are citizens of this state, that legislative aid without which they will be destitute of that protection and security to their property to which they are entitled equally with every other sect or denomination of Christians."[46] This law was a hard-fought victory for Maryland's former Jesuits, who finally secured their property 150 years after Lord Baltimore had restricted their property-holding. For Catholics, the security of their property was a tangible expression of their new republican liberty.

In the following decade, the General Assembly was bombarded with requests for incorporation from Catholics, German Reformed churchmen, German Evangelical Reformed Baptists, Presbyterians, Lutherans, and Methodists.[47] Even some Episcopal parish vestries applied.

Unlike the 1792 act, which incorporated the Catholic clergymen into a statewide body, these subsequent petitions for incorporation came from local congregations. The personnel of these corporate bodies varied; some only included laymen, while others consisted of a clergyman and a group of lay leaders. By the dawn of the nineteenth century, Maryland's Catholics, Presbyterians, Baptists, Methodists, and other denominations celebrated incorporation as a hard-fought right of disestablishment without debating whether it constituted a form of religious establishment.

Episcopalians also received greater assurances of their property rights and clarified their legal standing under the state's 1798 Vestry Act.[48] Under the terms of the new law, every parish vestry was incorporated, and their titles to all parish real estate and chattel were confirmed. Vestries were also able to buy and sell property without legislative permission under certain limits. Parish rectors had freehold over the glebes during their tenure. But the law also outlined the procedures for vestry elections, required vestrymen to take the standard oath of office for elected officials, and required vestries to keep registers of "all baptisms, marriages and funerals, of free persons in the parish by any minister of the protestant episcopal church." County magistrates were even empowered to fine delinquent vestrymen. The Vestry Act kept parishes under close legislative oversight, so much so that when Maryland's first Jewish governor, Marvin Mandel, took office in 1969, he often joked that he was still technically the head of the Episcopal Church in Maryland under the terms of the Vestry Act.[49] He would privately push to overturn this and other laws on the books that he believed knit together church and state unconstitutionally.

By the early nineteenth century, the legislature was so inundated by requests for incorporation from "many religious societies" that they moved from granting incorporation to denominations or congregations on an individual basis to embracing a general incorporation statute that would empower all Christian churches to incorporate.[50] The text of the 1802 law was nearly identical to the 1788 bill. The preamble declared that the legislature was "indispensably bound to secure and preserve the same equality of rights, privileges and advantages to all quiet and inoffensive Christian societies in this state" so that "religion may be encouraged and diffused." The law was front-page news in publications across the state, and several papers reprinted the text of the act in its entirety.[51]

The introduction of general incorporation in Maryland represented a multidenominational effort to make a key legal privilege of the former established church widely available to all Christians. Before the Revolution, Anglicans had relied on common-law incorporation to hold parish property, whereas the colony's non-Anglicans were left without a formal way to secure their property. Mortmain laws had prevented Catholic corporate property-holding, and formal petitions for incorporation from dissenting Protestants were rejected. After independence, other denominations initially sought incorporation through individual charters from the state. The torrent of petitions seeking incorporation from Catholics, Presbyterians, Methodists, and Lutherans marked an important step away from the framework of Anglican establishment; these groups were able to form corporations and secure their property as legal persons recognized in law. The legislature cited practical necessity to explain their adoption of general incorporation; there were just too many petitions arriving each session for them to handle. The growing popularity of incorporation made it far easier to codify the process under a single statute.

Patrick Allison, though, articulated the ideological importance of instituting a general act of incorporation. Such an act bypassed the incremental process of extending greater rights to religious societies one at a time and instead fundamentally leveled the playing field for all Christian denominations. General incorporation offered a statutory framework available to all denominations, which represented an inversion of the established church's reliance on customary incorporation. The general incorporation of churches in Maryland was not merely the legal framework that superseded colonial customary law but also a direct response to the way in which the established church had fundamentally exploited its exclusive ability to hold property to further its power. For Allison, general incorporation was more than a pragmatic victory; the law underscored the achievement of religious equality and religious liberty for Maryland's Christians. Incorporation enabled the security of property and therefore enabled equal access to religious liberty. General incorporation thus became a pillar of the establishment of religious freedom in Maryland.

The Episcopal Church remained wary of attempts to seize parish property, but none came. There were no organized campaigns for the confiscation of parish property in Maryland. Maryland's Catholics never argued that the state ought to seize Anglican parish property. Even in his private writings, Carroll did not so much as mention the prospect. Because the Catholic community held valuable, yet vulnerable, property of its own, its leaders were unlikely to argue for the confiscation of any church's property by the state, lest the pendulum swing back sometime in the future. Carroll and other former Jesuits were eager to secure corporate rights for their churches, not to weaken the perpetual and irrevocable nature of incorporated property. Even the strident Presbyterian Patrick Allison, who had spoken with righteous indignation about the injustice of the Episcopal Church retaining all parish property, never mounted a serious movement for confiscation. Rather than advocating for the state to seize parish property, these reformers threw their considerable weight into demanding incorporation be made available to non-Anglicans.

## Virginia's Rejection of Incorporation

Virginia took a different path. The story of Virginia's disestablishment is well-known, but returning to this familiar narrative with a focus on changing views about assessment, property, and incorporation illuminates how and why Virginia's project of disestablishment diverged so sharply from events in Maryland. The divergent priorities of non-Anglicans on either side of the Potomac led the two states to implement very different disestablishmentarian policies in practice and codify incompatible definitions of religious establishment in their laws.

In May 1784, the fight over incorporation was just brewing in Virginia. That month, the United Clergy of the Presbyterian Church sent a memorial to the assembly protesting laws that continued to give "substantial advantages" to the Episcopal Church.[52] Specifically, the Presbyterian clergy pointed to "injurious" laws that empowered vestries to continue raising levies for poor relief and gave Episcopal ministers more power to perform marriages than clergymen of other denominations. Finally, the Presbyterians' petition attacked the incorporated status of the Episcopal Church under common law. In their view, "The episcopal church is actually incorporated, and known in law as a body, so that it can receive and possess property for ecclesiastical purposes, without trouble or risk in securing it, while other Christian communities are obliged to trust to the precarious fidelity of trustees chosen for the purpose." It is essential to underscore that at this point Virginia's Episcopal parish vestries, churchwardens, and ministers were incorporated solely under common law; they had never received any form of charter. The 1784 Presbyterian Memorial did not protest the legitimacy of customary incorporation but attacked its continued exclusivity. The petition asked the legislature to "do away with any inequality" and to secure "the broad basis of perfect political equality" for "every religious denomination in the state" by revoking public powers from parishes and instituting a plan of general incorporation.

These Presbyterian petitioners occupied a position ideologically similar to Maryland's Catholics. The clergy attacked the Episcopal Church's exclusive access to incorporation under common law as an unjust holdover from the colonial religious establishment. They urged legislative action to make incorporation available to all religious societies. The Baptist General Committee also submitted a petition that month that attacked the marriage and vestry acts but did not mention the corporate status of the Episcopal Church.[53] If the Presbyterian clergy favored general incorporation in 1784, Baptists apparently remained neutral or ambivalent toward it.

A few weeks later, a memorial arrived from the Episcopal clergy.[54] Their petition requested that the General Assembly take action to repeal a number of outdated laws that "restrain[ed]" the church from self-government, including statutes that restricted their liturgy, the induction of their clergy, the election of vestries, their canons, and modes of faith. Much like their brethren in Maryland, Virginia's Episcopalian clergymen were uncertain about which colonial laws regulating the church were still in force and were worried that their reorganization under the new "appellation" of the Protestant Episcopal Church would lead to "cavils . . . disputes and litigations" over their claims to parish property. Thus, they asked for an act of incorporation "securing for ever to the Protestant Episcopal Church in Virginia the churches, glebe-lands, donations, and all other property belonging to the said established church."[55] While the Presbyterian clergy based their petition on the perceived strength of the Episcopal Church's incorporation under common law, the Episcopal Church sought a legislative boost to ensure and reaffirm these rights with a charter.

The Committee for Religion in the House of Delegates endorsed some measures from the Presbyterian, Baptist, and Episcopalian petitions submitted in 1784. They approved the Episcopal Church's request for an act of incorporation while also proposing a general act of incorporation for all religious societies in the state, per the Presbyterians' petition.[56] To remove vestiges of favoritism to the Episcopal Church, the committee agreed with requests to liberalize the laws regulating marriage and empowering vestries. Finally, they proposed a general assessment that would raise funds for all Christian churches in the state. Backed by Patrick Henry, this proposal closely resembled Paca's plan in Maryland. The legislature as a whole debated these proposals in the fall session of 1784. The Act of Incorporation for the Episcopal Church passed, as did the amendments to the marriage and vestry acts; no decision was made about a general act of incorporation, and the general assessment was postponed until the following year.

Even after the bill for incorporating the Episcopal Church had been proposed, neither leading evangelicals nor liberal political leaders raised fundamental objections to churches becoming incorporated.[57] John Blair Smith, the Presbyterian minister who had authored the Presbyterian clergy's petition earlier that same year, wrote to Madison during the summer of 1784 to voice his concerns about the bill. Smith clarified that incorporation itself was not the problem. He noted that "an incorporating act . . . would have been extremely proper" had the legislature not included a number of "unreasonable & highly improper, as well as dangerous" provisions. Smith balked at the Episcopal Church's request for permission from the legislature to alter their internal governance and reform their spiritual practices. Like his fellow Presbyterian minister Patrick Allison, Smith expressed dismay at the prospect of any group of clergymen asking the state "to *Enable,* them to regulate all the spiritual concerns of that Church." In so doing, the clergy "virtually declare[d] their Church a mere political machine, which the State may regulate at pleasure." Smith raised these concerns about the specifics of the act but did not object to the broader prospect of incorporation for religious societies.[58]

Writing to Thomas Jefferson, who was in Paris serving as the American Minister to France, James Madison echoed Smith and criticized several "exceptionable" provisions in the Incorporation Act. He resoundingly objected to the terms of the act that set the legislature in a position of "oversight" above the church. However, Madison acknowledged that "the necessity of some sort of incorporation for the purpose of holding and managing the property of the Church could not well be denied." The politically savvy Madison expected that voting against the incorporation act would "have doubled the eagerness and the pretexts for a much greater evil, a general assessment." Despite his reservations, Madison supported the 1784 Act of Incorporation in order to prevent any sort of religious tax from passing. John Marshall, then serving as a legislator, likewise voted for the bill, which passed that session.[59]

Neither John Blair Smith nor James Madison had expressed any concerns about the Episcopal Church retaining its glebes and churches. However, the fate of this property became one of evangelicals' central objections to the 1784 Incorporation Act. Virginia's Presbyterians and Baptists organized a petitioning campaign during 1786 in which five thousand Virginians demanded that the law be repealed.[60] Numerous petitions expressed fury over the Episcopal Church's exclusive right to parish property, including a group of inhabitants from Louisa County who opposed "incorporating the Episcopal Society, and vesting her with the Glebes, churches, surplus money and other Things, which we look upon to be the Property of the Publick."[61] These same petitioners argued that since this wealth had been "procured by the Law of Injustice and Hands of Oppression, we think it reasonable and just, that said property should be put to publick use" and closed with a final entreaty "that all Societies may be left to govern themselves." A group from Chesterfield County argued that glebes, churches, and other property truly belonged to all Virginians, "because [they were] the fruit of their honest Industry."[62]

Now that "the establishment [had been] justly Exploded, it is but reasonable that every Religious Denomination should have their equal part." Petition after petition calling for the repeal of the 1784 charter declared that all parish property belonged to public at large, whose taxes had funded its purchase and maintenance. Evangelicals put forward a charged vision of disestablishment in which the former establishment was not defused but destroyed.

These two demands—namely, to redistribute parish property to all denominations and to remove the legislature from a position of regulating the church—might have been answered by passing a narrower act of incorporation. Some petitions did simply request that the legislature repeal "every part of the Incorporating Act that we complain of."[63] However, to build as comprehensive a case as possible for repeal, evangelicals also began raising a wide range of arguments against incorporation. Criticism of the specific terms of the 1784 act gave rise to broader ideological objections to all forms of incorporation for religious societies, a development that did not happen in Maryland, where numerous evangelical congregations lobbied for and became incorporated in the 1790s.

There is a frenetic quality to these petitions as evangelicals mustered as many arguments as possible against incorporation. Some petitioners made scriptural arguments, asserting that incorporation of a church was "unprecedented in the New Testament."[64] The Baptist General Committee elaborated on this point, declaring that "New Testament Churches, we humbly conceive, are, or should be, established by the Legislature of Heaven, and not earthly power; by the Law of God and not the Law of the State; by the acts of the Apostles, and not by the Acts of an Assembly." These petitioners concluded that the law "appears to cast great contempt upon the divine Author of our Religion, whose Kingdom is not of this world."[65] Whenever a legislature made a church into a corporation, it overstepped its legitimate authority because God alone could authorize and sanction the activity of a church. This line of argument invoked scripture to define the legitimate sphere of state action, but evangelical opponents also voiced concerns about how the 1784 act gave the legislature a dangerous and unconstitutional role in overseeing the internal workings of the Episcopal Church. A memorial from Augusta County decried that the law, "established[d] an immediate, a dangerous, and unwarrantable connection between the Legislature and that Church" and effectively made the legislature "the Head of that church."[66] The Baptist

General Committee called the 1784 act a "Bitumen to Cement Church and State together; the foundation for Ecclesiastical Tyranny, and the first step towards an Inquisition" because it put the legislature in a position to regulate a private religious society.[67] The General Committee further claimed that the incorporation of religious societies fundamentally violated Article 16 of the Virginia Bill of Rights. These petitioners insisted that "if Religion or the duty which we owe to our Creator, and the manner of discharging it, can be directed, only by reason and conviction; not by force and violence, we cannot see with what propriety the General Assembly could incorporate the Protestant Episcopal Church." Laws, in their essential nature, amounted to a form of state force. Any attempt to incorporate the Protestant Episcopal Church by law used legislative coercion to establish the powers of a religious body and therefore necessarily violated an essential tenet of the Virginia Declaration of Rights. Underlying these constitutional objections was a definition of religious freedom premised on institutional separation of religion and government.

While evangelicals flooded the legislature with petitions calling to overturn the law, Episcopalians fiercely objected to repeal. They mounted their own counterpetition campaign across the state, and their petitions garnered 2,500 signatures.[68] The standing committee of the Episcopal Church in Virginia sent a rejoinder in December 1786 insisting that incorporation did not constitute a religious establishment so long as any and every denomination had the right to become incorporated. Moreover, they charged that the "title under which this Church enjoys the said glebes is the very same by which every man in the state enjoys that property which no one contests, and that it is a right of which they cannot be deprived, but by violence, nor without annihilating public faith, disturbing the principles of all government, and shaking the foundations of this state."[69] Episcopalians argued that revoking their charter or confiscating parish glebes would violate their right to private property and endanger the noble "principles of the Revolution."[70] Both camps invoked their fundamental rights under Virginia's 1776 constitution and Declaration of Rights when arguing for and against revoking of the Incorporation Act of 1784. Each side cast the repeal of the Incorporation Act as a crucial litmus test for the legacy of the Revolution and the sanctity of individual liberty in the new republic.

Why were Virginia's evangelicals so focused on the confiscation of parish property when the issue was never actively pursued by Maryland's nonconformists? There are several compelling explanations. First, Article 33 of Maryland's constitution had explicitly reserved all parish property to the Church of England forever.[71] Confiscation would have necessitated amending the 1776 constitution in Maryland. In Virginia, parish property had been protected through multiple statutes since the Revolution but was not explicitly mentioned in the state constitution.[72] Practically speaking, Virginians in favor of confiscation faced an easier task because they did not have to overcome the hurdle of a constitutional amendment. Second, in Maryland, the first private act of incorporation went to the Catholics, not the Episcopalians. Incorporation, then, expressed the expansion of religious liberty and religious equality in Maryland first and foremost in the popular mind. Because Episcopalians were the first denomination to receive a charter in Virginia, incorporation signified to evangelicals yet another unfair holdover of Anglican establishment. This difference in chronology shaped the course of the public debates. Third, these different religious groups had distinct understandings of the relationship between spirit and matter. For Catholics, God dwelt in the churches, chapels, and liturgical objects. This material theology made property inextricable from belief, and thus any attack on property was an attack on the right to free exercise. During the English Reformation, radical Protestants tore down, burned, stripped, and destroyed traditional Catholic spaces and objects and attempted to dematerialize their faith practices by insisting that investing tangible spaces or things with holiness was a form of idolatry. Baptists and Presbyterians in Virginia viewed church property through a wholly different lens than Catholics and did not regard confiscation of property as a fundamental attack on the right to free exercise.

The final reason lies in the differences between the nonconformist religious groups in either state. Maryland's Catholics simply had less incentive to call for confiscation. Given the fierce hostility Catholics had faced across the Anglo-American world for centuries, Carroll and his fellow Maryland Catholics were still fearful of losing their newly won civil rights or their property. Their political vulnerability made them less likely to directly attack the former establishment. The former Jesuits were far more focused on securing their own valuable estates than on claiming parish glebes. Opening the door to the confiscation of religious property might have jeopardized their own contested manors, which included at least 12,000 acres and more than two hundred enslaved people.[73] In addition, some of Maryland's leading Catholic families had faced and narrowly escaped state confiscation of their assets during the Revolution.[74] Having so recently achieved full civic rights and dodged popular threats to their estates, Catholic leaders espoused a conservative view of property rights and were unlikely to express democratic or levelling calls for the legislature to seize the glebes.[75]

By and large, Virginia's evangelical communities had far more to gain and far less to lose. The total value of Virginia's dissenters' property in the mid-1780s was far less than that of Maryland's Jesuits or Virginia's Episcopal parishes. A handful of Virginia's Presbyterian congregations had begun purchasing enslaved people in the decade before the Revolution.[76] For example, Peaks of Otter Presbyterian Church, which had sought incorporation in 1774, purchased one hundred acres and four people before the Revolution. By 1783, the church enslaved fourteen people.[77] Most congregations held far less property, though. Alexandria Presbyterian claimed to own a "10-acre lot of ground."[78] The Augusta Presbyterian Church claimed only "two small tracts of land."[79] While clearly there was a range in the value of different congregations' assets, most dissenting communities were unlikely to have wealthy investments rivaling those of nearby Anglican parishes, which might own four or five churches and chapels, a glebe, enslaved people, fine silver, a parish library, and a poorhouse.[80] Virginia's evangelical churches had only begun growing in the two decades before the Revolution, and many congregations were made up of less wealthy residents.[81] These congregations undoubtedly held far less property than their fellow Anglicans did in the 1780s. The fight for church property had very different stakes in the two Chesapeake states.

## Repealing Incorporation

Never happy with the Incorporating Act and sympathetic to the popular outcry against it, Madison began considering its repeal. First, though, he turned his attention to finally defeating general assessment with the passage of the celebrated Statute for Religious Freedom.[82] Madison's arguments against the assessment circulated in his *Memorial and Remonstrance* in the spring of 1785, and this document remains one of the most acclaimed statements about religious freedom. Its legislative companion, the Statute for Religious Freedom, which had been drafted by Jefferson in the 1770s, was passed at the next session of the legislature.[83] The law's bracing language captured the best of Jefferson the author; the passage of the law in the mid-1780s relied on Madison's strengths as a political tactician. The law gave statutory shape to Mason's broad statements in the Declaration of Rights and Madison's philosophical challenge to any form of a general assessment in the *Memorial and Remonstrance.*

The 1786 statute marked an important departure from the earlier process of disestablishment. Previously, the legislature had overturned specific colonial statutes one by one. The title of the 1786 statute, "An Act for establishing Religious Freedom," announced a new approach. The legislature appropriated the verb "establish," so long understood to convey an exclusive, state-sponsored church, and instead used it to construct a legal framework to bolster and ensure religious freedom for all. Whereas the colonial assembly had used statutes to privilege the established church, the republican legislature would now legislate to bolster religious freedom. The law explicitly prohibited religious taxation and disassociated civil rights from religious opinions. The 1786 statute positively "established" a comprehensive and inviolable vision of religious freedom protected under state law.

The following year, Madison returned to the question of repealing the Episcopal Church's charter. He recognized that revoking incorporation would present a thorny legal challenge. Among Madison's papers is a hurried page of notes he made sometime in early 1786 that has largely escaped the notice of scholars. Scrawled on the back of an old legislative resolution, the document recorded a discussion about repealing the act of incorporation made by "Mr. R" (presumably Edmund Randolph) and "Mr. Marshall" (assuredly John Marshall). The innocuous title Madison used, "Notes on Charters of Incorporation," obscured the specific topic under discussion. But the document's timing and content reveal that their discussion focused on repealing the 1784 Act of Incorporation. John Marshall, like Madison himself, had voted to incorporate the church in 1784.[84] Randolph and Marshall expressed strong objections to repealing the church's incorporation. The men characterized charters as "irrevocable" and compared rescinding incorporation to the "tyrannical acts" of Great Britain that had sparked the Revolution. Marshall said, "Laws of incorp[oratio]n. [are] distinct from general laws & not like them repealable: being compacts between two parties"; he elaborated that a "vested Right of any sort cannot be touched." The rancorous political fight over repealing the Episcopal Church's Act of Incorporation led Marshall to think through the rights of corporations vis-à-vis new state legislatures and assert their irrevocable nature.[85]

However, Marshall concluded his comments with an instructive, even prophetic, qualification when he invoked the first article of the Virginia Declaration of Rights. In a fragmentary note, he reiterated that no "compact" could deprive individuals of their inalienable rights, yet "if sense of people, Legislature may interpose—sense not yet expressed by majority." This final observation revealed that he was not commenting on the abstract question of revoking incorporation but specifically responding to the battle over the 1784 charter. Though Marshall clearly did not support a repeal, his words provided a way forward for opponents of the law.[86] If the people's fundamental rights had been betrayed by a charter, then the legislature could "interpose" on their behalf to justifiably revoke incorporation.[87]

Months after recording Randolph and Marshall's comments, Madison voted to revoke the Episcopal Church's incorporation in October 1786.[88] The Repeal Act included a specific provision "saving to all religious societies the property to them respectively belonging." Revoking the Episcopal Church's charter was the immediate outcome of the protest movement, but the legacy of these debates continued to resonate. Virginia's evangelicals had not only succeeded in reversing specific state policies but in reshaping the popular and constitutional definition of a religious establishment. Before they raised objections to the passage of the 1784 law, there was no widespread or codified opposition to a religious denomination securing its property through incorporation in Virginia. However, attacking the specific provisions of the law gave rise to a set of broader ideological arguments against incorporation. The shortcomings of the 1784 act led evangelicals to espouse the view that any form of state incorporation would unconstitutionally draw the state into regulating churches.

After the repeal of the Incorporation Act of 1784, no other religious societies became incorporated in Virginia. The legislature eventually enacted this prohibition into statute when it declared in 1799 that any former state laws that had "incorporated religious sects" were "inconsistent with the principles of the constitution, and of religious freedom, and manifestly [tend] to the re-establishment of a national church."[89] In 1851, the state formally amended its constitution to add this provision, which stood in place until 2002.[90] Evangelicals had persuasively argued that any form of incorporation transgressed the permissible boundary between church and state. In protesting against the chartering of the Episcopal Church, Virginia's evangelicals had articulated and enacted a broader definition of religious establishment that made religious incorporation impermissible.

Maryland and Virginia took divergent paths over the incorporation of religious societies. In both states, nonconformists set the agenda during disestablishment. Their experiences under the colonial established church shaped their views and priorities after the Revolution. Maryland settled on policies that made longstanding legal privileges available to all Christians. This version of disestablishment did not fundamentally sever ties between religion and government but instead set Christian denominations on equal footing. Long unable to use incorporation to protect their property, Catholics sought equal legal powers from the state government. Virginia's evangelicals drew on their experiences under punitive colonial laws and high taxes. Without a clear incentive to seek corporate privileges from the state, such as the need to secure valuable property, Virginia's nonconformists pushed back against incorporation as an unconstitutional connection between church and state. Material concerns shaped ideological change.

The question of incorporation ultimately led the two states to enact fundamentally different definitions of religious establishment. Marylanders had embraced private and general incorporation acts for the legal equality they bestowed on churches. Virginians, on the other hand, articulated a desire to separate churches as much as possible from the grasp of state oversight. Virginia's evangelicals expanded the parameters of religious establishment as a legal concept in their arguments against incorporation. The movement delegitimized any form of state regulation over churches. The issue of incorporation underscores the gulf between Virginia's disestablishment commitment to the separation of church and state and Maryland's commitment to equality of Christian churches in the state.

As the fight over incorporation in Virginia demonstrated, the definition of a religious establishment changed dramatically in the course of a few short years in response to the specific terms of the 1784 Incorporation Act. The goalposts of disestablishment continued to move during the 1780s, and the concept was still under construction as late as 1802. The political process refined the practical boundaries of an "establishment" as states put their principles into practice. Religious establishment was a moving target as the public developed new ideas about what constituted a state establishment of religion in the decades after the Revolution.

## Drafting the First Amendment

In their policies regarding incorporation, the Chesapeake states reached radically different definitions of what constituted a religious establishment. However, the significant divergence between Maryland's and Virginia's definitions of establishment remained out of sight during the drafting of the First Amendment. Soon, though, the discordant definitions of establishment and its implications for religious incorporation under the US Constitution would surface in the early nineteenth century.

Several state ratifying conventions had instructed Congress to add language protecting religious freedom when ratifying the Constitution, and there were also objections from some religious denominations that the document did too little to safeguard rights of conscience.[91] In response, James Madison had originally prepared an amendment that read: "The civil rights of none shall be abridged on account of religious belief or worship, nor shall any national religion be established, nor shall the full and equal rights of conscience be in any manner or pretext infringed."[92] Heated debates over the proposed language persisted during the summer of 1789. Whether raising objections to or praising Madison's amendment, congressmen drew on and articulated sharp regional differences about the proper relationship between church and state. The continued establishment of Congregationalism in much of New England, the recent disestablishment of the Anglican Church across the South, and the long history of nonestablishment in Rhode Island and Pennsylvania all shaped the views of the representatives and their constituents. New Englanders feared that such an amendment might force their home states to abandon their state establishments, while others argued that the amendment as written could actually threaten the foundations of all private religious institutions.

Marylander Daniel Carroll, the brother of John Carroll, was one of the loudest voices in favor of Madison's proposed amendment to the Constitution in the House of Representatives. In a speech in August 1789, Carroll indicated he "was much in favor of adopting the words" and thought they would be more powerful in "conciliating the minds of the people to the Government than almost any other amendment."[93] He declared that "the rights of conscience are . . . of a peculiar delicacy, and will little bear the gentlest touch of governmental hand; and . . . many sects have concurred that they are not well secured under the present Constitution." Carroll dismissed his colleagues' quibbling over the specific wording of the amendment. In a telling statement, the Catholic congressman said that he "would not contend with gentlemen about the phraseology, his object was to secure the substance."[94] Carroll claimed to be unconcerned with the specific wording of the amendment because he presumed that the meaning of "establishment" was straightforward enough not to be misconstrued. But, as the past decade of wrangling over incorporation suggested, the term was far from settled.

Carroll and Madison, both hailing from the Chesapeake, had personally taken part in the struggle over incorporation in their home states. Both men hoped that this amendment would convince wary religious communities that the new federal Constitution did not threaten the specific settlements between church and state reached in each state. The alliance between the Chesapeake representatives reflected the importance of protecting their hard-worn reforms.

The final language of the First Amendment reflects months of revision in the House of Representatives and the Senate. Congress had whittled down Madison's original language to read: "Congress shall make no law respecting an establishment of religion, or prohibiting the free exercise thereof." The amendment was finally ratified in 1791. The first two clauses of the ratified amendment were more ambiguous than the initial wording proposed by Madison. They evinced an agree-to-disagree compromise that gave the federal government neither too much nor too little power over the religious settlements only recently solidified in each state.[95] The different definitions of an "establishment" had not been carefully parsed during ratification but would be revealed in debates over specific policies like incorporation in the following decades.

## Incorporation and the Establishment Clause

Two decades later, in 1811, James Madison had become president of the United States. He issued his first veto to block a federal act of incorporation for Christ Church, an Episcopal congregation in the District of

Columbia.[96] In his veto message, Madison explained that the bill "exceeds the rightful authority to which governments are limited by the essential distinction between civil and religious functions and violates in particular the article of the Constitution of the United States which declares that 'Congress shall make no law respecting a religious establishment.'" He made two objections to the bill. First, the law included "sundry rules and proceedings relative purely to the organization and polity of the church incorporated, and comprehending even the election and removal of the minister." By outlining ministerial succession and other matters of internal organization, Madison believed the bill gave the color of law to the canons of the Episcopal Church and created a legal mechanism to enforce them. Such an arrangement created "a religious establishment by law, a legal force and sanction being given to certain articles in its constitution and administration."

Moreover, Madison attacked a provision in the bill enabling the church to "make such provision for the support of the poor of the said church, as shall by them be thought proper, and to provide also . . . for the education of the poor children of the said church." Nothing in the legislative text explicitly suggested the church would carry out these tasks in a public or official capacity, but Madison remained dubious. He reasoned that this grant of power would be "altogether superfluous if the provision is to be the result of pious charity." In fact, this bill set "a precedent for giving to religious societies as such a legal agency in carrying into effect a public and civil duty." Madison deemed this delegation of public power over education and welfare an unconstitutional form of establishment.

With this veto message, the president echoed the arguments made by Virginia's evangelicals almost thirty years earlier when protesting the state's 1784 Act of Incorporation of the Episcopal Church. Though initially ambivalent about the issue of incorporation, Madison had come to adopt the view that religious incorporation created an impermissible church-state connection. By their very nature, Madison argued that acts of incorporation codified some form of internal church government in law and set the state in a position of ecclesiastical oversight.[97] Congress's bill had erred further by attempting to delegate civic powers to a religious society. With this veto, Madison enacted his separationist definition of "establishment" to the federal level.[98]

News of the veto quickly spread, and reports appeared in many states over the following weeks.[99] The *Green-Mountain Farmer*, published in

Bennington, Vermont, celebrated the veto, exclaiming, "Happy America! Respect your Rights! Revere your inestimable republican government . . . and gratefully acknowledge the favor of Heaven, in granting you a Madison . . . to place a veto . . . as righteousness demands, unaw'd by man, and unallur'd by bribes."[100] However, Madison's action received immediate and scathing criticism from a Maryland newspaper. In a piece entitled "Democratic Qualms," an anonymous writer pointed out that the terms of this vetoed bill closely resembled the numerous acts passed by Maryland and other states to incorporate religious societies and congregations.[101] The author balked at Madison's veto message, which "condemns every state government in the union, for they have all passed similar acts." The newspaper derisively attacked the president's "ridiculous affectation" that he alone understood the Constitution and could "guard" its true meaning. The article specifically blasted Madison's interpretation of religious establishment as expressed in the First Amendment:

> What was the meaning of the Constitution in providing against a religious establishment? Does any man but Mr. Madison imagine it was to prevent the people of the District of Columbia from enjoying legal church regulations and from exercising corporate rights in the congregations? Does the legislature of Maryland believe it is creating a religious establishment, when it is occupied in granting charters to the churches of the different sects of Christians . . . Where all are equally protected and accommodated, where each sect and congregations has its own establishment . . . the best security against "a religious establishment," that is to say one preeminent establishment which is preferred and set up over the rest, against which alone the constitutional safeguard was created?[102]

This Marylander clearly had not followed events across the Potomac. But he reiterated the Maryland position that granting incorporation to all Christian churches gave each community greater legal standing and therefore protected nonestablishment. Just like Madison understood the First Amendment through his experiences in Virginia, this writer read the First Amendment through the lens of Maryland's embrace of incorporation. Articles critical of the veto appeared the following month in Pennsylvania and Massachusetts, which suggested widespread interest in the matter.[103] The public seemed to understand Madison's veto as a sweeping rejection of religious incorporation.

The House of Representatives did not know what to do when it received the president's veto message. There had not been a presidential veto since 1797, and several congressmen expressed confusion about the proper protocol for dealing with a vetoed bill. No one was sure if they had to vote immediately or whether they could refer the bill to a committee for amendment. After listening to Madison's response, the House decided to read the First Amendment aloud and consider its meaning. Having reacquainted himself with the Bill of Rights, Connecticut Congressman Timothy Pitkin said that "this question was new to him. He had no idea that the Constitution precluded Congress from passing laws to incorporate religious societies for the purposes of enabling them to hold property." Indeed, Pitkin stated that "he ha[d] always held the constitution to intend to prevent the establishment of a national church, such as the Church of England, a refusal to subscribe to the tendencies of which was to exclude a citizen from office, etc." Pitkin's interpretation of the Establishment Clause directly countered Madison's view. The Connecticut representative requested additional time for "reflection" upon the issue. However, Benjamin Pickman Jr. of Massachusetts dismissed the need to discuss the act or the underlying question of incorporation any further. Since the bill was "not an important one," and "a full discussion of the principles it involved would occupy the whole remainder of the session," Pickman suggested the "best course" was to move on to a vote. The veto override failed, and Madison's veto stood.[104]

This scene appears at turns amusing, astonishing, and enormously consequential. Confused about the protocol after a presidential veto and completely unsure about the meaning of the First Amendment, Congress stalled on the substantive questions. Then, seemingly motivated as much by a desire to leave Washington as to get at the true meaning of the Establishment Clause, the House chose not to interrogate the issue further. Their debates had exposed a wide gap between regional understandings of "establishment" in the early nineteenth century. Representative Pickman may have suggested that the incorporation of a small church in the capital city was insignificant, but this event should still be remembered as a decisive turn in American religious and constitutional history. Given the chance to consider the meaning of the Establishment Clause, Congress decided the matter was of too little importance to warrant further deliberation. Rather than override the veto, the House acquiesced to

Madison's understanding of establishment forged in the battles of Virginia's fight over incorporation.

Settling the matter of incorporation may have had long-term consequences for the definition of religious establishment, but it did not resolve the vocal demands of Virginia's non-Anglicans for the state to seize parish property. To Patrick Allison's great disappointment, Marylanders never seriously debated the confiscation of parish property. But for Virginia's Baptists, religious freedom would remain spurious without the seizure of parish property and disestablishment merely an unfulfilled promise. Episcopal parishes still had significant property holdings, which had been specifically preserved under the repeal of the incorporation act. For former dissenting communities, parish wealth was a material expression of continued inequality and injustice. Virginia's evangelicals set their sights on wresting this parish property from the Episcopal Church and toppling the edifice of establishment once and for all.

## Calls for Confiscation

Back in Virginia, the fight over parish property had only intensified after the state legislature's repeal of the 1784 incorporating act. Evangelicals contended that the establishment of religious freedom remained a false promise so long as the Episcopal Church retained all parish property. To these petitioners, parish churches, glebes lands, and enslaved people still held by Episcopal parishes were a material expression of their continued oppression.

Virginia's evangelicals launched a petitioning campaign over the next fifteen years to sway the legislature to seize parish property. In their 1787 appeal to the legislature, the Presbyterian General Committee made the constitutional case for confiscation by invoking two key phrases from the Virginia Declaration of Rights: the prohibition against emoluments in Section 4 and the protection of free and equal exercise of religion under Section 16.[105] Their petition framed the glebes as illegal "emoluments" given to the Episcopal Church without services rendered in return to public. In this version of events, the state was not a neutral arbiter but a bad actor that had forcibly seized "common property" and wrongfully "bestow[ed it] upon this infant church, to the exclusion of a great majority of the community."

While the Presbyterians' 1787 petition crafted a precise constitutional rationale for seizing the glebes, the Baptist Association's subsequent petitions seemed to throw as many arguments as possible against the wall to see what stuck. Ranging from principled and pragmatic to outlandish, they argued that confiscation would provide much needed public funds to the state government and that it was a form of reparation for years of intolerance. Most extreme, in their 1789 petition, the Baptists put forward a majoritarian claim to the glebes by declaring that property rights were "neither founded in Nature nor in Grace; but in Social Right."[106] Expressing a radical understanding of popular sovereignty, they maintained that "if a majority of Voices governed by the Principles of Right, say, that the Episcopal Church ought to have all the Property before mentioned, than s[ai]d church is entitled to it; otherwise the Law by which they had it, may be as easily repealed as any other Law whatever." Like populists elsewhere in America in the late 1780s, these Baptists argued that property rights should not take precedence over liberty, a line of argument that evinced the Revolution's contradictory impulses.

The federal Constitutional Convention had been called amidst anxiety among elites about this exact kind of levelling, democratic language, and the Baptists' argument realized Madison's worst fears of those unchecked majorities mentioned in the *Federalist,* no. 10 and the threat they posed to "personal security or the rights of property." Indeed, Madison had envisaged "a religious sect" that might "degenerate into a political faction" along with the "other improper or wicked project" such as the "equal division of property."[107] Fears that private property rights could be "repealed as easily" as any other law, as the Baptists' 1789 petition had claimed, confirmed the Federalists' greatest anxiety that the security of their property could be undermined at the whim of the masses.[108] The Baptist petitioners dismissed the "supposed danger" of their appeal, but their inclusion of this argument explicitly linked the fight over glebes to the larger conflict between popular sovereignty and private property.

The legislature issued a careful resolution in response to evangelicals' demands in the fall of 1789. The statement was crafted by the Committee for Religion, which included moderate delegates like Patrick Henry and Edmund Randolph who were seen as friendlier to the former establishment.[109] The committee declared that "the contest for the glebes, churches and chapels, is not of a religious nature, but is to be decided by the rules of private property."[110] The glebes, churches, and other property "whether purchased or given" belonged to the respective parishes, which were "capable in law of taking and holding them to their own use." Transferring any of this property to another sect or to former members would be "an unconstitutional invasion of right." The committee's succinct legal arguments dismissed the petitioners' rhetoric of religious oppression and their radical claim that property was a social right and declared, "The Legislative sanction for such a sale, would soon grow into a precedent for the constant intrusion of the State into all things which concern religion." This savvy response used evangelicals' longstanding plea for the legislature not to intrude on spiritual matters to defend the state's glebe policy and voiced a policy of nonintervention as the best means of preserving religious freedom.

The entire legislature signaled its approval for the resolution by voting to table the Baptists' petition in 1789 and rejecting the petition in 1790.[111] While the invocation of private property rights certainly appealed to Federalists, who hoped to prevent any levelling policies, the resolution also had support from leading anti-Federalists like Patrick Henry, who advocated for the restraint of governmental power.[112] In a final coup de grace, the legislature transferred any future discussion of the glebe issue from the Committee for Religion to the Committee for the Courts of Justice. Moving forward, the glebes would be treated by the legislature as a question of private property, not religious liberty.

If the legislators hoped to cow the Baptists by removing the question of the glebes from the realm of religion, they failed. Undaunted by the legislature's response, the Baptists quickly pivoted. The facts had not changed, but their arguments did. The community jettisoned any claim that property was a "social right" and instead adopted a liberal, natural rights framework to build a convincing case based on private property rights. They claimed the glebes had been paid for by "property which was drawn from [the parishioners] for the use of their own parishes."[113] The state had "confer[red] emoluments on a part of the community" by reserving the glebes to the Episcopal Church, which was a violation of all non-Episcopalians' "natural rights." To underscore their claim to private property, Baptists even began referring to themselves as "the parishioners." This label, which evangelical Virginians had forcibly resisted for decades, now gave them durable claims to parish property. Without the seizure of the glebes, they could not "consider themselves secure in their property, and equal privileges with the rest of their fellow men." Suddenly, these Baptist petitioners heartily agreed that any infringement of private property rendered all property claims insecure.[114] Only once the glebes were confiscated, they argued, would any private property be safe in Virginia. Baptists dropped populist, levelling arguments in favor of confiscation and instead claimed that seizing the parish glebes would be a vindication of their private property rights.

In the same decade that Baptists embraced the language of private property rights to demand confiscation, they were rapidly distancing themselves from earlier critiques of slavery.[115] Scholars have argued that white evangelicals abandoned their prerevolutionary commitment to spiritual equality in favor of "refinement and respectability." This retreat from social radicalism accompanied the explosive growth in the popularity of evangelical churches after the Revolution. In the 1790s, the political atmosphere became increasingly amenable to the Baptists' demands as their republican allies won more seats in the Virginia legislature.[116] Baptists embraced the republican rhetoric of private property just as they were coming into political power and abandoning antislavery.

In addition to the petitions sent by religious communities, the legislature would receive more than a hundred local petitions about parish property. Some were clearly submitted in tandem with denominational petitions.[117] However, many local requests were not a strategic backdoor to confiscation but reflected deep-seated confusion about the reformed legal relationship between church and state. Mired in conflicting property claims and uncertain about the practical implications of disestablishmentarian laws, local communities asked the legislature for clarification.

The repeal of the Incorporation Act proffered a civil mechanism—trusteeship—for churches to hold property without venturing into the thorny territory of incorporation. All denominations could appoint trustees "according to the rules of their sect . . . who shall be capable of managing and applying such property to the religious uses of such societies." To reiterate the point that denominations should be regulating their own affairs, the statute asserted that "so much of all laws now in force, as prevents any religious society from regulating its own discipline, shall be, and is hereby repealed."[118] Even after making this declaration, the state continued to exercise some supervision over parishes, going so far as to divide Hardy

Parish in two as late as 1790 and empowering the parish to sell its glebe.[119] Old habits died hard, apparently, as Episcopalians continued to look to the legislature for guidance and the state continued to treat parishes as semipublic bodies at times under its supervision. After queries arrived from vestries uncertain about their standing, the assembly expanded on the provision in the act of repeal in yet another act and unequivocally upheld vestries' title to parish property.[120]

Virginia's evangelicals called for the confiscation of only that parish property that had been purchased using tax funds; any privately donated property would remain in the hands of parishes, per the terms of the donors' instructions. The legislature had reasserted this rationale in its 1789 resolution.[121] However, the numerous charitable bequests left to parishes for the benefit of the poor complicated this distinction. One of the primary responsibilities, and certainly one of the highest expenses, of Virginia's colonial parishes had been poor relief. Trying to disentangle religion from government, communities questioned whether donations made to the parish specifically for the poor ought to belong to the newly private church or to the public at large. Practically speaking, it was often impossible to distinguish between parish property bequeathed a century earlier from parish property purchased with levy funds. Anyone familiar with parish vestry books would recognize the near impossibility of discriminating between these two sources of property. Lands given by donors were maintained by funds raised through the levy; income raised from enslaved people left to the parish was often not tracked separately from other sources of revenue. Across the state, Overseers of the Poor argued that donations made specifically for the care of the poor now belonged to them, as the public administrators of poor relief. These endowments sparked heated local disputes across the state.

In 1789, the Overseers of the Poor of Norfolk County hoped to take possession of a tract of land and "sundry" enslaved persons given by Matthew Godfrey in 1715/16 "to the Poor of Norfolk County for ever and ever."[122] Per the terms of Godfrey's will, the vestry held and managed the land and enslaved persons throughout the eighteenth century. This legacy was not managed as a separate endowment for poor relief but was pooled with the rest of the parish's funds.[123] However, after the creation of the state's new poor relief system in 1780, the Overseers of the Poor argued that they were "by law appointed guardians of the poor," so Godfrey's donation now came under their purview.[124] As the public body charged with caring for the poor, "the poor of all societies come under their notice as well as those of the Protestant Episcopal Church." The Overseers of the Poor invoked the specific wording of Godfrey's will, which specifically named the poor of Norfolk County as his intended beneficiary. They argued that the post-disestablishment administrative shift made the county the proper inheritor of both responsibility and property for the poor.

Godfrey's bequest not only sparked a clash between parish and county; there were also fights between localities. The city of Norfolk, which had formed part of Elizabeth River Parish at the time of the donation, also petitioned to claim its part of the land and enslaved community in 1789.[125] The county and the city were eager not to lose their share of the property. The county rejoined quickly to insist that if the city was to obtain any "proportion of land & slaves," they must "also receive their proportion of the poor."[126] Ultimately, the legislature agreed that the property should be sold, and the proceeds should be divided proportionally.

Disestablishment, so often narrated as a story of individual rights, also posed significant questions for communities. Parish property had been framed as an investment in the public good and for the community's welfare. Colonial testators had given their property in the context of a legally established religion in which the parish was concomitant with the whole community and served the public at large. Reformers argued that the state hand over bequests made for the parish poor to public administrators rather than allowing this property to remain under the control of a private religious sect. Fundamental to this argument was the belief that the Revolution had created a fundamentally new society, one that could not have been foreseen, and one in which republican institutions served the public good. The Revolution had destroyed the traditional church-state arrangement, and it was incumbent upon the legislature to ensure that the community did not lose their valuable assets as collateral damage. These queries were not about individual liberty but about the fabric of communal life in republican Virginia. This property mattered not only as an ideological issue but as a practical question of public resources. The assembly received a slew of local petitions about glebe lands after the repeal of incorporation grappling with the legal and material consequences of disestablishment. Local petitions presented circumstances that were not clear-cut and did not always reflect political or religious differences. They exposed the difficulty of transitioning the administration of public services from church to state and the desire for communities to settle disputes over property.

In practice, these petitions triangulated and left unresolved the same set of questions. First, who were the rightful successors to parishes? Second, what was the role of the continued state in disestablishment? Finally, what constituted an establishment if parishes were still under the direction of the legislature after "disestablishment"? However, while the denominational petitions operated in the abstract sphere of natural rights, local petitions highlighted the real property at stake. Angry neighbors with long-simmering grievances embodied the factions Madison had imagined in *Federalist*, no. 10.

And, of course, much of the property that elicited such fierce claims of ownership and cries for egalitarian laws was in fact enslaved people purchased to work at poorhouses, held as part of charitable endowments, and treated as appurtenances to the glebe lands. Communities and individuals, both for and against the sale of the glebes, demanded that the state respect equality under the laws by awarding them with property, namely the Black Virginians enslaved by the church. The liberty secured under republicanism and appeals to the state's duty to protect natural rights were limited to white Virginians, and debates over religious freedom were inseparable from the system of chattel slavery.

## The Glebe Acts

During the 1790s, as Virginia became increasingly evangelical and Virginia's House of Delegates became increasingly republican, Baptist petitioners garnered more political support for confiscation.[127] The state's Episcopalians, meanwhile, still appeared shell-shocked. Their position had only worsened since the mid-1780s—there were fewer ministers, fewer parishioners, and persistent internal disorganization. Still, the church began soliciting legal opinions to shore up its position. Bushrod Washington, nephew of George Washington and a future Supreme Court Justice, affirmed that Virginia's colonial vestries were incorporated, "notwithstanding the want of a formal charter," and that nothing during or since the Revolution had "destroy[ed] those rights." Washington argued that confiscation would unconstitutionally violate Episcopalians' "free exercise of their religion . . . by force and violence" by depriving them "of the means of supporting their clergy."[128]

While there had been scattered local responses from Episcopalians, it was not until 1796 that the denomination offered an official response. That year, the General Convention sent a petition echoing and elaborating on the legislature's 1789 resolution that the fight over the glebes was not a matter for the legislature but a dispute over private property. They argued that the popular call for the "sacrifice of private rights to a 'whole community'" meant that "the enjoyment of private rights is at one blow taken away." Indeed, the Episcopalians argued that "laws exist to *protect* private property and consequently, without criminal forfeiture can never be taken away," and any plan for glebe confiscation was "beyond the sphere of legislation." They stated they were "at loss to conceive upon what plausible pretence that petition might be supported." Their memorialists hoped that the assembly would not "yield to attempts which hitherto had always been thought unreasonable."[129] The House voted to postpone Episcopalian and Baptist petitions in 1796, effectively tabling them.

However, in January 1799, the legislature took a decisive step toward seizing the glebes by passing a law entitled "An act, to repeal certain acts, and to declare the construction of the Bill of Rights, and Constitution concerning religion." This statute, which was debated for more than a year, ultimately adopted the arguments made by Presbyterians and Baptists during the decade-long campaign for confiscation. This was not just an act of repeal but a bold indictment of the previous twenty years of legislation concerning religion. The law's preamble declared that several laws "do admit the church established under the regal government, to have continued so, subsequently to the constitution: have bestowed property upon that church: have affected a legislative right to establish any religious sect: and have incorporated religious sects." All these actions were "inconsistent with the principles of the constitution, and of religious freedom, and manifestly [tend] to the re-establishment of a national church." The fundamental premise of the 1799 law was that the legislature had actively and unconstitutionally perpetuated a form of religious establishment not only by incorporating religious denominations but also by protecting the property of the Episcopal Church. The statute reaffirmed that the Statute for Religious Freedom was the "true exposition" of Virginia's Constitution and Bill of Rights.[130]

While the 1799 law laid out the philosophical and legal groundwork for the state to confiscate parish property, it was not until 1802 that the legislature authorized a specific plan to seize church lands when it passed the Glebe Act. This 1802 statute declared "that all property formerly belonging to the Church, of every description, devolved on the good people of this commonwealth, on the dissolution of the British government here." The law claimed that all parish property, except for donations, rightfully belonged to the state. This sweeping claim included not only glebes but also "churches, and the property therein contained." However, the legislature only authorized the sale of glebe lands at that time, and only once the parish became "vacant," which meant that it no longer had an inducted rector. The text of the act framed these concessions as a magnanimous attempt "to reconcile all the good people of this commonwealth." The legislature declared it would be "inexpedient" though not illegal "at this time to disturb the possession of the present incumbents."[131] The legislature thus restricted the ability of counties to seize vacant glebes without yielding the ideological ground that the state had the right to seize all parish property if it so chose. Moreover, this logic fundamentally rejected that parishes were perpetual, corporate bodies. The only legal claim that the state would respect was the minister's freehold right to the glebe, which extinguished at his death or departure. This act followed the plan sketched by Jefferson in 1776 when he first outlined the laws that had to be repealed for the "establishment of the Church of England" to be "discontinued" in the state, which included the confiscation and sale of the glebes upon the death of the incumbent minister.[132]

In this formulation, the parish as an institution still retained an uncertain position between public and private. After a county seized parochial land, the "parishes" could still petition to determine how these resources would be deployed. The 1802 act's language suggests that the petitioners writing on behalf of the parish did not necessarily have to be practicing Anglicans; rather, the terms used to describe who could subscribe to such a petition—"freeholder" and "house-keeper"—denoted particular residency and property rights within the bounds of the parish as a geographical unit rather than membership in a private religious institution.[133] Thus, the legislature seemingly accepted the Baptists' argument that they, and all other Virginians, were still parishioners. With the passage of the 1802 act, it was no longer the hierarchical vestry but the will of the majority that would decide parochial matters, a reconception of the parish that reflected evangelical congregational practices as well as republican political ideology.

Under the Glebe Act, local communities had significant discretion over how to spend the money raised from the sale of glebes; however, the proceeds could not fund "any religious purpose whatsoever." The legislature had declared that previous laws had unconstitutionally granted property to a church; they would not be caught out using public money to fund religious life again, or enabling local officials to do so, either.

Together, the 1799 and 1802 Glebe Acts refined Virginia's definition of a religious establishment. Proposals throughout the 1780s to offer general incorporation to all religious denominations and to provide funds for all Christian teachers in the state had made nonpreference the standard of disestablishment. This definition, which closely resembled Maryland's position, had been championed by Patrick Henry but was ultimately defeated by Madison with the passage of the Statute for Religious Freedom. But even after the 1786 Statute for Religious Freedom rejected the general assessment, evangelicals had called for the legislature to distribute parish property, including churches and glebes, directly to religious denominations. This proposal had left open a possibility for the flow of funds from state to church. The Glebe Act closed this door firmly by prohibiting the use of glebe funds for "any religious purpose whatsoever." This provision shifted away from nonpreference or legislative entanglement to articulate a specific financial boundary between church and state. The legislature could not impose taxes for religion, nor could it dedicate these public funds for religious purposes.

With this provision in the Glebe Act, Virginia's definition of establishment recognized that material power and religious freedom were just as intertwined in the era of nonestablishment as they had been under the former establishment. In their protests, evangelicals had used the framework of emoluments to characterize the glebes. The Glebe Act not only accepted this rationale but added restrictions on public spending for the benefit of religion. The law underscored that the state's role was not merely to remain "nonintrusive" but to implement affirmative legislation to maintain the permissible relationship between church and state. The state could only guarantee religious freedom by actively policing a financial boundary between church and state. The law underscored that articulating the permissible use of public property was essential to securing religious freedom and preventing any form of religious establishment.

## The Glebe Act Before the Courts

The fight over Virginia's glebes soon moved from the legislature to the courts. Episcopalians around the state sought injunctions to prevent the seizure of their glebe property by county Overseers of the Poor who initiated confiscation proceedings. Both the Virginia Supreme Court of Appeals (the state's highest court) and the US Supreme Court would weigh in on the issue. Just as incorporation and property were intertwined in the minds of petitioners, the lawsuits challenging the Glebe Act reflected the inextricability of the two issues. Virginia's two most radical disestablishmentarian policies—the seizure of church property and the revocation and prohibition of incorporation—came under scrutiny as the courts considered the same set of questions that Virginia's petitioners and legislators had been debating for decades. Their decisions would implicitly endorse a particular interpretation of a religious "establishment."

A challenge to the law reached the Virginia Supreme Court of Appeals in 1802 after the vestry of Manchester Parish tried to prevent the Chesterfield County Overseers of the Poor from selling their glebe. The case, *Turpin v. Locket* (1804), halted the sale of glebe lands across Virginia as the state's highest court deliberated. The parish vestry argued that the state's actions had violated their private property rights and infringed their religious freedom. Virginia's chief justice was then Edmund Pendleton, a longtime vestryman of Drysdale Parish in Caroline County and a staunch Episcopalian. He had personally overseen the conviction of dissenters under the colony's establishmentarian laws before the Revolution and even provided the Episcopal Church with a legal opinion opposing confiscation.[134] Not surprisingly, Pendleton authored a decision in 1803 that ruled in favor of the Manchester Parish vestry and would have struck down the 1802 Glebe Act's confiscation of church property. However, the day before delivering his opinion in court, the eighty-two-year-old justice died suddenly, purportedly with the *Turpin* opinion in his pocket. Because Pendleton had not yet delivered his opinion in court, it did not stand. Theatrical in its many twists and turns, the case would have to be reargued once Pendleton's seat on the high court was filled.[135]

Pendleton's successor on the state's highest court was St. George Tucker, a rising star in the next generation of Virginia republicans. Ideologically aligned with Jefferson and Madison, Tucker reached a radically different conclusion than had his predecessor. Tucker recognized that under both common law and colonial statute, "the vestries in Virginia were a body politic, capable of purchasing and holding lands for the use of the ministers of their respective parishes; and capable of a perpetual succession." Moreover, all "the legal titles to all the glebe lands in Virginia" were "at the period of the Revolution vested in the vestries."[136] However, according to Tucker, the Revolution accomplished an immediate abolition of the established church, along with every other vestige of the monarchical government. Vestries were "subordinate parts of the body politic" and did not "continue to enjoy such parts of their ancient rights" as customary corporations once Virginia had declared independence.[137]

But did the legislature have the authority to revoke the 1784 Incorporation Act and to determine what happened to the property of a dissolved corporation? In short, yes. Tucker argued that the multiple statutes that had made the Episcopal Church into a private corporation and preserved its property had violated the provision for religious freedom and the prohibition against emoluments in Virginia's Declaration of Rights. Tucker concluded that the Glebe Acts of 1799 and 1802, which had repealed the earlier "repugnant" laws, should stand.[138] The legislature was fully within its rights to dissolve the vestries as corporations and to appropriate parish property for the use of the public at large. Doing so, in fact, reversed earlier unconstitutional abuse of property under the establishment. The Glebe Acts stood, and counties around the state began confiscating property.

For Virginians, Tucker's decision in *Turpin* was the final word on the matter of the glebes. But a decade later, another case about Virginian glebes wound its way through the courts, this time landing before the US Supreme Court. The same Episcopal Church whose incorporation had been the subject of Madison's 1811 veto once again found itself embroiled in controversy at the highest level of the federal government.

The case, *Terrett v. Taylor* (1815), resembled *Turpin v. Locket* in many ways. The key difference was jurisdiction. In *Terrett*, the vestry of Christ Church, in Washington, DC, sought to block the Fairfax County, Virginia, Overseers of the Poor from seizing its 517-acre glebe. Christ Church and its glebe lands had been part of Fairfax County in the colonial era but had been ceded by Virginia in 1801 to form the District of Columbia. The court found that the vestry held legal title to the glebe and determined that a county in Virginia had no right to seize land in Washington, DC.

Indeed, the decision could have just left it at that. However, Justice Story used his decision as an opportunity to offer a lengthy rebuke of Virginia's disestablishmentarian laws, which he believed had trounced private property rights and threatened the very foundation of all corporations.

Justice Story began his analysis by looking at the history of religious establishment in colonial Virginia. He concurred with Tucker that colonial Anglican vestries, churchwardens, and ministers of every parish had possessed distinct types of corporate power under common law. Here, Story diverged from Tucker and concluded that American independence had not undermined or modified parishes' legal status or their property. Instead, he contended that the status of parish property during the Revolution was altogether beside the point. The Virginia postrevolutionary legislature had incorporated the Episcopal Church in 1784 and guaranteed the Episcopal Church all parish property in six different statutes passed in 1776, 1777, 1784, 1785, 1786, and 1787.[139] With these many laws, the question of whether parishes' colonial property had become a public asset at the outset of the Revolution no longer mattered.

The justice then carefully examined the 1787 Repeal of Incorporation as well as the 1799 and 1802 laws that empowered the state to seize the glebes. He insisted that the laws incorporating the Episcopal Church and protecting its property had in no way contradicted the Virginia state constitution's principle of free exercise or its prohibition against emoluments. To Justice Story, it was Virginia's legislature that had violated the state constitution, "the principles of natural justice," "the fundamental laws of every free government," and "the spirit and the letter of the constitution of the United States."[140] After dwelling at great length on the unconstitutionality of Virginia's statutes, the justice ultimately relied on a much narrower jurisdictional rationale to uphold the vestry's claim that a county in Virginia could not seize lands outside the state. The vestry had won its case.

The Virginia Supreme Court of Appeals and the US Supreme Court provided contradictory answers to the fundamental questions that had divided Virginians for decades. Tucker's opinion in *Turpin* argued that the Revolution had dissolved the church's customary incorporation and destroyed its property claims. Afterward, the state had actively and unconstitutionally granted parish property to the newly founded Episcopal Church. Justice Story, on the other hand, concluded in *Terrett* that parochial corporate rights under common law endured the Revolution. The postrevolutionary state had incorporated the church, and the legislature could not simply repeal this charter and seize parish property without endangering the foundation of private property and corporate rights.

These opinions also endorsed distinct views about what type of state action constituted an "establishment" of religion. Tucker endorsed Virginia's stance that religious incorporation was a form of establishment and therefore unconstitutional in Virginia; Story rejected this interpretation and argued that if incorporation was available to all denominations, it was not an establishment. Neither decision framed its arguments as an appraisal of the lawfulness of Virginia's disestablishmentarian policies, but that was, in effect, what had happened. Tucker upheld the repeal of incorporation and the seizure of the glebes. The decision in *Terrett* set an important precedent for *Dartmouth College*, but as a matter of practical policy, the case had no significance outside of the District of Columbia. Tucker's ruling in *Turpin* stood in Virginia.[141]

THE FIRST Amendment declares, "Congress shall make no law respecting an establishment of religion." Nearly all the men who drafted this amendment and eventually voted to ratify it had lived under an established church. Catholic Marylander Daniel Carroll had been unable to vote, worship publicly, or be married by a priest of his own faith before the Revolution. James Madison, reared by his vestryman father and taught by a parish minister, witnessed persecution of his neighbors firsthand. Religious establishment was not an abstraction for this generation but a system of entrenched favoritism that afforded legal rights, civic powers, and public property to the state-sponsored church. By proscribing "an establishment of religion," they preserved a powerful memory of the established church in the Bill of Rights.

However, by the time the First Amendment was ratified in 1791, Maryland and Virginia had enacted radically different definitions of "establishment" in their state laws. A shared commitment to dismantling the Anglican Church did not necessarily lead Americans to embrace the same practical policies. At the outset of the Revolution, reformers in both states began overturning the powers of the Anglican Church one by one. Virginia and Maryland both rejected any form of religious assessment. Marylanders fought to secure incorporation for all Christian churches, whereas Virginians disparaged any religious incorporation as an example of legislative interference. Virginia counties confiscated and sold parish property, including glebes, churches, enslaved people, and silver. The legislature prohibited counties from using the proceeds to support "any religious purpose whatsoever." Maryland, like most states during this period, never went as far as seizing property. The two states' distinct policies reflected ideological fissures about what constituted an "establishment" of religion.

A similar array of contradictions and uncertainties was revealed in congressional debates about the First Amendment's implications for incorporation and the contention between the Virginia court's decision in *Turpin* and the US Supreme Court's opinion in *Terrett*. Moreover, in the following decades, the boundaries of an impermissible establishment continued to shift in both states. There was no single or stable definition of "establishment" in the wake of the Revolution, nor had Americans reached a firm consensus in the first decades of the nineteenth century. It was a developing, ambiguous, and contested concept that evolved in direct response to the policies pursued by reformers after 1783. Two hundred and fifty years after the Revolution, Americans are still questioning the boundaries of "an establishment."

# 5

# CONFISCATION IN REPUBLICAN VIRGINIA

In 1832, the Overseers of the Poor of Norfolk County asked the Virginia General Assembly to emancipate Billy Pugh, an enslaved man whose labor benefited the county welfare system for decades. Their petition explained that Pugh had "deported himself in the most respectful manner & having paid to the Poor by his heirs &c several thousand dollars."[1] The overseers made their math explicit by calculating the price of Pugh's freedom through his previous decades of labor and the continued enslavement of his children. The legislature assented on the condition that Pugh emigrate to Liberia. A week later, the county overseers received permission from the legislature to sell the rest of the county's enslaved community, including Pugh's family.

The plight of Pugh and the other men, women, and children enslaved by Norfolk County offers a new perspective on Virginia's disestablishment. Billy Pugh was just one of dozens of people enslaved by Norfolk County in the 1830s. This community was descended from three enslaved people who had been donated to Norfolk Parish as part of a charitable bequest in 1715 to support poor relief and the minister. Pugh and the rest of the enslaved community found themselves caught in the power struggle between church and state as three Episcopal parishes, the city of Norfolk, and Norfolk County all claimed their bodies and labor.[2] With the passage of the Glebe Act in 1802, the Virginia legislature handed control over this community to Norfolk County. Their forced separation and sale decades after the Glebe Act compel us to reconsider the course of disestablishment well into the nineteenth century. The Glebe Act did not simply wrest land from the church; the state also seized many types of property, including people held as property. White Virginians treated disestablishment as a material fight over public property; in this slave society, property meant people.

Another set of historical actors in this story, the Overseers of the Poor, also merit further investigation. Dismantling the established church required the legislature to overhaul local government, particularly the welfare system that Anglican parishes had long administered. Under Virginia's laws, county Overseers of the Poor surveilled the free Black community with increased powers and managed the process of glebe confiscation. The eagerness with which Norfolk's elected Overseers seized enslaved people and exploited them to fund public welfare shifts our focus away from the lofty language of constitutions, statutes, and high court decisions to consider how communities enacted disestablishment on the ground. The policy choices of local communities revealed an unwillingness to impose taxes or invest in costly public institutions. Schools and poorhouses funded by confiscated glebe property shuttered quickly when they proved expensive. Virginians discarded the old establishmentarian aims of enforcing Christian charity, maintaining communal consensus, and imposing moral oversight through local institutions. White public safety emerged as the unifying premise of republican government, the highest public good, and perhaps the only thing for which Virginian voters were willing to pay.

Ultimately, Virginians came to a new church-state settlement by seizing church property and power.[3] In the prolonged debates over disestablishment, Virginian evangelicals and their republican allies argued that glebes had been "common property, and designed for common benefit" and ought to have reverted to the public at large after disestablishment.[4] Though they invoked a universal public, there was no real consensus about who counted as "the public" or what constituted the public good. How would public welfare under republican government differ from the colonial Anglican parish system? Whom should public spending benefit? Should the state subsidize robust public services or prioritize keeping taxes low? Disestablishment was hammered out in the concrete choices over using common resources, and that process forged a new definition of the public good rooted in racial hierarchy. While debates over disestablishment were fought in the high-minded register of fundamental rights, material motives animated many of the fiercest conflicts. Disestablishment in the Chesapeake was as much a material process as an ideological one, and white Virginians argued that property rights were an essential component of religious freedom.

This chapter starts with the debates over confiscation of parish property and then looks at its implementation at the local level. Once counties were authorized to begin confiscating glebe property, popular debates continued over who could claim it, when it ought to be transferred, and what, if anything, still belonged to the Episcopal Church. Then, it turns to the reform of the public welfare system in the absence of an established church. Elected secular officials—county Overseers of the Poor—assumed responsibility for welfare and glebe confiscation while also gaining powers to supervise and control free people of color. Nineteenth-century white Virginians wove together glebe confiscation, poor relief, and racial surveillance under the banner of communal welfare. In the end, their choices revealed that racial hierarchy was the animating principle behind Virginia's policies over church property.[5]

## Property Confiscation Under the Glebe Act

When Virginia's highest court affirmed the Glebe Act in *Turpin v. Locket* (1804), it unleashed a sprawling process of property seizure across the state. The public officials tasked with implementing glebe confiscation were the Overseers of the Poor. In 1786, Virginia's legislature transferred responsibility for the welfare system from vestries to these new county officials. Overseers of the Poor were elected in every county and vested with "the power and authority" previously given to churchwardens and vestries to distribute poor relief, arrange the indenture of orphans, and punish vagrancy and bastardy.[6] Unlike vestries and churchwardens, the county Overseers lacked religious affiliation. In an adroit act of decontextualization, the legislature took what had long been ecclesiastical duties rooted in the established church's moral prerogative, stripped them of any religious association, and reinstated them as part of republican government. This overhaul of welfare was the practical counterpart to the more famous "Act for Establishing Religious Freedom," passed at the same legislative session, which abstractly guaranteed nonpreferential treatment for "all" Virginians regardless of their religion.[7] In practice, the state took on the church's traditional role of providing for the poor but reframed this responsibility as a secular public service.

Under the terms of the 1802 Glebe Act, confiscation proceeded on a parish-by-parish basis, as did decisions over how to spend the funds. Localities were free to use their glebe funds as they saw fit, so long as none of the money went to support "any religious purpose whatsoever." In counties with multiple parishes, each parish could independently direct their glebe funds.

Fifteen glebes had been sold before the passage of the Glebe Act in 1802 in vacant parishes without an active vestry or incumbent rector.[8] After the Glebe Act was upheld by the state's highest court in *Turpin v. Locket,* Overseers of the Poor in every county assumed authority to collect the proceeds from these sales.[9] In the decade after *Turpin,* counties appropriated another fifty-two glebes. By 1820, eighty-one glebes had been seized by counties, leaving just fourteen glebes in the hands of Episcopalians. Parishes that retained an inducted rector or could prove their glebe property came from private donations were able to avoid the initial flurry of confiscation. Slowly, though, even these glebes were seized and sold. In some cases, courts were unwilling to uphold parish claims in the face of local opposition, while elsewhere vestries declined to continue litigation to secure their glebes "because of the discord and unhappiness which would certainly attend it."[10] After the Civil War, only one glebe property remained in a parish's possession: the glebe of Suffolk Parish in Nansemond County.[11] (See the appendix for an index of all glebe sales, including their dates and their use after disestablishment.)

There are multiple ways to quantify the total amount of property confiscated statewide from parishes. The name of the 1802 law, "An act concerning the glebe lands and churches in this commonwealth," emphasized the *land* at stake, and scholars have likewise focused on the total acreage.[12] The average glebe farm was roughly 380 acres, so the seizure of Virginia's ninety-five glebes amounted to approximately 36,000 acres of land.[13] However, this figure underestimates the total area of land seized because counties often exceeded the precise terms of the act to claim churchyards, farms attached to poorhouses, and charitable endowments. Moreover, acreage alone does not covey the relative value of confiscated glebes, which often included fine homes, slave quarters, and access to waterways. A more laborious approach is to consider the money raised from the sale of seized parish property. Called "glebe funds," these discretionary accounts were managed by Overseers of the Poor and reflected the liquid capital raised from confiscation. Based on records from fourteen counties, the average glebe fund amounted to \$3,401. However, this average value obscures the significant variety between counties, which makes a statewide estimate challenging. These funds were often enough to cover the cost of poor relief for several years.[14] Indeed, at least three counties—Mathews, Essex, and Lancaster—still used these funds in the 1960s to support public housing and schools.[15]

## "Part of the Glebe": Enslaved People and Confiscation

But the greatest pitfall in calculating glebe funds either in terms of land or money is the erasure of enslaved people. Annexed legally to the glebe lands on which they labored, Black men and women were held in bondage by the church and became county property after confiscation. Focusing only on land obscures the lives of these men and women, and a key theme of this book is to restore their place in the history of disestablishment. Extant records show that Virginia's counties seized at least seventy-five enslaved persons from just nine of Virginia's ninety-five parishes. This figure represents a minimum and does not allow us to extrapolate any sort of average. At least half of Virginia's ninety-five colonial parishes held enslaved people, but it is difficult to gauge how this population changed between 1776 and 1804.[16] Many enslaved people self-emancipated during the war, and institutional record-keeping shows significant gaps in this period.[17] An ad placed in the *Norfolk Gazette and Publick Ledger* in 1807 exemplifies the difficulty in tracking the public confiscation of enslaved men and women held by parishes.[18] The notice claimed that two men, Jemmy and Jeffery, who had been sold "as part of the Glebe property" had fled to the Norfolk or Hampton area.[19] The ad ran for several months, which suggests the pair managed to evade recapture. The Christ Church Parish vestry book contains no record of Jemmy and Jeffery's purchase or labor, nor did the Overseers of the Poor mention them in their accounts.[20] We only know of their existence because they escaped. Their absence from any sort of institutional record cautions scholars about the difficulty of tracking confiscations of enslaved people.

Enslaved people were treated as "appurtenances" to glebe lands, which meant that legally they were attached to the land on which they lived and labored. By authorizing Overseers of the Poor to seize "all [glebe] lands and appurtenances," the Glebe Act allowed counties to seize both acreage and enslaved people. The willingness of the legislature to countenance these appropriations underscored the republican appetite to make enslaved property more easily transferable. By divorcing enslaved people from the church lands on which they had labored for generations, both could be sold more easily. The state signaled its view that parish donations were a holdover of the colonial era, and thus they no longer needed to heed their instructions. In many ways, this move paralleled the end of entail and the reclassification of enslaved people as chattel rather than real estate in Virginia's 1792 slave code.[21]

Parish slavery inflamed local tensions during confiscation. Part of this rancor reflected the tremendous monetary value of enslaved people as property, especially as the purchase price of enslaved people rose sharply during the early nineteenth century.[22] But the urgency of these disputes, even after the passage of the Glebe Act, also reflected the intrinsic tension of trying to treat people as property.[23] Enslaved people could resist, escape, fall ill, or act in myriad other ways to undermine their perceived value. On the other hand, an enslaved woman might bear children or young people might acquire valuable skills and begin to earn more as hired laborers. County Overseers' legal contortions to hasten the confiscation of enslaved people exposed the ideological contradiction inherent in claiming property rights in persons that enslavement could not erase.

In Halifax County, near the North Carolina border, the passage of the Glebe Act did nothing to quell a long-simmering conflict over the Antrim Parish glebe and the enslaved family of five who lived and labored there. A petitioning war over the glebe property stretched back to the 1780s as evangelical congregations, county officials, the parish vestrymen, and their minister all claimed ownership of the parish property. Following passage of the Glebe Act in 1802, the Halifax County Overseers of the Poor expressed their "great satisfaction" with the law because they mistakenly thought it would allow them to seize the glebe immediately.[24] However, Antrim Parish still had an inducted minister, the Rev. Alexander Hay, whose freehold rights to the glebe would extinguish only upon his death or resignation. The Halifax Overseers of the Poor did not wish to wait.

One available legal route was to argue that the minister, Alexander Hay, was no longer the rightful rector of the parish and thus had lost his tenured rights to the glebe property.[25] County officials accused Hay of not conducting divine services at all the parish chapels and "abandon[ing] their interests both temporal and spiritual." They argued he had failed as a "preacher of the gospel" and had "so far prostituted his holy calling" that he had surrendered his legal standing as rector of the parish. This petition called on the state to apply and interpret canon law to police the clergy, a request that flatly ignored the stated boundary between church and state.[26] Because parish rectors maintained their freehold rights under the traditional framework of establishmentarian laws, the Glebe Act left the door open to using these same laws to dispossess them of those rights.

The Overseers argued their case in the language of abstract rights, but their petition revealed a fixation with the enslaved couple and their three children. The petition hardly made mention of the glebe land itself. The Overseers accused Hay of leaving the glebe and "conveying the slaves along with him" and of "vainly pretending he acquired title to" the enslaved family and claiming he owned them "independent of all control." They complained of "abuses, to which said property may be liable" on the minister's watch. The Overseers' concerns over the enslaved family's purported movements underscored the risks of enslaved people escaping or moving freely, a message likely to resonate with the white legislators hearing their petition. Thus, the county officials suggested that Hay had proved himself untrustworthy and ought to be dispossessed of the glebe immediately before the public lost its valuable investment in human chattel.[27]

In rebuttal, the Antrim vestry and minister sermonized on the sanctity of property rights and reasserted the parish's claim to the enslaved family. Reverend Hay insisted that he had never moved the family off the glebe, let alone out of the county. He admitted that his claim extended only to "the use and benefit of them while he continues minister of Antrim Parish" but argued that "he cannot be disposesse[d] [of the enslaved people] without a violation of the rights of property and the common rights of a citizen." Hay and the vestry argued the Overseers had attempted to "violate the most sacred of all rights and to commence the most unjustifiable of all persecutions" in the guise of a "respect for right." When invoking the most "sacred of all rights," Hay and the vestry were, of course, referring to their property rights—and more specifically to their right to human property.

The Episcopalians flipped the familiar script on evangelicals and now claimed the mantle of persecuted Christians for themselves. Hay confessed that "an immense majority" in Halifax County had left the Episcopal Church and stood "against them." But he insisted that the parish "will never concede that any majority can trample on the constitutional rights of the minority." For Hay and the vestrymen, the struggle was a test of whether the legislature would bow to "the capricious and arbitrary will" of the majority or defend a citizen's right to his private property.[28] The parish declared that the legislature was not just bound by the state constitution but by "the gospel of Jesus Christ" and "the purest morality . . . never [to] remove that rock on which the church so founded; but that it will regard as sacred and inviolable those rights which are ours by the laws of the land, by the original laws of society, and by the equal laws of God." This statement intertwined republicanism and Christianity and made the absolute protection of private property an expression of divine, natural, and civil law. And, of course, this invocation of natural and divine right sought to bolster their claim to own people as property.[29]

Both sides in Halifax barely mentioned the glebe lands; their focus was squarely on the enslaved family. Their dueling petitions contained no concern for the well-being of this family but only their value as a material asset. While the law treated enslaved people as "appurtenances" to glebe lands, the community's preoccupation with the family underscored the absurdity of theoretically "attaching" people to land; land cannot escape or depart, but people can. The dehumanizing language of use, possession, acquisition, and benefit was undermined at every turn by the reality that enslaved people were, in fact, people. The parties' apparent urgency reflected the high monetary value of enslaved people and the inherent vulnerability of holding persons as property.

Hay and the parish vestry were also indignant that a county or a state would attempt to evaluate his performance as minister, something "amenable only to his own church" and not "under the cognizance of the General assembly of Virginia, or of the petitioners, the mass of whom . . . are in the interests of the Baptists." Hay defended the institutional independence of the Episcopal Church, but his impassioned argument also belied a strict separation of religion and government.[30] In the same petition, he implored the legislature to heed the Gospels as much as statutory law in respecting his property rights. But he differentiated between the legislature superintending ecclesiastical institutions and enforcing Christian principles; he rejected the former and extolled the latter.[31]

The state refused to intervene. Hay lived until 1819, when he apparently died while on a voyage for his health.[32] One can easily imagine the fury of Halifax's Baptists as the ailing rector traveled abroad while the glebe and enslaved community remained out of reach. One can likewise recognize, as none of the petitioners at the time did, the vulnerability and fear of the enslaved family left behind in Halifax and surrounded by neighbors eagerly awaiting any chance to seize them and their home. In 1820, the Overseers of the Poor swiftly sold the family and land for the sum of $6,682.25. There are no records of what happened to the enslaved family or whether any managed to stay together after being sold.

The dispute over the family enslaved by Antrim Parish reminds us of the predicament of enslaved people treated as the spoils of disestablishment. It also shows how disputes over property shaped the postrevolutionary church-state relationship. Each side framed the dispute as a test of their constitutional rights to religious freedom and property. For the Baptists, only state appropriation of the glebe would uphold the "true meaning of the Constitution" and deliver true religious liberty. To Hay and other Episcopalians, protecting the glebe would guarantee that their property rights and religious freedom did not "exist only in name" but were secured under the state constitution. Virginia's legislature did not intercede to divest Hay or other incumbent ministers of their glebes, and this precedent of noninterference mattered. The state's refusal to pass judgment on the spiritual fitness of ministers is an important legacy of the fights over parish property in the early nineteenth century.

## Property Seizure Beyond the Glebes

While the Glebe Act authorized Overseers of the Poor to claim glebe property, including land and enslaved men and women, the law expressly protected other property—"private donations," as well as "churches, and the property therein contained, [and] the church-yards."[33] In practice, counties frequently ignored these exemptions and seized reserved property anyway. The ruins of the old Berkley Parish Church in Spotsylvania were sold by the parish vestry for $120 in 1819. The buyer demolished the church and carted off "every part of it that was of any use."[34] Before the parish vestry could invest the funds in building a new sanctuary, however, county officials successfully petitioned the legislature and collected the proceeds from the sale. Under the strict terms of the Glebe Act, the Overseers had no claim to the property, but the legislature approved their petition anyway. Incidents like this blurred the boundary between seizable and reserved property under the law and reinforced a popular belief that all parish property did, in fact, belong to the public.

Counties also went after valuable communion silver, a source of lingering bitterness among Episcopalians. Silver chalices and plates were liturgical objects essential to the worship practices of Episcopalians but were derided by some evangelicals who saw them as idolatrous holdovers of Catholicism. William Meade, who served as Bishop of the Episcopal Diocese of Virginia from 1841 to 1862, wrote in 1857, "There is no part of the conduct of the opponents of the Episcopal Church which appears so unamiable and unjustifiable as that in regard to the Church plate. . . . The framers and supporters of the [Glebe Act] would have felt themselves insulted, if that insinuation have been made at the time of its passage."[35] Meade was wrong on this point, though. Within a few years of the Glebe Act's passage, the state gave permission to at least ten counties to claim communion silver, church bells, books, and other non-glebe property.[36] For instance, less than a decade after selling the Raleigh Parish glebe, the Amelia County Overseers of the Poor began hunting for ways to lower the cost of poor relief. In 1814, they sent an appeal to the legislature asking for permission to sell the "Plate, Bells, Books and other ornaments" that had belonged to the parish.[37] Their petition explained that the parish property had been acquired "when we were under the British government for the use of the episcopal religion," painting this parish wealth as ill-gotten gains and vestiges of the old monarchial system. Selling the valuable pieces of church silver would "be of great relief to the inhabitants of this county if the proceeds thereof was to be applied toward lessening the county levy or poor rates." The legislature approved Amelia's petition, and the county advertised the silver in the *Virginia Argus.*[38] The following year, the county Overseers established a poorhouse, partially paid for using the £119.18.6 raised from the sale of the church bell, communion silver, books, and other church furnishings.

Some congregants challenged county efforts to confiscate their parish silver. In Hanover County, the matriarch of one of Virginia's most prominent families, Frances Burwell Page Nelson Berkeley, moved the communion plate to her home for safekeeping after the death of the parish minister in 1804.[39] The silver had been a private donation to the parish and bore an inscription from its benefactor, which made it plainly obvious the plate could not be confiscated under the Glebe Act. Nonetheless, the Hanover County Overseers of the Poor sent deputies to her home who ordered Berkeley to hand over the parish silver. The Old Lady of

Hanover, as she was fondly called, flatly refused. Instead, she sent a note back to the Overseers that declared, "Tell the Gentlemen to come and take it." Her challenge went unmet.[40]

Another source of heated conflict over church property concerned charitable donations made for the support of poor relief. As discussed in chapter 2, wealthy donors in the colonial era often bequeathed land and enslaved people to parishes to fund poor relief and lower the annual levy. Treated as expressions of Christian charity and personal piety, these private bequests often prohibited the vestry from ever selling any of the enslaved persons or their descendants. Benefactors expected that enslaved communities would grow and thus endow the parish with generations of enslaved Black labor. The sea change of revolution and disestablishment complicated the issue—if the public administration of welfare services was transferred from parishes to counties, to whom did these public-spirited bequests belong? The Glebe Act protected private donations from seizure but did not address whether charitable gifts specifically made for poor relief fell under this protection. The murky status of colonial charitable donations showed just how profoundly disestablishment had reshaped the mechanics of local government.

In one of these cases, petitioners in Nansemond County angled to seize land and dozens of enslaved Black men and women from Suffolk (Lower) Parish immediately after the passage of the Glebe Act. The original donor gave instructions in 1731 that his bequest should support a free school and left instructions for "those gentlemen vestrymen" to "have the management of the disposal of the rents yearly, and the hire of my negroes aforesaid forever," as well as his house and books.[41] These instructions rested on the assumption that vestries and churchwardens existed in perpetuity and exercised corporate powers to hold and manage real and personal property (see chapter 2). In their challenge to the colonial legacy, antebellum petitioners did not challenge how the vestry held this property, nor did they argue that this endowment ought not to exist in perpetuity.[42] Instead, they argued that in the wake of disestablishment, the vestry was no longer the *appropriate* manager. The colonial testator, Yeates, "had no Idea" that the Revolution was on the horizon.[43] They argued that his gift was never "intended to be confined, to any particular sect persuation or society of people whatever, but was designed for the general & mutual advantage of every description of persons residing within the said bounds." Allowing the parish to retain this property was in fact "contrary to the true principle of Justice & totally inconsistent & repugnant to the true meaning and intent" of the bequest. County officials argued that revolutionary disestablishment had rendered his instructions obsolete, though not his altruistic intent. According to these petitioners, the only way to honor the donor's intent was to transfer this property from church to state. The legislature agreed and incorporated trustees (to be elected by white freeholders) to manage the school and its property moving forward.[44] The following year, the school's trustees earned more than £48 from hiring out nineteen enslaved people, including six children.[45]

The contest over this bequest reflected two distinct processes at work: the reform of public services as well as a redefinition of the "public" itself in the wake of disestablishment. By confiscating church buildings, silver, land, and enslaved people from parishes, counties dismantled the established church by taking its resources. The reallocation of this property cemented a new, nonsectarian definition of the public good in which welfare was an obligation of republican government to its citizens rather than the duty of a Christian state. Who counted as a "citizen," of course, was also being redrawn in this period, as whiteness replaced property-holding as the *sine qua non* of civic belonging.

## Popular Appropriation

Not all parish property was formally confiscated by state officials. The Episcopal Church had won the right to retain its churches, religious ornaments, and private donations, but the denomination could not maintain all these assets. As the number of parishioners dwindled, Virginia's parishes were saddled with too many churches and inadequate funds to maintain them all. Churches like St. Margaret's Parish Church in Caroline County, which had stood abandoned since the Revolution, were looted for valuable furnishings. By the nineteenth century, the old building was rumored to be haunted by the Devil himself. After leaving a militia muster one night, two boys decided to confront Satan and drive him out of the old church. Both drunk, they hatched a plan for one to stand guard by the entrance while the other entered the sanctuary brandishing a pole. Once inside the boys did in fact find a horned beast: an old bull who had taken up residence in the building. Provoked by the intruders, the animal charged at the boys and carried the unlucky guard out of the door. From then on,

A wood engraving from 1880 depicts the overgrown state of Blandford Church in Petersburg, Virginia. Completed in 1737, this parish church was abandoned in the early nineteenth century and deteriorated over the following decades. *Blandford Church, Virginia,* 1880. (Courtesy of the New York Public Library)

St. Margaret's was known as Old Bull Church.[46] This rumored encounter seemed to expose local anxieties that the decaying state of parish churches reflected not just a political change but a rapid fall from godliness.

Abandoned or underutilized churches were also ransacked for private gain. Hungars Parish Church in coastal Northampton County lost its organ to fishermen who melted down its pipes into weights for fishing nets.[47] The gilded altar of the St. Thomas Parish Church was torn down and turned into furniture, and its gravestones were removed and used as mill grindstones.[48] The grand Wicomico Parish Church had been stripped for parts: its windows, communion table, doors, bricks, and marble were long gone.[49] The authority of the established church had been expressed through and reinforced by its grand churches and extensive property. Popular destruction of these worship spaces and appropriation of their sacred ornaments expressed the establishment's fall from grace better than any single law or court decision.

In other instances, evangelical congregations in Virginia moved into derelict parish churches, often without formal agreements. Tillotson Parish Church in Buckingham County, for example, was unoccupied after the Revolution. A Baptist congregation began using the church in the early nineteenth century and still worships there today.[50] Likewise, Mattaponi Baptist Church in King and Queen County was originally the lower church of St. Stephen's Parish. Baptists from the Dover Association began using "the little brick church" in 1828 and later claimed ownership. In these instances, there was no formal transfer of title; rather, squatters' rights eventually prevailed. Because these arrangements did not rely on an act of legislature, they sidestepped the legal question of appropriating parish property for religious purposes. In other instances, some parish churches became "free churches," which were shared by multiple denominations.[51] Former parish spaces often underwent significant renovation when evangelical congregations began worshipping there. Baptists had long criticized the Anglican Church for its finery and pomp, which were seen as an expression of covetousness. One account referred to Episcopalians as "votaries of Mammon and of Belial" who worshiped "idols."[52] A group of inhabitants in Caroline County seeking to take over a former parish church noted that any objections to their plans betrayed the "popish" and "idolatrous habit of transforming our veneration from spirit to matter."[53] Treating former parish sanctuaries as anything other than buildings amounted to the "transubstantiation of brick and mortar into holiness." This evident derision of parish churches underscores that the stripping and destruction of parish churches was not just an expedient way to raise cash or lay claim to a worship space but was very much a theological statement in rejection of Anglican material practices. Evangelicals removed velvet, gilded altars, and other pieces of material finery, and this iconoclasm cleansed the "popish."[54] The removal of these objects sanctified the space in the eyes of its new occupants and underscored continued antipathy toward Episcopalian finery.

This widespread appropriation of parish property reflected a popular settlement that differed from the black letter of the law. Parish property had been envisaged as an investment in the public good and was amassed using communal resources. While the Glebe Act had reserved this property to the Episcopal Church, ordinary people still viewed these spaces as rightfully belonging to the public at large. As the religious affiliation of Virginians changed rapidly, Presbyterian, Methodist, and Baptist congregations felt entitled to claim underutilized churches as their own, even in violation of state law.

## Education and the New Public Good

Once counties had seized parish property, what did they do with it? The adage to "follow the money" proves instructive. About 34 percent of glebe proceeds went to education, and a handful of counties funded other public projects.[55] But the vast majority of counties spent the proceeds on poor relief, either by funding the annual budget for the Overseers of the Poor or by constructing poorhouses. The longevity of these projects is just as important in discerning public priorities as their sector or scale. Many of the original appropriations for education or poorhouses never came to fruition, and other public institutions folded after only a few years. There was almost no appetite for public spending once glebe funds ran out. This retreat from public institutions revealed that after independence, Virginia's counties operated very differently from colonial parishes, which had raised large sums annually to fund their spiritual and social work. Republican local government was leaner and less engaged in the daily lives of white Virginians by contrast.

A third of glebe funds were earmarked for the support of educational institutions. In the colonial era, parish ministers had often doubled as teachers, and they ran the few schools that existed in colonial Virginia.[56] Disestablishment left the state without its traditional means of schooling, which was a particular source of concern given widespread republican assumptions that an enlightened citizenry would be a bulwark of the new republic.[57] Despite the public discourse about the importance of education, Virginians did a remarkably poor job supporting public education after the Revolution.[58] Thomas Jefferson had pursued statewide public education twice, once in 1779 and again in 1817. He failed both times. Resistance to any form of direct taxation stymied efforts to organize a statewide school system. The opposition to funding public education manifested a deep conservativism running through Virginian republicanism and highlighted how deeply fault lines of class cut through the state's white male citizenry.[59] The value placed on personal property led many republicans to reject any proposals that required high levels of public spending. Elite Virginians argued that if they had to pay taxes to support public education while also educating their own children privately, it would be a form of double taxation and an attack on the "essence of property."[60] Glebe funds were alluring precisely because they offered a way to establish schools without raising taxes.

Glebe funds ultimately supported a wide variety of educational projects: universities, fee-charging academies, and free schools. Boosters of all three types of schools claimed their institutions would prove essential to the success of the republic, but differences between these institutions reveal the profoundly divergent impulses of antebellum republicanism. The most famous educational institution funded by glebe confiscation is the University of Virginia. The project grew out of two of Thomas Jefferson's defining passions—religious disestablishment and education. When Jefferson first wrote about disestablishment in 1776, he recommended that the state seize glebe lands as public property.[61] The thirty years of bitter legal and political fighting described in chapters 3 and 4 finally implemented Jefferson's revolutionary proposal. What became the University of Virginia started out as a far more modest proposal for a local school. Before the Revolution, Albemarle County had been divided into two parishes, St. Anne's and Fredericksville. In 1802, St. Anne's Parish did not have an incumbent minister, and the county immediately came into the proceeds from the sale of its glebe under the Glebe Act.[62] The following year, the legislature granted a charter to a local school, Albemarle Academy, funded by the sale of the land, but the project soon stalled.[63] The rector of Fredericksville Parish, Matthew Maury, died in 1808, and the glebe was sold the following year.[64] In 1811, the assembly granted permission for Albemarle's Overseers of the Poor to pool the funds from the sale of both glebes, invest them in the Bank of Virginia, and use the interest to fund "public schools in the said county" for "male and female child[ren]."[65] But again, this project failed to get off the ground, and Albemarle Academy never opened its doors.

The plan finally gained momentum after Thomas Jefferson joined the board of trustees in 1814.[66] Within a few months, it became clear that Jefferson and his fellow trustees were abandoning the original proposal for a local school and instead maneuvering to open a university comparable to the "best seminaries in other countries." Always a bellwether of republican contradictions, Jefferson recognized the importance of supporting public institutions to educate both the wealthy and the poor, but he framed their needs as distinct projects. He hoped the legislature would eventually provide a "more promising" system of primary education in the state, but he declared that "our Institution . . . shall have nothing to do" with this "1st grade of education."[67] Educating the "laboring" class may have been important, but it was not as important to Jefferson as establishing a leading university.[68] Jefferson's college would enroll only those "advanced" students who had received adequate primary education through private means. Though the former president had written about the importance of public education for all classes, the university he founded catered only to elite, white men. Jefferson complained of resistance to his plan from "some of the people of Albemarle" and of the difficulty he found "to eradicate the idea that it is a local thing, a mere Albemarle academy. I endeavor to convince them it is a general seminary of the sciences meant for the use of the state."[69] Not all residents were happy that plans for a local academy had been scrapped in favor of a state university they would likely never attend. The University of Virginia reflected not only the most ambitious but also the most exclusive institution built from glebe funds in the state.

Eventually the assembly chartered a new entity, Central College, which received $3,195 from Albemarle County's glebe funds.[70] This sum was a tiny fraction of the total budget needed to open the school, but it was enough seed money to purchase 183 acres and begin a fundraising campaign.[71] The university's backers declared that using the glebe proceeds to support the college was the best "application of those ancient acquisitions . . . more analogous to their original objects, and equally for the benefit of all interested in them."[72] This statement artfully reframed the glebe lands through a republican lens that would convert the old glebe lands into an investment in the common good fit for a new Virginia. Perhaps most analogous between this proposal and the original glebe system was the use of language of universal benefit in the face of stark exclusion on the basis of race, class, and gender.

In 1819, Central College became the University of Virginia.[73] In place of a chapel, Jefferson's university featured a library; it did not employ professors of divinity but professors of ethics. Jefferson wrote in emphatic terms about the importance of education for the success of the new republic—"Kno[w]lege is power . . . kno[w]lege is safety, and . . . kno[w]lege is happiness"—and proclaimed that providing the public with an opportunity for education was "the law of duty in every society of free agents, where every one has equal right to judge for himself."[74] The established church had imbued monarchy with divine authority and regulated society through religious doctrine. Now, there existed a republican university that equipped men to rule themselves, or at least certain white men who could afford to attend. Jefferson regarded the founding of UVA as one of his greatest accomplishments and hoped the university would remain part of his enduring legacy.[75] For Jefferson, the material dismantling of the established church secured Virginia's conversion from monarchy to republic.

Jefferson's university is an exceptional example of what happened to glebe funds, and the success of the project owed much to the determination and eminence of its primary supporter. Far more representative are the examples drawn from Caroline County, where residents were sharply divided about how to use their glebe funds. There were four parishes in Caroline County—St. Mary's, St. Margaret's, Drysdale, and St. Asaph's—and each parish used its glebe fund for different projects.

The first was Rappahannock Academy. In 1804, the inhabitants of St. Mary's Parish petitioned under the terms of the Glebe Act to sell their glebe, and in 1808 the legislature granted them a charter for a new school.[76] The new project was spearheaded by Caroline native John Taylor, a wealthy planter who had served in the Virginia Assembly and the US Senate. Taylor believed that educational institutions, not established religion, could best mold public morality and was an outspoken critic of religious establishment throughout his public career.[77] To Taylor, the glebe funds could serve no higher public purpose than educating young, virtuous male citizens. Soon after receiving their charter, Taylor and the school's other trustees tried to convince parishioners to sell the parish church for use as a new school building. The church needed major renovations, which the parishioners could not afford, and the trustees argued that under their plan, the "edifice may be saved from ruin and publick worship may be more effectually preserved."[78] The building would serve as a schoolhouse during the week, and parishioners could gather there for worship on Sundays. The parishioners agreed and sent yet another petition to the state legislature for permission to sell their church building to the school. This legislative deference underscored the widespread view that all parish property, including churches, was public, no matter the terms of the Glebe Act.

In their appeal, the trustees and parishioners sidestepped the question of whether it would violate the Glebe Act and instead focused on practical benefits.[79] The proceeds from selling the glebe would not cover the cost of a new school building even "one third of the size" of the large brick sanctuary. The St. Mary's petitioners argued their willingness to sell and renovate the church underscored the extent to which they were not treating it as a sanctified space. To the school's trustees, professors, and pupils, it would be just a school. However, the petitioners also tipped their hand by acknowledging that their plan was "in the service of knowledge, virtue, and religion" and would save their church from complete "destruction."[80] The terms of the Glebe Act may have formally prohibited using funds for any "religious purposes," but local petitions like those sent in support of Rappahannock Academy found a way of benefiting both religion and government.

The academy's trustees began purchasing real estate adjacent to Mount Church and had secured four hundred acres by 1813.[81] The acquisition of this much land underscored that Rappahannock Academy would either lease its grounds for additional income or directly cultivate the lands for its own support, which hewed closely to the traditional glebe system. References to "the servants" throughout the school's subsequent records—a phrase often used in Virginian sources to refer to enslaved persons—strongly indicates the latter possibility and suggests that the school owned or hired enslaved people who labored on its grounds.[82] When the school opened its doors in 1813, it remained an institution in service of a "public" good predicated on racial slavery.

Rappahannock Academy was not a public school in the modern understanding of the term. Virginia would not establish a statewide system of public schools that were free to attend and would receive state funding until 1845.[83] Still, the academy was a public institution, endowed with public resources at the behest of the voters and incorporated by the legislature. The school's trustees promised to open an accessible school where fees would be low enough that "no family need despair of being" turned away. In pitching its affordability, the trustees emphasized the public nature of the county-funded school and linked their proposal to the larger project of educating citizens to participate in "fair and free government."[84] In reality, the academy only served students who were white, male, and could afford to pay. For a year of lessons in writing, arithmetic, and literature, pupils paid $21, plus extra fees for boarding and supplies. The fees were high enough to have excluded the sons of skilled laborers, whose income was likely around $10 a month.[85] Though purportedly founded on principles of accessibility, the school exhibited a narrow definition of whom public institutions ought to serve.

Rappahannock Academy's trustees had been eager for all of Caroline's parishes to support the new school, but the other three refused to join the project.[86] The residents of St. Margaret's Parish petitioned the legislature to use their glebe fund to establish "a free school or Academy in the said Parish on the Lancastrean [*sic*] plan."[87] Introduced in English poorhouses in the 1790s, the Lancasterian method of teaching promised a means of affordably educating numerous students at once.[88] This model reached the United States in the first decade of the nineteenth century and became popular in almshouses and free schools. A free school was an expensive proposition, and the parish requested permission from the state to hold a lottery to augment their glebe fund. No records survive from the project, and it seems unlikely the school lasted more than a few years, if it ever opened at all. By 1821, the residents of St. Margaret's petitioned to sell off two of the parish's decrepit churches. This time, they asked the Overseers of the Poor to use the proceeds for poor relief and suggested a free school was no longer in operation.[89] Academies funded by glebes may have encountered criticism for their exclusivity, but county free schools were targeted as too ineffective for their cost.

When faced with the choice of public education or lower taxes, Virginians chose lower taxes. At least six glebe-endowed schools were swiftly abandoned within a few years, as soon as glebe funds ran dry.[90] Like the residents of St. Margaret's, King George County had moved immediately after confiscation to use their glebe fund to establish a free school in 1811. And, like the residents of St. Mary's, they converted the old parish church into a school building. The petitioners in King George County voiced their ardent belief "that in a Republican Government, the greatest good will be obtained from the establishment of seminaries of learning, where the youthful mind may be early impressed with virtue and morality, and where the children of the poor as well as the rich may receive the benefits of Education."[91] The success of the republic depended on accessible education that empowered citizens to govern themselves. The residents received permission to convert the parish church into a schoolhouse and use the glebe fund to support the school. By turning the resources of their former parish to the project of public education, the community hoped to combat the entrenchment of a class system that threatened its republican principles.

However, only a few years later, the community struggled to keep funding the school. In 1815, they sent another petition to the legislature asking for "the adoption of some system which will ensure the instruction of the ignorant . . . to educate the masses of the people, elevate their minds to a just appreciation of their rights, enable them to govern themselves and be worthy to be trusted with the government of others."[92] Without adequate support for public schooling, the community feared that their school was in danger, and by extension, their self-governing republic at risk.

By 1829, the King George free school was dead in the water, and residents petitioned the legislature to dissolve the school's charter. They reported that "the school fund has become almost entirely exhausted—the school has been for a long period discontinued and all hope of its survival is now utterly relinquished—the building is fast falling into decay and will soon become an unsightly heap of ruins."[93] Unable to secure greater funding from the state or win local financial support, the school had not survived long. The county's residents disagreed about what should happen to the ruined property. One group of petitioners hoped the building could revert back to a church and be returned to the parish for worship; others hoped that it would be sold and the funds handed over to the Overseers of the Poor.[94] In either case, the project of free public education using the glebe funds had failed in King George, just as it had in Caroline County.

The confiscation of the glebes had been championed on the grounds that common property ought to provide common benefits. Likewise, the founders of schools argued for the importance of educating citizens for the good of the whole republic. But, despite this universalizing language, the expense of these undertakings quickly proved higher than Virginians would tolerate. While 30 percent of glebe funds went to education, this number tells us only part of the story about the success and longevity of these institutions. The glebe schools that survived, including the University of Virginia and Rappahannock Academy, charged fees for enrollment. When glebe funds proved too meager to support county institutions, communities abandoned these projects rather than raise taxes. Communities chose to stop investing in public institutions when the cost of these projects shifted to taxpayers. While the parochial glebe system had been built on a system of high parish levies and long-term investment in community institutions, republican Virginians largely turned away from this model in favor of lower taxes and fewer publicly funded institutions. Ultimately, these choices would leave the welfare of the public in the hands of private efforts and set the stage for the Second Great Awakening's many private benevolent institutions.

## Poor Relief

Most counties spent the proceeds from glebe sales on poor relief, which in turn lowered county taxes. While St. Mary's and St. Margaret's parishes had used their glebe funds to support Rappahannock Academy, the two other parishes in Caroline County—Drysdale and St. Asaph's—gave their glebe funds directly to the Caroline County Overseers of the Poor. The Caroline Overseers spent $16,857 between 1814 and 1817 to support between 140 and 245 people annually while Caroline's taxpayers avoided paying a poor levy.[95] Immediate tax abatement proved more attractive to many of Caroline's residents than investing in an academy or a free school. Some scholars suggested that glebe funds were "frittered away" and poorly managed.[96] This reproach, though, does not acknowledge that the right to control this property was a hard-fought ideological victory. The use of these funds as a form of tax abatement was a reimbursement for levies unwillingly paid each year to the established church and carried particular symbolic weight for non-Anglicans. The right to control private property reflected a particular republican definition of liberty. The choice to use their glebe funds as a small form of tax relief was a political act in defiance of the traditional system; it also curbed the budget and power of local government.

Many counties took over parochial poorhouses or built new ones as part of the postrevolutionary system of relief. Despite the failure of its colonial poorhouse, discussed in chapter 1, Augusta County opened another poorhouse in 1820 using some of its glebe funds. In an 1829 report to the legislature, the Augusta Overseers concluded that the average annual cost per pauper rose after the construction of the poorhouse, from $63 to $68, but the total cost of poor relief fell from $1,718 to $1,502.[97] The officials happily reported that the project had saved them money because fewer residents applied for relief knowing they would have to enter the poorhouse. Likewise, the Prince Edward County Overseers of the Poor related that the construction of the poorhouse had lowered the cost of public welfare by requiring anyone receiving public support to the live at the workhouse.[98] They acknowledged that the new system "excluded a number of worthy poor, who could with small aid from the public, make out very well from their own exertions on their little farms," but they nonetheless chose to maintain the residency requirement. While colonial vestries had been wary of the high cost of relief and sought to mitigate annual spending, they never imposed stringent residency requirements on parishioners who received relief. In fact, colonial poorhouses in Augusta and Lynnhaven Parishes failed to lower costs precisely because vestries never forced parishioners to move in, and parishes continued to provide out-of-door relief to numerous recipients. Nineteenth-century Overseers of the Poor proved less lenient. By 1829, the metric of a successful welfare institution was how little it cost to run.

Some local administrators expressed skepticism that public welfare institutions benefitted either society at large or the relief recipients themselves. In the colonial era, vestries had described the poor as "blessed" and poorhouses as "pious" projects that would allow poor people to become "Religious, Virtuous, & Industrious."[99] Now Gloucester County's Overseers defended their decision to close the county poorhouse by arguing that it did more "harm" than "good" because it was "impossible to prevent a good deal of vice, whenever this description of people are congregated. We are persuaded, that it would contribute more to the improvement of their morals to separate them as far as possible from each other."[100] The Halifax County Overseers declared that the system only served "to increase pauperism generally, and to perpetuate it in families."[101] Indeed, the residents of Norfolk complained in 1831 that their new poorhouse seemed "too comfortable."[102] They argued that a "respectable looking poorhouse is an evil" because it encouraged paupers "to indulge in idleness and laziness," whereas a "forbidding exterior" would dissuade anyone from remaining long on county support. These Virginians argued that poor relief should be made as humiliating and unpleasant as possible to deter people from seeking welfare, which would thereby lower taxes.[103]

Some Overseers of the Poor also lamented their inability to punish moral crimes, unlike in the colonial era when churchwardens could present parishioners to the court. The Botetourt County Overseers called attention to "drunkards . . . [who] are enemies to themselves and a pest to society. And from that class the poor are much increased. From drunkenness, the morals of society are much injured. . . . The law on the subject of drunkenness is never enforced."[104] Updated bastardy laws also put new emphasis on Overseers' forcing white fathers of bastard children to pay support and less emphasis on their punishing white mothers for a moral crime.[105] Whereas enforcing Christian morality had been built into the parochial relief system, the republican overseers operated without a religious mandate or the same legal authority. Their sense of resignation signaled a significant departure from the parish welfare system, which had made social welfare and public morality one and the same and dedicated significant resources to both under the aegis of establishment.[106]

## Race and Relief

While county Overseers moved away from punishing the immorality of white Virginians, they received increased authority over people of color. In 1804, though, the state updated the terms of the apprenticing system to ensure that Black apprentices would not learn to read or write, which set them apart from white children whose contracts typically required schooling.[107] Two years later, the state overhauled its slave code and invested Overseers of the Poor with additional responsibilities over enslaved and free Black Virginians. The updated legislation reflected the federal prohibition of the international slave trade after 1807 and empowered Overseers to sell any persons illegally brought into their counties. The law also amended the oath of office taken by all Overseers of the Poor to include the provision, "*I, A. B. do swear, that I will faithfully enforce the laws to prevent the importation of slaves.*"[108] The new slave code prohibited any manumitted person from staying in Virginia longer than twelve months and authorized the Overseers to sell those who defied this stipulation back into slavery. Wary of the increasing population of free people of color, state legislators hoped this policy would discourage manumission, and after 1806, the number of new manumissions dropped precipitously.[109] Scholars have shown that numerous manumitted Virginians chose to remain in the state in violation of the law, and these transgressions were overlooked at the discretion of the Overseers.[110] But the law had impact even when Overseers of the Poor refrained from using their new authority. By investing those in charge of poor relief and apprenticing with the additional power to remove free Black inhabitants from the state, the legislature effectively disincentivized Black Virginians from seeking public support. The threat of sale against family members or neighbors was likely enough to discourage needy Black inhabitants from applying for poor relief and catching the attention of the Overseers. In one fell swoop, white legislators and administrators were able to keep welfare costs down and reassert a racial hierarchy.

The relief system enforced racial hierarchy not only by largely excluding free Black Virginians from benefits but also by relying on enslaved labor to fund poor relief. Whether Overseers hired enslaved people or seized them from parishes, they carried on the parochial tradition of using enslaved labor to fund poor relief. These practices underscored that "the poor" who deserved relief were understood to be white, and their welfare was served through the institutional enslavement of Black Americans.

In 1829, the state began requiring counties to submit their poor relief accounts annually, and the legislature specifically requested information on the racial composition of welfare recipients. Poor relief had long been granted on a racial basis; colonial vestries had granted poor relief less frequently to Black and Native American petitioners. But though vestries often identified the race of individual relief recipients, they made no comprehensive effort to track payments by race. The push to standardize social services across the state departed from the older, parochial model, which had relied on personal bonds of reciprocity and deference between the vestry and parishioners. Moreover, this new requirement formalized racial boundaries and underscored increasing preoccupation with overseeing the free Black community.[111]

Because the state requested figures dating back thirty years, we can tell that most counties granted poor relief overwhelmingly to white recipients.[112] Between 1800 and 1811, Chesterfield County extended poor relief to 736 white persons and 5 free Black persons.[113] In the following eleven years, 341 white persons received relief, while no Black residents did. Pittsylvania reported 1,253 white recipients of relief and just 5 Black recipients between 1800 and 1830.[114] Over the same decades, the Overseers of Norfolk County gave assistance to 1,764 white persons and no Black residents.[115] While free people of color made up 7 percent of the state's residents in 1810, they made up a disproportionately low percentage of poor relief recipients.[116] The records give no indication of whether Black and white applicants for relief were rejected at the same rate or whether the system itself discouraged Black Virginians from requesting relief in the first place. By overwhelmingly excluding people of color from welfare services, counties denied these men and women the material advantages of civic community and reserved the privilege of the social safety net for white Virginians.

It was not just the legislature who tied race to poverty; popular rhetoric insinuated that the indigence of free Black Virginians made them a greater threat to white safety and security. This line of thought sharpened after Nat Turner's Rebellion, a slave revolt in Southampton, Virginia, in 1831 that shook the white South to its core.[117] Turner was a messianic figure who led a dozen enslaved men to rebel against their bondage, which left numerous white individuals dead in the process. White enslavers killed scores of innocent people of color in retaliation. The uprising was a turning point in Virginia and unleashed panic among white Virginians, who would go on to sell tens of thousands of enslaved people to the Lower South. The state legislature imposed even more drastic restrictions on the bodies, rights, and movement of free people of color. A petition sent from white inhabitants of Nansemond County immediately afterward urged the state to "remove" all free Black Virginians. The 1831 Nansemond petition declared that "the mistaken humanity of the people of Virginia, and of your predecessors, has permitted to remain in this Commonwealth a class of persons who are neither Freeman nor slaves." Free Black Virginians were caught in a liminal state, "by nature preclude[ed] . . . of privileges of the former: and the laws of the land do not hold them allowed to be reduced to the condition of the latter." This "ill-fated class" would

Published in a Richmond broadside, this woodcut of Nat Turner's Rebellion reflected and amplified the widespread fear among white Southerners following the events. *Horrid Massacre in Virginia*, 1831. (Courtesy of the Small Special Collections Library, University of Virginia)

always remain "of necessity, degraded, profligate, vicious, turbulent and discontented." The petitioners accused free Black Virginians of "pursuing no course of regular business, and negligent of everything like economy and husbandry" and included a wildly inflated statistic that free Black residents were "more frequently than Whites (probably in tenfold proportion) sustained by the charitable provisions of our poor laws."[118] These white citizens argued that the exclusion of free Black Virginians from the rights of freemen and the ranks of the enslaved made their penury unavoidable.[119]

Moreover, they insisted that the supposed dependence of Black Virginians not only made them "a burden on the community" but a threat to this slave society.[120] According to the Nansemond petitioners, free Black Virginians' reliance on public assistance and their very refusal to remain in "servitude to business" stoked "impracticable hopes in the minds of those who are even more ignorant and unthinking," by which they meant the enslaved. This example purportedly gave enslaved people a "dangerous agency" and encouraged their "schemes, wild and visionary." Thus, these white petitioners argued that the peace, happiness, and safety of "society" could only be secured by removing all free Black persons from the state. This petition rested on a bifurcated racial logic that left no room for Black men and women who were free. The lone solution, in the minds of these petitioners, was for free Black Virginians to settle "in other lands [so that] they may become an orderly, sober, industrious, moral, enlightened and Christian community: and be the happy instruments of planting and dispersing these blessings over a barbarous and benighted continent." Poor relief and removal were closely interrelated in the popular anxieties of white Virginians about controlling enslaved people.

For white Virginians, the very presence of free Black residents destabilized the racial hierarchy on which slavery rested. Efforts to prevent free people of color from receiving poor relief not only made their lives as difficult as possible but discouraged any class-based alliance between white and free Black people.[121] Colonial vestries had closely monitored the behavior of Black and white people alike. The republican relief system operated on a larger, countywide basis and moved away from relying on bonds of deferential reciprocity or divine duty. Antebellum overseers stopped enforcing Christian morality and oversaw a system that prioritized racial order and lowering costs above all else.

## Absolute Property Rights in Persons

By the second decade of the nineteenth century, Overseers of the Poor were not satisfied with wresting control of enslaved people from parishes to support the traditional relief system; they also wanted the absolute right to sell them. Parochial bequests often prohibited the sale of any enslaved persons or their descendants indefinitely, but antebellum overseers began seeking permission from the legislature to contravene these terms and gain absolute property rights over these communities. Subsequent legal challenges raised questions about how far nineteenth-century Virginians would go to uphold a colonial donor's intent in light of the revolutionary upheavals that had transformed Virginia's religious institutions, laws, and government. In this reading, disestablishment was a radical, legally destabilizing process that threw long-standing property arrangements into question. Like common-law incorporation and royal charters, charitable bequests also came under attack in republican Virginia. Removing parishes from a position of public authority and transferring traditional welfare services from church to state had already called into question the terms of donations made for poor relief. The dismantling of establishment handed Overseers of the Poor and other public institutions the opportunity to assert absolute property rights over those enslaved people who had long been sheltered from sale.

For example, Gloucester County's three parishes—Ware, Abingdon, and Petsworth—had received land and enslaved people through multiple bequests in the late seventeenth and early eighteenth centuries. The original donors specified that their gifts should support parish poor relief and a free school under the direction of the vestries. Moreover, these legacies stipulated that none of the enslaved people were ever to be sold; the parishes only had the right to hire out enslaved laborers for a "term of years."[122] When the colonial assembly revised a statute concerning these parishes' endowments in 1756, it went to great lengths to uphold all of the original conditions imposed by the donors, even after the creation of new counties and parishes made the bequests exceedingly complex to honor and administer.[123]

Under the 1802 Glebe Act, the Gloucester County Overseers of the Poor seized these parish endowments, including enslaved people, along with the glebes.[124] Shortly thereafter, white residents in Gloucester petitioned to sell the enslaved men and women and use the money to fund a workhouse or free school. The community's petition conceded that this plan would violate the express terms of the colonial donations but justified this breach with an opaque reference to the "particular situation of slaves in the lower country at the present time." The event to which they referred, known as the German Coast Uprising, was a revolt of enslaved people in Louisiana two years earlier.[125] News of this insurrection had convinced Gloucester's white residents that it would be "more advantageous" for the Overseers to sell the "several slaves" and use "the monies arising from the sales" to support the "benevolent intentions" of the original donors.[126] Under this scheme, the petitioners claimed that the "happiness" of the "community" would be better served through the sale, and thus the new act actually better upheld the wishes of the original donors to benefit the public good.[127] This contorted reading of the donors' intent flatly ignored the specific provisions of these bequests. The parameters of colonial benevolence no longer suited the sensibilities of antebellum Virginiana.

The legislature swiftly assented to the petition and granted the Gloucester Overseers absolute rights over the community. The 1814 act authorizing the sale recapitulated much of the language from the local petition and thus endorsed the view that a perpetual endowment of enslaved people posed a threat to the white community. While Virginia's colonial assembly had bent over backwards to closely adhere to the many conditions set forth by the original donors, the republican legislature was willing to disregard the stipulations of colonial donors if the safety of the white community purportedly hung in the balance. But it was not just a change in public attitude that induced the legislature to override the terms of the bequest. The legal rupture of disestablishment had already rendered the original terms of the bequest obsolete by upending the parochial welfare system that the donation supported. The enslaved community had already been transferred from parish to county, despite the colonial donor's specific instructions, and it was just one further step to grant the county absolute rights over these men and women.

It was not always clear from Gloucester's petition or others like it whether counties sought to move away from institutional slaveholding or if they simply wanted to win absolute rights over enslaved people previously shielded from sale. One petition in Nansemond denigrated the community of enslaved people still protected under a parochial bequest for being lazy and "disorderly." This community had become too "choice in their masters" and "hire[d] but low" because they were unafraid of being sold. The petitioners sought to contravene the terms of the colonial bequest and "sell the slaves at their discretion (apart or the whole)." This language made it transparent that counties did not necessarily seek to get out of the business of slaveholding altogether but aimed to exert greater control over enslaved people through the threat of sale.[128]

Perhaps the clearest example of the shifting views toward institutional slaveholding is the tale of Billy Pugh, whose story opened this chapter. Pugh was descended from one of the three persons deeded to Elizabeth River Parish in 1715/16. The original grantor, Matthew Godfrey, had donated a couple named Prince and Nell and a girl (likely their daughter, Nance) to the parish. Godfrey provided detailed instructions for the future management of his estate. Neither the land nor "any of the said Negroes [n]or any of their increase" were to be "sold." Godfrey ostensibly aimed to keep Prince, Nell, and Nance together on parish land, but this provision extended only to the first generation of the family.[129] Thereafter, the descendants of Prince and Nell would "be let out from year to year for the good of the poor . . . as the vestry . . . shall see good and most profitable."[130] Three decades later, Norfolk Parish was benefitting from a new generation of enslaved laborers, just as Godfrey had planned. In the 1750s, the vestry recorded the proceeds from hiring out five enslaved persons (Davy, Soll, Ishmaell, Sarah, and Nell), and a few years later, one of the women bore another child.[131] The enslaved community of Norfolk Parish were held in bondage as a perpetual investment for the benefit of white parishioners. The precise terms of the original bequest took precedence half a century later when the colonial assembly passed new laws dividing Norfolk Parish into three new parishes.[132] The colony brokered a complex agreement about how to divide the proceeds from their labor without selling any of Nell and Prince's descendants. When the system was revised again in 1765, the assembly yet again honored Godfrey's instructions as closely as possible.[133]

After the county took over the poor relief system, the Norfolk County Overseers of the Poor claimed ownership of the enslaved persons by citing the terms of Godfrey's will. They argued that the gift was for the "benefit of the Poor of Norfolk County," and therefore it belonged to whichever institution had jurisdiction over poor relief. The legislature approved the transfer, but the Overseers' notes suggest that it was not until after the Glebe Act's passage in 1802 that their title to the property was secured.[134]

Billy Pugh was born around 1800 amid the upheavals of disestablishment. He and the rest of the enslaved community who once belonged to Norfolk Parish remained in bondage for the benefit of Norfolk County's poor white residents, now under the control of secular administrators.

In 1823, more than a century after Godfrey's original bequest, a group of Norfolk's citizens sought permission to contravene the terms of the donation. The descendants of Prince, Nell, and Nance "now amount to about 30," but "their annual product has at all times fallen short of the sum, which their price, if converted into money would procure in interest." The easy "conversion" of currency imagined here—from people to cash—underscored the driving motivation of some community members to break the terms of Godfrey's donation. Due to "the frequent changes of the overseers of the poor and the inability of numerous individuals acting in an official capacity to regulate and direct such property, the slaves themselves acquire habits of indolence and insubordination Alike fatal to the interests of their owners, to the good order of the community and their own contentment." The petitioners argued that the reality of corporate property-holding was fundamentally incongruous with benevolent paternalism. They suggested that direct, personal oversight was needed to ensure those held in bondage were obedient, industrious, and, purportedly, content. The "natural augmentation of numbers" would "only aggregate" the problem. Unabated and unmastered, the enslaved community threatened public order and the safety of white citizens.[135] However, the legislature did not act.

Nine years later, another request arrived from Norfolk requesting the sale of the enslaved community, this time from the county Overseers of the Poor. Their appeal came on the heels of Nat Turner's Rebellion. The Norfolk Overseers implored the legislature for permission to sell the men and women whom they had inherited from the parish who "now amount to about thirty and for the most part are a worthless and impossible family of slaves."[136] Of course, terming this community worthless while seeking permission to sell them was a patently self-interested argument. These individuals were worthless only in so far as they could not be sold by the Overseers. Nor, it seems, could the enslaved community be easily controlled without the threat of sale. The Overseers made their case, explaining that "difficulty arises in the management of a set of disorderly slaves, even when controlled by a single person, possessed of absolute power to dispose of them and that the difficulties are much increased when their governance is under the direction of a body so numerous as the board of overseers of the poor, with no other power then to hire them out from year to year."[137] The absolute power—the ability to sell, or even make the threat of sale—denied the Overseers their most important method of controlling the enslaved community.[138] The Overseers claimed these limits to their power deprived them of the ability to truly control these men and women. Enslaved people who were safe from the threat of sale were less productive and therefore, they argued, did not fulfill the objectives of the donors. Only by breaking the terms of the colonial endowment could the county exercise authority over the former enslaved people of the parish.

This time, the legislature assented, agreeing to break the terms of Godfrey's will and passing a law allowing the Overseers to "dispose of any negroes" belonging to the county.[139] The chasm created by Nat Turner's Rebellion persuaded the legislature that the presence of a large community of "disorderly" Black men and women was a threat to communal safety. This time, the legislature glossed over the terms of Godfrey's will and gave no justification for amending the terms of the endowment. But their motivation was clear. This group of enslaved people could not be controlled using the threat of sale, nor could they be carefully supervised under a single authoritative gaze. The institutional nature of the county's ownership effaced the pretense of benevolent paternalism to which white Virginians clung. White public safety became the paramount priority of government, and the legislature embraced a flexible reading of the hundred-year-old will to award the overseers absolute rights over the descendants of Nance and Prince.

Billy Pugh was not among those "disorderly" persons facing sale. A few weeks earlier, the Norfolk Overseers had petitioned the legislature asking that he be manumitted. The legislature agreed but only on the condition that Pugh leave the state and emigrate to Liberia. Starting in the mid-1820s, the work of the American Colonization Society had convinced many white Virginians that the forced migration of free people of color to Liberia was the only solution for maintaining order and safety in the state.[140] The sources only include a brief glimpse of Pugh's perspective in these proceedings: "Billy Pue not having time to see all the overseers of the poor I certify that it was their wish & desire to have signd it." This suggestive line does not reveal how Pugh viewed his conditional emancipation but instead captures a rushed administrative process and Pugh's limited say in the proceedings.

The heartbreaking plea of Mary Watkins, a woman of color who was freed under similar constraints in 1827, might provide some insight into how Pugh felt. Watkins and her son, Edward, had been manumitted in the will of her former master on the condition that they emigrate to Liberia. However, her husband was still enslaved in Virginia. She appealed to the legislature for permission to stay in the state, explaining that her husband was more "near & dear to her than almost her own existance and to leave her husband (who is now a slave) would be like suffering death."[141] Pugh faced a similarly excruciating choice; accepting his freedom meant leaving behind his enslaved children, their mother, and his home. To remain in Virginia, however, risked re-enslavement. The legislature gave neither Mary Watkins nor Billy Pugh the chance to live in Virginia as free people.

Disestablishment upended the traditional property claims of parishes to enslaved communities. This radical legal rupture removed parishes from a position of public authority and transferred traditional welfare services from church to state. Overseers of the Poor and other public institutions seized the opportunity to assert absolute property rights over those enslaved people who had previously belonged to parishes in perpetuity. And, of course, it was human property that elicited the fiercest claims of ownership and cries for egalitarian laws. White Virginians, both for and against the sale of the glebes, demanded that the state respect equality under the laws by awarding them with property—namely, the enslaved people held as property. The liberty secured under republicanism and appeals to the state's duty to protect natural rights were limited to white Virginians.

WHETHER COMMUNITIES chose tax abatement, poorhouses, free schools, or academies, Virginians translated republican principles into practical policy as they repurposed parish wealth. Glebe funds most often went to lower the annual tax burden. This choice expressed the view that control of private property preserved citizens' liberty. Other communities opened educational institutions using their glebe funds, but those that survived catered to middle-class and elite men. Free schools, on the other hand, often struggled to last more than a few years. Reformers had championed the confiscation of glebes in universalizing terms but only a portion of the community attended the institutions they built. Enslaved men and women who had belonged to parishes were either sold or remained in bondage and continued to serve the welfare of the white community. Those who received public assistance remained overwhelmingly white, while the state tasked Overseers of the Poor with surveilling free Black communities and monitoring their reliance on public support.

The diversity of local decisions about how to spend glebe funds reflected a transformation in communal life after disestablishment. Racism was a constant, as was resistance to taxes, but there was no longer a single hierarchical framework of religious orthodoxy or civic conformity to structure local government. The capacious terms of republicanism left room for a wide variety of community actions under its banner. Lowering taxes, cutting public spending, opening poorhouses, and funding schools all reflected different, and sometimes conflicting, objectives within republican thinking. The sell-off of glebe properties, if anything, exposed unresolved tensions over the best way to turn republican principles into practical policies. Examples from across the state underscored that the brand of republicanism forged during disestablishment retreated from the strong local institutions that had characterized parochial life and prioritized a leaner local government that made racial hierarchy its highest priority.

# 6

# INCORPORATION IN REPUBLICAN MARYLAND

"CITIZENS YOU have been on the brink of ruin!" warned the *Hornet,* a weekly newspaper in Frederick, Maryland, in the fall of 1809. Writing under the pseudonym "Federalist Methodist," the author raised the alarm about a recent plot to restore "an established church with a vengeance" in Maryland. According to the newspaper, the trouble started with a petition from the bishop and clergy of the Episcopal Church to incorporate their statewide governing body, the General Convention. What seemed like an innocuous request for incorporation, the author claimed, disguised a conspiracy between the Episcopal Church and its Federalist allies to strip Marylanders of their liberty and property. The author exhorted his readers, "Ye disciples of Washington, ye descendants of the heroes of '76 . . . ye friends of religious liberty" protect your "dear-bought liberty and independence."[1] This critic maintained that the legacy of the Revolution was hanging by a thread. A political firestorm followed, and the bill to incorporate the Episcopal General Convention was defeated.

Seven years after the passage of Maryland's General Incorporation Act for Christian Churches in 1802, the twin issues of religious propertyholding and incorporation still gripped the state. Anxiety over church property was deeply embedded in Maryland's debates over religious freedom, denominational equality, and the legitimate boundaries of state power. Maryland never confiscated property from the formerly established church like its neighbor, Virginia, yet its Anglican establishment had been a property regime. Thus, Maryland's republican disestablishment rested on a reformation of property rights as much as Virginia's had. In the early nineteenth century, Maryland was also transforming rapidly, and its religious denominations were adjusting, sometimes with painful results. The formerly established Episcopal Church, the newly empowered Catholic community, and Maryland's growing Jewish population all navigated the reformed church-state relationship in a changing Chesapeake. This chapter will examine their experiences in turn.

Plagued by many of the same concerns as Virginians about how to dismantle the inequities of establishment, Marylanders turned to different remedies. They constructed an establishment of religious freedom on very different terms than their neighbors to the south that eschewed confiscation and instead expanded corporate rights. While both Chesapeake states sought to establish religious freedom and pursue a republican vision of the public good, their actual policies, particularly when it came to property, diverged sharply. Events in Maryland thus clarify in granular detail why disestablishment cannot be considered a finite event with a clear start or end point. Three decades after the Revolution, Maryland's disestablishment was not finished by a long shot. Rather, it remained an ongoing negotiation over the permissible ties between religion and government, and the legal rights afforded to religious communities and individuals. Disestablishment was—and remains—an ongoing pursuit of the proper relationship between church and state.

## Maryland's Glebes

Maryland's parishes retained control over all colonial-era property after disestablishment, and events in Maryland provide an illuminating corollary to Virginia's policy of glebe confiscation. Article 33 of Maryland's constitution of 1776 had expressly affirmed that "the churches, chapels, glebes, and all other property now belonging to the church of England, ought to remain to the church of England forever."[2] But after a new denomination—the Episcopal Church—was created from the remnants of the old Anglican system in a parallel act of religious independence, Episcopalians in the state were anxious that their titles to parish property could be challenged. As we saw in chapter 4, evangelicals in Virginia did employ this precise line of reasoning in their calls for confiscation. Baltimore's zealous Presbyterian minister Patrick Allison may have denounced the settlement and framed it as a serious blow to religious equality, but neither evangelicals like Allison nor the state's Catholics mounted a serious attempt to seize glebes or other parish assets in Maryland. Episcopal parishes retained control of their glebes and other property without ever facing an organized campaign for state confiscation.

Still, the colonial Anglican Church had been built on a model of compulsory financial support, and the transition out of legal establishment proved difficult for the formerly established church. Not only had parishes lost the ability to raise annual levies in 1776, but two thirds of Maryland's clergy had been loyalists, and more than half of the state's parishes were without ministers in 1780.[3] After the Revolution, fewer British-born Anglican ministers were willing to emigrate to the new United States, which left Maryland's parishes competing for a smaller pool of ordained ministers.[4] Moreover, evangelical sects were rapidly expanding across the Chesapeake in the final third of the eighteenth century. Baptists, Methodists, and Presbyterians all gained numerous converts from the former established church in Maryland.[5]

Facing these many challenges, Episcopal parishes struggled to maintain their extensive property. Part of the problem was that many colonial parishes had operated three, four, or even five different churches and chapels to serve far-flung communities. Under the established system of worship, parishes had built and maintained this multicongregational structure to serve the dispersed population in their bounds. Stepney Parish in Somerset County, for example, struggled to support all its churches after independence. In 1776, Stepney had three churches and a chapel, all supported by taxes. By the late 1790s, the largest brick church reportedly still had an active congregation and was in good condition. But its second church would require at least some "expence [to] be made comfortable," and its third church stood in ruins, "the doors and windows are entirely demolished; it is open to cattle and every abomination under heaven."[6] A visiting clergyman castigated the Stepney vestry for letting these valuable sanctuaries go "to ruin." He argued that churches and chapels were material reflections of the "state of religion" in their communities. Deteriorating houses of worship reflected spiritual atrophy and would deter worshippers and clergymen. The material decay of churches and chapels was, to some extent, a process of rightsizing for a denomination that had lost public funding and parishioners since independence. But this widespread pattern of dilapidation exacerbated parishes' struggles to raise funds, retain worshippers, and hire ministers in the wake of disestablishment.

Many of Maryland's parishes introduced a subscription model in which parishioners pledged to give a particular amount each year to support the minister and parish. Under this framework, "parishioner" became a voluntary religious identity rather than a compulsory legal status of English subjecthood. The newly created Diocese of Maryland suggested that parishes raise funds by asking parishioners to rent pews in the churches and chapels. However, most congregations found this proposition ineffective. The vestry of All Hallows Parish in Worcester County concluded in 1797 that "we have tried it but with bad success." Somerset Parish's vestrymen in Somerset County likewise complained, "We cannot say that as yet it has been very flattering. A considerable no. of pews have been taken up, but many yet remain vacant." The vestry of Great Choptank Parish in Dorchester County explained that "we have tried the pew rent scheme. . . . Its success has perhaps been equal to what can be expected in the present state of religion. Still, we are of opinion that it has lessened our congregation. Some appear to remain at home on Sunday, because they are too parsimonious to rent a pew." The pew-rent scheme could not raise enough funds to combat the decreasing number of parishioners spread out between multiple chapels and churches in every parish. The proposal even seemed to dissuade poorer parishioners from attending worship altogether, which was certainly the last thing any church needed as it fought to retain worshippers.[7]

When voluntary contributions and pew-rent schemes failed, many of Maryland's parishes turned to their glebe properties to raise funds. Reports from parishes to the Bishop of Maryland from the late 1780s through the early 1810s show a number of ways that parishes used their glebes to remain financially solvent. Parishes with valuable glebes used profits from these estates to employ ministers, hire enslaved laborers, contribute to the support of the bishop, maintain their churches and chapels, and pay sextons and clerks. Even parishes with smaller or poor glebes could rent out the land and then use these funds to pay a minister to preach occasionally.

For example, William and Mary Parish in St. Mary's County was desperate to find a new minister after the death of their rector in 1807. The vestry reported in a letter to the bishop that the minister's passing was all "the more unfortunate at this particular period as a certain sect of dissenters is for the first time gaining proselytes here." The vestry asked the bishop to recommend a "worthy" clergyman to fill the post. However, with few available ministers in the state, their letter also went to great lengths to underscore the many advantages that a minister could expect, including "an excellent Glebe containing three hundred acres as good farming land as any in the neighborhood," which could "yield handsome support for a large family, [and] has generally been from £100 to $300." They even mentioned the plentiful oysters and fish in the coastal waters near the property. The vestry's letter concluded that the income from the glebe along with voluntary contributions and fees from funerals and marriages would provide an "amount exceeded by very few parishes in the state as remote from wealthy Towns as we are." They also placed a notice in the *Maryland Gazette* with the same details seeking a minister looking for a "permanent" situation.[8] Apparently, their advertising worked, and the parish recruited William Bradley to take the position.[9]

However, Bradley soon got a better offer from another parish, and William and Mary's vestry was left searching again for a rector. They turned to the Bishop of Maryland for help. The vestry acknowledged that "the advantages held out to [Bradley] were so flattering that none of his friends could attempt to dissuade him from it." The parish hoped to recruit a new minister "with as little delay" as possible because "our Glebe is now stocked with everything." Writing in March, the vestry expected that if a new clergyman could be found quickly, a valuable wheat crop could still be raised that year, as "the hands and overseer" were already living on the glebe. The passing references to the glebe being "stocked" with "hands" reveals the parish's continued reliance on enslaved labor. The parish had not listed enslaved people in its inventory of assets, which makes it far more likely that the vestry had hired enslaved laborers to live and work on the glebe for the coming year. The vestry included these details in their letter to the bishop to underscore the valuable living that awaited a minister in their parish.[10]

Together, these two letters from the vestry of William and Mary highlight how the scarcity of ministers created a competition between parishes hoping to recruit and retain a rector. The disparity between parishes' wealth engendered a system of trading up as clergy were eager to move from parish to parish in search of higher-paying offers. Wealthy parishes endowed with valuable real estate were at a significant advantage. As William and Mary's vestry had noted in their letter, urban parishes in wealthy towns were often able to pay higher salaries. St. Paul's Parish in Baltimore, for example, owned seventeen lots in the city.[11] The parish rented out thirteen of these lots for a total of £127 annually and raised nearly five times that amount annually from contributions and renting pews. The valuable income a minister could expect in the booming city certainly made it harder for rural parishes, even those with valuable glebes, to recruit and retain ministers. Episcopal clergymen acknowledged that they were eager to attain posts that paid well. The Rev. George Ralph wrote to the bishop in June of 1802 about his current situation in All Faith Parish. He had accepted a one-year position there, even though "the salary is trifling." He wrote that a "sense of duty prevailed, I hope, over interest." Ralph touted his decision to prioritize his spiritual calling above any earthly compensation. However, by sending this account of self-sacrifice to his superior, Ralph was angling for the bishop to recommend him for a plum position the following year.[12]

When vestries could not find tenants for their glebe lands or recruit ministers, their other resort was to sell their glebes to stave off financial collapse.[13] Between 1785 and 1840, more than 80 percent of Maryland's parishes sold their glebes. Glebe property offered a financial lifeline to Maryland's former established church and allowed parishes to invest the funds raised from selling off land into other types of capital that cost less to maintain but still provided a steady income.

## Parish Slavery After Disestablishment

Maryland's Episcopal parishes also sold enslaved people, whom parish vestries treated as a fungible asset to leverage after the loss of state support. In 1783, the vestry and churchwardens of Somerset Parish received permission from the legislature for the sale of "so many of the slaves belonging to their parish as will enable them to build a dwelling house" for a clergyman.[14] Little else is known about this enslaved community given the paucity of any records from Somerset before 1796. Their names and details were apparently not deemed important enough to be included in the parish register, the only extant colonial document. All surviving evidence suggests that the parish had sold the entire enslaved community by the 1790s when the vestry offloaded 150 acres of land and invested the funds.[15] Without the regular contributions of taxpayers to maintain the land and support the enslaved community, the vestry turned to other forms of capital and investments for financial support.

The Black community long enslaved by William and Mary Parish (also known as Piccowaxen Parish) in Charles County would also be broken apart and sold during disestablishment. As discussed in chapter 2, in the 1760s, the parish held at least twenty-two people in bondage, including eight children, and their labor had been used to bail out the indebted parish rector, Rev. John McPherson.[16] Even though some enslaved individuals, such as Will Wage (discussed in chapter 3), had managed to escape during the war, the community enslaved by William and Mary numbered at least twenty-eight by the 1790s.[17] Two documents from 1796—a freedom petition and a law passed by the Maryland Assembly—point to a tragic end to their story as the vestry moved to sell the entire community.

In 1791, an enslaved woman named Mary petitioned for her freedom from the vestry of William and Mary Parish in the Charles County Court. Over the next five years, her case made its way to the General Court of the Western Shore of Maryland, one of the state's two appeals courts. Intriguingly, Mary was represented by one of the state's leading attorneys, William Kilty, who would become a federal circuit court judge and later chancellor of Maryland, the highest judicial officer in the state.[18] Born in England, Kilty had emigrated to Maryland as a boy and trained in medicine before serving as a surgeon in the 5th Maryland Regiment during the American Revolution. Kilty later read law at the College of St. Omer's, a Jesuit college in France where many of Maryland's Catholic sons were sent to be educated. Despite his Catholic upbringing, he would be buried at St. Anne's Episcopal Church in Annapolis in 1821. Kilty enslaved three people in 1810, yet he had chosen to represent Mary and more than thirty others in their bids for freedom. Raised and educated as a Catholic but buried as an Episcopalian, a legal advocate for the enslaved and an enslaver, Kilty defied neat categorizations. Exactly how this well-known legal mind became involved in the case is unclear, but his participation was certain to raise the profile of the proceedings.[19]

Mary's freedom suit was based on the claim that her maternal ancestor had been illegally enslaved in Maryland generations earlier.[20] Perhaps her mother or grandmother, this female forebear was also called Mary (hereafter Mary the Elder) and had been "imported many years ago into this country from Madagascar" before being enslaved by the parish sometime before 1715. In fact, Mary was one of thirty-four people descended from Mary the Elder seeking their freedom from the parish.[21] Rather than review each individual petition, the court chose one petitioner, Mary, to stand in for the rest of the family. If the court accepted her claim, their decision would also have freed the rest of her family members.

According to Mary's appeal, Madagascar was not a country where "the slave trade was usually practiced" or "whence slaves were usually bought."[22]

Because Madagascar was a remote locale outside the customary framework of Anglo-American slave law, Mary the Elder was never "a slave according to the laws of this state." Thus, all of Mary the Elder's descendants were likewise "unjustly held and detained in slavery by the vestry of William and Mary Parish in Charles County." The case file included additional depositions from the oldest residents in the parish about Mary the Elder's complexion, status, and behavior to demonstrate she had been set apart from other enslaved people and treated differently. Thus, Mary's petition argued that Mary the Elder had been held in bondage unlawfully by the parish and all her descendants who were still enslaved ought to be free.

In their rebuttal, the Piccowaxen Parish vestry claimed that Madagascar was like any other African country engaged in the slave trade with Europeans. Nothing about Mary the Elder's bondage was exceptional, and she had been legitimately enslaved according to the laws of Maryland. Siding with the parish vestry, the court decreed that the only recourse for Mary to prove her claim was to "show her ancestor was free in her own country." This decision set Mary a patently impossible task by requiring her to present evidence that Mary the Elder had been a free woman eighty years earlier halfway around the world. With this unattainable standard, the case was dismissed in October 1796. The General Court's decision was later republished in the nineteenth century in several collections of precedents on the laws of slavery.[23] Notably, the published case report mentioned only one petitioner, "Negro Mary," which erased the thirty-three other people enslaved by the parish from the printed records.

The month after Mary's freedom suit was dismissed, the Maryland Assembly received a petition signed by the rector, vestrymen, church-wardens, and inhabitants of William and Mary Parish. Without mentioning the years of litigation or naming any of the enslaved individuals, these parish petitioners explained, "There are belonging to the said parish a number of negroes, many of whom are unfit for labour, and are expensive to the said parish."[24] They sought permission to "dispose of all or so many of the said negroes as they may think proper." The petition's unvarnished nastiness in seeking to sell enslaved people because they were too unwell or too old to labor cut across every pretext of Christian paternalism trotted out to defend slavery. And given that the parish had enslaved numerous children just three decades earlier, this rationale was almost certainly a misrepresentation of the facts. A significant financial windfall awaited the parish by auctioning off this large community.

The precise origins of the community enslaved by William and Mary are unknown. Neither the court nor the legislative records mention a specific donation or conveyance to the parish, which makes it more likely than not that the parish purchased enslaved people outright at some point.[25] The parish sent its petition two years before the 1798 Vestry Act asserted the relative autonomy of parishes over their property and thus clearly sought advance approval from the legislature. It stretches credulity that the timing of these two events—the enslaved petitioners' pursuit of their freedom and the parish's petition for sale—was mere coincidence. Perhaps the enslaved community had heard about the potential sale and chose to bring their suits preemptively in 1791. It seems just as likely, though, that their appeal for freedom convinced the vestry, rector, and parishioners that the enslaved community was not just too expensive but also too defiant to maintain. Whatever the order of events, the assembly gave its assent to the proposed sale.

A large Black community challenging its bondage through the courts, with the assistance of legal counsel no less, proved destabilizing to slavery as an institution itself. To the vestry, this bid for freedom and sophisticated recourse to the courts likely made the continued system of parish slavery a liability, rather than an asset. The records furnish few other answers about what happened to Mary or the other members of enslaved community of William and Mary Parish. Whether members of the community remained nearby or were sold far away, whether families remained together or were forcibly separated, the sources do not tell us. The parish continued to benefit from the enslaved community long after they were sold. In an 1844 report to the diocese, the William and Mary vestry listed a "funded endowment" acquired by "the sale of personal property" worth nearly $8,000 (about $337,000 in current dollars), which paid the annual salary of the rector and supported the costs of the parish.[26] This chattel was, of course, the enslaved community who had labored to support the parish and its ministry for generations in the eighteenth century.

Maryland's parishes underwent the transition from public to private by leveraging their property. The large-scale divestment in glebe lands and enslaved people revealed the financial legacy of legal establishment in a state without confiscation. Institutional slavery and plantation agriculture had enriched Maryland's parishes for close to a century. Taxpayer funds had been used to support the purchase and maintenance of enslaved people, whose labor filled the parishes' coffers in turn. Despite the end of the Anglican establishment, Maryland's 1776 constitution and subsequent disestablishmentarian legislation explicitly protected parishes' claims to "negroes" and all "other property."[27] This assurance of their property rights shielded parishes from appropriation but did nothing to insulate enslaved people from sale and separation. The dismantling of the parish glebe system and the attrition of parishioners to other denominations prompted the Episcopal Church to sell off land and enslaved people after the Revolution, without any apparent consideration for the communities torn asunder as a result.

## Incorporation, Again

Still, news of glebe confiscation in Virginia seemed to alarm Maryland's Episcopalians. Misleading accounts of the 1802 Glebe Act suggested to Marylanders that Virginia's legislature had authorized counties to sell glebes whenever "a majority of the housekeepers and freeholders of the parish shall petition for it" and called "for throwing open the churches, and allowing all sects an equal title to preach in them."[28] These details were wrong—Virginia's Overseers of the Poor could not confiscate glebe lands until the death or resignation of the incumbent minister, and church buildings were technically exempt from seizure—but the larger implication that parish property might be taken by the state at any time distressed Maryland's Episcopalians.

As the litigation over the Glebe Act played out in Virginia's courts, Maryland's clergy began considering how to secure their denomination's property. Under the state's 1798 Vestry Act, every vestry was incorporated, vested with all the real estate and chattel of the parish, and empowered to buy and sell property under certain limits.[29] Parish rectors had freehold over the glebes during their tenure. But the law did not provide for "vacant" parishes, which had neither an active vestry nor incumbent minister, nor were these parishes addressed by the state's 1802 general incorporation statute. This omission was troubling for church leaders, given that nearly half of the state's parishes sat vacant by 1800.[30] A statewide governing body with the flexibility to take control of an unknown amount of property until some unknown date in the future did not fit within the narrow parameters of either the Vestry Act or the general incorporation statute, so the Episcopal Diocese of Maryland sought a mechanism to secure the property of these parishes until a vestry or minister could be installed. At the 1807 session of the General Convention, the bishop and clergymen resolved to petition the assembly for a separate act of incorporation to enable the diocese to hold property and temporarily manage the property of vacant parishes.[31]

The incorporation petition quickly became embroiled in party politics. After two years of delays, the bill finally passed the House of Delegates, but it failed in the Senate, where it met stiff opposition from Jeffersonians ahead of the statewide elections in October 1809. Drawing on the long memory of Anglican establishment, republican opponents dubbed it the Church Bill, a nod to the much-reviled 1702 Church Act that had established the Church of England in the Maryland (see chapter 1). Their message was clear—this act of incorporation would amount to nothing short of the reestablishment of the Episcopal Church. An editorial opposing to the plan branded the bill a return to "ecclesiastical tyranny." One dangerous provision was the bill's use of the word "parish." While Episcopalians had begun using this term to refer to a voluntary community of believers, the phrase still carried the connotation of a civil body that forcibly included "all the inhabitants" within specific geographic bounds. To skeptical onlookers, this wording was a ploy designed to ensnare all Marylanders under the legal jurisdiction of an established church once again.[32] Rumors spread that the bill would reinstate the colonial-era clergy tax of thirty pounds of tobacco per poll to benefit the Episcopal Church; soon the people and "all their property" would be subject to "seizure and imprisonment, to satisfy the requisitions."

Most contentious was the absence of specific property limits. In the anticorporate rhetoric of Jeffersonian democrats, an unrestrained corporation was a Trojan horse that could accumulate so much wealth as to "endanger the government."[33] Critics were quick to claim that every other statute of incorporation for a religious society included explicit property limits, whereas this bill would allow the General Convention of the Episcopal Church to amass property unchecked. Critics insisted that incorporation of any church was legitimate only with strict limits on property-holding.[34] This new Episcopal establishment would "hurl down tyranny and destruction upon the members of every other religious society" and abrogate the "perfect freedom in the enjoyment of political and religious opinions" currently enjoyed in Maryland.[35] Unlike in Virginia, where republican objections to religious incorporation centered on the inadvisability of placing the legislature in a position of power above any religious bodies, these republican Marylanders problematized the lack of legal restrictions over the proposed corporation. Only through careful state oversight could religious corporations be kept in check.

The pitched partisan battle drew responses from Federalist editors, who decried "the false and infamous charge of an attempt by the federal party to have an established church and compelling all religious sects to pay towards its support" and the opposition's efforts to stir the people into "a state of phrenzy, of convulsive political madness."[36] Some supporters of the bill sought to extricate the incorporation issue from the divisive election but to no avail.[37] In response to the outcry, the Episcopal General Convention issued a statement insisting that the entire affair had been a simple misunderstanding. Surely no bill "so inoffensive and harmless to the rights and privileges of every other religious denomination" once "properly understood" could be seen as a threat.[38] Moreover, they pointed that the state had issued numerous special acts of incorporation for religious denominations, in addition to the general statute, and they were at a loss to see why their church should be treated any differently. They pointed to the statewide corporation of Catholic clergymen as a clear precedent. But their assertion that the incorporation bill was the same as any other fell on deaf ears. Privately, clergymen fumed at the "most wicked attempt" to stir up the "prejudices and passions of the ignorant" against the Episcopal Church.[39] Despite further attempts in the following year, the Episcopalians failed to win incorporation for their General Convention and dropped their request to be incorporated.

The political uproar over incorporation inspired a trio of changes—two laws and a constitutional amendment—to bolster religious liberty in Maryland. In the November session of 1809, republicans pursued three related motions in the Maryland House of Delegates. First, the republican-controlled house voted to reaffirm the act of general incorporation for Christian churches.[40] This endorsement was seemingly a pointed admonition of the Episcopal Church by reiterating that the state offered a general regulatory framework for religious corporations and their property available to all Christians. The legislature's refusal to incorporate the General Convention was emphatically not a blanket rejection of incorporation but was meant to chide the former establishment for seeking special treatment from the state.

Buoyed by the energy around religious liberty that fall, republicans in the legislature passed a second law that enabled Christians who refused to swear oaths to serve on juries. By 1794, the 1776 constitution had already been amended to allow qualified "Quakers, Menonists, Tunkers, or New Quakers" who were "conscientiously scrupulous of taking an oath on any occasion" to vote, hold office, and "hold offices of trust and profit" by a solemn affirmation.[41] The constitution was amended yet again in 1797 to explicitly allow members of the same religious groups to serve as "witnesses in all cases."[42] But questions lingered about whether members of these same religious communities could also undertake jury service without swearing oaths. This query had been raised repeatedly since the 1790s to no avail, but the political appetite for strengthening the legal protections for religious freedom in the fall of 1809 finally led republicans to enact a specific measure codifying the rights of nonjuring Christians.

Trying to settle the matter once and for all without having to address each right one by one, the legislature affirmatively extended "full participation of the rights of citizenship" to all these "scrupulous" believers.[43] However committed republicans were to protecting religious conscience, they nonetheless added a significant caveat to the new act by barring anyone unwilling to swear an oath from serving as a juror in freedom suits. Well aware of Quakers' and Mennonites' vocal antislavery convictions, the legislature made sure to prevent any of these committed Christians from potentially granting an enslaved person their freedom through the jury box.[44] With this exception, the goal of protecting slavery trumped any obligation to extend the full and equal rights of citizenship to religious minorities. Only those Christians whom the state trusted to protect slavery at every turn were granted their full and equal civil rights to serve on juries.

Finally, and most consequentially, the state altered the 1776 constitution to remove the power of the legislature to impose a general assessment for Christian churches "or any other tax, on the people of this state, for the support of any religion."[45] No system of general religious taxation had been proposed since 1785, when Paca's proposals for assessment were soundly defeated. However, the power of the legislature to impose "a general and equal tax for the support of the Christian levy for religion" survived in Article 33 of Maryland's Declaration of Rights. The recent controversy over the Episcopalians' incorporation petition made this dormant clause seem like a forgotten land mine, and republicans treated it as a dangerous threat that needed immediate attention. In a widely republished article praising the proposed constitutional amendment, republicans declared that "no door should be left open to the establishment of any institution, whatever partaking of the character of a religious establishment. Genuine religion rejects all such aid, which can only avail to promote views subversive to political liberty."[46] This position equated public "aid" of any kind to a religious society as a threatening form of religious establishment that sincere believers would reject out of hand. The republication of this article beyond Maryland suggested wider support for this ideological position. In January 1810, the amendment passed with an overwhelming majority of votes, 48–3. Far from a partisan issue, Maryland's legislature gave its overwhelming support to a constitutional amendment to prohibit religious taxation.

Maryland's constitution now included a blanket rejection of tax support for "any religion." This new amendment created a financial barrier between church and state in no uncertain terms. The state's Jeffersonians closed off any form of assessment as a backchannel to establishment, which moved Maryland's constitutional definition of "an establishment of religion" far closer to Virginia's separationist outlook. This consequential shift in the state's constitutional definition of establishment took place thirty-four years after independence and underscored the processual nature of disestablishment.

The church-state settlement in Maryland continued to evolve in the early nineteenth century, and concerns about property motivated many of these reforms. As in Virginia, questions about church property, assessment, and incorporation became inextricably linked in Maryland's public debates, and the laws governing all three issues shifted in tandem.

## "Belonging to the Corporation"

Episcopalians were not alone in adjusting to the transformed legal, economic, and political landscape of the Chesapeake in the wake of the Revolution. The state's Catholic community had long suffered under targeted laws that restricted their property-holding and free exercise. Rather than calling for confiscation of parish property, however, Catholic leaders threw their weight behind securing their assets and building public institutions befitting of their newly equal status in the republic. But these ambitious goals would also prove enormously expensive. Like the state's

Episcopalians, Maryland's Catholics would soon turn to selling off land and enslaved people to finance their plans.

In 1789, John Carroll had become Bishop of Baltimore, the first American bishop of the first American diocese. Three years later, he helped win a charter for the Catholic clergy in Maryland after 150 years of legal precarity. Legislative incorporation allowed the Catholic clergy to hold property jointly and thus resolved their longstanding concerns about separate claims held by individual priests under Maryland's restrictive colonial laws. The 1792 charter, which created the Corporation of Roman Catholic Clergy of Maryland (CRCC), represented a legal guarantee not just of Catholic property but also of their equal right to exist as a state-recognized body in Maryland. The ongoing suppression of the Jesuit Order also hung over this project. In 1773, Clement XIV had disbanded the Society of Jesus and instructed every bishop to seize Jesuit property in his jurisdiction. Without a bishop anywhere near Maryland, confiscation did not happen, and the former Jesuits carefully held onto their estates in the intervening two decades. The CRCC consolidated control over the nine mission plantations and hundreds of enslaved people, thereby securing them until the time the Society might be restored; at the very least, it shielded them from appropriation.[47]

Surveying his church in 1795, Bishop Carroll wrote that "churches either do not exist or they are in a wretched condition, due to the fact that the Catholics . . . [have] for so many years have been oppressed by harsh laws and have been reduced to a state of great poverty."[48] For generations, Catholics had either gathered for mass at the mission plantations or in private chapels inside the homes of the gentry, including Carroll's childhood home. The construction of public places of worship became an immediate priority as an expression of Catholics' equal rights. New churches would bolster the faithful by "adding solemnity to the public acts of Divine worship" and be more "suitable for celebrating the sacred liturgy."[49] In particular, Carroll was eager to construct a grand cathedral in Baltimore, which would be a "monument erected to the honor of God in a country, where error and heterodoxy" had long reigned.[50] The new bishop embarked on a zealous campaign to remake the landscape of American Catholicism that would proclaim its equal and public presence in the new republic.

Equally as pressing for Carroll was the creation of Catholic educational institutions commensurate with their new standing. Like the public celebration of mass, Catholic education had been prohibited under Maryland's colonial establishment. Catholic children were educated at home or in schools run quietly on the mission plantations, and there were no Catholic colleges anywhere in the United States. Educated as a young boy under these strictures, Carroll was intent on change and in 1789 helped secure land near the bustling port of Georgetown, Maryland, for a college. Soon known as Georgetown College (now Georgetown University), this new institution embodied all Carroll's ambitions for American Catholicism. He confided to a friend, "On this academy is built all my hope of permanency & success to our Holy religion in the United States."[51] By enrolling "students of every religious Profession," Carroll was exercising the equal religious liberty of Catholics under Maryland's constitution and rejecting any vestiges of the traditional view that made Catholicism seditious.[52] Yet another Catholic institution took root in Maryland in 1791. The Sulpician Order fled Paris amid the spiraling violence of the French Revolution and landed in Baltimore, where Carroll helped them resettle and resurrect their seminary in the rapidly expanding city. Carroll understood these Catholic schools would become part of the scaffolding of religious freedom in the new American experiment. Thus, within a mere decade, the institutional landscape of Catholicism in Maryland had been

This engraving portrays Georgetown College in a pastoral setting with fields under cultivation, implicitly recognizing that the Jesuit Order relied on plantation agriculture and slavery to finance the college. Casimir Bohn, *Georgetown College D.C.*, c. 1789–1815. (Courtesy of the Library of Congress)

radically transformed through equal guarantees of rights equal to Catholics and Protestants in Maryland law. By chartering their clergy, securing their property, building a cathedral, founding a college, and opening a seminary, Maryland's Catholic community exercised privileges denied them for centuries under the Anglo-American penal laws and sought to assert a new role for Catholicism in the American republic.

But the relationship between these new developments and the centuries-old mission plantations was complicated. The hostile realities of Anglican establishment had forced Maryland's Catholics to build a religious culture on the margins of Maryland society. In place of a traditional diocesan structure or parish life, the Jesuit missions had been a crucial sanctuary for Catholic worship and education. The Jesuit missions succeeded to a great degree by operating quietly on the edges of a hostile Anglo-American society. Their private nature endowed them with power and shielded them from establishmentarian persecution. With Maryland's new guarantees of equal religious and civil religious liberty for Catholics, the missions no longer served the same spiritual function they once did. Carroll's new vision for American Catholicism sought to celebrate the presence of Catholicism and integrate Catholicism into the American republic institutionally, socially and materially. His motivation was, in many ways, a direct inversion of the colonial missions.

But if the mission system was a holdover from the era of establishment, it was also the linchpin in Carroll's plans to remake American Catholicism because it provided two crucial things: income and capital. While Carroll bemoaned the destitution of Maryland's Catholics, they still held significant wealth through the mission system that could be leveraged to support an array of public projects. In the 1790s, the CRCC was one of the largest slaveholders in Maryland with some three hundred Black men, women, and children laboring in bondage on the thousands of acres of land the Catholics held in Maryland and Pennsylvania.[53] The wealth generated by their labor and, later, their bodies would provide much of the initial seed money for Carroll's ambitious program of public institutions across Maryland.

The corporation provided funds and labor to support the many new Catholic institutions in Maryland. The records suggest a fluid labor force moved between institutions. For example, two enslaved people from the Bohemia Mission, Jack and Peg, were sent to the seminary in Baltimore in

1795 to serve the priests there, while Alexius, an enslaved man, was sent from St. Thomas Mission to work for Bishop Carroll.[54] The corporation also channeled funds from the estates to Georgetown College, as captured in financial accounts listing credits and debits between White Marsh and St. Inigoes Missions and the college.[55] The corporation treated enslaved people as a mobile labor force who could help buoy these new institutions.

At the same time, the corporation's trustees were keen to preserve their claim to these enslaved laborers as chattel. For example, the CRCC trustees opted to grant the seminary the profits from Bohemia plantation in 1793, but two years later they scolded the Sulpicians for "interfering with the power of the Corporation concerning the disposal of money and other business" and reiterated that all the "money arriving from the sale of negroes" belonged solely to the corporation.[56] The context for this reproach was the sale of eight enslaved people from Bohemia in the preceding two years: Phillis and her three-week-old infant, Nel; Clara, Phillis's four-year-old daughter, who was separated and sold away from her mother and sister; Bob and his daughter, Lucy; and a couple, Ralph and Jany, and their daughter, Nelly.[57] A decade later, the corporation had diverted the income from Bohemia to support Georgetown College instead. Bishop Carroll then reprimanded the college president in 1805 for his "unfounded claim" to "the negroes" of Bohemia.[58] Amid the increasing institutional complexity of Catholic life in Maryland, the corporation sought to assert title to the hundreds of enslaved people laboring on the mission plantations and at other Catholic institutions in Maryland.

The corporation's financial situation rapidly worsened after 1800. Internally, there were accusations that poor management of the estates had made the missions less profitable. However, the Chesapeake was changing rapidly in the first decades of the nineteenth century in ways that undermined the traditional economic system of the region. Long-term market forces and the degradation of the soil had prompted Chesapeake planters to switch from growing tobacco to wheat even before the Revolution, and the collapse in tobacco prices in the 1790s accelerated this shift. Grain cultivation was less labor-intensive, and Chesapeake planters complained that there were too many enslaved people amid decreasing profits. At the same time, the upsurge in cotton production in the Lower South and the end of the international slave trade created a highly lucrative interstate slave trade. The sale of enslaved people in the Chesapeake, whether locally or thousands of miles south and west, became "an almost universal recourse to raise money."[59]

Faced with financial woes time and again after 1800, the corporation began selling enslaved people to raise funds. For instance, to pay off a debt of $1,200 in 1805 (approximately $32,300 in current dollars), the trustees of the corporation ordered the managers of their estates to arrange "the sale of superfluous slaves" to raise the funds as quickly as possible.[60] The CRCC treated enslaved people as a form of financial surety during this period of economic dislocation. As the nineteenth century wore on, the financial losses of the missions began to mount, and the clergy hotly debated whether to keep, sell, or free enslaved people over the following decades.

As the corporation became more "burdened with debt," some of the clergymen cast blame on the enslaved people themselves. One priest declared that "our poverty and the fruitlessness of our plantations" came down to the fact that "our slaves for the most part [are] corrupt and are corrupted without punishment. Because of this the idle, the fornicators, the adulterous, the drunks, and the thieves get away with it; they know the priests will not sell them to outsiders." Worse still, according to this priest, the Jesuits' reputation for leniency lowered the price of enslaved people at auction. As was the case in Virginia's parishes, these Christian enslavers claimed that it was financially impossible to continue the practice of institutional slaveholding without the threat of sale. After elaborating at length about all the expenses incurred in supporting the enslaved community, Br. Joseph Mobberly stated bluntly, "Having no Blacks the expenses would be very few."[61] In the wake of Nat Turner's Rebellion, some clergymen found yet another reason to recommend sale: the ethical quandary of punishing enslaved people had apparently become too onerous for the clergy. With the rising anxieties about slave rebellions, "masters will be obligated to take severe measures, often with weapons in hand, to prevent or suppress uprisings among the blacks. We sense how odious will be all the things our Fathers will have to do to cooperate with such measures. Already it is moral burden enough for them to be forced to sometimes punish defiant slaves with the whip." Once a pillar of the financial system of Maryland's Catholic community, chattel slavery was now treated as a drain on the church, while enslaved people were blamed for purportedly imposing a high moral and monetary cost on their enslavers.

Tensions intensified after the Jesuit Order was restored in 1814 and the corporation grudgingly agreed to submit to the authority of the Superior General, although they retained control over the property as a civil corporation.[62] Moreover, festering resentment between the Diocese of Baltimore and CRCC also threatened to spill into the courts as the new Bishop of Maryland asserted his claim to corporation property. With internal tensions at an all-time high and the plantations losing funds every year, the superior general of the Society of Jesus began considering how to restructure the mission system in Maryland. The president of Georgetown College, Thomas F. Mulledy, SJ, wrote to the superior general of the Society in Rome, Fr. Jan Philip Roothaan, SJ, with something of an ultimatum: "The missions and the College cannot successfully advance together—both equally can languish,—they cannot flourish." The missions had become unprofitable and the enslaved communities a costly, potentially dangerous burden. After experimenting with the sale of some enslaved communities in the 1820s, Roothaan gave his approval to the CRCC to sell the remainder of the enslaved people.

Writing from Rome in 1836, Father Roothaan outlined the conditions of the sale of remainder of the community. The Society would try to keep families together "as much as is possible" and "the benefit of exercising religion be given to the negroes, and the assistance of a priest." After laying out these conditions, Roothaan directed that the funds from the sale "*ought to be invested* so that it may grow," seamlessly reducing people to capital as he wrote.[63] With his approval in hand, the Maryland Jesuits proceeded to arrange the sale of 272 enslaved people to two Louisiana planters in 1838, all the while complaining that their expected payout from the sale had been substantially reduced due to the financial panic of 1837. The words of one enslaved woman forcibly being sold away were recorded by Fr. Peter Havermans, SJ. Writing with equal parts remorse and resignation, he described a pregnant woman who approached him to ask, "If ever someone should have reason for despair, do I not now have it? I do not know on what day the birth will come, whether on the road or sea. What will become of me? Why do I deserve this?"[64] He encouraged her to put her trust in God while he privately condemned the sale in his letters to Rome. His spiritual consolation, though, did nothing to prevent her forced migration from Maryland to Louisiana, nor could it even begin to offer a sufficient answer to the moral dilemma of slavery.

Begun two hundred years earlier, the Jesuit missions had provided a financial and spiritual lifeline to Maryland's Catholic communities. The dismantling of the mission plantation system paralleled choices made by white Episcopalians in Maryland and Virginia to divest from institutional slavery and plantation agriculture as the primary funding mechanism for their religious communities. But a century of slaveholding paid dividends, and the Catholic institutions of the new republic relied heavily on the proceeds and eventual sale of land and people for generations to come. Moreover, slavery persisted on Episcopal glebes and at Jesuit schools, most often in the form of hired labor. Retreating from large-scale institutional slaveholding did not disentangle Catholic or Episcopalian religious institutions from slavery.

## "The Scattered Israelites"

As Episcopalians and Catholics adapted to the republican reforms in Maryland, Jews also began to settle in Baltimore in greater numbers. Though still a small community by the 1820s, the growth of Baltimore's Jewish population reflected the transformation of the city itself, which would soon become the second largest in the United States.[65] But the expansion of this new religious community emphasized the stark inequalities remaining in Maryland law, which limited the body politic to Christians. In the following decades, Jewish Marylanders campaigned not only for individual civil and religious rights on an equal basis with Christians but state recognition and protection of their right to hold property through incorporation. Yet again, Maryland's church-state settlement would continue to evolve.

The 1776 Maryland Declaration of Rights counterposed universal promises of religious freedom against several explicit endorsements of Christianity. Article 33 began by declaring, "It is the duty of every man to worship God in such manner as he thinks most acceptable to him" and that no person could be "molested in his person or estate on account of his religious persuasion" nor compelled to attend a particular place of worship. However, the very next clause limited full and equal religious liberty to those "persons, professing the Christian religion." Article 33 further empowered the legislature to pass a "general tax" for the support of the Christian religion. Despite gestures toward more sweeping protections for religious freedom, these provisions erected an ecumenical Christian establishment.

Similarly, Article 36 began with capacious language to suggest that any oath "ought to be such, as those of the religious persuasion, profession, or denomination, of which such person is one, generally esteem the most effectual confirmation, by the attestation of the Divine Being," but Article 35 explicitly required a declaration of "belief in the Christian religion" for any office of trust or profit. Again, the constitution's abstract promise of rights fell far short of the specific framework laid out in the text, and its guarantees of religious liberty seemed to rest on a logic of equality among Christians rather than a more universal recognition of universal free exercise. Indeed, when describing Maryland's constitution in the 1780s, John Carroll felt no need to distinguish between "religious freedom" and the "equality of Christians."[66] His experiences in a state so long dominated by the conflict between Catholics and Protestants led him to use this language interchangeably without recognizing any friction between the comprehensive language of religious liberty and the stubborn legal preferences toward Christians in the state. A pointed partiality toward Christianity lingered in state law.

The growth of a non-Christian community highlighted the gulf between Christian equality and religious freedom. Jews in Maryland were granted some degree of protection for their free exercise but suffered from diminished civil rights under a state government that explicitly endorsed Christianity. Starting in the 1790s, Jewish leaders began to push for full and equal rights. The first official petition came before the Maryland legislature in 1797 from Solomon Etting and others protesting that "they are a sect of people called jews, and thereby deprived of many of the invaluable rights of citizenship, and praying to be placed upon the same footing with other good citizens."[67] Etting was a merchant who had arrived in Baltimore in 1791 and quickly become a leading republican political organizer while being denied the right to hold office himself. Raised in neighboring Pennsylvania, where Jews had rights equal to Christians, Etting felt the loss of his civil rights acutely when he settled in Maryland. Despite his many connections to the political and business communities in Baltimore, Etting's 1797 plea went nowhere. Four years later, he spearheaded another petition requesting the assembly abolish the "the incapacities which [the Jews] now labour under agreeably to the constitution and laws of this state."[68] The House of Delegates voted to table the proposal to alter the constitutional test oaths that prevented Jews from serving on juries, becoming attorneys, or holding office and ultimately did not pass the requested legislation.

A month after sending their ill-fated petition in 1801, Etting and Levi Solomon purchased the "Jews burying ground" from Charles Carroll of Carrollton, John Leggett, and William McMechen.[69] Though Article 34 of the Maryland Declaration of Rights stated that every "religious sect, order, or denomination" could hold up to two acres of land for a house of worship and a cemetery without needing legislative approval, apparently Etting and Solomon were wary that without any formal congregational recognition or corporate standing in the state, the property claim could be challenged. In a predicament deeply familiar to the Catholic Carroll, Baltimore's Jews were forced to rely on private individuals to acquire and hold property for their community.[70]

When the legislature passed a general statute of incorporation the following year, its protections were limited to "every Christian church, or society or congregation."[71] The act reiterated that all Christians should "enjoy equal rights and privileges, without partiality, preference or distinction"; and for "their welfare that they should be empowered to hold and acquire certain portions of property in a corporate or congregational capacity, and enter into various engagements if a civil or temporal nature, which can only be done by assistance of the general assembly." The legislature moored the "free and full exercise of [one's] religion" to the right to incorporate and hold property jointly but limited this privilege to Christians. So often called a general act of incorporation, the law's restrictive terms shut out Baltimore's Jews.

After several more failed petitions in the following years, the issue of Jewish civil rights lay quiescent for more than a decade. Not until 1818 did Thomas Kennedy, a Scottish-born Presbyterian, introduce a bill to extend to "the sect of people professing the Jewish religion, the same rights and privileges that are enjoyed by Christians." Kennedy put forward a bill that exempted Jews from the constitutionally required test oath declaring a belief in the Christian religion and instead allowed them to swear any oath on "the five books of Moses."[72] This bill did not eliminate the test oath but simply carved out an exemption for Jews. Kennedy's arguments in favor of the law vacillated between universalizing rhetoric in favor of complete religious freedom in which there were no "political distinctions" on the basis of religion and specifically setting Jews and Christians "on an equal footing."[73] Hailing from the western county of Washington nestled in the Appalachian Mountains, Kennedy lived far from Baltimore and claimed he had never met "any Jew in the world."[74] He nonetheless felt compelled to right the wrongs of "bigotry and persecution" and specifically cited his time among Catholics in Maryland for removing the "hereditary hatred" of Catholicism with which he had been raised in Scotland.[75] After forming close relationships with numerous Catholics in Maryland, he "found them . . . amiable in all respects." Kennedy claimed this experience had taught him the perils of religious intolerance. Prejudice, not pluralism, was the real danger. Branded the "Jew Bill" in the press, the proposed law was defeated. Kennedy would try and fail yet again.[76]

Reformers like Kennedy also insisted that Maryland's test oath was out of step with the federal Constitution's guarantees of religious liberty. State Delegate Henry Brackenridge argued that "Maryland has deprived, and still continues to deprive, American citizens of their just political rights" under the US Constitution and afforded to them in every other state constitution.[77] In the 1822–23 legislative session, Kennedy brought forward a constitutional amendment "to extend to all citizens of Maryland the same rights and privileges enjoyed under the Constitution of the United States" by abolishing Article 35's test oath.[78] While the proposed amendment did not entirely live up to its lofty name, it would have introduced a radical reworking of the state's revolutionary-era religious settlement. Kennedy's proposed language removed any form of religious qualification for jury service, officeholding, or any other position of trust or profit in the state. One proponent of the amendment, William Worthington, called the state's test oath a "wily enemy to equal rights" and emphasized that the Maryland Declaration of Rights had been written "at so early a period as August, '76, when something of monarchical and colonial prejudice and narrow-mindedness, still hung about us."[79] In the wake of the "fiery ordeal of a long revolutionary war" in which patriots of all faiths had proven their loyalty and risked their lives, the framers of the US Constitution would "not suffer" any such discrimination.[80] Thus, the US Constitution's Article 6, which prohibited any "Religious Test, was the very corner stone laid down by our illustrious progenitors, at the foundation of the Temple of Liberty."[81] The issue was crystallized in the case of Benjamin I. Cohen, who was unable to accept a commission in the state militia under the terms of the state constitution.[82] His plight was used to exemplify the consequences of Article 35, which denied Jewish Marylanders their full and equal rights as Americans.

Debates over the "Jew Bill" dominated the 1823 election. The amendment had passed the Maryland House of Delegates and Senate, but any constitutional amendment had to be passed in two consecutive years to take effect, which gave Maryland voters the opportunity to weigh in at the ballot box. Detractors warned that the bill would "open the door to infidels and atheists" to hold office.[83] Candidates for election that autumn ran on self-proclaimed "Christian" or "Anti-Jew Bill" platforms and trotted out familiar antisemitic arguments that the Jews had crucified Christ and branded Kennedy "Judas Iscariot." Their claims sought to stoke fear that "every man's property and life might depend on the oath of individuals, who not believing in future retribution, might from envy, hatred, and ill will, swear them away."[84] Allow non-Christians into office and onto juries, and turmoil would surely ensue.

Some critics even resorted to the Chesapeake's familiar racial fearmongering to suggest that the provision would even "admit the free negroes to vote or represent us," although this position required a radical reading of the federal Constitution as a document that conferred rights equally without respect to race.[85] Ultimately, Kennedy lost his bid for reelection, the bill failed, and the test oath remained constitutional in Maryland.

Finally, a narrowly tailored act passed in the 1824 session. While it did not eliminate the constitution's test oath requiring a belief in the Christian religion, the bill granted an exemption for Jews to take the oaths of office after making a "declaration of [their] belief [in the] future state of rewards and punishments."[86] Later that same year, Solomon Etting and Jacob Cohen were both elected to the Baltimore City Council. Not until the state drafted its Reconstruction-era constitution in 1867 was Maryland's religious test oath formally abolished.

Most historical accounts of Maryland's Jew Bill end there, but the Jewish community's push for equal rights did not. As in the case of every Christian denomination in the wake of independence, Baltimore's Jewish community set their sights on incorporation as an essential privilege for a religious community. In 1829, Jesse Hunt presented the House of Delegates with a petition from "sundry citizens of the city of Baltimore" seeking to become "incorporated under the name and style of 'The Scattered Israelites,' for the purpose of building a Synagogue in said city."[87]

This petition came not from the traditional Jewish elite of Baltimore, the Ettings and the Cohens, but a new group of German-speaking Jews. After the delegates initially rejected the petition, the governor purportedly intervened, and the bill was passed.[88]

The congregation, Nidhe Israel, became known as the Baltimore Hebrew Congregation. In 1845, when they finally raised the funds to construct a central synagogue, they invited the public to witness its dedication. The *Easton Star,* which had featured dozens of screeds against the Jew Bill in 1823, published a congratulatory report about the event, ultimately declaring: "Thus has an edifice been erected and consecrated to the most High god by a handful of Scattered Israelites, which will stand as a lasting memento of their devotedness to the Faith of their Fathers, and an ornament to the city of Baltimore."[89] Incorporation conferred state recognition that Jews' legal status was on par with Christians.

CONTINUING THE story of church and state into the nineteenth century reveals the ongoing process of disestablishment in Maryland. Concerns about material property set the agenda as Marylanders deliberated over assessment, incorporation, and property-holding. The inability to hold and pass communal assets prompted Episcopalians and Jews to seek incorporation. Anger about the potential use of tax funds to benefit certain religious groups drove the adoption of a constitutional prohibition against a general assessment and the creation of new financial barriers between church and state. Furthermore, the state's commitment to protecting slavery trumped a sweeping commitment to religious liberty, and the state denied the right of nonjuring, abolitionist Christians to serve on juries in freedom suits. Property remained of the utmost importance in negotiations over the legal parameters of church and state in republican Maryland.

Under the guarantees of the 1776 state constitution, Maryland's Episcopalians never faced a state program of property confiscation. The formerly established church leveraged the wealth begotten by the colonial establishment to adapt to its new status as a private religious society. As parishes auctioned off lands and enslaved people, they deconstructed the glebe system that had underwritten Maryland's established church in the colonial era. Catholics had won incorporation only in the 1790s, which enabled the church to secure its property and assert equal standing under the laws. Under Carroll's leadership, the church embarked on an ambitious campaign to create Catholic institutions fit for the new American republic. Catholics, like Episcopalians, chose to divest from the traditional plantation system that had propped up their spiritual communities in the colonial era. The suffering of enslaved communities torn apart by this transition underscores that disestablishment did not deliver a clear-cut victory for individual liberty. In fact, disestablishment affirmed a widespread commitment to racial slavery and coupled the expansion of religious freedom with the continued unfreedom of enslaved Americans.

Maryland's 1776 constitution was debated and renegotiated time and again as significant changes were made to the state's church-state settlement during the first three decades of the nineteenth century. The state's early commitment to the equality of Christians as the basis for religious freedom proved inadequate for guaranteeing rights to the growing community of Jews in the state. Maryland did not abandon its establishmentarian model entirely but slowly introduced separationist reforms to guarantee greater civil rights group by group and right by right. But it was not just religious diversity that triggered constitutional changes. Maryland also expanded the rights of nonjuring Christians but significantly did not guarantee their right to serve on a jury in sweeping terms. Because Maryland had retained an ecumenical establishment in its constitution, the state retained—and used—the power to abridge civil rights on the basis of faith.

# CONCLUSION

In many ways, Yeocomico Church in Westmoreland County, Virginia, epitomized the long arc of church and state in the Chesapeake. Built by Cople Parish in 1706, this brick sanctuary boasted an octagonal marble baptismal font, a fine walnut communion table, and large glass windows. Imposing and expensive, this parish church stood as a material testament to the power of the established Anglican Church, which exercised state power, managed public resources, and governed local life in the colonial Chesapeake. During the Revolution, Yeocomico Church went the way of the Anglican establishment itself—a victim of the violent upheavals of the war. British forces commandeered the church as a barracks, converting the churchyard into a makeshift abattoir and even dragging the communion table outside to use as a chopping block. A female parishioner secreted away the plate and altar cloth to a nearby plantation for safekeeping.

The sanctuary suffered once again during the War of 1812, this time when American militias camped inside, looting the church and even using the baptismal font as a punchbowl. A soldier from New Jersey who visited the site in 1814 reported that the derelict parish church had become "the terror of the neighborhood, from being the resort of runaway negroes and wandering vagrants" and recalled "the Lord's Prayer, the Ten Commandments, and other texts of Scripture, hung upon the walls, now much defaced, mouldered, and torn."[1] Decades later, this same eyewitness puzzled over "the mysterious desolation of the ancient Churches of Virginia . . . these sacred monuments of the faith of our fathers and the religious care of the Provincial Government." What this outsider failed to grasp was that these spaces endured popular hostility and widespread neglect precisely because they had so powerfully represented the old regime of establishment and monarchy.

Methodists began worshipping at the church as part of the widespread popular appropriation of parish property and later shared it with a revived Episcopalian community. During the 1840s, the Episcopalians sought to assert their title and prevent the Methodists from using the church further. Ardent pleas from both sides resuscitated many of the arguments made generations earlier by turning the dispute over church property into a fight for religious liberty itself.[2]

The Westmoreland Methodists begged the Virginia legislature to intervene on their behalf and ensure their continued access to the space. Rehearsing the history of disestablishment, these petitioners argued that after the Revolution, "the churches, communion silver, and the churchyards all belonged to the public." Their interpretation, of course, ignored the explicit terms of the Glebe Act and instead relied on the popular memory of disestablishment as a movement to deliver "the greatest good to the greatest number." This democratizing narrative emphasized the public good over appeals to private property rights.[3] To leave this church in the hands of the Episcopalians, the petitioners warned, would return Virginia to the oppressive former establishment. The Episcopalian parishioners countered with many of the same arguments made by their forebears. If Yeocomico Church became common property, they exhorted, "tremendous consequences must result! Universal Confiscation must follow."[4] The Episcopalians in Westmoreland maintained that any infringement of their claim to the church would destabilize property rights across the state and injure the religious freedom of all Virginians.

Seventy-odd years after independence, local communities were still divided over disestablishment. Postrevolutionary efforts to untwine church and state unfolded in fits and starts over generations. Reforms were met with a wide range of reactions—confusion, eagerness, apathy, and resistance. Both camps fighting over the old Cople Parish church made appeals to the principle of religious liberty, but each understood it very differently in practice. The fallout from the Revolution left Americans debating how to translate their ideals into policies and contemplating just how different their new republic could and should be.

This project began with local stories like the fight over the old Cople Parish church. As a graduate student, I went looking for religion in the eighteenth-century Chesapeake and was surprised to encounter the state at every turn. Vestry books were filled with the mundane affairs of local government—tax collection, property surveys, moral fines, lawsuits, court presentments, construction projects, welfare expenditures, and tobacco inspection. It was impossible to parse religion from government in the original sources because establishment made them inseparable in practice. Their wide-ranging activity and watchful oversight of local communities were at odds with the common depiction of the Anglican Church as spiritually vacant and institutionally weak, or, more broadly, with the way scholars tend to write about American religion to emphasize belief over practice and texts over material objects and spaces.[5]

The extensive literature on church and state has carefully narrated the political and legal processes driving disestablishment within the states and their implications for constitutional developments at the federal level. Scholars of religion have detailed how religious freedom transformed American religious life by spurring the energetic spread of evangelicalism, the "hothouse" of spiritual experimentation, and by encouraging the rise of reform movements bent on saving and improving the people.[6] Together, these bodies of work paint a picture of profound rupture and a vibrant American religious culture.

But what I didn't find in the literature was a clear explanation of what happened to communities where the civic work of the established church ground to a halt and where parish property, long deemed an investment in the common good, no longer belonged to the common public. With the issues of state power and church property in mind, I set out to explore establishment and its dismantling. The result was this book, *A Great Revolution in Church and State,* which advances three key arguments in response to these questions.

First, there was an essential contingency to disestablishment. Nothing was foreordained about American disestablishment. Revolutionary events unfolded without a coherent ideology or unified platform. Reforming church and state was a prolonged and meandering process, not a discrete event. Indeed, the demands of reformers evolved and diverged sharply over time. The guarantees of the 1776 state constitutions and modest reforms of wartime disestablishment gave way to more far-reaching changes in the following decades. This development was not the achievement of a long-term plan but a contingent and ever-evolving series of policies implemented in response to shifting demands and circumstances.

Newly independent Americans came to their understandings of an establishment of religion from the process of dismantling the established church. They embarked on this journey without a map or even a clear sense of the destination. Decades later, they still had not reached a coherent or stable agreement about where they had landed. The precise terms of an impermissible establishment of religion remained under construction well into the nineteenth century. In Maryland, the emphasis on the equality of Christians in the 1776 state constitution moved closer to the separationist model espoused by Virginia. Yet even in Virginia, discord remained over how to draw and enforce new lines between religion and government. The states embraced conflicting ideas about what constitutes an impermissible establishment of religion, all while agreeing they had established religious freedom.

Second, the established Anglican Church in the colonial Chesapeake expressed and exercised its public status and legal powers through its wealth. Parishes in the colonial Chesapeake claimed churches, land, libraries, silver, cash, and enslaved people using the powers extended to the established church in statutory and common law. Because property and property rights were so deeply bound up in the exclusive power of establishment, they both became central priorities for reformers. The prolonged fights over incorporation and confiscation illustrate how much material property—and the right to hold it—mattered to revolutionary Americans.

Their attention to property reflects the tangible assets at stake and the opportunities for communities to repurpose them as they built new public institutions in the absence of monarchy or establishment. Emphasizing the importance of property rights does not tarnish the sincerity of reformers' religious convictions or ideological principles; rather, it grounds the ideological discussion of rights in their real-world context. Concerns over material property drove the most significant ideological divergence between the two states' laws. Their discordant positions on church incorporation and confiscation fashioned distinct understandings of establishment.

Revolutionary-era fights over church property were deeply entwined with a commitment to racial slavery. Just recall how Maryland amended its laws to allow nonjuring Christians to serve on juries except in freedom suits. The vocal antislavery convictions of Quakers and Mennonites were a roadblock to their equal civil rights, and this conspicuous carve-out revealed that protecting slavery trumped Maryland's Christian equality. In Virginia, the confiscation of church lands and enslaved people funded poor relief and other civic institutions. This state action proceeded over the outraged protests of Episcopalians that the state was trampling on their religious liberty and their "sacred" right to private property, as one parish rector called his right to the glebe land and a family of enslaved people laboring there.[7] The legislature looked the other way when localities sought to sell off additional church assets and handed Overseers of the Poor more complete control over enslaved people who had been seized from the church. Real conflicts arose out of competing claims to religious liberty and a commitment to property rights in persons.

Finally, American reformers transformed church and state by reconfiguring the legal relationship between the two. The standard terms "disestablishment" and "the separation of church and state" capture only part of this process. Disestablishment emphasizes the derecognition of the former state church, while "the separation of church and state" points to the disentangling of religion and government. These terms convey the rejection of the church-state union without conveying the efforts to build something altogether different in its place. These shortcomings do not mean we ought to jettison these terms from our discussions; rather, it is valuable to recognize each as just one aspect of a more expansive revolutionary reform movement.

The established church had wielded immense power in the colonial Chesapeake. Parishes were busy administrators of daily life, and orthodoxy suffused laws in both colonies. Political loyalty was defined by confessional conformity. The Revolution was at once destructive of the imperial past and constructive of a new republican future. As newly independent Americans dismantled the Anglican establishment under which they had lived for generations, they also deliberated just what would take its place. Americans discarded divinity as the basis of sovereignty. The federal Constitution departed from English precedent by guaranteeing individual religious liberty in sweeping terms and rejecting a national establishment. State governments absorbed many of the church's traditional bureaucratic powers, reframing them not as the dictates of faith but as the obligations a republican government owed its citizens. Evangelicals and Catholics became powerful political voices and set the agenda for a reformed republic. A great revolution tore down the old establishment of religion, fashioned a new establishment of religious freedom in its place, and remade the landscape of American life.

# APPENDIX

## Virginia's Parish Glebes: Their Date of Confiscation and Use After Disestablishment

Virginia's 1802 Glebe Act left the confiscation process in the hands of local county administrators, and the state legislature did not comprehensively track the subsequent sale or use of the glebes. However, it is possible to cobble together the story of what happened in almost every parish using a wide variety of records: local histories, deed books, newspaper ads, acts of legislation, court cases, institutional records, Overseers of the Poor accounts, and architectural studies. It can be difficult to differentiate between the date when the parish minister died, when the glebe property and its profits came into the hands of the Overseers of the Poor, or when any or all the property was sold. For example, in Albemarle County, the rector of St. Anne's Parish died in 1808, the glebe lands were sold in 1809, and an act of the legislature was passed to appropriate the funds for a school in 1811, but in the end, the proceeds were simply invested. In 1817, these funds were transferred to Central College, which later become the University of Virginia. Still, the institutional records provide a clear trail for historians. However, in many other cases, only one of these pieces of information might be available, and in a handful of counties, there are no clear records at all. Much of the information in the following table comes from *Acts Passed at a General Assembly of the Commonwealth of Virginia,* later titled *Acts of the General Assembly of Virginia,* cited as *Acts VA*. Full citations for other sources are given below.

| Locality | Parish | Date | Use after disestablishment | Sources |
|---|---|---|---|---|
| Accomack County | Accomack | 1805 | Margaret Academy | Turman, *Eastern Shore of Virginia*, 161. |
| Accomack County | St. George | 1804 | Margaret Academy | Turman, *Eastern Shore of Virginia*, 161. |
| Albemarle County | Fredericksville | 1809 | University of Virginia | *Acts VA* (1810–11), ch. 23, 29–30. |
| Albemarle County | St. Anne's | 1780 | University of Virginia | Hening, *SL*, 10:112–13; Inhabitants of St. Anne's Parish, Albemarle County, Dec. 7, 1803, LPDC, LVA; Woods, *Albemarle County*,127; *Acts VA* (1810–11), ch. 23, 29–30. |
| Amelia County | Raleigh | 1805 | Overseers of the Poor | Amelia County: Report, 1829, Box 1, Folder 7, OP Annual Reports, APA, LVA. |
| Amherst County | Amherst | 1778 | County court | Hening, *SL*, 9:567–68; Virginia Department of Historic Resources, "The Glebe: Amherst County, VA," National Register of Historic Places Nomination Form (Washington, DC: U.S. Department of the Interior, National Park Service, 2008), Section 7. |
| Amherst County | Lexington | 1778 | County court | Hening, *SL*, 9:567–68. |
| Augusta County | Augusta | 1802 | Overseers of the Poor; Later Staunton Academy | William Patrick, "To the Citizens of Augusta County: The Undersigned Feels It a Duty . . . as Overseers of the Poor . . . to Expose the Falsity of Some Reports . . . Respecting the Money Arising from the Sale of the Glebe Lands" (Staunton, VA: L. Collett, 1812), Broadsides Collections, LVA. |
| Bedford County | Russell | 1779 | County court | Hening, *SL*, 10:109–10. |
| Berkeley (Jefferson) County | Norborne | 1807 | Overseers of the Poor | *Acts VA* (1807–8), ch. 98, 81. |

| Locality | Parish | Date | Use after disestablishment | Sources |
|---|---|---|---|---|
| Botetourt County | Botetourt | 1777 | Liberty Hall, Botetourt Seminary, and Wythe Academy | *Acts VA* (1793–94), ch. 70, 47. |
| Brunswick County | Meherrin | 1818 | Poorhouse and workhouse | *Acts VA* (1817–18), ch. 227, 222–23. |
| Brunswick County | St. Andrew's | 1818 | Poorhouse and workhouse | *Acts VA* (1817–18), ch. 227, 222–23. |
| Buckingham County | Tillotson | 1794 | Overseers of the Poor | *Acts VA* (1794–95), ch. 31, 19. |
| Caroline County | St. Asaph's | c. 1808 | Overseers of the Poor | Caroline County, Report: 1829, Box 2, Folder 7, OP Annual Reports, APA, LVA. |
| Caroline County | St. Margaret's | 1813 | Free school or academy | Inhabitants of St. Margaret's Parish: Petition, Caroline County, December 17, 1813, LPDC, LVA. |
| Caroline County | St. Mary's | 1805 | Rappahannock Academy | Inhabitants of St. Mary's Parish: Petition, 1804-12-08, Caroline County, LPDC, LVA; *Acts VA* (1804–5), ch. 32, 31; Rappahannock Academy, Record Book of the Trustees of Rappahannock Academy, 1810–22, 2, Accession 24654c, Organization records collection, LVA. |
| Caroline County and King and Queen County | Drysdale | c. 1808 | Overseers of the Poor | Caroline County, Report: 1829, Box 2, Folder 7, OP Annual Reports, APA, LVA; Freeholders & Citizens: Petition, King and Queen County, Dec. 13, 1808, LPDC, LVA. |
| Charles City County | Westover | 1807 | Charles City Charity School (school and poorhouse) | Mason, *Colonial Churches of Tidewater Virginia,* 127; *Acts VA* (1809–10), ch. 87, 76. |

(*continued*)

| Locality | Parish | Date | Use after disestablishment | Sources |
|---|---|---|---|---|
| Charlotte County | Cornwall | 1802 | Overseers of the Poor | Charlotte County: Report, 1829, Box 3, Folder 2, OP Annual Reports, APA, LVA. |
| Chesterfield and Powhatan Counties | King William | 1813 | Overseers of the Poor | Freeholders & Inhabitants of King William Parish: Petition, Powhatan County, November 2, 1814, LPDC, LVA; *Acts VA* (1813–14), ch. 52, 66, 1313–14. |
| Chesterfield County | Dale | 1826 | Overseers of the Poor | *Intelligencer & Petersburg Commercial Advertiser,* July 21, 1826, p. 3 (available on microfilm 51, LVA). |
| Chesterfield County | Manchester | 1804 | Overseers of the Poor | *Turpin v. Locket,* 6 Call 113 (1804). |
| Culpeper County | St. Mark's | After 1834 | Overseers of the Poor | Slaughter, *History of St. Mark's Parish,* 60–61. |
| Cumberland and Powhatan Counties | Littleton | 1826 | Overseers of the Poor | Powhatan County, Deed Book 9, 279. |
| Dinwiddie County | Bath | 1803 | Overseers of the Poor | Dinwiddie Land Book, 1803b, 7. |
| Elizabeth City County | Elizabeth City | 1806 | Overseers of the Poor; Hampton Academy | Hellelfinger, *Kecoughtan old and new,* 28. |
| Essex County | South Farnham | Before 1842 | Poorhouse | *Acts VA* (1843–44), ch. 105, 79–80. |
| Essex County | St. Anne's | 1822 | County glebe fund | Freeholders of St. Anne's Parish: Petition, Essex County, Dec. 6, 1821, LPDC, LVA; *Acts VA* (1821–22), ch. 69, 54–55. |
| Fairfax County | Truro | n/a | n/a *(No glebe at the time of the Revolution)* | Slaughter, *History of Truro Parish in Virginia,* 90. |
| Fauquier County | Hamilton | 1806 | Overseers of the Poor | Fauquier County, Deed Book 16, 654–56; *Acts VA* (1807–8), ch. 98, 81. |

| Locality | Parish | Date | Use after disestablishment | Sources |
|---|---|---|---|---|
| Fauquier County | Leeds | c. 1812 | Use unknown; date of seizure estimated based on date of rector's death or departure. | Brydon, "List of Clergy of the Episcopal Church Ordained After the American Revolution," 427. |
| Frederick County | Frederick | 1822 | Overseers of the Poor | *Acts VA* (1821–22), ch. 76, 61. |
| Gloucester County | Abingdon | 1813 | Gloucester Charity School | Freeholders & Housekeepers: Petition, Gloucester County, Dec. 16, 1813, LPDC, LVA; *Acts VA* (1813–14), ch. 56, 118–20. |
| Gloucester County | Petsworth | 1813 | Gloucester Charity School | Freeholders & Housekeepers: Petition, Gloucester County, Dec. 16, 1813, LPDC, LVA; *Acts VA* (1813–14), ch. 56, 118–20. |
| Gloucester County | Ware | 1813 | Gloucester Charity School | Freeholders & Housekeepers: Petition, Gloucester County, Dec. 16, 1813, LPDC, LVA; *Acts VA* (1813–14), ch. 56, 118–20; Mason, *Colonial Churches of Tidewater Virginia,* 127. |
| Goochland County | St. James's Northam | 1811 | Overseers of the Poor | Goochland County, Deed Book 21, 205. |
| Halifax County | Antrim | 1820 | Overseers of the Poor | Halifax County: 1829 Report, 1829, Box 5, Folder 7, OP Annual Reports, APA, LVA. |
| Hanover County | St. Martin's | 1804 | Overseers of the Poor | "Advertisement," *Virginia Argus* (Richmond) 12, no. 1193, Oct. 6, 1804, 2. |
| Hanover County | St. Paul's | 1778 | Overseers of the Poor | Hening, *SL,* 9:442. |

(*continued*)

| Locality | Parish | Date | Use after disestablishment | Sources |
|---|---|---|---|---|
| Hardy and Hampshire Counties | Hampshire | 1790 | County court | Hening, *SL*, 13:189–91. |
| Hardy County | Hardy | 1800 | Overseers of the Poor | *Acts VA* (1799–1800), ch. 12, 8. |
| Henrico County | Henrico | 1831 | Overseers of the Poor | *Overseers of the Poor v. Hart (1831)*, in *Cases Decided in the Supreme Court of Appeals of Virginia*, Vol. 30, 2nd ed. (Richmond, VA: 1857), 1–4; Burton, *Annals of Henrico Parish*, 36; *Enquirer* (Richmond), June 24, 1831, 4. |
| Isle of Wight County | Newport | 1802 | Poorhouse | Overseers of the Poor: Petition, Isle of Wight County, Dec. 15, 1819, LPDC, LVA; *Acts VA* (1819–20), ch. 90, 78–79. |
| James City (York) County | Bruton | 1821 | Alderman of Williamsburg | *Acts VA* (1813–14), ch. 54, 116; *Acts VA* (1819–20), ch. 95, 82–83; *Acts VA* (1841–42), ch. 129, 91; *Enquirer* (Richmond), June 19, 1821, 1. |
| James City County | James City | 1816 | Poorhouse and school | *Acts VA* (1816–17), ch. 79, 147–48. |
| King and Queen County | St. Stephen's | c. 1811 | Overseers of the Poor | Overseers of the Poor: Petition, King and Queen County, Dec. 7, 1812, LPDC, LVA. |
| King and Queen County | Stratton Major | c. 1811 | Overseers of the Poor | Overseers of the Poor: Petition, King and Queen County, Dec. 7, 1812, LPDC, LVA; Freeholders of the Parish of Stratton Major: Petition, King and Queen County, Dec. 21, 1815. OP Annual Reports, APA, LVA. |

| Locality | Parish | Date | Use after disestablishment | Sources |
| --- | --- | --- | --- | --- |
| King George County | Hanover | 1807 | The Free School of Hanover Parish | *Acts VA* (1807–8), ch. 39, 41; Freeholders of Hanover Parish: Petition, King George County, Dec. 11, 1807, LPDC, LVA; *Norfolk Gazette and Publick Ledger* (Virginia), March 30, 1807, 4. |
| King George County | St. Paul's | 1811 | Free school or schools of St. Paul's Parish | Inhabitants of St. Paul's Parish: Petition, King George County, Dec. 15, 1811, LPDC, LVA; *Acts VA* (1811–12), ch. 67, 101–4; *Acts VA* (1812–13), ch. 67, 89. |
| King William County | St. David's | 1814 | King William Asylum for the Poor; later Overseers of the Poor | *Acts VA* (1814–15), ch. 54, 115; *Acts VA* (1827–28), ch. 86, 55. |
| King William County | St. John's | 1814 | King William Asylum for the Poor; later Overseers of the Poor | *Acts VA* (1814–15), ch. 54, 115; *Acts VA* (1827–28), ch. 86, 55. |
| Lancaster County | Christ Church | 1815 | Overseers of the Poor; Lancaster Glebe Fund | *Acts VA* (1846–47), ch. 168, 156–58; Rawley, "Glebe Lands on Carter's Creek Lancaster Co.," 1358–63. |
| Loudoun and Fairfax Counties | Cameron | 1804 | Overseers of the Poor | *Turpin v. Locket,* 6 Call 113 (1804); *Alexandria Advertiser and Commercial Intelligencer* (Virginia), Aug. 30, 1802, 1; Inhabitants of Cameron Parish: Petition, Fairfax County, 1820-12-13, LPDC, LVA. |

(*continued*)

| Locality | Parish | Date | Use after disestablishment | Sources |
|---|---|---|---|---|
| Loudoun County | Shelburne | 1840 | Overseers of the Poor | Virginia Historic Landmarks Commission Staff (Nov. 1974), "National Register of Historic Places Inventory—Nomination Form: Glebe of Shelburne Parish" (PDF), National Park Service. |
| Louisa County | Trinity | 1806 | Overseers of the Poor | *Enquirer* (Richmond) June 17, 1806, 4; Louisa County: Report, 1829, Box 11, Folder 5, OP Annual Reports, APA, LVA. |
| Lunenburg County | Cumberland | c. 1821 | Overseers of the Poor | "Legislative Acts/Legal Proceedings," *Enquirer* (Richmond) 18, no. 68, Dec. 22, 1821, [3]. |
| Madison and Culpeper Counties | Bromfield | 1804 | Overseer of the Poor | Inhabitants of Bromfield Parish: Petition, Madison County, Dec. 8, 1804, LPDC, LVA. |
| Mathews County | Kingston | 1809 | Overseers of the Poor | *Acts VA* (1809–10), ch. 69, 59–60. |
| Mecklenburg County | St. James's | 1803 | Overseers of the Poor | James Stanley et al. to Howell Taylor, Indenture, April 16, 1803, Mecklenburg County, Deed Book 11, Microfilm Reel 6, 374–76, LVA. |
| Middlesex County | Christ Church | c. 1807–1813 | Overseers of the Poor | *Norfolk Gazette and Publick Ledger* (Virginia), Jan. 19, 1807; *Acts VA* (1809–10), ch. 29, 32. |
| Nansemond County | Suffolk (Lower) | n/a | n/a *(Glebe never seized)* | Dunn, *History of Nansemond County* (1907), 47. |
| Nansemond County | Upper Parish | c. 1818 | Glebe sold; funds managed by the Overseers of the Poor | Nansemond County: Report, 1829, Box 8, Folder 5, OP Annual Reports, APA, LVA; Bragg, *History of Nansemond County* (1909), 47. |
| New Kent and James City Counties | Blisland | 1807 | Workhouse and school; later primary school | *Acts VA* (1807–8), ch. 90, 76–78; Freeholders & Housekeepers of Blisland Parish: Petition, James City County, Dec. 15, 1824, LPDC, LVA. |

| Locality | Parish | Date | Use after disestablishment | Sources |
|---|---|---|---|---|
| New Kent County | St. Peter's | 1807 | Workhouse and school | *Acts VA* (1807–8), ch. 90, 76–78. |
| Norfolk | St. Bride's | c. 1802 | Overseers of the Poor | Brydon, "List of Clergy of the Episcopal Church Ordained After the American Revolution," 397–434. |
| Norfolk County | Elizabeth River | 1806 | Norfolk Academy | Morrison, *Beginnings of Public Education in Virginia,* 140; *Norfolk Gazette and Publick Ledger* (Virginia), Feb. 13, 1807, 3. |
| Norfolk County | Portsmouth | 1816 | Overseers of the Poor; academy | *Norfolk Gazette and Publick Ledger* (Virginia), January 16, 1809, 4; Norfolk County: Report, 1829, Box 9, Folder 1, OP Annual Reports, APA, LVA. |
| Norfolk County | St. Bride's | c. 1804 | Use unknown; date of seizure estimated based on date of rector's death or departure. | Brydon, "List of Clergy of the Episcopal Church Ordained After the American Revolution," 431. |
| Northampton County | Hungars | 1859 | Overseers of the Poor | Gordon, "Landscape of Faith." |
| Northumberland County | St. Stephen's | Before 1818 | Northumberland Academy | *Acts VA* (1817–18), ch. 100, 147–48; Morrison, *Beginnings of Public Education in Virginia,* 152–53. |
| Northumberland County | Wicomico | Before 1818 | Northumberland Academy | *Acts VA* (1817–18), ch. 100, 147–48; Morrison, *Beginnings of Public Education in Virginia,* 152–53. |
| Nottoway County (before 1776 Amelia) | Nottoway | 1799 | Overseers of the Poor | *Acts VA* (1798–99), ch. 32, 17. |

(*continued*)

| Locality | Parish | Date | Use after disestablishment | Sources |
|---|---|---|---|---|
| Orange County | St. Thomas' | 1810 | Orange County Humane Society | *Acts VA* (1810–11), ch. 61, 81–83. |
| Pittsylvania County | Camden | 1779 | County court | Hening, *SL*, 9:567–68. |
| Powhatan County | Southam | 1807 | Overseers of the Poor | *Acts VA* (1807–8), ch. 65, 58–59; *Virginia Gazette, and General Advertiser* (Richmond), April 12, 1808, 1. |
| Prince Edward County | St. Patrick's | 1777 | County court after 1792 | Hening, *SL*, 13:555–56. |
| Prince George County | Bristol | 1816 | Overseers of the Poor | *Acts VA* (1805–6), ch. 13, 10; *Acts VA* (1815–16), ch. 82, 200. |
| Prince George County | Martin's Brandon | 1806 | Overseers of the Poor | *Acts VA* (1806–7), ch. 40, 20; Louisa County, Report, 1829, Box 7, Folder 3, OP Annual Reports, APA, LVA. |
| Prince William County | Dettingen | 1800 | Overseers of the Poor | Prince William County: Report, 1829, Box 11, Folder 3, OP Annual Reports, APA, LVA. |
| Princess Anne County | Lynnhaven | 1802 | Overseers of the Poor | Princess Anne County: Report, 1829, Box 11, Folder 5, OP Annual Reports, APA, LVA. |
| Richmond County | Lunenberg | c. 1805 | Lunenberg and Farnham Charity School | *Acts VA* (1808–9), ch. 80, 73–74; Citizens of Lunenburg Parish: Petition, Richmond County, Dec. 3, 1812, LPDC, LVA. |
| Richmond County | North Farnham | c. 1805 | Lunenberg and Farnham Charity School | *Acts VA* (1808–9), ch. 80, 73–74; Citizens of North Farnham Parish: Petition, Richmond County, Dec. 3, 1812, LPDC, LVA. |
| Shenandoah County | Beckford | 1799 | Shenandoah County Almshouse | *Acts VA* (1798–1799), ch. 32, 17; Painter, *Alms House of Shenandoah County.* |

| Locality | Parish | Date | Use after disestablishment | Sources |
|---|---|---|---|---|
| Southampton County | St. Luke's | c. 1802 | Use unknown; date of seizure estimated based on date of rector's death or departure. | Brydon, "List of Clergy of the Episcopal Church Ordained After the American Revolution," 433. |
| Southampton County (Isle of Wight before 1785) | Nottoway | c. 1802 | Use unknown; date of seizure estimated based on date of rector's death or departure. | Brydon, "List of Clergy of the Episcopal Church Ordained After the American Revolution," 433. |
| Spotsylvania County | Berkeley | 1829 | Overseers of the Poor | Spotsylvania County, Deed Book CC, 146–48. |
| Stafford County | Brunswick | 1810 | Free school (Potomac Academy) | Inhabitants: Petition, Stafford County, Dec. 12, 1810, LPDC, LVA; *Acts VA* (1810–11), ch. 51, 85–86. |
| Stafford County | Overwharton | 1810 | Free school (Potomac Academy) | Inhabitants: Petition, Stafford County, Dec. 12, 1810, LPDC, LVA; *Acts VA* (1810–11), ch. 51, 85–86. |
| Surry County | Southwark | 1804 | Overseers of the Poor | Surry County: Report, 1829, Box 13, Folder 9, OP Annual Reports, APA, LVA. |
| Warwick County | Warwick | 1806 | Construction of county buildings | Mason, *Colonial Churches of Tidewater Virginia*, 259. |
| Westmoreland County | Cople | 1812 | Westmoreland Poor School | *Acts VA* (1812–13), ch. 56, 86–89. |
| Westmoreland County | Washington | 1812 | Westmoreland Poor School | *Acts VA* (1812–13), ch. 56, 86–89. |
| York County | Charles | 1819 | Overseers of the Poor | *Acts VA* (1819–20), ch. 92, 79–80. |
| York County | Yorkhampton | 1806 | Free schools | Trustees of Yorktown: Petition, York County, Dec. 15, 1807, LPDC, LVA. |

## Sources

Bragg, D. J. *The History of Nansemond County, Virginia.* Suffolk, VA: 1909.

Brydon, G. MacLaren. "A List of Clergy of the Protestant Episcopal Church Ordained After the American Revolution, Who Served in Virginia Between 1785 and 1814, and a List of Virginia Parishes and Their Rectors for the Same Period." *William and Mary Quarterly,* 2nd ser., 19 (1939): 397–434.

Burton, Lewis William. *Annals of Henrico Parish.* Richmond, VA: 1904.

Dunn, Joseph Bragg. *The History of Nansemond County.* 1907.

Gordon, Sarah Barringer. "The Landscape of Faith: Religious Property and Confiscation in the Early Republic." In *Making Legal History: Essays in Honor of William E. Nelson,* edited by Daniel J. Hulsebosch and R. B. Bernstein. New York: NYU Press, 2013.

Hellelfinger, Jacob. *Kecoughtan old and new, or, Three hundred years of Elizabeth City Parish.* Hampton, VA: 1910.

Hening; William Waller. *The Statutes at Large; Being a Collection of All the Laws of Virginia, from the First Session of the Legislature in the Year 1619.* Richmond, VA: Printed by George Cochran (cited as Hening, *SL*).

Legislative Petitions Digital Collection, Library of Virginia, Richmond (cited as LPDC, LVA).

Mason, George Carrington. *Colonial Churches of Tidewater Virginia.* Richmond: Whittet and Shepperson, 1945.

Morrison, Alfred James. *The Beginnings of Public Education in Virginia, 1776–1860: Study of Secondary Schools in Relation to the State Literary Fund,* vol. 187. Richmond, VA: 1917.

Overseers of the Poor Annual Reports and Checklists, 1800–1909. Auditor of Public Accounts (1776–1928), Accession 739, State Government Records Collection, LVA (cited as OP Annual Reports, APA, LVA).

Painter, Fred P. *The Alms House of Shenandoah County: A Brief History.* Stephens City, VA: Commercial Press, 1979.

Rawley, Heath J. "The Glebe Lands on Carter's Creek Lancaster Co., VA." *Northern Neck Historical Magazine* 15 (1965): 1358–63.

Slaughter, Philip. *A History of St. Mark's Parish, Culpeper County, Virginia.* Baltimore: Innes & Co., 1877.

Slaughter, Philip. *The History of Truro Parish in Virginia.* Edited by Edward L. Goodwin. Philadelphia: 1908.

Turman, Nora Miller. *The Eastern Shore of Virginia, 1603–1964.* Onancock, VA: Eastern Shore News, 1964.

Woods, Edgar. *Albemarle County in Virginia.* Charlottesville, 1901.

# NOTES

## Introduction

1. "The Will of John Yeates, Sept. 18th, 1731," in W. E. MacClenny, "Yeates' Free Schools," *William and Mary Quarterly*, 2nd ser., 5 (1925): 33.
2. Inhabitants on the South Side of the Nansemond River: Petition, Nansemond County, December 21, 1802, Legislative Petitions Digital Collection, Library of Virginia, Richmond, available online at http://www.virginiamemory.com/collections/petitions (hereafter cited as LPDC, LVA).
3. John Carroll to Cardinal Antonelli, March 13, 1786, in *The John Carroll Papers*, ed. Thomas O'Brien Hanley, 3 vols. (Notre Dame, IN: University of Notre Dame Press, 1976), 1:208.
4. I use the words "reform" and "reformers" throughout this book. The utility of the term "reformation" itself has been the subject of intense debate as scholars have queried its semantics and critiqued its inherent value. My choice of language is not meant to suggest that American revolutionaries somehow finished the theological project begun by Protestants in 1517, nor should it be seen to perpetuate a whiggish narrative in which the Reformation and the American Revolution were part of a grand march toward individual freedom. Instead, I use this terminology advisedly to talk broadly about a varied group of revolutionaries bent on tearing down the established church. Evangelicals and Catholics allied with rationalist liberal thinkers to pull down the establishment and create something new. They certainly did not agree on what should be built in its place, let alone on theology or the political future of the republic, but the term "reformer" captures their shared desire to re-form church and state on new terms. For more on the language of reformation, see Benjamin Guyer, *How the English Reformation Was Named: The Politics of History* (Oxford: Oxford University Press, 2022); Christopher Haigh, *English Reformations: Religion, Politics, and Society Under the Tudors* (Oxford: Oxford University Press, 1993); Peter Marshall, *Reformation England, 1480–1642*, 3rd ed. (London: Bloomsbury Academic, 2022); Alexandra Walsham, *Charitable Hatred* (Manchester, UK: Manchester University Press, 2006); Brad S. Gregory, *The Unintended Reformation: How a Religious Revolution Secularized Society* (Cambridge, MA: Harvard University Press, 2012).

5. For more on the importance of imperial Protestantism and its collapse, see Katherine Carté, *Religion and the American Revolution: An Imperial History* (Chapel Hill: University of North Carolina Press, 2021).
6. See Rhys Isaac, *The Transformation of Virginia, 1740–1790* (Chapel Hill: University of North Carolina Press, 1982); Frank Lambert, *The Founding Fathers and the Place of Religion in America* (Princeton, NJ: Princeton University Press, 2003), 46–72; Timothy Breen, *Tobacco Culture: The Mentality of the Great Tidewater Planters on the Eve of the Revolution* (Princeton, NJ: Princeton University Press, 1985); Allan Kulikoff, *Tobacco and Slaves: The Development of Southern Cultures in the Chesapeake, 1680–1800* (Chapel Hill, NC: Institute of Early American History and Culture, Williamsburg, VA, by the University of North Carolina Press, 1986). Classic denominational histories include George MacLaren Brydon, *Virginia's Mother Church and the Political Conditions Under Which It Grew*, 2 vols. (Richmond: Virginia Historical Society, 1947–52); William Meade, *Old Churches, Ministers and Families of Virginia*, 2 vols. (Philadelphia: Lippincott, 1857).
7. For a helpful historiographical discussion of the "functionalist" approach to colonial Anglicanism, see Lauren Winner, *A Cheerful and Comfortable Faith* (New Haven, CT: Yale University Press, 2010), 3–5, 190n7, 195n42.
8. Jewel Spangler, *Virginians Reborn: Anglican Monopoly, Evangelical Dissent, and the Rise of the Baptists in the Late Eighteenth Century* (Charlottesville: University of Virginia Press, 2008); Monica Najar, *Evangelizing the South: A Social History of Church and State in Early America* (New York: Oxford University Press, 2008); Jon Ragosta, *Wellspring of Liberty: How Virginia's Religious Dissenters Helped Win the American Revolution and Secured Religious Liberty* (Oxford: Oxford University Press, 2010), 16–18; Thomas Buckley, *Church and State in Revolutionary Virginia, 1776–1787* (Charlottesville: University of Virginia Press, 1977), 8–12.
9. John Nelson's extraordinarily researched *Blessed Company* is the most comprehensive work on colonial Anglicanism and emphasizes the close cooperation between parishes and counties in local government. See Nelson, *A Blessed Company: Parishes, Parsons, and Parishioners in Anglican Virginia, 1690–1776* (Chapel Hill: University of North Carolina Press, 2001). Lauren Winner and Louis Nelson offer another important corrective by focusing on the material religion of Southern Anglicanism. See Winner, *A Cheerful and Comfortable Faith*; Louis Nelson, *The Beauty of Holiness: Anglicanism and Architecture in Early South Carolina* (Chapel Hill: University of North Carolina Press, 2009); Jacob M. Blosser, "Pursuing Happiness in Colonial Virginia: Sacred Words, Cheap Print, and Popular Religion in the Eighteenth Century," *Virginia Magazine of History and Biography* 118

(2010): 209–45; Joan R. Gundersen, *The Anglican Ministry in Virginia, 1723–1766: A Study of a Social Class* (New York: Garland, 1989); "The Non-Institutional Church: The Religious Role of Women in Eighteenth-Century Virginia," *Historical Magazine of the Protestant Episcopal Church* 51 (1982): 347–57; Edward L. Bond, *Spreading the Gospel in Colonial Virginia: Sermons and Devotional Writings* (Lanham: Lexington Books, 2004).

10. Dell Upton, *Holy Things and Profane: Anglican Parish Churches in Colonial Virginia* (New Haven, CT: Yale University Press, 1997); Winner, *Cheerful and Comfortable Faith;* L. Nelson, *Beauty of Holiness;* Louis P. Nelson, "Sensing the Sacred: Anglican Material Religion in Early South Carolina," *Winterthur Portfolio* 41 (2007): 203–321.

11. For discussions of Catholicism in Maryland, see Antoinette Sutto, *Loyal Protestants and Dangerous Papists: Maryland and the Politics of Religion in the English Atlantic, 1630–1690* (Charlottesville: University of Virginia Press, 2015); Patricia Bonomi, *Under the Cope of Heaven: Religion, Society, and Politics in Colonial America* (New York: Oxford University Press, 1986), 13, 21–24; David W. Jordan, "Political Stability and the Emergence of a Native Elite in Maryland," in *The Chesapeake in the Seventeenth Century: Essays on Anglo-American Society,* ed. David L. Ammerman and Thad Tate (New York: Norton & University of North Carolina Press, 1979), 243–72; Maura Jane Farrelly, *Papist Patriots: The Making of American Catholic Identity* (New York: Oxford University Press, 2012). Some older studies of Anglicanism in Maryland include Nelson Waite Rightmyer, *Maryland's Established Church* (Baltimore: Church Historical Society for the Diocese of Maryland, 1956); Gerald Hartdagen, "The Vestry as a Unit of Local Government in Colonial Maryland," *Maryland Historical Magazine* 67 (1972): 363–88; Carol Van Voorst, *The Anglican Clergy in Maryland, 1692–1776* (New York: Garland, 1989); Albert Warwick Werline, *Problems of Church and State in Maryland During the Seventeenth and Eighteenth Centuries* (South Lancaster, MA: College Press, 1948).

12. Major works on the Chesapeake emphasize the importance of the county court to law and government while often overlooking the parish or leaving it out altogether. See A. G. Roeber, *Faithful Magistrates and Republican Lawyers: Creators of Virginia Legal Culture, 1680–1810* (Chapel Hill: University of North Carolina Press, 1981), and "Authority, Law, and Custom: The Rituals of Court Day in Tidewater Virginia, 1720 to 1750," *William and Mary Quarterly,* 3d ser., 37 (1980): 30; Kulikoff, *Tobacco and Slaves,* 203; Lois Green Carr, "County Government in Maryland 1689–1709" (PhD diss., Harvard, 1968). For a useful overview, see Nelson, *Blessed Company,* 334n1.

13. While John Nelson's exceptional study emphasizes parishes' role in local government, I reorient my analysis around the parish as a legal institution through its powers under common law and statute and its responsibilities to execute the law. Nelson, *Blessed Company,* 13–16, 35–36, 41–47.
14. *Godwin v. Lunan,* Jeff. 96 (Va. Gen. Ct. 1771), 103.
15. State legislation remains the focus of most scholarship about disestablishment. See Thomas Buckley, *Church and State in Revolutionary Virginia, 1776–1787* (Charlottesville: University Press of Virginia, 1977); Carl H. Esbeck, "Disestablishment in Virginia, 1776–1802," and Michael D. Breidenbach, "Church and State in Maryland: Religious Liberty, Religious Tests, and Church Disestablishment," in *Disestablishment and Religious Dissent: Church-State Relations in the New American States,* ed. Carl H. Esbeck and Jonathan Den Hartog (Columbia: University of Missouri Press, 2019), 139–80, 309–26; Ragosta, *Wellspring of Liberty,* 111–60. For discussions of disestablishment and the First Amendment, see Lambert, *The Founding Fathers and the Place of Religion in America,* 207–98; Sidney Meade, *The Nation with the Soul of a Church* (New York: Harper & Row, 1975); Philip Hamburger, *Separation of Church and State* (Cambridge, MA: Harvard University Press, 2009), 19–108; Steven Green, *The Second Disestablishment* (New York: Oxford University Press, 2010), 13–78; T. Jeremy Gunn and John Witte Jr., eds., *No Establishment of Religion: America's Original Contribution to Religious Liberty* (New York: Oxford University Press, 2012).
16. Thomas Curry provides one of the best comparative accounts of the two states' disestablishments. See Curry, *The First Freedoms: Church and State in America to the Passage of the First Amendment* (New York: Oxford University Press, 1987), 134–58. Some of the most valuable work on Virginia includes Buckley, *Establishing Religious Freedom*; Ragosta, *Wellspring of Liberty*; Spangler, *Virginians Reborn.* On Maryland, see Michael D. Breidenbach, "Church and State in Maryland: Religious Liberty, Religious Tests, and Church Disestablishment," in Esbeck and Den Hartog, *Disestablishment and Religious Dissent,* 309–26; Werline, *Problems of Church and State in Maryland.*
17. For example, see Frederick V. Mills, "Disestablishment," in *Encyclopedia of Religion in the South,* 2nd ed., ed. Samuel S. Hill and Charles H. Lippy (Mercer, GA: Mercer University Press, 2005), 260–61. For some examples in Supreme Court jurisprudence, see *Everson v. Board of Education,* 330 U.S. 1 (1947), 11–14. The case lays out Virginia's history in detail and then only points to differences in other states in a footnote.
18. For example, Frederick V. Mills dates disestablishment in Maryland to 1776 and in Virginia to 1786. In choosing these dates, Mills is presumably pointing to the passage of the Maryland Declaration, which ended the

compulsory system of parochial taxation that supported the established church in 1776. In Virginia, though, he chooses 1786, the year in which the legislature rejected the general assessment plan, repealed the incorporation of the Protestant Episcopal Church, and passed the Statute for Establishing Religious Freedom. Virginia had revoked parishes' ability to levy taxes for ministerial salaries in 1776 on a temporary basis and then enacted the provision on a permanent basis in 1779. While Maryland rejected a general assessment plan in 1785, it was not until 1809 that the legislature formally amended its state constitution to prevent the state from levying religious taxes. Thus, Mills could have chosen numerous dates for disestablishment in both states, depending on the specific definition of disestablishment: 1776, 1785, or 1809 in Maryland; 1776, 1779, or 1786 in Virginia. It is essential for scholars not to presuppose the meaning of disestablishment but to specify how they are defining the term in their narratives and for the field more generally to move toward consensus about which markers denote disestablishment. See Mills, "Disestablishment," *Encyclopedia of Religion in the South,* 260–61.

19. Sidney Ahlstrom argues that only a basic form of disestablishment had been achieved in 1786 in Virginia; he contends that a complete disestablishment of the Anglican Church was not realized until 1799, when the legislature finally stripped parishes "of their customary public or landed support" by beginning the process of confiscating church glebes. For Ahlstrom, the legislature's law claiming the power to confiscate parish property constituted true disestablishment of religion. By Ahlstrom's definition, Maryland has never fully disestablished the Anglican Church because the state preserved all of the church's property. See Ahlstrom, *A Religious History of the American People,* 2nd ed. (New Haven, CT: Yale University Press, 2004), 369. Thomas Curry emphasizes that Maryland's disestablishment only went so far as to make Christian groups equal and that the state retained religious tests until the twentieth century. See Curry, *First Freedoms,* 158.

20. Important models for studying the centrality of property to disestablishment include Sarah Barringer Gordon's scholarship on antebellum state regulation of church property-holding and her work on confiscation. See Gordon, "The First Disestablishment: Limits on Church Power and Property Before the Civil War," *University of Pennsylvania Law Review* 162 (2014): 307–372; "The Landscape of Faith: Religious Property and Confiscation in the Early Republic," in *Making Legal History: Essays in Honor of William E. Nelson,* eds. Daniel J. Hulsebosch and R. B. Bernstein (New York: NYU Press, 2013), 13–48. Thomas Buckley and H. J. Eckenrode both emphasized glebe property in Virginia's disestablishment. See Buckley, *Establishing*

*Religious Freedom: Jefferson's Statute in Virginia* (Charlottesville: University of Virginia Press, 2013), 136–86; Eckenrode, *Separation of Church and State in Virginia* (Richmond, VA: 1910), 151–55. Denominational histories also recount the loss of property. See Brydon, *Virginia's Mother Church,* 2:500–509. Historians of colonial Catholicism have long focused on property rights. See Gerald P. Fogarty, "Property and Religious Liberty in Colonial Maryland Catholic Thought," *Catholic Historical Review* 72 (1986): 573–600; Patrick J. Dignan, *History of the Legal Incorporation of Catholic Church Property in the United States,* 1784–1932 (New York: P. J. Kenedy & Sons, 1935). For more recent property-focused work beyond the Chesapeake, see Erik Nordbye, "The Rights of God's Stewards: Property, Conscience, and the Great Awakening in Canterbury, Connecticut," *New England Quarterly* 95 (2022): 570–609; and Miles Smith IV, "South Carolina," in Esbeck and Den Hartog, *Disestablishment and Religious Dissent,* 180–201.

21. William Blackstone devotes significant attention to the established church in his discussion of corporations in his classic text on the common law. See William Blackstone, *Commentaries on the Laws of England,* "Of Corporations," 1:458–60, Avalon Project, https://avalon.law.yale.edu/subject_menus/blackstone.asp.

22. Joseph Stancliffe Davis's landmark history of American corporations briefly mentions colonial parishes before dismissing them as mere "quasi-corporations" rather than "true" corporations. Scholars ever since have followed Davis's lead by omitting unchartered corporations from their discussions. When recent accounts of American corporate history emphasize the very low number of corporations in the colonial and Revolutionary periods, they rely on Davis's tallies and leave out parishes and other common-law corporations. See Davis, *Essays in the Earlier History of Corporations* (Cambridge, MA: Harvard University Press, 1917), 6, 79–80; Adam Winkler, *We the Corporations* (New York: Liveright Publishing, 2018), 4, 408n2; Eric Hilt, "Early American Corporations and the State," in *Corporations and American Democracy,* ed. Naomi R. Lamoreaux and William J. Novak (Cambridge, MA: Harvard University Press, 2017), 40–42, 48, 400n14; Pauline Maier, "The Revolutionary Origins of the American Corporation," *William and Mary Quarterly,* 3rd ser., 50 (1993): 51–84.

23. Scholars of the English parish have traced the emergence of corporate powers but do not come to a clear consensus about whether common-law incorporation—authorized by customary usage rather than royal charter—constituted "true" or "quasi" corporate status. Beat Kümin recognized the "peculiar legal status" of medieval parishes as "quasi-corporate bodies" that could sue and be sued and hold property jointly. See Kümin, *The Shaping of a Community: The Rise and Reformation of the*

*English Parish c. 1400–1560* (London: Scolar Press, 1996), 2, 19–27, 149–52, 257–59. Alice E. McCampbell states that in the seventeenth century, London's vestries were not corporations but churchwardens were. See McCampbell, "The London Parish and the London Precinct, 1640–1660," *Guildhall Studies in London History* 11/3 (1976): 112, 116. Sidney and Beatrice Webb discuss the customary corporate powers of parishes. See Webb and Webb, "What Happened to the English Parish," *Political Science Quarterly* 17 (1902): 224. Steven Hindle asserts that the "parish assumed a corporate identity," particularly in lawsuits brought by churchwardens against parishioners. See Hindle, "The Political Culture of the Middling Sort, c. 1550–1700," in *The Politics of the Excluded, c. 1500–1850*, ed. Tim Harris (New York: Palgrave, 2001), 139–40. The few historians who have considered the corporate powers of Anglican parishes in the Chesapeake colonies also do not agree. Gerald Hartdagen finds that vestries possessed corporate powers in colonial Maryland, while Elliott Cramer concludes that vestries developed quasi-corporate powers in colonial Maryland. See Hartdagen, "The Anglican Vestry in Colonial Maryland: A Study in Corporate Responsibility," *Historical Magazine of the Protestant Episcopal Church* 40 (1971): 315–35; Cramer, "Constituting Christianity: The Episcopal Church and the Law in Early Maryland, 1692–1816," chap. 8, (forthcoming PhD diss., Yale University, New Haven, CT, 2026). Throughout this book, I take a functional approach and defer to the colonial sources that consistently recognized colonial vestries as corporations.

24. Legal treatises and opinions authored by colonial lawyers recognized the corporate status of vestries, churchwardens, and rectors in the Chesapeake. See George Webb, *Office and Authority*, 71, 76; "Argument for Bruton Parish the Plaintiff" (1718) cited in *Virginia Magazine of History and Biography* 12 (1914): 401–9; William Paca and Samuel Chase, "To the Rev. Mr. Jonathan Boucher," *Maryland Gazette*, January 14, 1773.

25. This difference between Chesapeake custom and formal English doctrine was one of the many ways that colonial vestries were far more powerful than those in England (see discussion in chapter 1). Chesapeake vestries' insistence on their corporate rights suggests the enduring power of this local custom through the eighteenth century. The relationship between custom and common law in the colonies has produced a rich literature, and I draw particularly on David Thomas Konig, *Law and Society in Puritan Massachusetts: Essex County, 1629–1692* (Chapel Hill: University of North Carolina Press, 1981); William E. Nelson, *The Common Law in Colonial America*, 4 vols. (New York: Oxford University Press, 2008–18), and *Americanization of the Common Law: The Impact of Legal Change on Massachusetts Society, 1760–1830* (Cambridge, MA: Harvard University

Press, 1975); Mary Sarah Bilder, *The Transatlantic Constitution: Colonial Legal Culture and the Empire* (Cambridge, MA: Harvard University Press, 2008).

26. See St. George Tucker in *Turpin v. Locket,* 10 Va. 113, 131–39 (1804); Joseph Story in *Terrett v. Taylor,* 13 U.S. (9 Cranch) 43, 46–47 (1815).
27. For more on the broader series of legal reforms after the American Revolution, see Claire Priest, "The End of Entail: Information, Institutions, and Slavery in the American Revolutionary Period," *Law and History Review* 33 (2015): 277–319; Holly Brewer, "Entailing Aristocracy in Colonial Virginia: Ancient Feudal Restraints and Revolutionary Reform," *William and Mary Quarterly,* 3rd ser., 54 (1997): 307–46; Kathryn Preyer, "Crime, the Criminal Law, and Reform," *Law and History Review* 1, no. 1 (1983): 53–85; Charles T. Cullen, *St. George Tucker and Law in Virginia, 1772–1804* (New York: Garland, 1987); Alan Taylor, *The Internal Enemy: Slavery and War in Virginia, 1772–1832* (New York: Norton, 2013), 39–46; Bruce Mann, *Republic of Debtors: Bankruptcy in the Age of American Independence* (Cambridge, MA: Harvard University Press, 2009).
28. I rely on a large body of scholarship for my discussion of republicanism. See Joyce Appleby, *Capitalism and a New Social Order: The Republican Vision of the 1790s* (New York: NYU Press, 1984); Linda K. Kerber, *Women of the Republic: Intellect and Ideology in Revolutionary America* (Chapel Hill: Omohundro Institute of Early American History and Culture, University of North Carolina Press, 1997); Bernard Bailyn, *The Ideological Origins of the American Revolution,* 3rd ed. (Cambridge, MA: Harvard University Press, 2017); Gordon Wood, *The Creation of the American Republic, 1776–1787,* 2nd ed. (Chapel Hill: Omohundro Institute of Early American History and Culture, University of North Carolina Press, 1998). Important works that consider the relationship between race and republicanism include John Saillant, *Black Puritan, Black Republican: The Life and Thought of Lemuel Haynes, 1753–1833* (New York: Oxford University Press, 2002), 47–82; Gary Nash, *Race and Revolution* (Oxford: Rowman & Littlefield, 1990), 26–28, 75–81; Joanne Pope Melish, *Disowning Slavery: Gradual Emancipation and "Race" in New England, 1780–1860* (Ithaca, NY: Cornell University Press, 1998), 1–5, 50–79; Michael A. Morrison and James Brewer Stewart, eds., *Race and the Early Republic: Racial Consciousness and Nation-Building in the Early Republic* (Lanham, MD: Rowman & Littlefield, 2001).
29. Rebecca Anne Goetz, *The Baptism of Early Virginia: How Christianity Created Race* (Baltimore: Johns Hopkins University Press, 2012); Jennifer Oast, *Institutional Slavery: Slaveholding Churches, Schools, Colleges, and Businesses in Virginia, 1680–1860* (Cambridge: Cambridge University

Press, 2016); Steven Craig Wilder, "War and Priests: Catholic Colleges and Slavery in the Age of Revolution," in *Slavery's Capitalism*, ed. Sven Beckert and Seth Rockman (Philadelphia: University of Pennsylvania Press, 2016), 227–42; Steven Craig Wilder, *Ebony and Ivy: Race, Slavery, and the Troubled History of America's Universities* (New York: Bloomsbury, 2014); Thomas Murphy, SJ, *Jesuit Slaveholding in Maryland, 1717–1838* (New York: Routledge, 2001).

30. US Constitution, Amendment I.
31. The shortcomings of disestablishment that scholars have rightly pointed out are in fact reflective of the mutability of "establishment" as a legal concept. There was no unified sense of the movement we now call disestablishment at the time of the founding. See David Sehat, *The Myth of American Religious Freedom* (New York: Oxford University Press, 2011); Steven Green, *The Second Disestablishment* (New York: Oxford University Press, 2010); Tracy Fessenden, *Culture and Redemption: Religion, the Secular, and American Literature* (Princeton, NJ: Princeton University Press, 2007).
32. John Carroll to Cardinal Antonelli, March 13, 1786, in *John Carroll Papers*, 1:208. See editorial discussion in "Act for Establishing Religious Freedom, [31 October] 1785," Founders Online, https://founders.archives.gov/documents/Madison/01-08-02-0206.

## 1. Established by Law

1. Belinda Nash and Danielle Sheets, *A Place in Time: The Age of the Witch of Pungo* (Virginia Beach, VA: W. S. Dawson Co., 2013); "Grace Sherwood: The One Virginia Witch," *Harper's Monthly Magazine* 69 (1884): 99–101. For an excellent scholarly examination of Grace Sherwood's case and its local memory, see Scott O. Moore, *The Witch of Pungo: Grace Sherwood in Virginia History and Legend* (Charlottesville: University of Virginia Press, 2024). See also Cynthia A. Kierner, "Grace Sherwood: The Virginia Witch," in *Virginia Women: Their Lives and Times*, ed. Cynthia A. Kierner (Athens, GA: University of Georgia Press, 2015), 11–32.
2. For example, see Emerson Baker, *A Storm of Witchcraft: The Salem Trials and the American Experience* (New York: Oxford University Press, 2014), 206; Jon Butler, Grant Wacker, and Randall Balmer, *Religion in American Life: A Short History* (New York: Oxford University Press, 2011), 86.
3. See Carol F. Karlsen, *Devil in the Shape of a Woman* (New York: Norton, 1987); Paul Boyer and Stephen Nissenbaum, *Salem Possessed* (Cambridge, MA: Harvard University Press, 1974).

4. Princess Anne County Court, "Records, 1706 January 2–July 10, of the Court of Princess Anne County, Va., concerning the trial of Grace Sherwood for witchcraft," Manuscripts Vault, Mss4 P9354 a, 2, Virginia Museum of History and Culture, Richmond (hereafter VMHC).
5. "Records, 1706 January 2–July 10," 2, VMHC.
6. "Records, 1706 January 2–July 10," 5, VMHC.
7. Nash and Sheets, *A Place in Time.*
8. "Records, 1706 January 2–July 10," 5, VMHC.
9. "Records, 1706 January 2–July 10," 5–6, VMHC.
10. George Webb, *The Office and Authority of a Justice of Peace* (Williamsburg, VA: 1736), 361–62.
11. Col. Edward Moseley, Capt. Horatio Woodhouse, Capt. Henry Chapman, and Major Henry Spratt all presided over Grace Sherwood's trial and served as vestrymen. Compare "Records, 1706 January 2–July 10," 1–6, VMHC; George Carrington Mason, ed., *The Colonial Vestry Book of Lynnhaven Parish, Princess Anne County, Virginia, 1723–1786* (Newport News: VA, 1949).
12. Numerous scholars have noted that many of the same local gentlemen were both justices of the peace and vestrymen. This dual officeholding strengthened the hold of the planter elite over Chesapeake society, but the jurisdictions of the parish and the county were still distinct. Gentlemen sat on the county court in their capacity as JPs, but they presented parishioners, disbursed funds, and oversaw processioning, tobacco inspection, and indentures in their capacity as parish representatives. See Rhys Isaac, *The Transformation of Virginia, 1740–1790* (Chapel Hill: University of North Carolina Press, 1982), 133–35; Charles S. Sydnor, *Gentlemen Freeholders: Political Practices in Washington's Virginia* (Chapel Hill: University of North Carolina Press, 1952), 80, 89–92.
13. Princess Anne County Court, "Processioners' Report on Lands, Oct. 19–Nov. 4, 1731," Minute Book, No. 2 [Orders], 1709–17, Princess Anne County Records, Microfilm 38, 269–71, LVA.
14. See Kierner, "Grace Sherwood," 17.
15. Mason, *Colonial Vestry Book of Lynnhaven Parish,* 40–41.
16. Mason, *Colonial Vestry Book of Lynnhaven Parish,* 46, 48, 51, 53, 57–58, 93, 96, 100, 107, 109.
17. James Maury, "To Christians of Every Denomination" (Annapolis: Green, 1771), 31; Rev. James Maury to Commissary Dawson, October 6, 1755, cited in "Letters of Patrick Henry, Sr., Samuel Davies, James Maury, Edwin Conway and George Trask," *William and Mary Quarterly* 1, no. 4 (1921): 278.

18. For an overview of scholarship that emphasizes the prolonged and processual nature of the English Reformation, see Peter Marshall, "(Re)defining the English Reformation," *Journal of British Studies* 48, no. 3 (2009): 564–86. For more on the slow process of religious reform in England, see Eamon Duffy, *The Stripping of the Altars: Traditional Religion in England, c. 1400–c. 1580* (New Haven, CT: Yale University Press, 1992); Nicholas Tyacke, ed., *England's Long Reformation: 1500–1800* (London: UCL Press, 1997); Margaret Aston, *Broken Idols of the English Reformation* (Cambridge: Cambridge University Press, 2016).
19. Richard Hooker, *Of the Laws of Ecclesiastical Polity: Preface, Book I, Book VIII,* ed. Arthur Steven McGrade (Cambridge: Cambridge University Press, 1989), 130.
20. Brian Walsh, *Unsettled Toleration: Religious Difference on the Shakespearean Stage* (Oxford: Oxford University Press, 2016), 1.
21. John Buckeridge, *A Sermon Preached Before His Majestie at Whitehall, March 22, 1617* (London: 1618), cited in Glenn Burgess, "Divine Right of Kings Reconsidered," *English Historical Review* 107 (1992): 857.
22. William Waller Hening, ed., *The Statutes at Large; Being a Collection of All the Laws of Virginia, from the First Session of the Legislature in the Year 1619* (Richmond: J & G Cochran, 1821), 1:68–69 (hereafter cited as Hening, *SL,* followed by volume and page numbers).
23. Brent Tarter, "Lawes Divine, Morall, and Martiall," in *Encyclopedia Virginia,* Virginia Humanities, Last modified January 20, 2012, https://www.encyclopediavirginia.org/Lawes_Divine_Morall_and_Martiall.
24. For more on religious difference in early Jamestown, see *Spreading the Gospel in Colonial Virginia: Sermons and Devotional Writings,* ed. Edward L. Bond (Lanham, MD: Lexington Books, 2004), 5–10.
25. Hening, *SL,* 1:155, 157–61, 223, 229, 249–51, 278, 298, 317, 399–400.
26. On religious diversity in early Virginia, see Philip D. Morgan, "Religious Diversity in Colonial Virginia: Red, Black, and White," in *From Jamestown to Jefferson: The Evolution of Religious Freedom in Virginia,* ed. Paul Rasor and Richard E. Bond (Charlottesville: University of Virginia Press, 2011); Kevin Butterfield, "Puritans and Religious Strife in the Early Chesapeake," *Virginia Magazine of History and Biography* 101 (2001): 5–36.
27. Butterfield, "Puritans and Religious Strife in the Early Chesapeake," 8–10.
28. For more on the Society of Friends in the colony, see Kenneth L. Carroll, "Quakerism on the Eastern Shore of Virginia," *Virginia Magazine of History and Biography* 74 (1966): 170–89.
29. George Webb, *The Office and Authority of a Justice of Peace* (Williamsburg: 1736).

30. "The Charter of Maryland: 1632," Avalon Project, Yale Law School, https://avalon.law.yale.edu/17th_century/ma01.asp.
31. For more on the growing tensions between Calvert and the Jesuits, particularly over land, see Robert Emmett Curran, *Papist Devils: Catholics in British America, 1574–1783* (Washington, DC: Catholic University of America Press, 2014), 45–56; Antoinette Sutto, "Lord Baltimore, the Society of Jesus, and Caroline Absolutism," *Journal of British Studies* 48, no. 3 (2009): 631–52; Russell R. Menard, "Maryland's 'Time of Troubles,'" *Maryland Historical Magazine* 76 (1981): 124–40; John D. Krugler, "Lord Baltimore, Roman Catholics, and Toleration," *Catholic Historical Review* 65 (1979): 67–72; Thomas Hughes, SJ, *The History of the Society of Jesus in North America, Colonial and Federal,* 4 vols. (New York, 1907–17), 1:499–501, 556–59; Gerald P. Fogarty, "Property and Religious Liberty in Colonial Maryland Catholic Thought," *Catholic Historical Review* 72 (1986): 573–600.
32. "An Act Concerning Religion," September 21, 1649, Avalon Project, http://avalon.law.yale.edu/18th_century/maryland_toleration.asp.
33. Archives of Maryland Online, 5:131. This database is at https://msa.maryland.gov/megafile/msa/speccol/sc2900/sc2908/html/volumes.html. The volumes are listed in order at the above URL.
34. Kenneth L. Carroll, "Quaker Opposition to the Establishment of a State Church in Maryland," *Maryland Historical Magazine* 65, no. 2 (1970): 155.
35. Archives of Maryland Online, 5:137, 147.
36. Archives of Maryland Online, 8:137–38.
37. See Carroll, "Quaker Opposition to a State Church in Maryland," 149–70.
38. Archives of Maryland Online, 13:430.
39. For a chronological discussion of these acts, see Carroll, "Quaker Opposition to a State Church in Maryland"; Spencer Ervin, "The Established Church of Colonial Maryland," *Historical Magazine of the Protestant Episcopal Church* 24 (1955): 232–92.
40. Carroll, "Quaker Opposition to a State Church in Maryland," 149–71.
41. Archives of Maryland Online, 8:107, 448; 20:144; 22:487; 26:46, 289, 340, 349; 27:371; 33:109, 189. For more on anti-Catholic laws adopted in Maryland, see Maura Jane Farrelly, *Papist Patriots: The Making of American Catholic Identity* (New York: Oxford University Press, 2010), 188–218.
42. Hening, *SL,* 3:171. For continued arguments about the applicability of the English Act of Toleration to Virginia, see Rev. James Maury to Commissary Dawson, October 6, 1755, cited in "Letters of Patrick Henry, Sr., Samuel Davies, James Maury, Edwin Conway and George Trask," *William and Mary Quarterly,* ser. 2, 1, no. 4 (1921): 278; "An Address to the Anabaptists Imprisoned at Caroline," *Virginia Gazette,* Feb. 20, 1772 (Purdie and

Dixon). For a discussion of licensing, see Isaac, *Transformation of Virginia*, 149–53, 199–205.

43. John Nelson's study of parishes refers to the "parish-county" as a "dual institution" of local government. His work offers an important revision by highlighting the importance of parishes in Virginia's system of government. See *A Blessed Company: Parishes, Parsons, and Parishioners in Anglican Virginia, 1690–1776* (Chapel Hill: University of North Carolina Press, 2001), 4, 13.
44. For more on the development of the parish and its central role in English life, see Beat Kümin, *The Shaping of a Community: The Rise and Reformation of the English Parish c. 1400–1560* (Aldershot, UK: Scolar Press, 1996); Valerie Hitchman and Andrew Foster, eds., *Views from the Parish: Churchwardens' Accounts, c. 1500–c. 1800* (Newcastle, UK: Cambridge Scholars Publishing, 2015); Katherine French, Gary Gibbs, and Beat Kümin, eds., *The Parish in English Life, 1400–1600* (Manchester, UK: Manchester University Press, 1997); Katherine French, *The People of the Parish: Community Life in a Late Medieval English Diocese* (Philadelphia: University of Pennsylvania Press, 2001).
45. The Convention of the Clergy of Virginia to the Bishop of London, April 10, 1719, in *Historical Collections Relating to the American Colonial Church*, vol. 1, *Virginia*, ed. William Stevens Perry (Hartford, CT: Church Press Co., 1878), 213.
46. Colonial vestries exercised far more power than their English counterparts. In England, the term "vestry" referred to a meeting or assembly of the parishioners called to make decisions about the parish. During the English Reformation, an institution known as the select vestry emerged as a corporate, decision-making body in some parishes, but its members still were elected annually. See Nelson, *Blessed Company*, 39–40, 373n7; Kümin, *Shaping of a Community*, 250–53.
47. In Virginia, the right of advowson, or installing the parish rector, technically belonged to the royal governor, but vestries claimed the right to "present" all candidates for induction to the governor, thereby seizing control of a crucial lever of power. Virginian vestries often put prospective clergyman through a trial period, which newly arrived clergymen viewed as not just imperious but impious. See Nelson, *Blessed Company*, 127–33.
48. Gov. Alexander Spotswood to the Vestry of St. Ann's, Essex County, VA, September 3, 1718, quoted in Perry, *Historical Collections*, vol. 1, *Virginia*, 204.
49. By law, the two longest-serving lay vestrymen of every Maryland parish had to give up their seats each year, and the freeholders elected two new vestrymen in their stead on Easter Monday. See Bacon's *Laws of Maryland*, at Archives of Maryland Online, 75:714–16.

50. 1704 and 1727 Statutes; Regulation for Payment of Parochial Charges. See Bacon's *Laws of Maryland,* at Archives of Maryland Online, 75:131.
51. Maryland's vestries and parishioners had no control over the appointment of clergymen. For example, when St. James Parish in Anne Arundel County needed a new minister, Gov. Charles Calvert, "recomend[ed] and appointed the Said Peter Tustian to be Rector of your Parrish, and Direct you to receive him as Incumbent thereof." See Edith Stansbury Dallam, ed., *St. James' Parish: old Herring Creeke Parish: a History, 1663–1799* (Lothian, MD: Vestry of St. James' Parish, 1976), 193.
52. Virginia's vestries were not entirely autonomous, however. The House of Burgesses retained the right to dissolve vestries and exercised this power from time to time when they determined a vestry had failed in its legal duties. The legislature required serious accusations to dissolve a vestry, though, and for the most part, Virginian vestries operated autonomously, much to the chagrin of many clergymen and civil leaders. Hening, *SL,* 7:144–46, 154–55.
53. Churchwardens are remarkably absent from accounts of government and law in the Chesapeake, presumably because so few of their records survive. However, copies of churchwardens' records appear in the vestry books of Bristol Parish and Henrico Parish, which detail their activity. See R. A. Brock, ed., *The Vestry Book of Henrico Parish, Virginia 1730–'73* (Richmond, VA: 1874), 151–52; C. G. Chamberlayne, ed., *The Vestry Book and Register of Bristol Parish, 1720–1789* (Richmond, VA: 1898), 129–39, 189–201, 203–7, 213–14, 216–17, 226–29, 263.
54. Robert Carter, "Rules for the conduct of churchwardens," 1775, 10, Carter family papers, 1651–1861, VMHC. See also Hening, *SL,* 5:226.
55. *The Vestry Book of Truro Parish, 1732–1802,* 53, https://www.pohick.org/history/colonial-origins/pages/the-truro-parish-colonial-vestry-book.
56. The quality of the Anglican clergy in the Chesapeake has been debated at length in the literature, as have the efforts to oversee and discipline the clergy. For discussion of Virginia, see Isaac, *Transformation of Virginia,* 144–45, 150, 281–89; Nelson, *Blessed Company,* 149–61, 409n75; Joan R. Gundersen, "The Search for Good Men: Recruiting Ministers in Colonial Virginia," *Historical Magazine of the Protestant Episcopal Church* 48, no. 4 (1979): 453–64. For a discussion of clerical authority and oversight in Maryland, see Carol Van Voorst, *The Anglican Clergy in Maryland, 1692–1776* (New York: Garland, 1989).
57. "The Vestry of Coventry Parish to Horatio Sharpe," *Proceedings of the Council of Maryland, 1761–1769,* Archives of Maryland Online, 32:229.
58. Rev. Robert Paxton, "Of Justice and Equity," cited in Bond, *Spreading the Gospel,* 149. Paxton drew extensively on the works of Archbishop John

Tillotson, whose published sermons were among the most popular devotional writings in the colonial Chesapeake. See Tillotson, *The Works of the Most Reverend Dr. John Tillotson, Lord Archbishop of Canterbury* (London: J. and R. Tonson, 1752), 37.

59. Lt. Governor Spotswood to the Council of Trade and Plantations, December 15, 1710, in *The Calendar of State Papers, Colonial: North America and the West Indies 1574–1739*, 25:313–18, Colonial State Papers, ProQuest.
60. For the evolution of Virginia's church attendance laws during the colonial era, see Hening, *SL*, 1:123; 2:48; 3:170–71, 360; 5:226. For more on their enforcement in Virginia, see Nelson, *Blessed Company*, 244–49, 286.
61. Collect for the King, The Communion, *The Book of Common Prayer* (Cambridge, 1760).
62. Dell Upton, *Holy Things and Profane: Anglican Parish Churches in Colonial Virginia* (New Haven, CT: Yale University Press, 1997), 55, 74, 97–98, 120, 163.
63. This quotation comes from a popular English sermon about public worship that was frequently cited and circulated in the colonies. William Beveridge, "A Sermon Concerning the Excellency and Usefulness of the Common Prayer" (London: 1683), 24.
64. Rev. Miles Selden, "The Great Duty of Publick Worship," in Bond, *Spreading the Gospel*, 535, 537.
65. Rev. James Blair, "The Fifth Petition of the Lord's Prayer," in Bond, *Spreading the Gospel*, 224.
66. Blair, "Fifth Petition," in Bond, *Spreading the Gospel*, 224.
67. Lt. Governor Gooch to the Council of Trade and Plantations, July 18, 1732, in *The Calendar of State Papers, Colonial: North America and the West Indies 1574–1739*, 39:173–78, Colonial State Papers, ProQuest.
68. Bacon's *Laws of Maryland*, at Archives of Maryland Online, 75:344–46.
69. Hening, *SL*, 3:461. An example of the slave code being copied into the vestry book in order to be recited at worship can be found in Charles Gibson Chamberlayne, *The Vestry Book of Christ Church Parish, Middlesex County, Virginia, 1663–1767* (Richmond, VA: Old Dominion Press, 1927), 189–97.
70. *Virginia Gazette*, January 20, 1737, 2. For more on this, see A. G. Roeber, "'The Scrutiny of the Ill Natured Ignorant Vulgar': Lawyers and Print Culture in Virginia, 1716 to 1774," *Virginia Magazine of History and Biography* 91 (1983): 398.
71. Vestries in Maryland also purchased published copies of the laws. For example, see "Vestry Proceedings, St. Ann's," *Maryland Historical Magazine* 10, no. 2 (1915): 133.
72. Hening, *SL*, 3:515.
73. Lt. Governor Spotswood to the Earl of Dartmouth, Virginia, June 30, 1713, cited in Alexander Spotswood, *The Official Letters of Alexander*

*Spotswood, Lieutenant-Governor of the Colony of Virginia . . .* , ed. Robert Alonzo Brock (Richmond, VA: 1882), 2:30.

74. Laws in Virginia and Maryland both stipulated numerous public notices be posted on the church door. In Virginia (at Hening, *SL*), see, for example, laws requiring notices be posted about land sales, 8:590; court summons, 4:83; 5:220–25; docking of entail, 8:276–77; the annual levy, 6:41; processioning, 3:421; elections, 7:520; stray animals, 4:48; public auctions, 3:275–76. In Maryland (at Archives of Maryland Online), see laws about posting notice on the church door about land disputes, 36:517–18; court summons, 841:95; 543:257; public petitions, 61:519–23.
75. See Hening, *SL*, 1:261; 2:333; 5:19; 7:96.
76. Hening, *SL*, 3:460.
77. Mason, *Colonial Vestry Book of Lynnhaven Parish*, 23.
78. For evidence of female parishioners in Maryland receiving loans from the vestry, see Dallam, *St. James*, 243. For an example of a female parishioner's influence on vestry activity, see the instruction of Mrs. Bladen directing the vestry to build a private vault to bury her family in "Vestry Proceedings, St. Ann's Parish, Annapolis, MD," *Maryland Historical Magazine* 6 (1911): 349. For more on women's role in directing private religion within Anglican homes in the colonial Chesapeake, see Lauren F. Winner, *A Cheerful and Comfortable Faith: Anglican Religious Practice in the Elite Households of Eighteenth-Century Virginia* (New Haven, CT: Yale University Press, 2010).
79. Lt. Governor Gooch to the Council of Trade and Plantations, February 12, 1731, in *The Calendar of State Papers, Colonial: North America and the West Indies 1574–1739*, 38:41–42, Colonial State Papers, ProQuest.
80. Archives of Maryland Online, 50:198–99.
81. "An Address to the Anabaptists Imprisoned at Caroline," *Virginia Gazette* (Purdie and Dixon), February 20, 1772.
82. Jeffrey Robert Young, ed., *Proslavery and Sectional Thought in the Early South, 1740–1829* (Columbia: University of South Carolina Press, 2006), 81.
83. Young, *Proslavery and Sectional Thought*, 92.
84. Young, *Proslavery and Sectional Thought*, 81.
85. Archives of Maryland Online, 203:99.
86. Maryland's attendance laws exempted dissenters from attending parish worship but not Catholics. See Archives of Maryland Online, 24:265–73.
87. Archives of Maryland Online, 24:265–73. For more on the restrictions of Catholics' religious and political rights under the Anglican establishment, see Farrelly, *Papist Patriots*, 188–217.

88. An example of vestrymen signing these oaths is preserved in vestry book of Little Chuckatuck Parish (Nansemond County, VA) and transcribed in William Meade, *Old Churches, Ministers and Families of Virginia,* 2 vols. (Philadelphia: Lippincott, 1857), 1:307.
89. For more on the tithable system in Virginia and its relationship to racialized and gendered understandings of labor, see Kathleen Brown, *Good Wives, Nasty Wenches, and Anxious Patriarchs* (Chapel Hill: University of North Carolina Press, 1996), 116–28. For more on the relationship between labor, gender, and race in the wider seventeenth-century British Atlantic, see Jennifer L. Morgan, *Laboring Women: Reproduction and Gender in New World Slavery* (Philadelphia: University of Pennsylvania Press, 2004); Brooke Newman, *A Dark Inheritance: Blood, Race, and Sex in Colonial Jamaica* (New Haven, CT: Yale University Press, 2018).
90. Chamberlayne, *Vestry Book of Christ Church,* 142.
91. C. G. Chamberlayne, ed., *The Vestry Book of Blisland (Blissland) Parish, New Kent and James City Counties, Virginia, 1721–1786* (Richmond: 1935), 109.
92. For example, in Lynnhaven Parish, records show an average parish levy between 1723–76 of 31 pounds of tobacco and that a minister's income accounted for 39 percent of the annual levy between 1723–76. See Mason, *Colonial Vestry Book of Lynnhaven Parish,* 44. John Nelson shows that parish levies were usually higher than the county or provincial levy. See Nelson, *Blessed Company,* 43–45. Over a century ago, Phillip Bruce came to the same conclusion. See Bruce, *Institutional History of Virginia in the Seventeenth Century,* 2 vols. (New York: 1910), 1:77.
93. This figure was calculated from the levies recorded in 1734, 1741, 1746, 1750, 1754, and 1759 by the county's four parishes: Saint Paul's Parish, Queen Ann Parish, King George Parish, and Prince George Parish. Levy Book A, Prince George's County, C1245, Maryland State Archives, Annapolis (hereafter cited as MSA).
94. Bacon's *Laws of Maryland,* at Archives of Maryland Online, 75:687. The decrease in salary from forty to thirty pounds per poll was enacted after the tobacco inspection laws raised the standard of tobacco. The law lowered a number of public salaries and rates in order to account for the increase in the real price of the tobacco that served as currency. See Mary McKinney Schweitzer, "Economic Regulation and the Colonial Economy: The Maryland Tobacco Inspection Act of 1747," *Journal of Economic History* 40 (1980): 563.
95. Augusta Parish, Vestry Book, Augusta County, VA, Accession 20429, 345, Church records collection, LVA.

96. Mason, *Colonial Vestry Book of Lynnhaven Parish,* 95. Though beyond the scope of this project, more detailed analysis of the relationship between parochial poor relief and race deserves closer attention in future studies.
97. See, for example, how the Blackwater Monthly Meeting in Surry County Virginia distributed poor relief to Friends seeking assistance and support for orphaned children in the community: Martha A. Putnam, *Early Quaker Records of Southeast Virginia* (Berwyn Heights, MD: Heritage Book, 2020), 15–16.
98. For example, the Meeting Minutes of Cedar Creek Monthly Meeting note, "Thomas Clark was appointed to inspect the needs of the poor," in 1747. Mary Marshall Brewer, ed., *Quaker Records of Cedar Creek Monthly Meeting, Virginia, 1739–1793* (Lewes, DE: Colonial Roots, 2002). See also Najar, *Evangelizing the South,* 91–93.
99. See discussion of "sufferings" in the minutes of the Blackwater and Chuckatuck Monthly Meetings of Friends in Putnam, *Early Quaker Records of Southeast Virginia,* 16, 52.
100. Augusta Parish, Vestry Book, LVA, 362.
101. Chamberlayne, *Vestry Book and Register of Bristol Parish,* 168, 182.
102. Mason, *Colonial Vestry Book of Lynnhaven Parish,* 33–47.
103. For more on how Virginian women cultivated powerful local networks through practices like midwifery, see Joan R. Gundersen, "Kith and Kin: Women's Networks in Colonial Virginia," in *The Devil's Lane: Sex and Race in the Early South,* ed. Catherine Clinton and Michele Gillespie (New York: Oxford University Press, 1997), 90–108.
104. For example, the 1761 St. James Parish levy reflects wide-ranging types of expenditures. The accounts of the annual levies are often vague and list only the name of the recipient and the amount of money he or she received without any additional explanation. However, the vestry's orders for goods and services in the meeting minutes clarify them. See, for example, the 1761 levy in Dallam, *St. James' Parish,* 385.
105. Dallam, *St. James' Parish,* 247.
106. The levy of 1754 makes no mention of the loan but simply lists a payment of 3,500 pounds of tobacco to Cha. Drury as a line-item expense. Dallam, *St. James' Parish,* 233, 394.
107. Dallam, *St. James' Parish,* 233.
108. Such was the case in Lynnhaven Parish, Virginia. Anthony McKeel served as sexton in the brick church most years from 1752 to 1772, in addition to receiving reimbursements for medical care and poor relief payments some years. Thereafter, Frances McKeel, likely his wife, took over the role from 1773 to 1778. See Mason, *Colonial Vestry Book of Lynnhaven Parish,*

46, 48–51, 61, 64, 68–74, 76, 78, 81, 83, 86, 88, 92, 95, 99, 101, 103, 105, 107, 109, 111, 112.

109. The parish undertook major construction projects to build and rebuild the church, the chapels, the poor house, and the glebe house in 1727–29, 1731, 1733, 1740, 1751, 1757, and 1770. See Mason, *Colonial Vestry Book of Lynnhaven Parish,* 6–8, 10, 12–13, 17–21, 24, 28–31, 41, 43, 52, 54, 60, 87, 90, 87, 91, 93–95, 97.

110. Archives of Maryland Online, 46:122; Vestry Minutes, Shrewsbury Parish, Kent County, MD, SCM 339-1, 61–62, MSA.

111. Hening, *SL,* 1:158.

112. Rev. James Blair, "The Peacemakers," 180. On the importance of holy rites, see Robert Paxton, "Of the Lord's Supper," 160–70. Both cited in Bond, *Spreading the Gospel.*

113. Hening, *SL,* 3:258–61. Maryland adopted the same framework in 1724. Bacon's *Laws of Maryland,* Archives of Maryland Online, 75:360, 708–9.

114. Archives of Maryland Online, 24:268.

115. Augusta County Court, Order Book 8, June 22, 1763, in Lyman Chalkley, ed., *Chronicles of the Scotch-Irish Settlement in Virginia, Extracted from the Original Court Records of Augusta County, 1745–1800,* 3 vols. (Rosslyn, VA: National Society of the Daughters of the American Revolution, 1912), 1:107.

116. John Page, *A Deed of Gift to My Dear Son,* in Bond, *Spreading the Gospel,* 99, 103.

117. Archives of Maryland Online, 52:503.

118. Marriage by banns cost only 5 shillings current money. See Hening, SL, 6:84. Maryland also set prices for marriages by statute. See Bacon's *Laws of Maryland,* at Archives of Maryland Online, 75:686.

119. Joseph A. Waddell, *Annals of Augusta* (Staunton, VA: 1902), 292.

120. Some dissenting communities disowned members who were married by the parish rector. For example, in 1773, Ann Thompson was disowned by the Blackwater Monthly Meeting of Friends in Virginia's Surry County after getting "married by a hireling priest." Putnam, *Early Quaker Records of Southeast Virginia,* 17.

121. Augusta County, County Court Judgments, May 1767, Record Book E, reproduced in Chalkley, *Chronicles of the Scotch-Irish Settlement in Virginia,* 1:463.

122. Archives of Maryland Online, 52:503.

123. Archives of Maryland Online, 52:508–10.

124. Dallam, *St. James' Parish,* 291; Vestry Minutes, Shrewsbury Parish, Kent County, MD, SCM 339-1, 87, MSA.

125. Dallam, *St. James' Parish,* 299.
126. Archives of Maryland Online, 52:504.
127. Records show that when counties collected fines for moral crimes, these funds did not specifically go to poor relief but were simply added to the county's coffers. See Prince George Parish, Levy Book A, Prince George's County, C1245, 31, MSA.
128. This phrase comes from the vestry's investigation in 1775 into the marriage of William Merritt and his deceased wife's granddaughter, Martha Vansant. The parish condemned the marriage and presented the pair to the Kent County Court for an incestual relationship. Vestry Minutes, Shrewsbury Parish, Kent County, MD, SCM 339-1, 127, MSA.
129. "An Act for the Punishing the Offences of Adultery and Fornication" (1715), Bacon's *Laws of Maryland,* at Archives of Maryland Online, 75:222.
130. Vestry Minutes, Shrewsbury Parish, Kent County, Md., SCM 339-1, 25, 27, 33, 35, 38, 40, 43, 47, 72, MSA.
131. Somerset County Court, March 1729, Archives of Maryland Online, 567:105; see also Archives of Maryland Online, 30:244.
132. Chamberlayne, *Vestry Book and Register of Bristol Parish,* 167–68.
133. These were small sums in proportion to the parish's total budget, at most 2–4 percent, but still allowed the parish to provide additional relief disbursements.
134. Wilmer L. Hall, ed., *The Vestry Book of the Upper Parish, Nansemond County, Virginia, 1743–1793* (Richmond: Commonwealth of Virginia, 1949), 55.
135. Najar, *Evangelizing the South,* 91.
136. Fairfax County, Order Book, 1754–1756, Microfilm Reel 37, passim, LVA.
137. The Augusta Parish vestry book contains hundreds of bastardy bonds and lists punishments imposed on single women for bearing children. For instance, the Augusta County Court convicted Catherine Quinn for bastardy in 1747. Deeming her a "lewd woman," she was sentenced to whipping and her son was bound out by the churchwardens. See Augusta Parish, Vestry Book, 34, 47. LVA.
138. Chamberlayne, *Vestry Book and Register of Bristol Parish,* 45. See a similar case in Augusta Parish from 1756 of a parent requesting an indenture for their child due to financial hardship. See Augusta Parish, Vestry Book, 391, LVA.
139. For example, see *Vestry Book of Saint Peter's Parish, 1682–1758,* 217.
140. For example, see Chamberlayne, *Vestry Book and Register of Bristol Parish,* 59.
141. Goetz, *Baptism of Early Virginia,* 78–85.
142. Under the legal doctrine of *partus sequitur ventrem,* a woman's legal status determined the status of her children. While mixed-race children born to

white mothers were free people of color, Virginia law required them to be bound out under the age of 31. See Hening, *SL*, 2:170; 3:86, 453.

143. This statute was first passed in 1691 and updated again in 1733 and 1752. Hening, *SL*, 3:86–87.
144. Chamberlayne, *Vestry Book and Register of Bristol Parish*, 134.
145. Dallam, *St. James' Parish*, 187, 257.
146. *Vestry Book of Saint Peter's Parish, 1682–1758, New Kent County* (Richmond, VA: National Society of the Colonial Dames for the State of Virginia), 168.
147. Processioning had been required by law since 1662 but was haphazardly enforced. By the terms of the 1705 act, justices of the peace and vestrymen were personally fined if they failed to organize processioning. The regular entry of processioners' returns into vestry books from across the colony reflected that the legislation was closely observed. See Hening, *SL*, 2:102.
148. Brock, *Vestry Book of Henrico Parish*, 53, 70.
149. A 1723 law in Virginia, "An Act for the better and more Effectual Improving the Staple of Tobacco," had initially given parishes the right to appoint tobacco inspectors. For the full text of the 1723 and 1727 acts, see C. G. Chamberlayne, "The Tobacco Acts of 1723 and 1729," *Virginia Magazine of History and Biography* 20 (1912): 158–78. For an example of Virginian vestries appointing inspectors, see C. G. Chamberlayne, ed., *The Vestry Book of Petsworth Parish, Gloucester County, Virginia, 1677–1793* (Richmond, VA: 1933), 214. In 1730, the legislature transferred this power from vestries to the county courts. For a discussion of the 1730 law, see Stacy L. Lorenz, "'To Do Justice to His Majesty, the Merchant and the Planter': Governor William Gooch and the Virginia Tobacco Inspection Act of 1730," *Virginia Magazine of History and Biography* 108, no. 4 (2000): 345–92.
150. The text of the 1747 Tobacco Inspection Act can be found in Archives of Maryland Online, 44:595–638. The act was amended in 1748 and then overhauled in 1763. Bacon's *Laws of Maryland*, at Archives of Maryland Online, 75:584–633.
151. This quotation from the *Maryland Gazette* is cited in Schweitzer, "Economic Regulation and the Colonial Economy," 559.
152. While much has been written about the beneficial economic effects of the act, the role of the parish in the administration of tobacco inspection has been overlooked by scholars. See Schweitzer, "Economic Regulation and the Colonial Economy," 551–69, 559.
153. Vestry Minutes, Shrewsbury Parish, Kent County, MD, SCM 339-1, 36–109, MSA.

154. Vestry Minutes, Shrewsbury Parish, Kent County, MD, SCM 339-1, 87, MSA.

## 2. Property and Power

1. For more on Commissary Blair, see John Nelson, *A Blessed Company: Parishes, Parsons, and Parishioners in Anglican Virginia, 1690–1776* (Chapel Hill: University of North Carolina Press, 2001), 108, 110–11; Thad W. Tate, *Dictionary of Virginia Biography,* "James Blair (ca. 1655–1743)," Encyclopedia Virginia, Virginia Humanities, updated 2016, https://www.encyclopediavirginia.org/Blair_James_ca_1655-1743.
2. Blair, "A Proposition," quoted in *Historical Collections Relating to the American Colonial Church,* vol. 1, *Virginia,* ed. William Stevens Perry (Hartford, CT: Church Press Co., 1878), 1:334–44.
3. Blair, "A Proposition," quoted in Perry, *Historical Collections,* 1:338.
4. Blair, "A Proposition," quoted in Perry, *Historical Collections,* 1:339.
5. Nelson, *Blessed Company,* 139.
6. For a discussion of "establishment" as a series of privileges and disadvantages, see Michael W. McConnell, "Establishment and Disestablishment at the Founding, Part I: Establishment of Religion," *William & Mary Law Review* 44 (2003): 2105, http://scholarship.law.wm.edu/wmlr/vol44/iss5/4; Vincent Phillip Muñoz, "The Original Meaning of the Establishment Clause and the Impossibility of Its Incorporation," *Journal of Constitutional Law* 8, no. 4 (2006): 585.
7. On iconoclasm in the English Reformation, I draw especially on Margaret Aston, *Broken Idols of the English Reformation* (Cambridge: Cambridge University Press, 2016); Eamon Duffy, *The Stripping of the Altars: Traditional Religion in England, c. 1400–c. 1580,* 2nd ed. (New Haven, CT: Yale University Press, 2005); James G. Clark, *The Dissolution of the Monasteries: A New History* (New Haven, CT: Yale University Press, 2021); Kenneth Fincham and Nicholas Tyacke, *Altars Restored: The Changing Face of English Religious Worship, 1547–c. 1700* (Oxford: Oxford University Press, 2007).
8. See Lauren A. Winner, *A Cheerful and Comfortable Faith: Anglican Religious Practice in the Elite Households of Eighteenth-Century Virginia* (New Haven, CT: Yale University Press, 2010).
9. On the importance of *The Book of Common Prayer,* see Nelson, *Blessed Company,* 3, 66, 190–91.
10. Dell Upton, *Holy Things and Profane: Anglican Parish Churches in Colonial Virginia* (New Haven, CT: Yale University Press, 1997), 33–34, 55, 97.

11. See Cary Carson et al., "Impermanent Architecture in the Southern American Colonies," *Winterthur Portfolio* 16 (1981): 135–96.
12. Rhys Isaac and Dell Upton offer shrewd readings of the social dynamics at work in these ordered spaces. See Upton, *Holy Things;* Rhys Isaac, *The Transformation of Virginia, 1740–1790* (Chapel Hill: University of North Carolina Press, 1982).
13. Though Louis Nelson was specifically discussing early South Carolinian Anglican churches, his insights readily apply to the Chesapeake. See Louis P. Nelson, "Sensing the Sacred: Anglican Material Religion in Early South Carolina," *Winterthur Portfolio* 41 (2007): 203–321; see also Louis P. Nelson, *The Beauty of Holiness: Anglicanism and Architecture in Early South Carolina* (Chapel Hill: University of North Carolina Press, 2009); Winner, *Cheerful and Comfortable Faith,* 13.
14. George Carrington Mason, ed., *The Colonial Vestry Book of Lynnhaven Parish, Princess Anne County, Virginia, 1723–1786* (Newport News: VA, 1949), 50.
15. For example, see the vestry book of Kingston Parish in Mathews County. There are but two direct references to the community enslaved by the parish scattered throughout the colonial vestry records. In 1755, the vestry made a note that their rector should "not be Liable to Any Charge on acct of the Negroe boys runing away that belongs to the parish." Another reference to an enslaved boy appears in 1757, though it is not clear whether he was the same child. Nowhere previously in the Kingston Parish records, which begin in a scattered fashion in 1690 and are complete after 1741, are there any overt references to an enslaved community. Nor were any members of the enslaved community mentioned again until 1783, when the churchwardens were ordered to "collect Rents of the Glebe and hire of the negroes belonging thereto," as well as arranging their hire for the following year. Later, there is a reference to the hiring out of enslaved woman named Judah in 1787 until she could be sold at auction. The enslaved community who lived and labored on the glebe for generations is hardly acknowledged anywhere in Kingston's records. Still, their presence is recorded in other ways, such as the construction and repairs of quarters on the glebe. See C. G. Chamberlayne, ed., *The Vestry Book of Kingston Parish, Matthews County, Virginia (until May 1, 1791, Gloucester County) 1679–1796* (Richmond, VA: 1929), 55, 64, 69, 70, 88, 115, 117, 119, 123.
16. Patrick Allison, *Candid Animadversions on a Petition,* 2nd ed. (Baltimore: William Goddard and James Angell, 1793), 24.
17. Archives of Maryland Online, 61:367.
18. Archives of Maryland Online, 61:465.

19. *Maryland Journal,* October 20, 1778, 2.
20. *Votes and Proceedings of the House of Delegates of the State of Maryland,* November Session, 1783, 213 Microfilm SC M 3197, MSA.
21. My findings accord with Jennifer Oast's conclusions that there is evidence that half of parishes owned enslaved people. See Oast, *Institutional Slavery: Slaveholding Churches, Schools, Colleges, and Businesses in Virginia, 1680–1860* (New York: Cambridge University Press, 2016), 20. There is no evidence in extant records of the fifteen following parishes owning enslaved persons: Albemarle (Surry/Sussex Counties), Augusta (Augusta), Blisland (New Kent/James City Counties), Bristol (Prince George County), Fredericksville (Albemarle), Henrico (Henrico), St. George (Accomack), St. George's (Spotsylvania), St. Patrick's (Prince Edward), St. Peter's (New Kent), Stratton Major (King and Queen), Upper Parish (Nansemond), Ware (Gloucester), and Wicomico (Northumberland County). Records demonstrate the following parishes enslaved at least one person: Antrim (Halifax), Bruton (James City/York), Christ Church (Middlesex County), Cumberland (Lunenberg), Elizabeth River (Elizabeth River), Hungars (Northampton), Kingston (Mathews), Suffolk (Lower) Parish (Nansemond), Lynnhaven (Princess Anne), Petsworth (Gloucester), St. Bride's (Norfolk), Portsmouth (Norfolk), Abingdon (Gloucester), and. St Paul's (Hanover).
22. Charitable bequests to parishes are also discussed at length in chapters 5 and 6.
23. Technically, some endowments were supposed to be managed by vestries, but parish records suggest that these funds were comingled with other parish income. For example, the records of Elizabeth River Parish show that the income produced by the enslaved people who were given as a charitable bequest was not tracked separately from the annual budget. See Alice Granbery Walter, ed., *Vestry Book of Elizabeth River Parish, 1749–1761* (New York: Alice Granbery Walter, 1969), 3, 6, 20. Christ Church Parish in Middlesex County collected funds from an endowment for a free school without operating it. Guy Fred Wells, *Parish Education in Colonial Virginia* (New York: Teachers College, Columbia University, 1923), 43–44.
24. Mason, *Colonial Vestry Book of Lynnhaven Parish,* 69.
25. Mason, *Colonial Vestry Book of Lynnhaven Parish,* 111.
26. For more on the language of "breeding," see Daina Ramey Berry, *The Price for Their Pound of Flesh: The Value of the Enslaved, from Womb to Grave, in the Building of Nation* (Boston: Beacon Press, 2017), 10–32, 78–79; Gregory D. Smithers, *Slave Breeding: Sex, Violence, and Memory in African American History* (Gainesville: University of Florida Press, 2012); Deborah Gray White, *Ar'n't I a Woman: Female Slaves in the Plantation South*

(New York: Norton, 1985). On the prevalence of this language among Virginia's religious institutions, see Oast, *Institutional Slavery,* 16–18.

27. William Waller Hening, ed., *The Statutes at Large; Being a Collection of All the Laws of Virginia, from the First Session of the Legislature in the Year 1619* (Richmond: J & G Cochran, 1821), 3:453 (hereafter cited as Hening, *SL*).
28. C. G. Chamberlayne, ed., *The Vestry Book and Register of Bristol Parish, 1720–1789* (Richmond, VA: 1898), 134.
29. For the record of Isaac Jackson's hire, see "Memorandum Books, 1769," fn. 24, Founders Online, https://founders.archives.gov/documents/Jefferson/02-01-02-0003. For the record of Jefferson's representation of Manly, see "Memorandum Books, 1772," fn. 26, Founders Online, https://founders.archives.gov/documents/Jefferson/02-01-02-0006.
30. "Memorandum Books, 1772," fn. 26, Founders Online.
31. Edith Stansbury Dallam, ed., *St. James' Parish: old Herring Creeke Parish: a History, 1663–1799* (Lothian, MD: Vestry of St. James' Parish, 1976), 121.
32. Dallam, *St. James' Parish,* 119.
33. Dallam, *St. James' Parish,*131, 139, 145.
34. Perry, *Historical Collections,* vol. 4, *Maryland,* 4:232.
35. For example, St. Paul's Parish in Hanover occasionally hired enslaved laborers for specific tasks or construction projects, as well as on annual basis to work at the Poor House. Upper Parish in Nansemond County paid "John Streeter for the hier of his Negrow woman at the poors house" in 1758. See C. G. Chamberlayne, ed., *The Vestry Book of St. Paul's Parish, Hanover County, Virginia, 1706–1786* (Richmond: Library Board, 1940), 181, 445, 450, 451, 501, 517, 531, 539; Wilmer L. Hall, ed., *The Vestry Book of the Upper Parish, Nansemond County, Virginia, 1743–1793* (Richmond: Commonwealth of Virginia, 1949), 127.
36. C. G. Chamberlayne, ed., *The Vestry Book of Petsworth Parish, Gloucester County, Virginia, 1677–1793* (Richmond, VA: 1933), 332.
37. "St. Margaret's Church, Annapolis," Episcopal Diocese of Maryland, "On the Trail of Souls," https://trailofsouls.org/st-margarets-church-annapolis/.
38. Nelson, *Blessed Company,* 262, 407n56, 441n8.
39. Carol Lee Van Voorst, "The Anglican Clergy in Maryland, 1692–1776" (PhD diss., Princeton University, Princeton, NJ, 1978), 265.
40. Rev. Charles Clay, Account Book, 1773–1818, Clay family papers, 1769–1951, VMHC.
41. Rev. William West, Account Book, 1765–74 V.F., 10, 13, 15, Episcopal Diocese of Maryland Archives, Baltimore (hereafter cited as EDMA).
42. Maryland Historical Trust, "Kintail Glebe Springhouse (The Glebe)," HA-872, Architectural Survey File, Maryland Inventory of Historic Properties, 23, https://apps.mht.maryland.gov/medusa/PDF/Harford/HA-872.pdf.

43. Charles Wetherell, "'Boom and Bust' in the Colonial Chesapeake Economy," *Journal of Interdisciplinary History* 15 (1984): 185–210.
44. Entailing land was one common method Virginians used to preserve property across the generations. See Claire Priest, "The End of Entail: Information, Institutions, and Slavery in the American Revolutionary Period," *Law and History Review* 33 (2015): 277–319; Holly Brewer, "Entailing Aristocracy in Colonial Virginia: Ancient Feudal Restraints and Revolutionary Reform," *William and Mary Quarterly*, 3rd ser., 54 (1997): 307–46.
45. Very few scholars have considered the corporate powers of parishes. Gerald Hartdagen considered the parish as a corporation, and his conclusions inform the direction of my inquiry. See Hartdagen, "The Anglican Vestry in Colonial Maryland: A Study in Corporate Responsibility," *Historical Magazine of the Protestant Episcopal Church* 40 (1971). Sarah Barringer Gordon draws attention to the issue of the incorporation of religious societies following the Revolution in two recent works. Her research proves invaluable to understanding the growth of corporate religious societies in the early republic. I locate some of the same developments in colonial parishes. See Gordon, "The African Supplement: Religion, Race, and Corporate Law in Early National America," *William and Mary Quarterly*, 3rd ser., 72 (2015): 385–422, and "The First Disestablishment: Limits on Church Power and Property Before the Civil War," *University of Pennsylvania Law Review* 162 (2014): 316–24.
46. As Paul Musselwhite convincingly argues, Chesapeake plantation owners sought to consolidate power by preventing the rise of cities and towns that might become rivals to their political, economic, and social power. See Musselwhite, *Urban Dreams, Rural Commonwealth: The Rise of Plantation Society in the Chesapeake* (Chicago: University of Chicago Press, 2018).
47. Dell Upton, *Architecture in the United States* (New York: Oxford University Press, 1997), 110–14, 205–18; Isaac, *Transformation of Virginia*, 16–17, 36–39, 351–54.
48. See Joseph Stancliffe Davis, *Essays in the Earlier History of Corporations* (Cambridge, MA: Harvard University Press, 1917); Adam Winkler, *We the Corporations* (New York: Liveright Publishing, 2018), 4, 408n2; Eric Hilt, "Early American Corporations and the State," in *Corporations and American Democracy*, ed. Naomi R. Lamoreaux and William J. Novak (Cambridge, MA: Harvard University Press, 2017), 40–42, 48, 400n14; John Morley, "The Common Law Corporation: The Power of the Trust in Anglo-American Business History," *Columbia Law Review* 116, no. 8 (2016): 2145–97; Pauline Maier, "The Revolutionary Origins of the American Corporation," *William and Mary Quarterly*, 3rd ser., 50 (1993): 51–84.

49. William Blackstone, *Commentaries on the Laws of England,* "Of Corporations," 1:458, Avalon Project, https://avalon.law.yale.edu/subject_menus/blackstone.asp.
50. Blackstone, *Commentaries on the Laws of England,* 1:458.
51. Blackstone, *Commentaries on the Laws of England,* 1:460.
52. Blackstone, *Commentaries on the Laws of England,* 1:460.
53. Blackstone, *Commentaries on the Laws of England,* 1:458, 459.
54. George Webb, *The Office and Authority of a Justice of Peace* (Williamsburg: 1736).
55. For an excellent discussion of Webb and the importance of this legal text, see Warren M. Billings, "A Virginia Original: George Webb's *Office and Authority of a Justice of Peace,*" in *"Esteemed Bookes of Law" and the Legal Culture of Early Virginia,* ed. Warren M. Billings and Brent Tarter (Charlottesville: University of Virginia Press, 2017), 199–225.
56. Webb, *Office and Authority of a Justice of Peace,* 71.
57. Webb, *Office and Authority of a Justice of Peace,* 76.
58. *Terrett v. Taylor,* 13 U.S. (9 Cranch) 43 (1815).
59. Hening, *SL,* 1:399–400; 3:151.
60. Hening, *SL,* 1:478–79.
61. Hening, *SL,* 2:171.
62. For example, in 1753, the vestry of Upper Parish in Nansemond County hired an attorney to help them secure title to lands acquired in the seventeenth century. See Hall, *Vestry Book of the Upper Parish,* 88. Washington Parish in Westmoreland County had to sue to protect their land from other claimants. *Legan Lessee of R'd Bernard v. Washington Parish,* 2 Va. Colonial Dec. B272 (1738), 4.
63. For one example, see the 1757 "An Act to impower the Vestry of the Parish of Saint George, in the County of Spotsylvania, to sell their Glebe," Hening, *SL,* 7:143.
64. Hening, *SL,* 7:234.
65. Hening, *SL,* 8:365; 9:239.
66. For some examples, see Hening, *SL,* 7:314–15; 9:240.
67. Hening, *SL,* 8:607–9.
68. Hening, *SL,* 8:608. Similarly, in 1744, when the legislature "dissolved" the vestry of Truro Parish in Fairfax County and called for the election of twelve new vestrymen, the bill specified that the vestry would retain all its property, and its rights were not affected by the dismissal of its current vestrymen. Hening, *SL,* 5:274–75.
69. Hening, *SL,* 8:415–16.
70. Alexander Spotswood to the Board of Trade, August 14, 1718, in *Letters of Alexander Spotswood,* 292.

71. "Argument for Bruton Parish the Plaintiff," (1718) cited in *Virginia Magazine of History and Biography* 12 (1914): 401–9.
72. "Argument for Bruton Parish the Plaintiff," *Virginia Magazine of History and Biography,* 408.
73. Alexander Spotswood to the Board of Trade, August 14, 1718, in *Letters of Alexander Spotswood,* 292.
74. Jack P. Greene, *The Quest for Power: The Lower Houses of Assembly in the Southern Royal Colonies: 1689–1776* (Chapel Hill: University of North Carolina Press, 1963), 347–48.
75. Vestries' insistence on their corporate rights suggests the enduring power of this distinctive local custom through the eighteenth century. The relationship between custom and common law in the colonies is the subject of a rich literature, and I draw particularly on David Thomas Konig, *Law and Society in Puritan Massachusetts: Essex County, 1629–1692* (Chapel Hill: University of North Carolina Press, 1981); William E. Nelson, *The Common Law in Colonial America,* 4 vols. (New York: Oxford University Press, 2008–18), and *Americanization of the Common Law: The Impact of Legal Change on Massachusetts Society, 1760–1830* (Cambridge, MA: Harvard University Press 1975); Mary Sarah Bilder, *The Transatlantic Constitution: Colonial Legal Culture and the Empire* (Cambridge, MA: Harvard University Press, 2008).
76. Archives of Maryland Online, 13:430.
77. Kenneth L. Carroll, "Quaker Opposition to the Establishment of a State Church in Maryland," *Maryland Historical Magazine* 65 (1970): 149–71.
78. Archives of Maryland Online, 19:427.
79. Archives of Maryland Online, 24:93.
80. Thanks to Elliott Cramer for bringing this quotation to my attention. See Board of Trade, "Representation upon an Act past in Maryland in April 1700, for [the] Service of Almighty God &c.," February 11, 1700/1, CO 5/726, 29, [UK] National Archives, Kew, in Adam Matthew, Colonial America Database, https://www.colonialamerica.amdigital.co.uk.
81. Archives of Maryland Online, 24:265.
82. Archives of Maryland Online, 24:270–72.
83. William Paca and Samuel Chase, "To the Rev. Mr. Jonathan Boucher," *Maryland Gazette,* January 14, 1773.
84. For more on the controversy, see Anne Y. Zimmer, "The 'Paper War' in Maryland, 1772–73: The Paca-Chase Political Philosophy Tested," *Maryland Historical Magazine* 71, no. 2 (1976): 177–93; Anne Y. Zimmer and Alfred H. Kelly, "Jonathan Boucher: Constitutional Conservative," *Journal of American History* 58, no. 4 (1972): 906–8; Robert J. Brugger, *Maryland, a Middle Temperament* (Baltimore: Johns Hopkins University Press, 1988), 110–14.

85. Paca and Chase, *Maryland Gazette,* January 14, 1773.
86. Zimmer and Kelly, "Jonathan Boucher," 906.
87. Once back in England, Boucher published a six-hundred-page repudiation of what he called the "American revolt." See Boucher, *Reminiscences of an American Loyalist, 1738–1789* (Boston: Houghton Mifflin Company, 1925).
88. Jonathan Boucher, "To Samuel Chase, and William Paca, Esqrs.," *Maryland Gazette,* February 4, 1773.
89. In Maryland, debates over to what extent the colony had an authoritative homegrown constitution became particularly heated on the eve of the Revolution. See Farrelly, *Papist Patriots,* 198–240.
90. For records of Paca's and Chase's service as vestrymen, see "Vestry Proceedings, St. Ann's," *Maryland Historical Magazine* 10, no. 2 (1915): 135–38.
91. Vestry Minutes, St. Paul's Parish, Prince George's County, Md., SCM 255, 135–38, MSA.
92. See the "Vestry of Lynnhaven Parish" listed in Princess Anne County, Deed Book 8, 532, LVA; Princess Anne County Deed Book 9, 103, LVA; Princess Anne County, Deed Book 14, 42, LVA. See the "Parish of Lynnhaven," listed in Princess Anne County, Deed Book 9, 103, LVA. See the "Churchwardens of Lynnhaven Parish" listed in Princess Anne County, Deed Book 9, 91, LVA; Princess Anne County, Deed Book 9, 343, LVA.
93. However, as exemplified in cases such as *Godwin et al v. Lunan* (1771) and *Legan's Lessee v. Washington Parish* (1738), sometimes the vestry or the parish were named as litigants, rather than the churchwardens, particularly when lawsuits concerned real estate.
94. For example, see the records of five parish lawsuits in the New Kent County Court listed in *The Vestry Book of Saint Peter's Parish, 1682–1758, New Kent County* (Richmond, VA: National Society of the Colonial Dames for the State of Virginia), 77, 86, 103, 176, 216–17. See examples of four lawsuits brought by Bristol Parish in the Prince George County Court Minute Book, 1737–40, Microfilm Reel 9, 94–103, 279–80, 305, 516, LVA.
95. The authority of churchwardens to make presentments for moral crimes is discussed in chapter 2. Scholars have paid considerable attention to churchwarden's prosecutorial powers without emphasizing their standing to sue. See Monica Najar, *Evangelizing the South: A Social History of Church and State in Early America* (New York: Oxford University Press, 2008), 89–102; Nelson, *Blessed Company,* 239–80.
96. R. A. Brock, ed., *The Vestry Book of Henrico Parish, Virginia 1730–'73* (Richmond, VA: 1874), 148.
97. Hall, *Vestry Book of Upper Parish,* 17.
98. *Vestry Book of Saint Peter's Parish,* 216.

99. Chamberlayne, *Vestry Book and Register of Bristol Parish,* 196.
100. Chamberlayne, *Vestry Book of Petsworth Parish,* 303.
101. For more on the Jesuits' acquisition of land, see Antoinette Sutto, "Lord Baltimore, the Society of Jesus, and Caroline Absolutism," *Journal of British Studies* 48, no. 3 (2009): 638–39, 650. For more on the significance of property-holding for Jesuits, see Gerald P. Fogarty, "Property and Religious Liberty in Colonial Maryland Catholic Thought," *Catholic Historical Review* 72 (1986): 573–600; Thomas Hughes, SJ, *The History of the Society of Jesus in North America, Colonial and Federal,* 4 vols. (Cleveland: Burrow Brothers, 1907–17), Text, vol. 1:578–616.
102. See "Lewager's Diary on new Conditions and Oath," in Thomas Hughes, *History of the Society of Jesus, Documents, Vol. 1, Part 1,* 164–65.
103. For more on the history and development of mortmain in England, see Sandra Raban, *Mortmain Legislation and the English Church, 1279–1500* (Cambridge: Cambridge University Press, 1982); A. H. Oosterhoff, "The Law of Mortmain: An Historical and Comparative Review," *University of Toronto Law Journal* 27 (1977): 257–334; Gareth Jones, *History of the Law of Charity, 1532–1827* (Cambridge: Cambridge University Press, 1969).
104. Sutto, "Lord Baltimore, the Society of Jesus, and Caroline Absolutism," 638–39, 650.
105. Eighteenth-century legal writers identified a host of regulations on churches and schools as Maryland's homegrown mortmain statutes. See Bacon, *Laws of Maryland,* "Mortmain," 688; for an index of Maryland's statutes regulating parish property-holding, see Bacon, *Laws of Maryland,* 651, 715, all at Archives of Maryland Online, vol. 75.
106. "Official Report from the Superior, Father G. Hunter, to the Provincial, Father Dennett," July 23, 1765, cited in Hughes, *History of the Society of Jesus, Documents, Vol. 1, Part 1,* 335–37.
107. Peter Atwood, SJ, "The title of our Lands deduced from the first taker-up to the present . . . ," in Hughes, *History of the Society of Jesus, Documents, Vol. 1, Part 1,* 211.
108. John Carroll, "The Plan of Clergy Organization," in *The John Carroll Papers,* ed., Thomas O'Brien Hanley, 3 vols. (Notre Dame, IN: University of Notre Dame Press, 1976), 1:61.
109. "Ordinance of the Jesuit Provincial," in Hughes, *History of the Society of Jesus, Documents, Vol. 1, Part 1,* 267.
110. "Ordinance of the Jesuit Provincial," in Hughes, *History of the Society of Jesus, Documents, Vol. 1, Part 1,* 267–68.
111. Matthias Manners, SJ, to John Lewis, SJ, December 14, 1773, Box 30, folder 7, 1, Archives of the Maryland Province of the Society of Jesus, Georgetown University Library, Washington, DC (hereafter cited as MPA).

112. Matthias Manners, SJ, to John Lewis, SJ, December 14, 1773, 1, MPA.
113. "Official Report from the Superior, Father G. Hunter, to the Provincial, Father Dennett," July 23, 1765, in Hughes, *History of the Society of Jesus, Documents, Vol. 1, Part 1*, 335–37.
114. Matthias Manners, SJ, to John Lewis, SJ, December 14, 1773, 2, MPA.
115. Matthias Manners, SJ, to John Lewis, SJ, December 14, 1773, 2, MPA.
116. Matthias Manners, SJ, to John Lewis, SJ, December 14, 1773, 1, MPA.
117. Matthias Manners, SJ, to John Lewis, SJ, December 14, 1773, 3, MPA.
118. For a summary of the property belonging to the Third Haven Meeting of Friends in 1815, see "An Act to ratify and protect the Title of the Third Haven Monthly Meeting of Friends," Archives of Maryland Online, 192:1771–73.
119. Deed (August 16, 1701), Talbot County (Land Records) Liber RF 9, 71–72, MSA.
120. Deed (August 22, 1705), Talbot County (Land Records) Liber RF 9, 340–43, MSA.
121. Deed (March 25, 1745), Talbot County (Land Records) Liber JL 16, 267–69, MSA.
122. Deed (August 22, 1705), Talbot County (Land Records) Liber RF 9, 342, MSA.
123. Deed (September 2, 1723), Somerset County Court (Land Records) GH, 71–72, MSA.
124. Deed (September 2, 1723), Somerset County Court (Land Records) GH, 72, MSA.
125. "Presbyterian Society of Baltimore to Gov. Robert Eden," 1774, Black Book, vol. 10, pt. 1: Proprietary Papers, No. 75, Maryland State Papers (Black Books, 1713–85), MSA.
126. An unsigned draft of a charter exists among the state papers, although it is unclear how or why it stalled. "Henry Harford, Lord Proprietary. Charter of incorporation for the Presbyterian Society of Baltimore" [Draft], Black Book, vol. 10, pt. 1: Proprietary Papers, No. 75, Maryland State Papers (Black Books, 1713–85), MSA. See also "A Movement for the Incorporation of the Presbyterian Church in Baltimore City," *Maryland Historical Magazine* 4 (1909): 228.
127. For more on the rise of evangelicalism in Virginia, see Isaac, *Transformation of Virginia*; Najar, *Evangelizing the South*; Spangler, *Virginians Reborn*.
128. Jurists on both sides of the Atlantic debated whether English laws restricting mortmain had applied in colonies like Virginia where they were not explicitly adopted. In the nineteenth century, English and American courts consistently found that such laws only applied in colonies like Maryland, where they were formally adopted. See *Attorney General v. Stewart* (1817)

2 Mer. 143, 35 Eng. Rep. 33 (Ch); *Perrin v. Carey*, 24 U.S. (11 Wheat.) 465 (1826); *Lathrop v. The Commercial Bank of Scioto*, 8 *Rep. Select Cases Decided in the Court of Appeals of Kentucky*, 121–29 (Ky. Ct. App. 1839). For more generally on the application of English statutes to Virginia, see John Ruston Pagan, "English Statutes in Virginia, 1660–1714," in Billings and Tarter, *"Esteemed Bookes of Law,"* 57–94.

129. Carroll, *Quakerism on the Eastern Shore of Virginia*, 177–79.
130. Augusta County, Deed Book 19, No. 1, 443–44, LVA.
131. Princess Anne County, Deed Book 9, 509, LVA.
132. Fincastle Presbyterian Congregation: Petition, Botetourt County, December 19, 1805, Legislative Petitions Digital Collection, Library of Virginia, Richmond, available online at http://www.virginiamemory.com/collections/petitions (hereafter cited as LPDC, LVA).
133. Members of the Augusta Presbyterian Church: Petition, Augusta County, December 10, 1805, LPDC, LVA.
134. *Journals of the House of Burgesses of Virginia, 1773–1776* (Richmond: 1905), 103.
135. Patrick J. Dignan provides examples of requests for incorporation from Presbyterian, Congregational, Huguenot, and Lutheran congregations all being rejected. The only non-Anglican denomination able to incorporate in New York was the Dutch Reformed Church. See Dignan, *History of the Legal Incorporation of Catholic Church Property in the United States, 1784–1932* (New York: P. J. Kenedy & Sons, 1935), 27–30. Susanna Linsley's dissertation helpfully discusses how incorporation was an important privilege of the Anglican establishment in New York and Charleston. See Linsley, "The American Reformation: The Politics of Religious Liberty, Charleston and New York 1770–1830" (PhD diss., University of Michigan, 2012), 37–50.
136. Morley, "The Common Law Corporation," 2145–97.

## 3. Pulling Down the Church

1. William Waller Hening, ed., *The Statutes at Large; Being a Collection of All the Laws of Virginia, from the First Session of the Legislature in the Year 1619* (Richmond: J & G Cochran, 1821), 9:75 (hereafter cited as Hening, *SL*).
2. Winifred Sackville-Stoner, *St. Paul's Episcopal Church, Norfolk, Virginia, U.S.A.* (Norfolk: 1903), 9.
3. Hening, *SL*, 9:328.
4. George Carrington Mason, "The Colonial Churches of Norfolk County, Virginia," *William and Mary Quarterly* 21, no. 2 (1941): 148–52.

5. Inhabitants on the South Side of the Nansemond River: Petition, Nansemond County, December 21, 1802, Legislative Petitions Digital Collection, Library of Virginia, Richmond, available online at http://www.virginiamemory.com/collections/petitions (hereafter cited as LPDC, LVA).
6. Baptist Church at Occoquan, October 12, 1776, Prince William County, LPDC, LVA.
7. Rhys Isaac, *The Transformation of Virginia, 1740–1790* (Chapel Hill: University of North Carolina Press, 1982), 292; Woody Holton, *Forced Founders: Indians, Debtors, Slaves, and the Making of the American Revolution in Virginia* (Chapel Hill: Omohundro Institute of Early American History and Culture, University of North Carolina Press, 1999), 198.
8. This term can still be valuable. I continue to use "disestablishment" to describe the broad movement against the established church but do so with the recognition that it was not a phrase employed by revolutionary Americans.
9. The phrase gained popularity during the 1860s amid the debates over the Church of Scotland in the UK. *Oxford English Dictionary Online,* s.v. "disestablishment."
10. The editors of Jefferson's and Madison's papers both used the word "disestablishment" throughout their editions. However, the sources themselves never include this term. For example, the editors entitle a document "Rough Draft of Jefferson's Resolutions for Disestablishing the Church of England and for Repealing Laws Interfering with Freedom of Worship," though the word "disestablish" appears nowhere in the document. Jefferson's words were, "Notes & proceedings on discontinuing the Establmt of the Church of Engld." See Thomas Jefferson, "I. Rough Draft of Jefferson's Resolutions for Disestablishing the Church of England and for Repealing Laws Interfering with Freedom of Worship, [before 19 November 1776]," Founders Online, https://founders.archives.gov/documents/Jefferson/01-01-02-0222-0002.
11. "I. Rough Draft of Jefferson's Resolutions for Disestablishing the Church of England"; "James Madison to James Monroe, 12 April 1785," Founders Online, https://founders.archives.gov/documents/Madison/01-08-02-0141.
12. H. J. Eckenrode was the state librarian of Virginia and reproduced many of the legislative petitions about disestablishment in his published volume on the topic. See Eckenrode, *Separation of Church and State in Virginia* (Richmond: 1910), 46, 47, 77, 123.
13. Inhabitants: Petition, Prince Edward County, October 10, 1776, LPDC, LVA.

14. Inhabitants: Petition, Prince Edward County, October 10, 1776, LPDC, LVA; John Carroll to Charles Plowden, February 27, 1785, in *The John Carroll Papers,* ed. Thomas O'Brien Hanley, 3 vols. (Notre Dame, IN: University of Notre Dame Press, 1976), 1:168.
15. Bernard Bailyn, *Ideological Origins of the American Revolution* (Cambridge, MA: Harvard University Press, 1992), 231–45; Edmund Morgan, *American Slavery, American Freedom: The Ordeal of Colonial Virginia* (New York: Norton, 1975), 376; Peter A. Dorsey, "To 'Corroborate Our Own Claims': Public Positioning and the Slavery Metaphor in Revolutionary America," *American Quarterly* 55 (2003): 353–86; David Brion Davis, *The Problem of Slavery in the Age of Revolution, 1770–1823* (Ithaca, NY: Cornell University Press, 1975), 39–40, 263, 560–64.
16. Okoye argued that it was not only a familiar institution but also the worst "nightmare" of white Americans. F. Nwabueze Okoye, "Chattel Slavery as the Nightmare of the American Revolutionaries," *William and Mary Quarterly,* 3rd ser., 37 (1980): 12.
17. John Carroll to Cardinal Antonelli, March 13, 1786, in *John Carroll Papers,* 1:208.
18. *Maryland Gazette,* August 19, 1773, quoted in Albert Warwick Werline, *Problems of Church and State in Maryland During the Seventeenth and Eighteenth Centuries* (South Lancaster, MA: College Press, 1948), 159.
19. Ronald Hoffman, in collaboration with Sally D. Mason, *Princes of Ireland, Planters of Maryland: A Carroll Saga, 1500–1782* (Chapel Hill: Omohundro Institute of Early American History and Culture, University of North Carolina Press, 2002), 277.
20. For more on the Tobacco Inspection Act, see Carol Van Voorst, "The Anglican Clergy in Maryland, 1692–1776" (PhD diss., Princeton University, Princeton, NJ, 1978), 87–97. For more on the Two-Penny Act, see Jon Kukla, "New Light on the Parsons' Cause in Colonial Virginia," *Anglican and Episcopal History* 86, no. 4 (2017): 367–95.
21. For two thorough discussions of the episcopate controversy, see Frederick V. Mills, *Bishops by Ballot: An Eighteenth-Century Ecclesiastical Revolution* (New York: Oxford University Press, 1978); and Carl Bridenbaugh, *Mitre and Sceptre: Transatlantic Faiths, Ideas, Personalities, and Politics* (New York: Oxford University Press, 1962).
22. My interpretation differs from scholars who emphasize the weakness of the church before the Revolution. Jewel Spangler, for example, described the established church as being on its "last legs" in 1774. See Spangler, *Virginians Reborn: Anglican Monopoly, Evangelical Dissent, and the Rise of the Baptists in the Late Eighteenth Century* (Charlottesville: University of Virginia Press, 2008), 200.

23. Oaths of Allegiance and Abjuration: "I *A. B.* do sincerely Promise and Swear, That I will be Faithful, and bear True Allegiance to His Majesty King WILLIAM. *So help me God. I, A. B.*, do Swear, That I do from my Heart Abhor, Detest, and Abjure, as Impious and Heretical, that Damnable Doctrine and Position, *That Princes Excommunicated or Deprived by the Pope, or any Authority of the See of* Rome, *may be Deposed or Murthered by their Subjects, or any other whatsoever.* And I do Declare, That no Foreign Prince, Person, Prelate, State, or Potentate, hath, or ought to have, any Jurisdiction, Power, Superiority, Preeminence, or Authority. Ecclesiastical or Spiritual within this Realm. *So help me God.*" English Bill of Rights, 1689. The assembly required these oaths by law, as seen in Hening, *SL*, 7:141, and an example of vestrymen signing these oaths is preserved in the vestry book of Little Chuckatuck Parish (Nansemond County, VA) and transcribed in William Meade, *Old Churches, Ministers and Families of Virginia*, 2 vols. (Philadelphia: Lippincott, 1857), 1:307.
24. Hoffman and Mason, *Princes of Ireland*, 297.
25. Maura Jane Farrelly, *Papist Patriots: The Making of American Catholic Identity* (New York: Oxford University Press, 2010), 230.
26. Hoffman and Mason, *Princes of Ireland*, 287–93; Farrelly, *Papist Patriots*, 228–36.
27. Archives of Maryland Online, 78:10.
28. *Dunlap's Gazette and Baltimore General Advertizer*, Nov. 18, 1776, cited in Werline, *Church and State in Maryland*, 194.
29. Ordinances of the Convention, July 1775, in *The Proceedings of the Convention of Delegates for the Counties and Corporations in the Colony of Virginia* (Richmond, VA: 1816), 39.
30. John Ragosta, *Wellspring of Liberty: How Virginia's Religious Dissenters Helped Win the American Revolution and Secured Religious Liberty* (New York: Oxford University Press, 2010), 9, 71–73.
31. Journal of the Convention, August 16, 1775, in *Proceedings of the Convention of Delegates for the Counties and Corporations in the Colony of Virginia* (Richmond, VA: 1816), 17.
32. Virginia Declaration of Rights of 1776, Section 1, America's Founding Documents, National Archives Online. For more on Mason's role in drafting Virginia's Declaration of Rights and his role in debates over religious liberty in Virginia, see Daniel L. Dreisbach, "George Mason's Pursuit of Religious Liberty in Revolutionary Virginia," *Virginia Magazine of History and Biography* 108, no. 1 (2000): 25–44.
33. Virginia Declaration of Rights of 1776, Section 2, America's Founding Documents, National Archives Online.

34. Jonathan Boucher, "On Civil Liberty: Passive Obedience and Non-Resistance," (1775), in *A View of the Causes and Consequences of the American Revolution; in Thirteen Discourses, Preached in North America Between the Years 1763 and 1775* (London: G. G. and J. Robinson, 1797), 545.
35. The collect before the communion reminded the congregation to submit to God's "chosen servant, George, our King and Governor . . . (knowing whose Minister he is) . . . we and all his subjects (duly considering whose authority he hath) may faithfully serve, honour, and humbly obey him." The Communion, Collect for the King, *Book of Common Prayer,* 1760 ed.
36. Virginia Declaration of Rights of 1776, Section 16, America's Founding Documents, National Archives Online.
37. Maryland Declaration of Rights, and the Constitution and Form of Government of 1776, Article 33, Avalon Project.
38. Virginia Declaration of Rights, Section 16, America's Founding Documents, National Archives Online.
39. Maryland Declaration of Rights, Articles 35 and 36, Avalon Project.
40. See Edward Eitches, "Maryland's 'Jew Bill,'" *American Jewish Historical Quarterly* 60 (1971): 260–61.
41. Maryland, Declaration of Right, Article 34, Avalon Project. It was common for states to restrict the amount of property held by religious societies. See Gordon, "The First Disestablishment," 312, 323.
42. Maryland's constitution required "every person, appointed to any office of profit or trust" to disavow the king of Great Britain, swear allegiance to the state of Maryland, and subscribe a "declaration of a belief in the Christian religion." Maryland Constitution of 1776, Article 55, Avalon Project.
43. Nelson Rightmyer, *Maryland's Established Church* (Baltimore: Church Historical Society for the Diocese of Maryland, 1956), 117–18.
44. Hening, *SL,* 9:165–66.
45. Inhabitants: Address, May 29, 1777, Mecklenburg, LPDC, LVA.
46. Hening *SL,* 10:198.
47. May 29, 1778, *Journal of the House of Delegates of the Commonwealth of Virginia (1777–1780),* 24–25.
48. Elizabeth River Parish, June 16, 1783, Norfolk County, LPDC, LVA; Inhabitants of Tanner Creek & Norfolk Borough, November 18, 1796, Norfolk County, LPDC, LVA.
49. Excerpts from the Durham Parish vestry records cited in Henry F. Thompson, "The Parish Records of Maryland," *Maryland Historical Magazine* 2 (1907): 132–33.
50. Edward L. Bond and Joan R. Gundersen, "The Episcopal Church in Virginia, 1607–2007," *Virginia Magazine of History and Biography* 115, no. 2 (2007): 207.

51. Cited in Barry Paige Neville, "For God, King, and Country: Loyalism on the Eastern Shore of Maryland During the American Revolution," *International Social Science Review* 84, no. 3/4 (2009): 141.
52. Sylvia Frey, *Water from the Rock: Black Resistance in a Revolutionary Age* (Princeton, NJ: Princeton University Press, 1991), especially, 55–80, 145–51; Holton, *Forced Founders*, 152–60.
53. Cassandra Pybus discusses the varied estimations of the number of escaped enslaved people during the war and provides a revised estimate. See Pybus, "Jefferson's Faulty Math: The Question of Slave Defections in the American Revolution," *William and Mary Quarterly*, 3rd ser., 62 (2005): 258.
54. The spelling of "McPherson" and "Piccowaxen" vary in some of the original sources. *Maryland Journal* (Baltimore), October 20, 1778.
55. Frey, *Water from the Rock*, 145, 151; Pybus, "Jefferson's Faulty Math," 258–59.
56. Archives of Maryland Online, 105:230–31.
57. *Virginia Gazette* (Williamsburg), February 26, 1779.
58. *Virginia Gazette* (Williamsburg), February 26, 1779.
59. Paula E. Dumas, *Proslavery Britain: Fighting for Slavery in an Era of Abolition* (London: Palgrave Macmillan, 2016), 21–24.
60. Banastre Tarleton, *A History of the Campaigns of 1780 and 1781 in the Southern Provinces of North America* (Dublin: 1787), 414.
61. Rev. Archibald McRoberts to Col. Davies, August 9, 1781, Providence, VA, Calendar of State Papers, Virginia, Vol. 2, 308–9.
62. Meade, *Old Churches, Ministers and Families of Virginia*, 1:449–50.
63. Rev. Archibald McRoberts to Col. Davies, August 9, 1781, Providence, VA, Calendar of State Papers, Virginia, vol. 2, 308–9.
64. Tarleton, *History of the Campaigns of 1780 and 1781*, 92.
65. Pybus, "Jefferson's Faulty Math," 258.
66. For a discussion of how the British forces put Black men and women to work, see Jim Piecuch, *Three Peoples, One King: Loyalists, Indians, and Slaves in the Revolutionary South, 1775–1782* (Columbia: University of South Carolina Press, 2008), 219–22.

## 4. The Establishment of Religious Freedom?

1. John Carroll to Cardinal Antonelli, March 13, 1786, in *The John Carroll Papers*, ed. Thomas O'Brien Hanley, 3 vols. (Notre Dame, IN: University of Notre Dame Press, 1976), 1:208.
2. See editorial discussion in "Act for Establishing Religious Freedom, [31 October] 1785," Founders Online, https://founders.archives.gov/documents/Madison/01-08-02-0206.

3. Frederick V. Mills, "Disestablishment," in *Encyclopedia of Religion in the South,* 2nd ed., ed. Samuel S. Hill and Charles H. Lippy (Mercer, GA: Mercer University Press, 2005), 260–61; Jon Kukla, *Patrick Henry: Champion of Liberty* (New York: Simon & Schuster, 2017), 279–82; Thomas E. Buckley, *Church and State in Revolutionary Virginia, 1776–1787* (Charlottesville: University of Virginia Press, 1977), 78–105; see Jon Ragosta, *Wellspring of Liberty: How Virginia's Religious Dissenters Helped Win the American Revolution and Secured Religious Liberty* (New York: Oxford University Press, 2010), 111–60.
4. For example, see Mills, "Disestablishment," in Hill and Lippy, *Encyclopedia of Religion in the South,* 260–61. For some examples in Supreme Court jurisprudence, see *Everson v. Board of Education,* 330 U.S. 1 (1947) and *Abington School District v. Schempp,* 374 U.S. 203, 374 U.S. 214 (1963). The case lays out Virginia's history in detail and then only points to differences in other states in a footnote.
5. Blackstone, *Commentaries on the Laws of England,* 1:460.
6. John Carroll to Ferdinand Farmer, December 1784, in *John Carroll Papers,* 1:156.
7. John Carroll to Charles Plowden, February 27, 1785, in *John Carroll Papers,* 1:168.
8. John Carroll to Cardinal Antonelli, February 27, 1785, in *John Carroll Papers,* 1:170–71.
9. John Carroll to Cardinal Antonelli, March 1, 1785, in *John Carroll Papers,* 1:181.
10. John Carroll to Cardinal Antonelli, March 13, 1786, in *John Carroll Papers,* 1:208.
11. For more, see Raymond A. Schroth, SJ, "Death and Resurrection: The Suppression of the Jesuits in North America," *American Catholic Studies* 128 (2017): 51–66.
12. Maryland Constitution of 1776, Article 34, Avalon Project, Yale Law School, https://avalon.law.yale.edu/17th_century/ma02.asp.
13. Thomas Murphy's work on Jesuit slaveholding briefly discusses the importance of postrevolutionary incorporation. See Murphy, SJ, *Jesuit Slaveholding in Maryland, 1717–1838* (New York: Routledge, 2001), 49, 65–66, 71.
14. Murphy, *Jesuit Slaveholding in Maryland,* 49.
15. John Carroll to Charles Plowden, October 4, 1790, in *John Carroll Papers,* 1:475.
16. Archives of Maryland Online, 203:207–10.
17. Maryland Declaration of Rights, and the Constitution and Form of Government of 1776, Article 33, Avalon Project.
18. Archives of Maryland Online, 203:207–10.

19. "The Memorial and Petition of the Subscribers, in behalf of themselves and others the Clergy of the Episcopal Churches," in William Stevens Perry, ed., *Journals of General Conventions of the Protestant Episcopal Church, in the United States, 1785–1835* (Claremont, NH: Claremont Manufacturing, 1874), 3:20.
20. "A Declaration of certain fundamental Rights and Liberties of the Protestant Episcopal Church of Maryland," in Perry, *Journals of General Conventions,* 3:22.
21. The notes from the clergy's August meeting are rerecorded in Perry, *Journals of General Conventions,* 3:21.
22. Perry, *Journals of General Conventions,* 3:26–27.
23. Patrick Allison, *Candid Animadversions, respecting a petition* (Baltimore: Hayes and Killen, 1783), 9.
24. Maryland Constitution of 1776, Article 33, Avalon Project.
25. Allison, *Candid Animadversions* (1783), 3, 6.
26. Allison, *Candid Animadversions* (1783), 6.
27. Allison, *Candid Animadversions* (1783), 15.
28. Thomas J. Curry, *The First Freedoms* (New York: Oxford University Press, 1986), 154–58.
29. However, the legislature did pass an act incorporating the Society for Widows and Orphans. This bill escaped blowback because it was narrowly framed as an act of incorporation for a charitable project. Archives of Maryland Online, 203:426.
30. John Carroll to Charles Plowden, February 27, 1785, in *John Carroll Papers,* 1:168.
31. "Copy of a Petition, now Signing," March 25, 1785, *Baltimore Advertizer,* quoted in Curry, *First Freedoms,* 156.
32. Archives of Maryland Online, 380:19.
33. This bill resembled statutes recently adopted by other states. For more on general acts of incorporation, see Sarah Barringer Gordon, "The First Disestablishment: Limits on Church Power and Property Before the Civil War," *University of Pennsylvania Law Review* 162 (2014): 317–25.
34. *Votes and Proceedings of the Senate of the State of Maryland,* November Session, 1784, 12, Microfilm MSA SC M 3185, MSA; *Votes and Proceedings of the House of Delegates of the State of Maryland,* November Session, 1788, 92–94, Microfilm MSA SC M 3197, MSA. The first page of the bill and any records of its discussion is missing from the records of the House of Delegates, but the full text of the act is available in the *Journal of the Maryland State Senate.* See *Votes and Proceedings of the Senate of the State of Maryland,* November Session, 1788, 33–37, Microfilm MSA SC M 3185, MSA.

35. *Votes and Proceedings of the Senate of the State of Maryland,* November Session, 1788, 33, Microfilm MSA SC M 3185, MSA.
36. *Votes and Proceedings of the Senate of the State of Maryland,* November Session, 1788, 76, Microfilm MSA SC M 3185, MSA.
37. *Votes and Proceedings of the Senate of the State of Maryland,* November Session, 1788, 91, Microfilm MSA SC M 3185, MSA.
38. *Maryland Journal* (Baltimore), January 9, 1789.
39. Albert Warwick Werline, *Problems of Church and State in Maryland During the Seventeenth and Eighteenth Centuries* (South Lancaster, MA: College Press, 1948), 184.
40. The House of Delegates voted not to debate the bill in 1791. Compare *Votes and Proceedings of the House of Delegates of the State of Maryland,* November Session, 1788, 92–95, Microfilm MSA SC M 3197, MSA, with *Votes and Proceedings of the House of Delegates of the State of Maryland,* November Session, 1791, 113, Microfilm MSA SC M 3197, MSA.
41. Allison, *Candid Animadversions* (1793), 21.
42. Allison, *Candid Animadversions* (1793), 22.
43. Allison, *Candid Animadversions* (1793), 29.
44. The text of 1779 Vestry Act can be found in Archives of Maryland Online, 203:216; see also Allison, *Candid Animadversions* (1793), 24.
45. Allison, *Candid Animadversions* (1793), 24, 22.
46. Archives of Maryland Online, 644:49.
47. The following religious societies and congregations received an act of incorporation between 1793–1800: Vestry of Saint-John's Parish, in Prince George's County (1793), 645:89; German reformed congregation of Baltimore-town (1795), 647:12; The Trustees of the Roman Catholic Church in the Town of Baltimore (1795), 647:10; The Committee of the Presbyterian Church in the City of Baltimore (1797), 652:49; German Evangelical Reformed Church in Baltimore (1797), 652:44; The Committee of the Baptist Church in the City of Baltimore (1798), 653:19; The Trustees of the Roman Catholic Church in Cob Neck (1799), 100:32; Presbyterian Church of Snow Hill (1800), 94:7; Lutheran Church in Baltimore (1800), 94:6; Presbyterian Church in Baltimore (1800), 94:6; Light-street Methodist Episcopal Church (1800), 94:31; Old-town Methodist Episcopal Church (1800), 94:31: all references can be found at Archives of Maryland Online.
48. Archives of Maryland Online, 653:13–17.
49. George B. Delaplaine Jr., "The Reverend Governor: Maryland's Separation—or Lack Thereof—Between Church and State," *Maryland Life* (July 2006), 56.

50. Archives of Maryland Online, 192:294–98.
51. For example, see *Maryland Herald and Hager's-Town Weekly Advertiser,* March 16, 1803; *Republican Gazette and General Advertiser,* March 11, 1803.
52. Thomas Cary Johnson, *Virginia Presbyterianism and Religious Liberty in Colonial and Revolutionary Times* (Richmond, VA: Presbyterian Committee of Publication, 1907), 92–97; *Journal of the House of Delegates of the Commonwealth of Virginia,* May 26, 1784 (May 1784 Session) (Richmond: 1828), 21.
53. Baptist Association Petitions, May 26, 1784; *Journal of the Virginia House of Delegates of the Commonwealth of Virginia,* May 26, 1784, 20.
54. *Journal of the Virginia House of Delegates of the Commonwealth of Virginia,* June 4, 1784, 36.
55. For the full text of the memorial, see George MacLaren Brydon, *Virginia's Mother Church and the Political Conditions Under Which It Grew,* vol. 2 (Richmond: Virginia Historical Society, 1952), 592–93.
56. *Journal of the Virginia House of Delegates of the Commonwealth of Virginia,* November 17, 1784 (October 1784 Session), (Richmond: 1828), 27.
57. Philip Hamburger discusses the favorable view of Baptists toward incorporation in colonial New England and the ambivalence in North Carolina. See Hamburger, *Separation of Church and State* (Cambridge, MA: Harvard University Press, 2009), 178–179n60.
58. John Blair Smith to James Madison, June 21, 1784, Founders Online, https://founders.archives.gov/documents/Madison/01-08-02-0043.
59. James Madison to Thomas Jefferson, January 9, 1785, Founders Online, https://founders.archives.gov/documents/Madison/01-08-02-0122.
60. Eckenrode, *Separation of Church and State in Virginia,* 120. Thomas Buckley helpfully maps the petitions for and against by county and denomination. See Buckley, *Church and State in Revolutionary Virginia,* 168.
61. Inhabitants: Petition, Louisa County, October 31, 1786, Legislative Petitions Digital Collection, Library of Virginia, Richmond, available online at http://www.virginiamemory.com/collections/petitions (hereafter cited as LPDC, LVA).
62. Inhabitants: Petition, Chesterfield County, November 24, 1786, LPDC, LVA.
63. Eckenrode, *Separation of Church and State in Virginia,* 124–25.
64. Eckenrode, *Separation of Church and State in Virginia,* 121.
65. Eckenrode, *Separation of Church and State in Virginia,* 119.
66. Eckenrode, *Separation of Church and State in Virginia,* 124.
67. Representatives of Several Baptist Associations: Petition, November 1, 1786, LPDC, LVA.

68. Eckenrode, *Separation of Church and State in Virginia,* 125.
69. Standing Committee of the Convention of the Protestant Episcopal Church: Petition, December 5, 1786, LPDC, LVA.
70. Inhabitants of St. Asaph's Parish: Petition, Caroline County, December 4, 1786, LPDC, LVA.
71. Maryland Constitution of 1776, Article 33, Avalon Project.
72. Hening, *SL,* 9:164–67; 10:111; 11:532–37.
73. "Official Report from the Superior, Father G. Hunter, to the Provincial, Father Dennett," July 23, 1765, cited in Thomas Hughes, *History of the Society of Jesus in North America Colonial and Federal, Documents, Vol. 1, Part 1* (New York: Longmans, Green, and Co., 1910), 335–37.
74. For more on how the confiscation of loyalist property affected Catholics, see Ronald Hoffman in collaboration with Sally D. Mason, *Princes of Ireland, Planters of Maryland: A Carroll Saga, 1500–1782* (Chapel Hill: Omohundro Institute of Early American History and Culture, University of North Carolina Press, 2002), 321–33.
75. Gerald P. Fogarty, "Property and Religious Liberty in Colonial Maryland Catholic Thought," *Catholic Historical Review* 72 (1986): 599–600.
76. Jennifer Oast, *Institutional Slavery: Slaveholding Churches, Schools, Colleges, and Businesses in Virginia, 1680–1860* (New York: Cambridge University Press, 2016), 88–93.
77. Oast, *Institutional Slavery,* 93.
78. Members of the Presbyterian Church: Petition, Alexandria City, October 30, 1786, LPDC, LVA.
79. Nelson, *Blessed Company,* 51.
80. Isaac, *Transformation of Virginia,* 164–66, 173, 384n9.
81. Members of the Augusta Presbyterian Church: Petition, Augusta, December 10, 1805, LPDC, LVA.
82. The *Memorial and Remonstrance* and Statute for Religious Freedom have received significant attention from scholars of law and religion. See Thomas Buckley, *Establishing Religious Freedom: Jefferson's Statute in Virginia* (Charlottesville: University of Virginia Press, 2013); Jon Ragosta, *Religious Freedom: Jefferson's Legacy, America's Creed* (Charlottesville: University of Virginia Press, 2013); Curry, *First Freedoms,* 143–47.
83. Hening, *SL,* 12: 84–86. See editorial discussion in "Act for Establishing Religious Freedom, [31 October] 1785," Founders Online, https://founders.archives.gov/documents/Madison/01-08-02-0206.
84. Eckenrode, *Separation of Church and State in Virginia,* 101.
85. James Madison, "Notes on Charters of Incorporation, [January?] 1786," Founders Online, https://founders.archives.gov/documents/Madison/01-08-02-0244.

86. Marshall would also vote against glebe confiscation in 1789. See Eckenrode, *Separation of Church and State in Virginia,* 137.
87. James Madison, "Notes on Charters of Incorporation," Founders Online.
88. Hening, *SL,* 12:266–67. The legislature reaffirmed parishes' title to property in 1788. Hening, *SL,* 12:705–706.
89. *Acts Passed at a General Assembly of the Commonwealth of Virginia,* December Session, 1798 (Richmond: Meriwether Jones & John Dixon, 1799) (hereafter cited as *Acts VA*) (1798–99), ch. 9, "An act, to repeal certain acts, and to declare the construction of the Bill of Rights, and Constitution concerning religion," 8.
90. "The General Assembly shall not grant a charter of incorporation to any church or religious denomination, but may secure the title to church property to an extent to be limited by law." Virginia Constitution (1851), Article 32. Jerry Falwell sued the state to challenge its prohibition on incorporation and won. See *Falwell v. Miller,* 203 F. Su 2d 624 (W.D. Va. 2002).
91. Virginia, North Carolina, New York, and Rhode Island all proposed amendments to the federal Constitution that offered specific language about the free exercise of religion. See Pauline Maier, *Ratification: The People Debate the Constitution, 1787–1788* (New York: Simon & Schuster, 2010), 163, 207, 225, 263, 303, 453–54; Michael W. McConnell, "The Origins and Historical Understanding of Free Exercise of Religion," *Harvard Law Review* 103 (1990):1409–517; Daniel L. Dreisbach, "The Constitution's Forgotten Religion Clause: Reflections on the Article VI Religious Test," *Journal of Church and State* 38 (1996): 261–95; Gary D. Glenn, "Forgotten Purposes of the First Amendment Religion Clauses," *Review of Politics* 49 (1987): 340–67.
92. *Annals of Congress,* First Congress, First Session, June 8, 1789, 451, online at https://www.congress.gov/annals-of-congress/page-headings/1st-congress.
93. *Annals of Congress,* First Congress, First Session, August 15, 1789, 758.
94. *Annals of Congress,* First Congress, First Session, August 15, 1789, 757–58.
95. For a thoughtful discussion of these implications, see Vincent Phillip Muñoz, "The Original Meaning of the Establishment Clause and the Impossibility of Its Incorporation," *Journal of Constitutional Law* 8, no. 4 (2006): 585–639.
96. "An act incorporating the Protestant Episcopal Church in the town of Alexandria, in the District of Columbia," January 28, 1811, in *The Debates and Proceedings in the Congress of the United States* (Washington, DC: Gales and Seaton, 1853), 22:105.
97. Michael W. McConnell offers a different interpretation by arguing that Madison's "reasons for vetoing the federal bill, however, were narrow and

should not be interpreted as opposing all incorporations of religious bodies." See McConnell, "The Supreme Court's Earliest Church-State Cases: Windows on Religious-Cultural-Political Conflict in the Early Republic," *Tulsa Law Review* 37, no. 7 (2001): 15.

98. "From James Madison to the House of Representatives, 21 February 1811," Founders Online, https://founders.archives.gov/documents/Madison/03-03-02-0233.

99. *American Watchman and Delaware Republican* (Wilmington), March 2, 1811; "Democratic Qualms," *Poulson's American Daily Advertiser* (Philadelphia), March 4, 1811; "Democratic Qualms," *Berkshire Reporter* (Pittsfield, MA), March 16, 1811; *Scioto Gazette* (Chillicothe, OH), March 13, 1811; *Rhode-Island Republican* (Newport), March 27, 1811; *Green-Mountain Farmer* (Bennington, VT), April 1, 1811; *Farmers' Repository* (Charles Town, VA), March 1, 1811; *Federal Republican* (Baltimore), February 26, 1811; *Star* (Raleigh, NC), March 7, 1811; *New Hampshire Patriot and State Gazette* (Concord), March 9, 1811; *American Advocate* (Hallowell, ME), March 13, 1811.

100. *Green-Mountain Farmer* (Bennington, VT), April 1, 1811.

101. "Democratic Qualms," *Federal Republican* (Baltimore), February 26, 1811, 2. See the specific acts the author cites in Archives of Maryland Online, 653:13–17; 644:49.

102. "Democratic Qualms," *Federal Republican* (Baltimore), February 26, 1811, 2.

103. "Democratic Qualms," *Poulson's American Daily Advertiser* (Philadelphia), March 4, 1811; "Democratic Qualms," *Berkshire Reporter* (Pittsfield, MA), March 16, 1811; *American Watchman and Delaware Republican* (Wilmington, DE), March 2, 1811.

104. *Annals of Congress,* 11th Congress, 3rd Session, February 21, 1811, 982–85, 995–98.

105. Ministers & Lay Representatives of the Presbyterian Church in Convention: Petition, October 31, 1787, LPDC, LVA.

106. Baptist Associations: Petition, November 14, 1789, LPDC, LVA.

107. *Federalist,* no. 10, November 23, 1787.

108. Baptist Associations: Petition, November 14, 1789, LPDC, LVA.

109. Both Patrick Henry and Edmund Randolph served on the committee. Henry had advocated for a general assessment only to be defeated by Madison. Randolph had been an ardent defender of the Anglican Church. John Ragosta, however, argues that Henry was opposed to the Episcopal Church retaining its glebe lands. See Ragosta, *Patrick Henry: Proclaiming a Revolution* (New York: Routledge:, 2016), 77.

110. *Journal of the House of Delegates of the Commonwealth of Virginia,* November 27, 1789 (Richmond: 1828), 83–84.

111. *Journal of the House of Delegates of the Commonwealth of Virginia,* December 9, 1789, 113; *Journal of the House of Delegates of the Commonwealth of Virginia,* November 17, 1790, 73.
112. Eckenrode, *Separation of Church and State in Virginia,* 136–37.
113. General Committee of Baptists: Petition, October 10, 1792, LPDC, LVA.
114. Baptist General Committee: Petition, November 17, 1795, LPDC, LVA.
115. Numerous scholars have looked closely at this reversal, but the connection between their changing position on slavery and their embrace of natural rights in the fight over the glebes during the same period has not been made explicit. For more on evangelicals and slavery, see James David Essig, "A Very Wintry Season: Virginia Baptists and Slavery, 1785–1797," *Virginia Magazine of History and Biography* 88 (1980): 170–85; Charles F. Irons, *The Origins of Proslavery Christianity: White and Black Evangelicals in Colonial and Antebellum Virginia* (Chapel Hill: University of North Carolina Press, 2008), 55; Donald G. Matthews, *Religion in the Old South* (Chicago: University of Chicago Press, 1977); Janet Moore Lindman, *Bodies of Belief: Baptist Community in Early America* (Philadelphia: University of Pennsylvania Press, 2008), 33–52; Janet Moore Lindman, "Acting the Manly Christian: White Evangelical Masculinity in Revolutionary Virginia," *William and Mary Quarterly,* 3rd ser., 57 (2000): 393–416; Jewel Spangler, "Becoming Baptists: Conversion in Colonial and Early National Virginia," *Journal of Southern History* (2001): 243–86; Najar, *Evangelizing the South,* 137–62.
116. For more on the changing political alignment of Virginia, see Eckenrode, *Separation of Church and State in Virginia,* 130–50; Thomas Buckley, SJ, "Evangelicals Triumphant: The Baptists' Assault on the Virginia Glebes, 1786–1801," *William and Mary Quarterly,* 3rd ser., 45 (1988): 33–69.
117. Thomas Buckley argues that Baptists had more success seizing glebes on a parish-by-parish basis. See Buckley, *Establishing Religious Freedom,* 95.
118. Hening, *SL,* 12:266–67.
119. Inhabitants of Hardy & Hampshire: Petition, Hardy County, October 28, 1790, LPDC, LVA.
120. Hening, *SL,* 13:705–6.
121. *Journal of the House of Delegates of the Commonwealth of Virginia,* November 27, 1789 (October 1789), (Richmond: 1828), 83–84.
122. The will of Matthew Godfrey from 1715/6 is included in a legislative petition from 1832. The pages are unnumbered, but the discussion of his donation is on page 7 of the will. See Citizens: Counter-Petition, Norfolk County, December 31, 1832, LPDC, LVA.
123. See Alice Granbery Walter, ed., *Vestry Book of Elizabeth River Parish, 1749–1761* (New York: Alice Granbery Walter, 1969), 3, 6, 50.

124. Overseers of the Poor: Petition, Norfolk County, November 5, 1789, LPDC, LVA.
125. Inhabitants: Petition, Norfolk City, November 2, 1789.
126. Overseers of the Poor: Petition, Norfolk County, November 5, 1789, LPDC, LVA.
127. Richard Beeman, *The Old Dominion and the New Nation* (Lexington: University of Kentucky Press, 1972), 198–99.
128. Bushrod Washington, "Opinion on Glebes and Churches," December 27, 1797, Papers of Bushrod Washington, Washington Papers Project, University of Virginia, http://bushrod.washingtonpapers.org/node/1707.
129. Convention of the Protestant Episcopal Church: Petition, November 22, 1796, LPDC, LVA.
130. *Acts Passed at a General Assembly of the Commonwealth of Virginia* (hereafter cited as *Acts VA*) (1798–99), ch. 9, "An act, to repeal certain acts, and to declare the construction of the Bill of Rights, and Constitution concerning religion," 8–9.
131. This stipulation respected the property rights of the inducted rector as a *persona ecclesiae* to the use of the glebe during his lifetime. Waiting for parishes to become vacant only slightly slowed the pace of land seizures because there was a dearth of Episcopal ministers in the state. For a discussion of the Episcopal clergy in Virginia after the Revolution, see G. MacLaren Brydon, "A List of Clergy of the Protestant Episcopal Church Ordained After the American Revolution, Who Served in Virginia Between 1785 and 1814, and a List of Virginia Parishes and Their Rectors for the Same Period," *William and Mary Quarterly,* 2nd ser., 19 (1939): 397–434.
132. "I. Rough Draft of Jefferson's Resolutions for Disestablishing the Church of England . . . ," Founders Online, https://founders.archives.gov/documents/Jefferson/01-01-02-0222-0002.
133. Definition of freeholder: "A person who possesses a freehold estate." The latter is defined as "an estate in land or other real property, of uncertain duration; that is, either of inheritance of which may possible last for the life of the tenant at the least, (as distinguished from a leasehold;) and held by free tenure, (as distinguished from copyhold or villeinage.)" Definition of housekeeper: "One who is in actual possession of and who occupies a house, as distinguished from a 'boarder,' 'lodger,' or 'guest.'" In Henry Campbell Black, *A Dictionary of Law* (St. Paul: West Publishing Co., 1891), 520, 588.
134. Kukla, *Patrick Henry,* 127; Buckley, *Establishing Religious Freedom,* 159.
135. "The Episcopal Church in Virginia, 1607–2007," *Virginia Magazine of History and Biography* 115 (2007): 214–15.
136. *Turpin v. Locket* (1804), 10 Va. 113, 139.
137. *Turpin v. Locket* (1804), 10 Va. 113, 139.

138. *Turpin v. Locket* (1804), 10 Va. 113, 152.
139. *Revised code,* vol. 1, 79.
140. *Terrett v. Taylor,* 13 U.S. (9 Cranch) 43, 49.
141. Hoping to use the Supreme Court's rulings in *Terrett* and later in *Dartmouth College,* the vestry of Shelburne Parish sued in equity to prevent the sale of their glebe lands by the Overseers of the Poor of Loudoun County. Henry St. George Tucker, the son of former Virginia justice St. George Tucker, ruled on the matter while serving as chancellor in the Court of Chancery in Winchester in 1830. Not only did he reject the court's legal rationale in *Terrett,* but he also went even further to declare that "the question in this case is not touched by the constitution of the United States, which was not adopted until two years afterwards. . . . This is a subject over which the supreme court of the United States have no manner of jurisdiction." *Selden v. Overseers of Poor of Loudoun,* 38 Va. 127 (1840); Henry St. George Tucker, "The Opinion of Chancellor Tucker in the Case of Selden and Others against the Overseers of the Poor of Loudoun and Others," *Commentaries on the Laws of Virginia,* vol. 2 (Winchester, VA: 1837), 12.

## 5. Confiscation in Republican Virginia

1. Overseers of the Poor: Petition, Norfolk County, December 22, 1832, Legislative Petitions Digital Collection, Library of Virginia, Richmond, available online at http://www.virginiamemory.com/collections/petitions (hereafter cited as LPDC, LVA).
2. The original bequest had been given to Norfolk Parish, which was divided into three parishes: Elizabeth River, Portsmouth, and St. Bride's. Norfolk County and the city of Norfolk (sometimes called the Borough of Norfolk) made claims to the enslaved people. See Overseers of the Poor: Petition, Norfolk County, November 5, 1789, LPDC, LVA; Mayor, Recorder, & Aldermen: Petition, Norfolk (Borough/City), October 16, 1792, LPDC, LVA; Inhabitants: Petition, Norfolk (Borough/City), November 2, 1789, LPDC, LVA.
3. The only other state to confiscate church property during disestablishment was Vermont. For more on the distinctions between Virginia and Vermont's disestablishmentarian policies, see Alyssa Penick, "From Disestablishment to Dartmouth College v. Woodward: How Virginia's Fight over Religious Freedom Shaped the History of American Corporations," *Law and History Review* 39 (2021): 507.
4. Ministers & Lay Representatives of the Presbyterian Church in Convention: Petition, October 31, 1787, LPDC, LVA.

5. The emphasis on consolidating white support mirrors the dynamics Robert Parkinson identified across Revolutionary America. See Parkinson, *The Common Cause: Creating Race and Nation in the American Revolution* (Chapel Hill: Omohundro Institute of Early American History and Culture, University of North Carolina Press, 2016).
6. William Waller Hening, ed., *The Statutes at Large; Being a Collection of All the Laws of Virginia, from the First Session of the Legislature in the Year 1619* (Richmond: J & G Cochran, 1821), 12:27–30 (hereafter cited as Hening, *SL*).
7. Hening, *SL*, 12:84–86.
8. The legislature had given its permission in these instances either to vestries selling worn-out land or to counties without active Episcopal vestries or ministers.
9. For example, see Inhabitants of St. Anne's Parish, Albemarle County, December 7, 1803, LPDC, LVA.
10. For King William Parish in Powhatan and Chesterfield Counties, see Freeholders, Housekeepers, & Inhabitants of King William Parish: Petition, Powhatan County, December 13, 1834, LPDC, LVA. For more on Hungars Parish in Northampton County, see Sarah Barringer Gordon, "The Landscape of Faith: Religious Property and Confiscation in the Early Republic," in *Making Legal History: Essays in Honor of William E. Nelson*, ed. Daniel J. Hulsebosch and R. B. Bernstein (New York: NYU Press, 2013), 34. For more on Henrico Parish in Henrico County, see William Meade, *Old Churches, Ministers and Families of Virginia*, 2 vols. (Philadelphia: Lippincott, 1857), 1:144; Overseers of the Poor: Petition, Henrico County, December 17, 1817, LPDC, LVA.
11. Perhaps Nansemond's Overseers never felt the need to aggressively pursue glebe confiscation because they had already successfully seized valuable charitable donations from the parish, which they used to support a free school and poor relief. H. J. Eckenrode, *Separation of Church and State in Virginia* (Richmond, VA: 1910), 153; George MacLaren Brydon, *Virginia's Mother Church and the Political Conditions Under Which It Grew*, 2 vols. (Richmond: Virginia Historical Society, 1947–52), 2:511–12n30; Virginia Department of Education, *Virginia School Report, 1885* (Richmond: 1885), 280.
12. Scholars have typically described the loss of property during confiscation in acreage, implying that seizure was limited to real estate. See Alan Taylor, *Thomas Jefferson's Education* (New York: Norton, 2019), 57; Brydon, *Virginia's Mother Church*, 2:493; Thomas Buckley, SJ, "Evangelicals Triumphant: The Baptists' Assault on the Virginia Glebes, 1786–1801," *William and Mary Quarterly*, 3rd ser., 45 (1988): 33–69, 55; Buckley, "After Disestablishment: Thomas Jefferson's Wall of Separation in Antebellum Virginia," *Journal of Southern History* 61, no. 3 (1995): 449.

13. John Nelson, *A Blessed Company: Parishes, Parsons, and Parishioners in Anglican Virginia, 1690–1776* (Chapel Hill: University of North Carolina Press, 2001), 51.
14. Eckenrode and Brydon claimed that glebes were roughly worth $8,000–10,000. They relied on an estimate from a petition sent by the Presbyterian General Committee in 1783 that the total value of the glebes was roughly £300,000. The reliability of this figure, though, is dubious. The Presbyterians had an incentive to emphasize the high value of this land in making their case for its seizure as a public asset. Clergy of the Presbyterian Church: Petition, May 26, 1784, LPDC, LVA; Eckenrode, *Separation of Church and State in Virginia*, 77; Brydon, *Virginia's Mother Church*, 2:501, 509.
15. For example, see "Essex Seeks Approval to Use Its Glebe Funds," *Richmond Times-Dispatch* (VA), January 10, 1962; "Additional $30,000 School Loan Is Okayed by Mathews Board," *Daily Press* (Newport News, VA), January 28, 1965; "Century-Old Fund Aids Schools in Lancaster," *Richmond Times-Dispatch*, January 2, 1955.
16. This figure is based on extant records. There is no surviving evidence of the fifteen following parishes owning enslaved persons: Albemarle (Surry/Sussex Counties), Augusta (Augusta), Blisland (New Kent/James City Counties), Bristol (Prince George County), Fredericksville (Albemarle), Henrico (Henrico), St. George (Accomack), St. George's (Spotsylvania), St. Patrick's (Prince Edward), St. Peter's (New Kent), Stratton Major (King and Queen), Upper Parish (Nansemond), Ware (Gloucester), and Wicomico (Northumberland County). Records demonstrate the following parishes owned enslaved persons: Antrim (Halifax), Bruton (James City/York), Christ Church (Middlesex County), Cumberland (Lunenberg), Elizabeth River (Elizabeth River), Hungars (Northampton), Kingston (Mathews), Suffolk (Lower) Parish (Nansemond), Lynnhaven (Princess Anne), Petsworth (Gloucester), St. Bride's (Norfolk), Portsmouth (Norfolk), Abingdon (Gloucester), and. St Paul's (Hanover). My estimate accords with Jennifer Oast's findings. See Oast, *Institutional Slavery: Slaveholding Churches, Schools, Colleges, and Businesses in Virginia, 1680–1860* (Cambridge: Cambridge University Press, 2016).
17. Unknown numbers of enslaved people in Virginia were sold or fled during the Revolution. Estimates range from 5,000 to 100,000 individuals. For more on the debate over this figure, see Cassandra Pybus, "Jefferson's Faulty Math: The Question of Slave Defections in the American Revolution," *William and Mary Quarterly*, 3rd ser., 62 (2005): 243–64.
18. *Norfolk Gazette and Publick Ledger* (VA), January 19 and August 5, 1807.

19. The parish minister, Henry Heffernen, was still alive, so it seems that the parish must have struck some sort of deal with the Overseers of the Poor to sell the glebe and use the proceeds to maintain the minister during his lifetime. George MacLaren Brydon, "A List of Clergy of the Protestant Episcopal Church Ordained After the American Revolution, Who Served in Virginia Between 1785 and 1814, and a List of Virginia Parishes and Their Rectors for the Same Period," *William and Mary Quarterly,* 2nd ser., 19 (1939): 430.
20. This omission could suggest that they worked and lived on the glebe and their labor directly supported the minister, or they might have been hired out, and the churchwardens tracked the proceeds separately. Newspaper advertisements remain the only extant record that Christ Church Parish in Middlesex County owned enslaved people. See C. G. Chamberlayne, ed., *The Vestry Book of Christ Church Parish, Middlesex County, Virginia, 1663–1767* (Richmond, VA: Old Dominion Press, 1927).
21. See Richard Beeman, *The Old Dominion and the New Nation* (Lexington: University Press of Kentucky, 1972).
22. For detailed data on the increasing price of enslaved people over this period, see Daina Ramey Berry, *Berry Slave Value Database, 10 U.S. States, 1797–1865* (Ann Arbor, MI: Inter-university Consortium for Political and Social Research, 2018), https://doi.org/10.3886/ICPSR37099.v1.
23. Stephanie Smallwood identifies the "universal contradiction inherent in the idea of human beings as property" and the ways in which enslaved people resisted commodification. Smallwood, *Saltwater Slavery: A Middle Passage from Africa to American Diaspora* (Cambridge, MA: Harvard University Press: 2009), 182. Jennifer Morgan's masterful *Reckoning with Slavery* details how "the logics of property" sought "to distance the enslaved from the kinship ties that marked them as rooted in human communities," as well as the ways in which Black people "worked to invert them." Morgan, *Reckoning with Slavery: Gender, Kinship, and Capitalism in the Early Black Atlantic* (Durham, NC: Duke University Press, 2021), 177–78.
24. Overseers of the Poor & Others: Petition, Halifax County, December 21, 1802, LPDC, LVA.
25. The Overseers in Halifax were not alone in trying to use canon law to dispossess a rector of the glebe. Overseers of the Poor in Northumberland and Norfolk tried the same tack. See *Young v. Pollock* (1806) in *Reports of Cases Argued and Determined in the Supreme Court of Appeals of Virginia* (New York: Joseph Gold, 1814), 2:517–18; and *Claughton v. MacNaughton* (1811), in ibid., 2:513–17.

26. Thomas Buckley argued that dissenters rejected legislative "intervention," but church and state remained nonetheless "entangled." However, these invitations for direct disqualification of a minister's freehold based on his poor spiritual performance evidence a call for more direct oversight, at least of the Anglican Church. See Buckley, *Church and State in Virginia,* 182; and Buckley, "Establishing Religious Freedom," 141–43.
27. The parish's 1802 petition mentions an enslaved "man and a woman," as well as their three children. Minister & Members of Antrim Parish: Remonstrance, Halifax County, December 21, 1802, LPDC, LVA.
28. Minister & Members of Antrim Parish: Remonstrance, Halifax County, December 21, 1802, LPDC, LVA.
29. Minister & Members of Antrim Parish: Remonstrance, Halifax County, December 21, 1802, LPDC, LVA.
30. Hay exemplified the expectation that the legislature would uphold Christian values without governing its churches. See Carl H. Esbeck, "Dissent and Disestablishment: The Church-State Settlement in the Early American Republic," *Brigham Young University Law Review* (2004): 1579–80.
31. Minister & Members of Antrim Parish: Remonstrance, Halifax County, December 21, 1802, LPDC, LVA.
32. This information comes from the obituaries in a denominational publication. See "Miscellaneous," *Christian Journal, and Literary Register* 4 (New York: 1820), 64.
33. *Acts Passed at a General Assembly of the Commonwealth of Virginia* (hereafter cited as *Acts VA*) (1801–2), ch. 5, "An Act concerning the Glebe Lands and Churches within this Commonwealth," 9.
34. School Commissioners: Petition, Spotsylvania County, December 31, 1819, LPDC, LVA.
35. Meade, *Old Churches, Ministers and Families of Virginia,* 1:422.
36. *Acts VA* (1805–6), ch. 74, 43–45; *Acts VA* (1809–10), ch. 33, 33–34 (Plate in Surry County); *Acts VA* (1811–12), ch. 65, 100 (Essex County and King and Queen County authorized to sell plate); *Acts VA* (1812–13), ch. 58, 89–90 (Overseers in Richmond County to sell plate); *Acts VA* (1813–14), ch. 55, 117 (bell and plate of St. Peter's Parish in New Kent County); ch. 63, 126 (books, ornaments, and plate of St. Margaret's Parish in Caroline); *Acts VA* (1814–15), ch. 78, 137 (bell, plate, books, and ornaments belonging to parish in Amelia County); ch. 65, 130 (church plate and bells belonging to several parishes in Middlesex, Mathews, and Warwick Counties).
37. Inhabitants: Petition, Amelia County, October 17, 1814, LPDC, LVA.
38. *Acts VA* (1814–15), ch.78, 137; *Virginia Argus* (Richmond), September 9, 1815, 4.

39. Amelia County: Report: 1829, Box 1, Folder 7, Overseers of the Poor Annual Reports and Checklists, 1800–1909, Auditor of Public Accounts (1776–1928), Accession 739, State Government Records Collection, LVA (hereafter cited as OP Annual Reports, APA, LVA).
40. Meade, *Old Churches, Ministers and Families of Virginia*, 1:422.
41. "The Will of John Yeates, Sept. 18th, 1731," in W. E. MacClenny, "Yeates' Free Schools," *William and Mary Quarterly*, 2nd ser., 5 (1925): 30–31.
42. These petitioners did not invoke the rule against perpetuities or raise concerns about the threat posed by property-hungry corporations, both of which would have reflected popular anxieties in republican Virginia. They were focused solely on claiming this wealth for the state from the church. For more on popular concerns about perpetual endowments, see Stanley N. Katz, Barry Sullivan, and C. Paul Beach, "Legal Change and Legal Autonomy: Charitable Trusts in New York, 1777–1893," *Law and History Review* 3 (1985): 51–89.
43. Inhabitants on the South Side of the Nansemond River: Petition, Nansemond County, December 21, 1802, LPDC, LVA.
44. *Acts VA* (1802), ch. 46, "An Act to incorporate Trustees in the lower parish of Nansemond for the purposes therein mentioned," 35–36.
45. Virginia Department of Education, *Virginia School Report, 1885* (Richmond: 1885), 280.
46. Meade, *Old Churches, Ministers and Families of Virginia*, 1:410.
47. Writers Program of the WPA, comp., *Virginia: A Guide to the Old Dominion* (New York: Oxford University Press, 1941), 382.
48. Meade, *Old Churches, Ministers and Families of Virginia*, 1:391.
49. Meade, *Old Churches, Ministers and Families of Virginia*, 2:133.
50. Williams, "Survey Report: Buckingham Baptist Church: 1937 May 12," Virginia Historical Inventory Project, available online through the Library of Virginia, https://www.lva.virginia.gov/public/guides/opac/vhiabout.htm.
51. Dell Upton identified three formerly Anglican colonial churches taken over by Baptists following the Revolution: Mangohick Church, Stratton Major Parish Church, and Mattaponi Church. See Upton, *Holy Things and Profane: Anglican Parish Churches in Colonial Virginia* (New Haven, CT: Yale University Press, 1997), 235n5. For additional examples of parish churches that were used by other denominations in the nineteenth century, see Rosa G. Williams, "Survey Report: Buckingham Baptist Church: 1937 May 12"; Dorothy Diffenderfer, "Survey Report: Denbigh Baptist Church: 1937 May 18"; Louise Macon, "Survey Report: Millifield Church: 1938 Apr. 1," Virginia Historical Inventory Project, LVA.
52. Robert Baylor Semple, *A History of the Rise and Progress of the Baptists in Virginia* (Richmond: 1810), 179.

53. Inhabitants of St. Mary's Parish: Petition, Caroline County, December 11, 1810, 2, LPDC, LVA.
54. For example, the lower church of Christ Church Parish in Middlesex County was taken over by Baptists, who removed the sounding board, pulpit, and desk in an apparent effort "to destroy every vestige of Episcopal taste and usage." Meade, *Old Churches, Ministers and Families of Virginia,* 1:372.
55. Freeholders, Housekeepers, & Inhabitants of King William Parish: Petition, Powhatan County, December 16, 1813, LVA, LPDC. See also *Acts VA* (1813–14), ch. 52, "An act authorising the sale of the Glebe and King William Parish in the counties of Chesterfield and Powhatan, and for other purposes there in mentioned," 113–15. However, the law was repealed the following year, and it is not clear whether any part of the transportation project was ever carried into effect. Freeholders & Inhabitants of King William Parish: Petition, Powhatan County, November 2, 1814, LVA, LPDC; *Acts VA* (1814–15), ch. 66, "An Act to repeal the Act authorizing the sale of the Glebe and King William parish in the counties of Chesterfield in Powhatan," 131.
56. For more discussion of parochial education, see Guy Fred Wells, *Parish Education in Colonial Virginia* (New York: Teachers College, Columbia University, 1923).
57. For more on the parish school system in Virginia, see Taylor, *Thomas Jefferson's Education,* 13–29.
58. Johann Neem discusses the slower grow of public education in the antebellum South and highlights the particular shortcoming of Virginians on this point. See Neem, *Democracy's Schools: The Rise of Public Education in America* (Baltimore: Johns Hopkins University Press, 2017), 9–10, 63, 75–79.
59. For a discussion of the ideological conservativism of Southern republicanism, see Adam L. Tate, "Republicanism and Society: John Randolph of Roanoke, Joseph Glover Baldwin, and the Quest for Social Order," *Virginia Magazine of History and Biography* 111, no. 3 (2003): 263–98. Even works that emphasize democratization of Virginia's politics admit that it was later in coming and more limited than in other states. See William G. Shade, *Democratizing the Old Dominion: Virginia and the Second Party System, 1824–1861* (Charlottesville: University Press of Virginia, 1996). Alan Taylor calls attention to how social class shaped educational proposals in republican Virginia. See Taylor, *Thomas Jefferson's Education,* 3–4, 15, 82–84, 189–91, 217–22. Peter Onuf discusses the "class bias" of educational reform in the early republic. See Onuf, "State Politics and Republican Virtue: Religion, Education, and Morality in Early American Federalism," in

*Toward a Usable Past: Liberty Under State Constitutions,* ed. Paul Finkelman and Stephen E. Gottleib (Athens: University of Georgia Press, 1991), 104. Harry Watson describes this pattern in the South more generally. See Watson, "The Man with the Dirty Black Beard: Race, Class, and Schools in the Antebellum South" *Journal of the Early Republic* 32, no. 1 (2012): 1–26.

60. John Randolph of Roanoke quoted in Robert Orvis Woodburn, "An Historical Investigation of the Opposition to Jefferson's Educational Proposals in the Commonwealth of Virginia" (PhD diss., American University, 1974), 117–19.
61. "I. Rough Draft of Jefferson's Resolutions for Disestablishing the Church of England and for Repealing Laws Interfering with Freedom of Worship, [before 19 November 1776]," Founders Online, https://founders.archives.gov/documents/Jefferson/01-01-02-0222-0002.
62. The St. Anne's Parish glebe had been sold in 1780, and the churchwardens held onto the funds. The residents of the parish petitioned the legislature to hand these funds to the county. See Hening, *SL,* 10:112–13; Inhabitants of St. Anne's Parish, Albemarle County, December 7, 1803, LPDC, LVA; Edgar Woods, *Albemarle County in Virginia: Giving Some Account of What It Was by Nature, of What It Was Made by Man, and of Some of the Men Who Made It* (Charlottesville, VA: 1901), 127.
63. *Acts VA* (1802–3), ch. 34, "An act to establish an Academy in the county of Albemarle, and for other purposes," 23–34. The law included no explicit mention of using glebe funds to support this school; however, records from the county's Overseers suggest that they never received the glebe funds. This fact, plus the similar timing of the sale and the law, suggests that the money had been earmarked for public education. See Albemarle County, Report: 1829, Box 1 Folder 3, OP Annual Reports, APA, LVA.
64. Woods, *Albemarle County in Virginia,* 127.
65. *Acts VA* (1810–11), ch. 23, "An Act to appropriate certain funds arising from the sale of the Glebe Lands, in Albemarle County to the establishment of Public Schools in the said County," 29–30.
66. "Minutes of the Albemarle Academy Board of Trustees, 25 March 1814," Founders Online, https://founders.archives.gov/documents/Jefferson/03-07-02-0183-0002.
67. Thomas Jefferson to Peter Carr, 7 September 1814, Founders Online, https://founders.archives.gov/documents/Jefferson/03-07-02-0462.
68. For a thorough discussion of Jefferson's views on public education, see Taylor, *Thomas Jefferson's Education,* 161–91.
69. Joseph C. Cabell to Thomas Jefferson, 5 March 1815, Founders Online, https://founders.archives.gov/documents/Jefferson/03-08-02-0249;

Thomas Jefferson to Joseph C. Cabell, 10 September 1817, Founders Online, https://founders.archives.gov/documents/Jefferson/03-12-02-0011.

70. *Acts VA* (1815–16), ch. 75, "An act for establishing a College in the County of Albemarle," 191–94; *Journal of the House of Delegates of the Commonwealth of Virginia,* January 6, 1818 (Richmond: 1828), 117.

71. Conveyance of Lands for Central College from John M. Perry and Frances T. Perry to Alexander Garrett, 23 June 1817, Founders Online, https://founders.archives.gov/documents/Jefferson/03-11-02-0396.

72. *Journal of the House of Delegates of the Commonwealth of Virginia,* January 6, 1818 (Richmond: 1828), 117.

73. *Acts VA* (1818–19), ch. 19, "An act for establishing an University," 15–18.

74. Thomas Jefferson to George Ticknor, 25 November 1817, Founders Online, https://founders.archives.gov/documents/Jefferson/03-12-02-0170.

75. Thomas Jefferson: Design for Tombstone and Inscription, [before 4 July 1826, 4 July 1826], Founders Online, https://founders.archives.gov/documents/Jefferson/98-01-02-6185. For discussion of this epitaph, see Michael P. Zuckert, "Thomas Jefferson and Natural Morality: Classical Theory, Moral Sense, and Rights" in *Thomas Jefferson, the Classical World, and Early America,* ed. Peter S. Onuf and Nicholas P. Cole (Charlottesville: University of Virginia Press 2011), 56; Francis D. Cogliano, *Thomas Jefferson: Reputation and Legacy* (Edinburgh: Edinburgh University Press, 2006), 137–69.

76. Inhabitants of St. Mary's Parish: Petition, Caroline County, December 8, 1804; Freeholders & Housekeepers of St. Mary's Parish: Petition, Caroline County, December 8, 1808, LPDC, LVA.

77. Garrett Ward Sheldon and C. William Hill Jr., *The Liberal Republicanism of John Taylor of Caroline* (Madison, WI: Fairleigh Dickinson University Press, 2008); Robert E. Shalhope, *John Taylor of Caroline: Pastoral Republican* (Columbia: University of South Carolina Press, 1980).

78. Rappahannock Academy, *Record Book of the Trustees of Rappahannock Academy, 1810–1822,* Accession 24654c, page 2, LVA.

79. Inhabitants of St. Mary's Parish: Petition, Caroline County, December 11, 1810, LPDC, LVA.

80. Record Book of the Trustees of Rappahannock Academy, 3; Inhabitants of St. Mary's Parish: Petition, Caroline County, December 11, 1810, LPDC, LVA.

81. Trustees of the Rappahannock Academy: Petition, Caroline County, December 16, 1813, LPDC, LVA; Record Book of the Trustees of Rappahannock Academy, 7.

82. Record Book of the Trustees of Rappahannock Academy, 17.

83. Beeman, *Old Dominion and the New Nation,* 241–42.
84. Inhabitants of St. Mary's Parish: Petition, Caroline County, December 11, 1810, LPDC, LVA.
85. In Maryland and western Virginia, the income of agricultural laborers hovered around $10 between 1800–20. See Donald R. Adams Jr., "Prices and Wages in Maryland, 1750–1850," *Journal of Economic History* 46 (1986): 625–45; Adams, "Prices and Wages in Antebellum America: The West Virginia Experience," *Journal of Economic History* 52 (1992): 206–16.
86. Inhabitants of St. Mary's Parish: Petition, Caroline County, December 11, 1810, LPDC, LVA.
87. Inhabitants of St. Margaret's Parish: Petition, Caroline County, December 17, 1813, LPDC, LVA.
88. Dell Upton, "Lancasterian Schools, Republican Citizenship, and the Spatial Imagination in Early Nineteenth-Century America," *Journal of the Society of Architectural Historians* 55, no. 3 (1996): 238–53.
89. Freeholders & Housekeepers of St. Margaret's Parish: Petition, Caroline County, December 17, 1821, LPDC, LVA.
90. Schools in Essex, King George, Nansemond, and Prince George, which had originally received glebe funds, were closed after inhabitants petitioned the legislature. See Residents: Petition, Prince George County, December 2, 1806; Overseers of the Poor in the Lower Parish: Petition, Nansemond County, December 11, 1829; Inhabitants: Petition, King George County, January 2, 1829; Citizens: Polls, Essex County, December 12, 1842, LPDC, LVA.
91. Inhabitants of St. Paul's Parish: Petition, King George County, December 15, 1811, LPDC, LVA.
92. Citizens: Petition, King George County, December 11, 1815, LPDC, LVA.
93. Inhabitants: Petition, King George County, December 9, 1829, LPDC, LVA.
94. Inhabitants: Petition, King George County, January 2, 1829, LPDC, LVA; Inhabitants: Petition, King George County, December 9, 1829, LPDC, LVA.
95. Caroline County, Report: 1829, Box 2, Folder 7, OP Annual Reports, APA, LVA.
96. Eckenrode, *Separation of Church and State in Virginia,* 153; Carl H. Esbeck, "Disestablishment in Virginia, 1776–1802," in *Disestablishment and Religious Dissent: Church-State Relations in the New American States,* ed. Carl H. Esbeck and Jonathan Den Hartog (Columbia: University of Missouri Press, 2019), 170.
97. Augusta County: 1829 Report, Box 1, Folder 10, OP Annual Reports, 1829, APA, LVA.

98. Prince Edward County: Report, 1829, Box 10, Folder 8, OP Annual Reports, 1829, APA, LVA.
99. St. Anne's Parish Vestry Book (Albemarle County, VA), front cover. Accession 20804, Church Records Collection, LVA; C. G. Chamberlayne, ed., *The Vestry Book and Register of Bristol Parish, 1720–1789* (Richmond, VA: 1898), 165–66.
100. Gloucester County: 1829 Report, Box 5, Folder 1, OP Annual Reports, APA, LVA.
101. Halifax County: 1829 Report, Box 5, Folder 7, OP Annual Reports, APA, LVA.
102. Citizens: Counter-Petition, Norfolk County, December 31, 1832, LPDC, LVA.
103. The state did not track relief by gender, nor did county overseers. However, there are many more specific female recipients mentioned in the Overseers of the Poor's reports to the state. Moreover, the cultural association between independence and masculinity likely discouraged more men from seeking welfare than women. Keri Leigh Merrit argued that in a culture built on the logic of racial hierarchy and masculine honor, a white man seeking financial relief was not only deemed shameful but also dangerous. She wrote that "poor whites had long posed a threat to the maintenance of the peculiar institution" because of their "disconnectedness from slavery." Merrit, *Masterless Men: Poor Whites and Slavery in the Antebellum South* (New York: Cambridge University Press, 2017), 9, 125.
104. Botetourt County: 1829 Report, Box 2, Folder 3, OP Annual Reports, APA, LVA.
105. "An Act for providing for the Poor, and declaring who shall be deemed Vagrants" (1792), in *Virginia Revised Code,* 2nd ed. (Richmond: 1814), 1:257–58.
106. These attitudes lend credence to arguments made by scholars that disestablishment and the Second Great Awakening went hand in hand. As nineteenth-century public administrators washed their hands of moral regulation, churches and benevolent institutions were energetically taking up the cause. For a discussion of the work of private institutions in the Second Great Awakening, see Robert H. Abzug, *Cosmos Crumbling: American Reform and Religious Imagination* (Oxford: Oxford University Press, 2004); William G. McLoughlin, *Revivals, Awakening, and Reform* (Chicago: University of Chicago Press, 1978), 98–140.
107. *Acts VA* (1804–5), ch. 11, "An Act to further amend the Act, entitling 'An Act to reduce into one the several Acts concerning Slaves, Free Negroes, and Mulattoes,'" 9.
108. *Acts VA* (1805–6), ch. 63, "An Act to amend the several laws concerning slaves," 252.
109. For more about manumissions and the law in Virginia between the 1780s and 1820s, see Eva Sheppard Wolf, *Race and Liberty in the New Nation:*

*Emancipation in Virginia from the Revolution to Nat Turner's Rebellion* (Baton Rouge: Louisiana State University Press, 2006).

110. Wolf includes additional examples of Overseers of the Poor selling manumitted persons. See Eva Sheppard Wolf, *Almost Free: A Story About Family and Race in Antebellum Virginia* (Athens: University of Georgia Press, 2012), 53–77.
111. These records have been sorely underutilized by scholars as they contain a wealth of information about antebellum Virginia. This book does not provide a comprehensive discussion of antebellum poor relief, but the subject deserves more attention from historians.
112. Some counties did extend relief at higher rates to free Black residents. In Botetourt County, for example, free people of color were nearly 10 percent of poor relief recipients between 1800 and 1830. See Botetourt County, Overseers of the Poor: Report, 1829, Box 2, Folder 3, OP Annual Reports, APA, LVA. Jennifer Ann Gallagher likewise found that the Overseers of Montgomery County, Virginia, frequently provided poor relief to Black residents. See Gallagher, "'Remove Him to the Poorhouse': Poor-Relief in Montgomery County, VA, 1830–1880" (MA thesis, Virginia Polytechnic Institute and State University, 2019).
113. Chesterfield County, Overseers of the Poor: Report, 1829, Box 3, Folder 4, OP Annual Reports, APA, LVA.
114. Pittsylvania County, Overseers of the Poor: Report, 1829, Box 10, Folder 5, OP Annual Reports, APA, LVA.
115. Norfolk County, Overseers of the Poor: Report, 1829, Box 9, Folder 1, OP Annual Reports, APA, LVA.
116. Wolf, *Race and Liberty in the New Nation,* 111.
117. For more on Nat Turner's Rebellion and its legacy, see Randolph Ferguson Scully, *Religion and the Making of Nat Turner's Virginia: Baptist Community and Conflict, 1740–1840* (Charlottesville: University of Virginia Press, 2008); Patrick H. Breen, *The Land Shall Be Deluged in Blood: A New History of the Nat Turner Revolt* (New York: Oxford University Press, 2015); David F. Allmendinger Jr., *Nat Turner and the Rising in Southampton County* (Baltimore: Johns Hopkins University Press, 2014); Kenneth S. Greenberg, ed., *Nat Turner: A Slave Rebellion in History and Memory* (New York: Oxford University Press, 2003).
118. According to the records of Nansemond County's Overseers of the Poor, 25 percent of relief recipients between 1818 and 1830 were Black. This statistic is far higher than in other Virginian counties but does not come close to substantiating the petition's claim. See Nansemond County: Report, 1829, Box 8, Folder 5, OP Annual Reports, APA, LVA.
119. Citizens: Petition, Nansemond County, December 22, 1831, LPDC, LVA.

120. Citizens: Petition, Nansemond County, December 22, 1831, LPDC, LVA.
121. Timothy Lockley's excellent study of antebellum poverty argues that preventing poor, white Southerners from becoming "disaffected with the status quo" was essential to the maintenance of racial slavery and ensuring "the solid south." See Lockley, *Welfare and Charity in the Antebellum South* (Gainesville: University of Florida Press, 2007), 217.
122. Freeholders and Housekeepers, Gloucester County, December 16, 1813, LPDC, LVA; Gloucester County: 1829 Report, Box 5, Folder 1, OP Annual Reports, APA, LVA; *Acts VA* (1813–14), ch. 56, "An Act appropriating the proceeds of the Glebe Lands, and other Property, belonging to the parishes of Abingdon, Ware, and Petsworth the County of Gloucester," 117–19.
123. Hening, *SL*, 7:41–42.
124. Freeholders and Housekeepers, Gloucester County, December 16, 1813, LPDC, LVA.
125. For more on the 1811 German Coast insurrection, see Nathan A. Buman, "Historiographical Examinations of the 1811 Slave Insurrection," *Louisiana History: The Journal of the Louisiana Historical Association* 53 (2012): 318–37. For a discussion of how the event shaped popular opinion, see Brian Gabrial, *The Press and Slavery in America, 1791–1859: The Melancholy Effect of Popular Excitement* (Columbia: University of South Carolina Press, 2016), 17–28.
126. *Acts VA* (1813–14), ch. 56, "An Act appropriating the proceeds of the Glebe Lands, and other Property, belonging to the parishes of Abingdon, Ware, and Petsworth the County of Gloucester," 118.
127. Freeholders and Housekeepers, Gloucester County, Dec. 16, 1813, LPDC, LVA.
128. Inhabitants: Petition, Nansemond County, December 9, 1815.
129. Citizens: Counter-Petition, Norfolk County, December 31, 1832, LPDC, LVA.
130. Citizens: Counter-Petition, Norfolk County, December 31, 1832, LPDC, LVA.
131. Alice Granbery Walter, ed., *Vestry Book of Elizabeth River Parish, 1749–1761* (New York: Alice Granbery Walter, 1969), 6, 20.
132. Hening, *SL*, 7:418.
133. Hening, *SL*, 8:154–56.
134. Overseers of the Poor: Petition, Norfolk County, December 31, 1832, LPDC, LVA.
135. Citizens: Petition, Norfolk County, December 12, 1823, LPDC, LVA.
136. Overseers of the Poor: Petition, Norfolk County, December 31, 1832, LPDC, LVA.

137. Overseers of the Poor: Petition, Norfolk County, December 31, 1832, LPDC, LVA.
138. For a discussion of enslavers using the threat of sale as a mechanism of control, see Walter Johnson, *Soul by Soul: Life Inside the Antebellum Slave Market* (Cambridge, MA: Harvard University Press, 1999), 22–29.
139. Overseers of the Poor: Petition, Norfolk County, December 31, 1832, LPDC, LVA.
140. For discussions of how Virginians imagined Liberia and encouraged the manumission of enslaved men and women on the condition that they emigrate there, see Jane Ailes and Marie Tyler-McGraw, "Leaving Virginia for Liberia: Western Virginia Emigrants and Emancipators," *West Virginia History,* new series, 6 (2012): 1–34; Marie Stango, "Vine and Palm Tree: African American Families in Liberia, 1820–1860" (PhD diss., University of Michigan, 2016); Brandon Mills, "'The United States of Africa': Liberian Independence and the Contested Meaning of a Black Republic," *Journal of the Early Republic* 34 (2014): 79–107; Marie Tyler-McGraw, "Richmond Free Blacks and African Colonization, 1816–1832," *Journal of American Studies* 21 (1987): 207–22.
141. Mary Watkins: Petition, Powhatan County, December 12, 1828, LPDC, LVA.

## 6. Incorporation in Republican Maryland

1. *Hornet,* August 23, 1809; August 30, 1809; *American Watchman,* September 9, 1809; *Federal Republican,* September 5, 1809; *Republican Star,* September 12, 1809.
2. Maryland Constitution of 1776, Article 33. One of the most easily accessible versions of the 1776 Maryland Constitution mistakenly replaces the word "glebe" with "globe" in its text of Article 33 (as of August 2023). This typo underscores the extent to which church property has been widely overlooked as a constitutional issue in Maryland and the question of glebe lands largely forgotten. See "Constitution of Maryland—November 11, 1776," Avalon Project, Yale Law School, https://avalon.law.yale.edu/17th_century/ma02.asp.
3. Nelson Waite Rightmyer, *Maryland's Established Church* (Baltimore: Church Historical Society for the Diocese of Maryland, 1956), 119.
4. See Sandra Ryan Dresbeck, "The Episcopalian Clergy in Maryland and Virginia, 1765–1805" (PhD diss., University of California, Los Angeles, 1976).
5. For a discussion of Methodists in Maryland during and after the Revolution, see Dee E. Andrews, *The Methodists and Revolutionary America,*

*1760–1800: The Shaping of an Evangelical Culture* (Princeton, NJ: Princeton University Press, 2000), 56–59, 80, 129–33, 138, 160–61, 188–89. For a discussion of the postrevolutionary rise of evangelicalism across the south, see Christine Leigh Heyrman, *Southern Cross: The Beginnings of the Bible Belt* (Chapel Hill: University of North Carolina Press, 1997).

6. Rev. Thomas Scot, "Seventh District Report: Stepney Parish," Queries 14–15, 1798, V.F., Episcopal Diocese of Maryland Archives (hereafter cited as EDMA).
7. Rev. John Kemp, "Seventh District Report: All Hallows Parish," Part 2, Query 9, 1797, V.F., EDMA.
8. *North American and Mercantile Daily Advertiser,* January 12, 1808.
9. William Hebb to Bishop Thomas John Claggett, May 16, 1807, 1–2, V.F., EDMA.
10. William Hebb to Bishop Claggett, March 18, 1810, 1, V.F., EDMA.
11. St. Paul's Parish, Baltimore, "Account of the Glebe belonging to the Vestry of St. Paul's Parish in Baltimore County," June 1789, V.F., EDMA.
12. Rev. George Ralph to Bishop Claggett, June 5, 1802, 3, V.F., EDMA.
13. For examples of parishes discussing selling real estate to raise funds, see Vestry of St. Margaret's Westminster Parish, Anne Arundel County to Bishop Claggett, November 6, 1809, V.F., Oversize, EDMA; Rev. Thomas Scot, "Seventh District Report: Stepney Parish," Queries 14–15, 1798, V.F., EDMA; Bishop Thomas John Claggett to a Vestry, c. 1809?, V.F., EDMA.
14. Votes and Proceedings, December 6, 1783, MSA SCM 3197, 213, MSA.
15. Somerset Parish Vestry Accounts, 1796–1818, 18, MSA SC 2241 SCM 338, MSA.
16. Archives of Maryland Online, 61:465.
17. *Maryland Journal,* October 20, 1778.
18. Kilty's signature appears on numerous documents in the court record and matches numerous verified copies of his signature on archival documents. "Negro Mary v. Vestry of William and Mary Parish, Charles Co. (Petition for Freedom), Oct. 1796," General Court of the Western Shore (Judgments, "N," 1794–1805) S498-164, MSA.
19. H. L. Koopman, "Kilty's Manuscript Travesty of the Iliad," *Maryland Historical Magazine* 13, no. 2 (1918): 103–4.
20. "Negro Mary v. Vestry of William and Mary Parish, Charles Co. (Petition for Freedom), Oct. 1796," General Court of the Western Shore, MSA.
21. The thirty-four individual petitioners seeking their freedom from William and Mary Parish are identified in the Court's Docket: Adam, Casey, Clem, Claire, Elizabeth, Charity, Edy, Shadrach, Meshach, Abednego, Esther, Eleanor, George, Hannah, Henry, Henry, Harriott, Henson, Jacob, Jane, Joseph, John, Murria, Rebecca, Mary Adams, Mary, Mary, Sarah,

Sarah, Sinah, Susanna, Samuel, Thomas, and Winny. The petitions are all filed together. See May 1794, Docket, General Court of the Western Shore, S492–22, 158–93, MSA.

22. For more on the characterization of Madagascar as a country outside the customary laws of slavery, see Wendy Wilson-Fall, *Memories of Madagascar and Slavery in the Black Atlantic* (Athens: Ohio University Press, 2015), 1–5.
23. Thomas Harris and John McHenry, *Maryland Reports: Being a Series of the Most Important Law Cases* (New York: I. Riley, 1813), 3:501–2; Jacob D. Wheeler, *A Practical Treatise on the Law of Slavery* (New York: Allan Pollock Jr., 1837), 11–12.
24. Archives of Maryland Online, 105:230–31.
25. Parishes seeking permission to sell property bequeathed during the colonial era usually included the specific terms of the donation decades after the passage of the 1798 Vestry Act. For example, see Archives of Maryland Online, 635:21.
26. This figure is from the 1844 report of William and Mary Parish to the Diocese, and its relative value in 2023 was calculated using measuringworth.com. Parish Reports to Bishop William Whittingham, 1844–47, EDMA.
27. "A Supplement to the act for the establishment of select vestries" (1779), Archives of Maryland Online, 203:216; Maryland Constitution of 1776, Article 33.
28. This announcement also included a detailed statement from the Episcopal Church refuting the legislation and foreshadowing the pending arguments in *Turpin v. Locket* (1804). *Republican or Anti-Democrat* (Baltimore), January 4, 1802, 2.
29. Archives of Maryland Online, 653:13–17.
30. *Journal of a convention of the Protestant Episcopal Church in the state of Maryland* (Baltimore: 1803), 7.
31. *Journal of a convention of the Protestant Episcopal Church in the state of Maryland* (Baltimore: 1807), 9.
32. *Hornet,* August 30, 1809.
33. *Hornet,* August 23, 1809.
34. Their arguments conveniently overlooked the obvious precedent in the 1792 act incorporating the Catholic clergy, which did not impose strict property limits or the subsequent amendments and improvements to the act passed during the intervening years. Archives of Maryland Online, 644:49; 607:96–97; 192:832.
35. *Hornet,* September 27, 1809.
36. *Federal Republican,* October 6, 1809.
37. *Federal Republican,* September 5, 1809.

38. *Journal of a convention of the Protestant Episcopal Church in the state of Maryland* (Baltimore: 1809), 5.
39. James Kemp to John Henry Hobart, October 30, 1809, in *Archives of the General Convention*, vol. 6 (New York: 1912), 309.
40. *Votes and Proceedings of the House of Delegates of the State of Maryland*, November Session, 1809, page 99, Microfilm MSA SC M 3198, MSA.
41. Archives of Maryland Online, 380:2–3.
42. Archives of Maryland Online, 380:6.
43. Archives of Maryland Online, 570:28.
44. The amendment to add the exception in the case of freedom petitions is recorded in *Votes and Proceedings of the House of Delegates of the State of Maryland*, November Session, 1809, page 51, Microfilm MSA SC M 3198, MSA. A similar law was adopted in Virginia in 1795. See Alan Taylor, *The Internal Enemy: Slavery and War in Virginia, 1772–1832* (New York: Norton, 2013), 108.
45. *Votes and Proceedings of the House of Delegates of the State of Maryland*, November Session, 1809, page 104, Microfilm MSA SC M 319, MSA. See also Archives of Maryland Online, 380:19.
46. *National Intelligencer* (Washington, DC), November 22, 1809, 2; *Republican Star* (Easton, MD), November 28, 1809, 3; *Farmers' Repository* (Charles Town, WV), December 1, 1809, 3; *American Watchman* (Wilmington, DE), November 25, 1809, 2.
47. Thomas Hughes, *History of the Society of Jesus in North America Colonial and Federal, Documents, Vol. 1, Part* 2 (New York: Longmans, Green, and Co., 1910), 676, 694, 696–97, 699.
48. Carroll to Michael Alvarez y Cortes, April 9, 1796, *The John Carroll Papers*, ed. Thomas O'Brien Hanley, 3 vols. (Notre Dame, IN: University of Notre Dame Press, 1976), 2:172.
49. John Carroll, "Pastoral of Bishop Carroll Concerning the Cathedral at Baltimore, 1808," cited in *American Catholic Historical Researches* 9, no. 3 (1892): 143.
50. For more on the significance of the cathedral, see Michael DeStefano, "John Carroll, the Amplitude Apologetic and the Baltimore Cathedral," *American Catholic Studies* 122, no. 2 (2011): 31–61.
51. Carroll to Plowden, March 13, 1788, cited in Hughes, *History of the Society of Jesus, Documents, Vol. 1, Part 2*, 696.
52. John Carroll, "Proposals for Establishing an Academy at George Town, Patowmack-River, Maryland," 1787, Archives of the Maryland Province of the Society of Jesus, Box 102 Folder 14, Georgetown University Manuscripts, Booth Family Center for Special Collections, Washington, DC.

53. As Thomas Murphy, SJ, has persuasively argued, Maryland's Jesuits used slaveholding as a way to assert their rights as English subjects in Maryland. See Murphy, "'Negroes of Ours': Jesuit Slaveholding in Maryland, 1634–1838" (PhD diss., University of Connecticut, 1998), 49–60.
54. Maryland Province Archives, "A payment for Alexius, August 15, 1796," Georgetown Slavery Archive, https://slaveryarchive.georgetown.edu/items/show/419.
55. "Present State of the College," 1820, Georgetown Slavery Archive, https://slaveryarchive.georgetown.edu/items/show/190.
56. "Money arriving from the Sale of Negroes," Proceedings of the Corporation of Roman Catholic Clergy, August 25, 1795, Georgetown Slavery Archive, http://slaveryarchive.georgetown.edu/items/show/169.
57. "People Bought and Sold at Bohemia Plantation," 1794–1795, Georgetown Slavery Archive, http://slaveryarchive.georgetown.edu/items/show/331.
58. "'An Unfounded Claim': Bishop Carroll berates the President of Georgetown College for his claims to the people enslaved at Bohemia, December 1807," Georgetown Slavery Archive, http://slaveryarchive.georgetown.edu/items/show/110.
59. Quotation from a Maryland newspaper found in Ira Berlin, *Many Thousands Gone: The First Two Centuries of Slavery in North America* (Cambridge, MA: Harvard University Press, 2009), 265. See also Daina Ramey Berry, *The Price for Their Pound of Flesh: The Value of the Enslaved, from Womb to Grave, in the Building of Nation* (Boston: Beacon Press, 2017).
60. "The Corporation of Roman Catholic Clergymen orders the sale of 'superfluous slaves' to pay debts, July 1805," Georgetown Slavery Archive, http://slaveryarchive.georgetown.edu/items/show/263.
61. Joseph P. Mobberly, SJ, Papers, "'What the Farm Expends on the Blacks,' Mobberly Diaries, Part 1, 1820," Georgetown Slavery Archive, http://slaveryarchive.georgetown.edu/items/show/151.
62. Robert Emmett Curran, "'Splendid Poverty': Jesuit Slaveholding in Maryland," in *Facing Georgetown's History: A Reader on Slavery, Memory, and Reconciliation,* ed. Adam Rothman and Elsa Barraza Mendoza (Washington, DC: Georgetown University Press, 2021), 36.
63. "Fr. Roothaan, SJ lays out the conditions for the sale of enslaved persons, 27 December 1836," Georgetown Slavery Archive, http://slaveryarchive.georgetown.edu/items/show/94.
64. Archivum Romanum Societatis Iesu, "'What will become of me?': Fr. Havermans reports on the anguish of the slaves, October 20, 1838, and November 12, 1838," Georgetown Slavery Archive, https://slaveryarchive.georgetown.edu/items/show/226.

65. For more on the history of Baltimore's Jewish community, see Deborah R. Weiner and Eric L. Goldstein, *On Middle Ground: A History of the Jews of Baltimore* (Baltimore: Johns Hopkins University Press, 2018), 17–52.
66. For examples of Carroll's slippage between discussing religious freedom in universal terms and equality among Christians under Maryland's constitution, see John Carroll to Cardinal Antonelli, March 13, 1786, 1:208; John Carroll to Ferdinand Farmer, December 1784, 1:156; John Carroll to Charles Plowden, February 27, 1785, 1:168, all in *John Carroll Papers.*
67. *Votes and Proceedings of the House of Delegates of the State of Maryland,* November Session, 1797, page 69, Microfilm MSA SC M 3197, MSA.
68. *Votes and Proceedings of the House of Delegates of the State of Maryland,* December Session, 1801, pages 40, 101, Microfilm MSA SC M 3198, MSA.
69. Isidore Singer, ed., *The Jewish Encyclopedia* (New York: Funk and Wagnalls Co., 1902), 2:478–79.
70. "Solomon Etting," *Maryland Historical Magazine* 15, no. 1 (1920): 9–10.
71. Archives of Maryland Online, 192:294–98.
72. Emanuel Milton Altfeld, *The Jew's Struggle for Religious and Civil Liberty in Maryland* (Baltimore: 1924), 78.
73. Altfeld, *Jew's Struggle,* 75, 77.
74. Altfeld, *Jew's Struggle,* 79.
75. Altfeld, *Jew's Struggle,* 81, 101.
76. For more on Maryland's so-called Jew Bill, see Adam Jortner, *A Promised Land: Jewish Patriots, the American Revolution, and the Birth of Religious Freedom* (New York: Oxford University Press, 2024), 241–53; Edward Eitches, "Maryland's 'Jew Bill,'" *American Jewish Historical Quarterly* 60 (1971): 258–59; Eric Eisner, "'Suffer Not the Evil One': Unitarianism and the 1826 Maryland Jew Bill," *Journal of Religious History* 44 (2020): 338–55; Eric Eisner, "The Most Generous, Disinterested, and Philanthropic Motives: Race and the 1826 Maryland Jew Bill," *American Jewish History* 107 (2023): 757–79.
77. H. M. Brackenridge, *Speeches on the Jew Bill: In the House of Delegates of Maryland* (Philadelphia: J. Dobson, 1829), 67.
78. *Votes and Proceedings of the General Assembly of the State of Maryland,* December Session, 1822, 4, Microfilm MSA SC M 12329, MSA.
79. Brackenridge, *Speeches on the Jew Bill,* 103.
80. Brackenridge, *Speeches on the Jew Bill,* 103, 106.
81. Brackenridge, *Speeches on the Jew Bill,* 106.
82. Brackenridge, *Speeches on the Jew Bill,* 114.
83. *Easton Gazette,* January 25, 1823.
84. *Republican Star,* August 19, 1823.

85. *Baltimore Patriot,* September 27, 1823.
86. Archives of Maryland Online, 629:154; 815:42–43.
87. *Proceedings of the House of Delegates of the State of Maryland,* December Session, 1829, page 160, Microfilm MSA SC M 3200, MSA.
88. Altfeld, *The Jew's Struggle,* 45–46; *Proceedings of the House of Delegates of the State of Maryland,* December Session, 1829, 331, 531, Microfilm MSA SC M 3200, MSA. The text of the incorporation act appears in Archives of Maryland Online, 540:456.
89. *Easton Star,* October 14, 1845.

## Conclusion

1. William Meade, *Old Churches, Ministers and Families of Virginia,* 2 vols. (Philadelphia: Lippincott, 1857), 2:155.
2. "Yeocomico Church, Montross, Westmoreland, Virginia," in National Register of Historic Places, 69-11-35-0102, https://npgallery.nps.gov/NRHP/getasset/b89aeb80-67fb-4554-9c56-35af24826ae6; James Scott Rawlings, *Virginia's Colonial Churches: An Architectural Guide* (Richmond, VA: Garrett & Massie, 1963), 50–58; Meade, *Old Churches, Ministers and Families of Virginia,* 2:147–58.
3. Both petitioners are filed together in William Norvell Ward: Petition, Westmoreland County, January 3, 1844, 11, Legislative Petitions Digital Collection, Library of Virginia, Richmond, available online at http://www.virginiamemory.com/collections/petitions (hereafter cited as LPDC, LVA).
4. William Norvell Ward: Petition, Westmoreland County, January 3, 1844, 7, LPDC, LVA.
5. Talal Asad contends that the way scholars identify what counts as "religious" is "the product of a unique post-Reformation history" and "has a specific Christian history." Winifred Sullivan offers a complementary argument in her discussion of the Supreme Court's First Amendment jurisprudence. Sullivan suggest that American jurisprudence, and Americans more broadly, employ a definition of religion rooted in the reformed Protestant tradition that emphasizes belief over practice. Talal Asad, *Genealogies of Religion: Discipline and Reasons of Power in Christianity and Islam* (Baltimore: Johns Hopkins University Press, 1993), 28, 42; Sullivan, *The Impossibility of Religious Freedom* (Princeton, NJ: Princeton University Press, 2007), 1–12.
6. See, especially, Christine Heyrman, *Southern Cross: The Beginnings of the Bible Belt* (Chapel Hill: University of North Carolina Press, 1997); Jon Butler, *Awash in a Sea of Faith* (Cambridge: Harvard University Press, 1990);

Daniel Walker Howe, *What Hath God Wrought: The Transformation of America, 1815–1848* (New York: Oxford University Press, 2009); Jewel Spangler, *Virginians Reborn: Anglican Monopoly, Evangelical Dissent, and the Rise of the Baptists in the Late Eighteenth Century* (Charlottesville: University of Virginia Press, 2008); Katherine Carté, *Religion and the American Revolution: An Imperial History* (Chapel Hill: University of North Carolina Press, 2021).

7. Minister & Members of Antrim Parish: Remonstrance, Halifax County, December 21, 1802, LPDC, LVA.

# INDEX

*Italicized page numbers refer to illustrations.*

## The Revolutionary Age

*Suffering for the Crown: The Hudson Valley Loyalists and the Violence of Revolution*
Kieran J. O'Keefe

*The Burden of Independence: American Revolution on Trial*
T. H. Breen

*The American Revolution at 250: Twenty-Four Historians Reflect on the Founding*
Francis D. Cogliano, editor

*The Global Age of Revolutions: A History from 1650 to Today*
Bryan A. Banks and Cindy Ermus, editors

*Barbary Entanglements: Realizing American Independence on the World Stage*
John M. Chamberlin

*The Course of Human Events: The Declaration of Independence and the Historical Origins of the United States*
Steven Sarson

*Napoleon in America: Bonaparte and the Rhetoric of US Empire*
Mark F. Ehlers

*Before Manifest Destiny: The Contested Expansion of the Early United States*
Nicholas G. DiPucchio

*Revolutionary Diplomacy: Spanish Statecraft and the Birth of the United States*
Thomas E. Chávez

*Declarations of Independence: Indigenous Resilience, Colonial Rivalries, and the Cost of Revolution*
Christopher R. Pearl

*Dishonored Americans: The Political Death of Loyalists in Revolutionary America*
Timothy Compeau

*The American Liberty Pole: Popular Politics and the Struggle for Democracy in the Early Republic*
Shira Lurie

*European Friends of the American Revolution*
Andrew J. O'Shaughnessy, John A. Ragosta, and Marie-Jeanne Rossignol, editors

*The Tory's Wife: A Woman and Her Family in Revolutionary America*
Cynthia A. Kierner

*Writing Early America: From Empire to Revolution*
Trevor Burnard

*Spain and the American Revolution: New Approaches and Perspectives*
Gabriel Paquette and Gonzalo M. Quintero Saravia, editors

*The American Revolution and the Habsburg Monarchy*
Jonathan Singerton

*Navigating Neutrality: Early American Governance in the Turbulent Atlantic*
Sandra Moats

*Ireland and America: Empire, Revolution, and Sovereignty*
Patrick Griffin and Francis D. Cogliano, editors

www.ingramcontent.com/pod-product-compliance
Lightning Source LLC
LaVergne TN
LVHW101842191026
850388LV00025B/207
* 9 7 8 0 8 1 3 9 5 5 3 1 5 *